Management of Health Information: Functions and Applications

The Health Information Management Series

Rozella Mattingly

Shirley Anderson
Series Editor

Delmar Publishers

I(T)P™ An International Thomson Publishing Company

Albany • Bonn • Boston • Cincinnati • Detroit • London • Madrid
Melbourne • Mexico City • New York • Pacific Grove • Paris • San Francisco
Singapore • Tokyo • Toronto • Washington

NOTICE TO THE READER

Cover Credit: Brucie Rosch

Publishing Team:
Publisher: David C. Gordon
Acquisitions Editor: Marion Waldman
Developmental Editor: Jill Rembetski
Editorial Assistant: Sarah Holle

Project Editor: Melissa Conan/William Trudell
Production Coordinator: Cathleen Berry
Art and Design Coordinator: Richard Killar
Marketing Manager: Darryl L. Caron

COPYRIGHT © 1997
By Delmar Publishers
a division of International Thomson Publishing Inc.

The ITP logo is a trademark under license

Printed in the United States of America

For more information, contact:

Delmar Publishers
3 Columbia Circle, Box 15015
Albany, New York 12212-5015

International Thomson Publishing Europe
Berkshire House 168-173
High Holborn
London, WC1V7AA
England

Thomas Nelson Australia
102 Dodds Street
South Melbourne, 3205
Victoria, Australia

Nelson Canada
1120 Birchmount Road
Scarborough, Ontario
Canada M1K 5G4

International Thomson Editores
Campos Eliseos 385, Piso 7
Col Polanco
11560 Mexico D F Mexico

International Thomson Publishing Gmbh
Königswinterer Strasse 418
53227 Bonn
Germany

International Thomson Publishing Asia
221 Henderson Road #05-10
Henderson Building
Singapore 0315

International Thomson Publishing - Japan
Hirakawacho Kyowa Building, 3F
2-2-1 Hirakawacho
Chiyoda-ku, 102 Tokyo
Japan

1 2 3 4 5 6 7 8 9 10 XXX 02 01 00 99 98 97 96

Library of Congress Cataloging-in-Publication Data

Mattingly, Rozella.
   Management of health information : functions and applications / Rozella Mattingly.
      p.   cm. — (The Health information management series)
   Includes index.
   ISBN 0-8273-6057-6
   1. Medical informatics.   2. Information resources management.   I. Title.   II. Series.
   R858.M386 1996
   362.1'068'4—dc20   95-47449
                                                                                        CIP

Delmar Publishers' Online Services

To access Delmar on the World Wide Web, point your browser to:
http://www.delmar.com/delmar.html
To access through Gopher: gopher://gopher.delmar.com
(Delmar Online is part of "thomson.com", an internet site with information on more than 30 publishers of the International Thomson Publishing organization.)
For information on our products and services:
email: info@delmar.com
or call 800-347-7707

To my granddaughters Lauren, Michelle, and Stephanie, whose budding managerial skills are already evident in interactions with classmates. They contribute to my enthusiasm for leaders who will access the knowledge critical to creating tomorrow's managerial environment.

Contents

Preface

Entering health care as a beginning health information manager is exciting. Choosing the workplace environment is no less exciting; the possibilities are so varied. Opportunities for health information managers exist throughout the health-care spectrum. *Management of Health Information: Functions and Applications* identifies these settings and offers suggestions for rewarding careers. These suggestions include opportunities in acute-care facilities, but do not presume beginning managers will choose this setting. As other health-care organizations become even more numerous, opportunities in these settings will increase.

This text is written primarily for students enrolled in health information management courses. It may also function as an important resource for busy managers seeking an update on trends in management.

Management of Health Information: Functions and Applications is structured for use as a primary text in courses where managing health information is taught. Management principles found in introductory management texts are briefly outlined and then an integrated approach to health information management is built from these principles. Student learning will be enhanced by:

- Reading a basic management text or taking an introductory management course
- Experiencing clinical or practice courses in a health information setting

The objectives for preparing *Management of Health Information: Functions and Applications* are to:

- Create an understanding of management principles as they apply to various health information management settings

- Offer students an opportunity to learn from seasoned health information managers through text examples and through review questions asking students to interact with managers and with one another in their learning experience
- Build managerial skills for later courses where students are exposed to the technical knowledge viewed from a managerial perspective in this text

Integral to this text's contents are the comments from successful managers who shared insights into their roles in today's health-care environment and how they expect to apply management functions in their changing role as health-care information brokers. They have also shared management situations that enrich this text as case studies. In addition to interviews with seasoned managers, this text includes the thinking of experts in management and health information management as found in a variety of journals, magazines, and publications from the American Health Information Association (AHIMA) and other national organizations. The resources for suggested reading found at the end of each chapter include few books, since there are few books printed devoted to health information management.

Content Overview

Six sections separate the topics in *Management of Health Information: Functions and Applications*. Section I, Introduction to Managing Health-Care Information, introduces management functions and includes a chapter on decision making. AHIMA has developed competencies, domains, and tasks expected of newly graduated health information administrators and technicians. These are addressed in Sections II–V as the major management functions of **planning** (Section II), **organizing** (Section III), **leading** (Section IV), and **controlling** (Section V). Because planning is a function that flows throughout the other three functions, planning activities are also included in other sections of the text. For each function, the brokers' activities are defined in the professional model of practice language: data capture, analysis, integration, and information dissemination.

Section VI, Special Issues for Health Information Managers, discusses special managerial activities involving committees, time management, and managing change. *Management of Health Information: Functions and Applications* emphasizes the crucial role health information managers play as brokers of information resources throughout an organization.

Features

- **Learning Objectives** provide the learner with measurable goals while studying each chapter.
- **Key Terms** are listed alphabetically at the beginning of each chapter, then in bold type on their first appearance in the text. The terms are also defined in the **Glossary** at the end of the text.
- **Management Terminology** has been standardized for easy comprehension. Since learners need to recognize synonyms, the Glossary includes additional terms that are currently in use for the same body of knowledge. For example, *health information manager* refers to any professional performing management functions in health information. These management roles include the traditional manager of a department, the associate manager, the assistant manager, the supervisor of a department section, and team leaders or lead positions within sections. Also, the role of office manager in an alternative health-care setting is included in this phrase.

This text employs two terms, *section* and *team*, to designate a group of employees who perform a specific role in a health information management department. In actuality, a specific department may not have designated teams within sections. When the topic within this text demands that an entire section be involved, a slash is used to show this encompassing definition.

- **Review Questions** are provided at the end of each chapter to reinforce understanding of the key concepts. **Field Practice Questions** are included in selected chapters for those learners who wish to explore concepts further in a practice setting.
- **Decision Making** is crucial to effective managers. Thus, Chapter 3 is devoted entirely to decision making. The steps in making decisions are outlined and then developed further through the use of case studies and review questions.

- **Continuous Quality Improvement** is a management concept being emphasized in health care today. In addition to devoting a chapter to performance improvement in Section V, concepts used in quality or performance improvement are incorporated throughout the text as an integral part of management functions. It is anticipated that continuous quality improvement will become a natural part of management functions, not a concept layered onto present functions.

- **Case Studies** from a variety of health-care organizations, including vendors and related corporations, as well as acute-care settings, are included at the end of selected chapters. These examples expose the learner to a broad range of issues facing health-care managers today.

- **Managers Who Make a Difference** are true stories of managers who have successfully faced a variety of challenges. These vignettes are included in certain chapters to connect theoretical concepts to reality.

- **Practice Examples** included within some chapters take the learner through the problem-solving process.

- **Tips for Managing Resources** are integrated throughout the text with an emphasis on efficiently and effectively managing resources, determining the types of resources needed, outlining efficient ways of becoming familiar with current and emerging technology, and advocating innovative ideas for decision makers.

- **Customer Focus:** The basic philosophy that health information management departments are part of service organizations evolves throughout this text with the concept that managers serve customers or clients, whatever the setting. Examples used in this text include activities where a department customer may be the physician, an attorney, the patient, an upper-level administrator, or government regulator.

Planning and managing a consulting service is included, since increasing numbers of professionals are choosing consulting careers.

Assumptions

One's personal style of managing begins long before the pages of this text are opened. Past experiences, such as planning a family holiday celebration, involve some facet of management: planning, organizing, leading, and controlling. Prior work experiences also shape ideas of how managers get things done, as one can draw on the successes and failures of former managers.

This text will challenge you, the beginning manager, to look at the management of resources as an art that impacts both your professional and personal life. As you read, think back frequently to past observations of managers and their styles as this text expands your horizons. This will give reality to your learning experiences. Be ready to be intrigued; managing is exciting, stimulating, challenging, and ever-changing.

Acknowledgments

Encouragement and counsel from peers, family, and friends sustained me and focused my efforts during the preparation of this text. While I gratefully acknowledge each of them, the total list of contributors in this sense is too long to document. I do want to mention by name those who shared specific knowledge, personal stories, and professional competence.

Shirley Anderson, whose unselfish sharing added so much to this book, I especially wish to thank. With professional competence she helped guide the content and format of this text. Those who contributed personal experiences for "Managers Who Make a Difference" and "Practice Examples" include Judy Cordeniz, Karen Darnell, Darice Gryzbowski, Robbyn Lessig, Shereen Martin, Mary Moody, and E'Vette Zeitlow. They are busy professional managers with daily pressures to face; I am deeply grateful for the time they gave to assist me by sharing their stories. A writer and long-time colleague I also want to recognize is Jennifer Cofer. Since our professional interactions in Iowa in the 1970s, I have been enriched as I contemplated her vision for the future of the profession and her concise writing style.

To bring visual interest, I contacted several firms for assistance. Those who contributed so generously include Fox Bay, Mecon, Metamorphosis, and Steelcase. In addition, Susan Fenton of the Department of Veterans Affairs and Barbara Mountford of Applied Data Systems gave valuable assistance.

Of course, bringing the text into print is the task of the publisher. Working with Jill Rembetski and Marion Waldman in this effort has been a joy. Jill was always there to offer suggestions, to improve a paragraph, to encourage. Marion offered confidence and assurance; thanks to both of you.

I would like also like to acknowledge the efforts of the following reviewers:

Shirley Anderson, Ph.D., RRA
Professor
Department of Health Information
    Management
St. Louis University
St. Louis, MO

Sue Ellen Bice, M.S., RRA
Program Coordinator
Health Information Technology/
    Medical Records
Mohawk Valley Community College
Utica, NY

Melanie Brodnik, Ph.D., RRA
Director and Assistant Professor
Medical Record Administration
The Ohio State University
Columbus, OH

Shirley Higgin, RRA
Program Director and Instructor
Health Information Technology
Spokane Community College
Spokane, WA

John Lynch, Ph.D., RRA
Director and Associate Professor
Health Information Administration
    Program
University of Wisconsin, Milwaukee
Milwaukee, WI

Mary McCain, MPA, RRA
Chair
Department of Health Information
    Management
University of Tennessee
Memphis, TN

Jody Smith, MSM, RRA
Chair
Department of Health Information
    Management
St. Louis University
St. Louis, MO

Peggy H. Wood, M.Ed., RRA
Chair
Department of Health Information
    Management
East Carolina University
Greenville, NC

Introduction to Managing Health-Care Information

Introduction to the Health Information Management Profession and the Health-Care Environment

Learning Objectives

After completing this chapter, the learner should be able to:

1. Identify the major components in a definition of management.
2. Provide ideas for maintaining knowledge of health-care trends.
3. Explain how data and the resulting information are used in health-care organizations today.
4. Discuss advocacy and its role in the effective use of health-care information.
5. Define a health information consultant's role in alternative delivery settings.
6. List two unique health information needs facing home health-care organizations.
7. Give three areas of expertise that HIM professionals offer the home health-care setting.
8. Describe several advantages that a computer-based patient record system can offer HIM managers and their customers in the future.

Key Terms

Broker

Clinical management

Computer-based patient record
   (CPR)

Consultant

Critical pathways

Decision support systems

Electronic patient record (EPR)

Executive information systems
   (EIS)

Information superhighway

Knowledge couplers

Longitudinal patient record

Matrix organizational structure

Paradigm shift

Patient-focused centers

Quality improvement

Resources

Strategic planning

Introduction

The management skills needed to create an environment that facilitates the timely, accurate, and comprehensive electronic transfer of health-care data is a challenge for health information management (HIM) professionals. In addition, managing the data and subsequent integration of the data into meaningful direct patient-care information is only one aspect of the managerial skills needed. Just as crucial to success is the knowledge that entry-level HIM practitioners must have of management theories and practice. HIM professionals make decisions that demand effective planning, organization, motivation, and communication skills. Decisions are enhanced by using controlling tools and time management techniques. Each of these facets of managing requires a degree of human resource interaction. Thus, while automated technologies enhance the careers of health-care professionals and offer increased satisfaction, managers continue to need a broad educational core of knowledge. By integrating automated technology skills and management concepts into a framework of professional practice standards, beginning practitioners can fulfill their career goals while meeting customer needs.

Who are the customers to be served by HIM professionals? First they are the patients, their families, and the teams who provide direct patient care within a facility. HIM customers include physicians caring for patients within the facility as inpatients or outpatients. These physicians need timely appropriate information for providing care in an efficient and effective manner such as that provided by **decision support systems**. In a broader sense, physicians and their office staff are customers with a variety of information needs that are well served by HIM managers responsible for capture, analysis, integration, and dissemination of health-care data.

The teams providing direct patient care include nurses, respiratory therapists, physical therapists, occupational therapists, pharmacists, radiation therapists, and speech therapists. In addition, physician assistants, nurse practitioners, and other specialty nurses work in a variety of settings where timely and accurate health-care information is needed.

Customers of health-care information also include those professionals performing risk management, utilization review, and performance improvement activities. Integrating the data gathered as patient care is given with the demographic and financial data and making the resulting information available to these professionals is crucial to the long-term health of the facility.

But, just as important to the health of the facility is the information processing for **executive information systems (EIS)** used by administration. HIM managers can offer timely and accurate information in a format that serves upper-level management, community networks, and regional and national databases. By integrating a facility's database information and disseminating it, appropriate to each customer's needs, HIM managers serve as **brokers** of health-care data. Add to these information needs the demand for research data from many different sources such as physicians, other health-care professionals, planning teams, or scientific researchers and then the exciting career possibilities for HIM professionals truly begin to emerge.

Health-care decision makers demand timely, accurate information for their professional activities. As bits of data are captured throughout an organization, they may be of little value to decision makers until analyzed and integrated into useful information. Brokers, with health information management knowledge and skill, are the appropriate disseminators of this health-care information. The tasks involved in analyzing, integrating, and disseminating information require that HIM brokers manage the resources within their sphere of responsibility to accomplish these objectives efficiently and effectively.

In this chapter, after a detailed definition of management, HIM brokering activities are outlined and discussed. Major health-care settings are described in the next section; the unique opportunities HIM professionals have as brokers of information and managers of resources in these settings are outlined.

The last section of this chapter takes a glimpse through the window of the future where HIM managers will be responsible for **electronic patient records (EPR)** that can link with **computer-based patient records (CPR)** and the information needed by health-care decision makers of tomorrow. By learning and then practicing the knowledges and skills of today, HIM professionals can open windows into tomorrow and accept the challenge of being members of teams that will create and sustain the excellence of health care into the twenty-first century.

Management Defined

Definitions of management have emphasized the need to manage human beings while accomplishing the objectives of an organization. Because health-care settings are increasingly becoming an integral part of today's information/communication society, the definition of management must include all resources, not only people. Management is defined as a process of activities for creating objectives and for teaming with people to meet these objectives through efficient and effective use of resources.

As mentioned, this definition uses the term **resources** in its broadest meaning. Health-care managers have access to a range of resources, among them data and personnel. The terms *efficient* and *effective* are used in this definition because they are crucial ingredients for success in managing with limited resources. These terms complement each other, for one could manage efficiently using the wrong resources for the task and thus not be effective. Or, a manager may be very effective in delivering the services needed, but may be organized inefficiently and thus use precious resources wastefully.

The term *broker* is used in this text to emphasize the roles that data and the resulting information play in managerial activities in health-care facilities. Managing and brokering information in today's health-care society brings an exciting opportunity for those who choose a career in health information management. HIM brokers offer managerial expertise in the capture, analysis, integration, and dissemination of data. By learning unique skills for creating timely, valuable information from these data, they broker information to customers. The future holds excitement for the HIM broker who disseminates essential health-care information to improve not only the quality of patient care, but also the quality of decisions made throughout the health-care organization.

HIM Managing and Brokering Activities

Figure 1-1 details HIM activities and shows the far-reaching consequences as information is disseminated. The flow of information in Figure 1-1 demonstrates how data gathered at each point of patient–caregiver contact in an acute-care facility are analyzed, integrated, and then disseminated as valuable information. This portrayal of data through a facility emphasizes HIM managing and brokering activities as captured data are transformed and disseminated to end users. The first column includes professionals or departments where patient-care data are generated and initial data capture begins. Here the data become a part of the patient's health record.

HIM professionals analyze these data, change portions into appropriate format and standards, then merge the resulting information into database systems and registries. Gleaning information from the electronic patient records for patient-specific coding and abstracting, HIM professionals ensure that business services has the information for timely reimbursement. The coded data are then available in the database systems to integrate for other users.

The fourth column in Figure 1-1 gives examples of the scope of activities taken by HIM managers as the integrated information is shared and utilized for various purposes. Dissemination of information continues and then reaches its major focus in the last column. Patient-care decision support systems are developed or modified as integrated information is shared with patient caregivers. **Strategic planning** decisions are enhanced as EIS information is updated and available in a timely, comprehensive, and meaningful way by upper-level management and members of the board of trustees. Thus, decisions for organizational effectiveness through strategic planning and resource allocation are enhanced.

The flow of information to business services shows the interdependence created by the enterprise network. Not only does business services have timely reimbursement data, but electronic management of receivables can be maintained with the integrated information. Just as important to the health of the facility, the flow back to the patient caregivers indicates the continuous pattern of the process and ability to modify clinical deci-

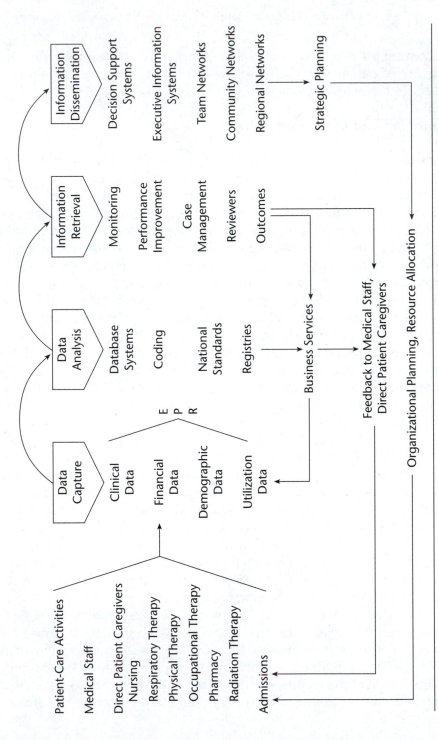

Figure 1-1. Integrated Information Management for Health Information Managers in Acute-Care Facilities

sion support systems. Through this brokering activity, excellence in patient care is monitored and performance improvement activities occur.

Important creative HIM activities are not revealed in Figure 1-1, however. In addition to the information management activities outlined, HIM professionals need skill in reaching out to potential customers, assessing their requirements, and designing information models to meet their needs. In so doing, they become information engineers. Opportunities for information leadership exist for the HIM professional who is ready and willing to accept the outreach challenge.

An Overview of Managing Health Information

Managing in today's complex health-care society involves applying creative solutions in the search for efficient and effective means for getting things done. A manager's set of tools for accomplishing delegated tasks tends to change as new technologies make possible the use of resources in ways unthinkable just a few years ago. By using these tools appropriately, HIM managers have the opportunity to redesign methods and create systems for a health-care environment that increasingly gives value to information and information management.

Unique Management Features

Health-care organizations have unique features that challenge managers including the complexity of services and the variety of education and experiences of employees. For example, one task in an HIM department may involve manual labor extensively, such as filing health records. The employee who spends 4 hours a day performing this task may spend another 3 hours at a computer entering data elements abstracted from incomplete records. Teams performing such a diversity of tasks require the HIM professional to use special managerial skills to create an environment of adaptability and flexibility. The demand for accuracy and excellence equally impacts both aspects of the employee activities mentioned above—the manual and the automated. The manager is challenged to create a culture that gives equal value and importance to both highly technical tasks and manual tasks.

Since the mid-1980s, an evolution toward productivity, efficiency, and effectiveness in health-care organizations has occurred with accelerating pace. This evolution has led to greater emphasis on cost containment and quality patient care. Increasing productivity, efficiency, and effectiveness in HIM departments are emphasized throughout the text.

Information Managers in Health-Care Facilities

With the advances in science and technology, greater recognition of the HIM professional as a key component player in the delivery of health care results. Frequently these technological advances allow for preventive care or ambulatory treatment rather than expensive inpatient care. This move will only increase the demand for information flowing to the various health-care service organizations such as physician office practice centers, wellness centers, and urgent care centers. As these health-care organizations become more complex and more frequently the setting for health-care delivery, the need for timely, accurate, and comprehensive information increases.

Definition of Health-Care Organizations

Managers of health-care information will typically work in health-care organizations. An organization is defined as a systematic arrangement of people and things to accomplish specific purposes. Health-care facilities are seen as organizations where health-care professionals come together, with standards and guidelines, to assess, diagnose, plan, and treat patients, and then document these activities. In keeping with these definitions, a major goal for HIM managers is to provide the resources for managing the information/communication flow within health-care organizations such as hospitals.

Delegation of HIM Responsibility

Responsibility for quality health care and optimum performance at all levels of the organization rests with the board of trustees or directors who then delegate responsibility to the president or chief executive officer (CEO). The president or CEO, in turn, delegates responsibility to the managers within the organization. Thus, HIM professionals are delegated their managerial responsibility by the board of trustees or directors of the organization.

Health-Care Facilities and Information Needs

With appropriate systems, HIM managers can provide data for clinical decision making at the point of patient care and then make it available as needed through a truly computerized patient record. Direct providers of care perform at optimum when information is at their fingertips and when documentation of their care is entered in the CPR by those same fingertips or by a voice recognition process. As these activities involving patient care are documented and create the information needed by others, the data are analyzed and managed by HIM professionals. In this way data become information of value and the managers become brokers of accurate, timely, and comprehensive health-care information. Obstacles to creating a true CPR are slowly being overcome. HIM brokers, investing in the time to obtain crucial current knowledge, can play a key role in CPR development. As they gain knowledge, they can, for example, educate their teams through in-service training. Giving recognition to employees who expand their knowledge through formal courses is another way to heighten interest in updating technological knowledge.

Advocacy

The role of the HIM professional in health-care organizations encompasses several facets of brokering health-care information. Advocacy is a major facet of brokering. This includes advocating quality patient care and documentation through the development of a comprehensive, **longitudinal patient record** for every patient by the year 2001, which is the target date for a nationally standardized CPR as declared by the federal government's Institute of Medicine (IOM) (Dick and Steen, 1991).

Advocacy includes embracing change and persuading others in the organization to share the enthusiasm. Communication and systems thinking skills will aid the HIM professional in championing change when working collaboratively to identify opportunities for improvement. Developing these advocacy skills will enhance the HIM professional's role in creating cultural change toward the goal of economical quality care and ensuring accurate and useful data as longitudinal CPRs are created.

Types of Health-Care Facilities and HIM Roles

HIM professionals find the need to adapt their expertise to the type of health-care facility in which they work. This section describes several of the typical settings and the positions that managers enjoy in these settings.

Acute-Care Facilities

Typically, regional hospitals are structured to meet the health-care needs of a regional area, whereas smaller community hospitals meet the basic health-care needs of the community. In some instances, community hospitals may specialize in specific therapies or advanced technologies identified as important for the community. Hospitals are considered one of the most complex organizations in modern society (see Figure 1-2). With the governing board holding legal authority and responsibility, and with the medical staff making decisions regarding patient care, administration is delegated responsibility for day-to-day operations.

Expanding Roles in Acute-Care Facilities

Today HIM professionals are a part of hospital organizations in a variety of positions. Figure 1-3 shows these possibilities.

There are also rewarding careers for HIM professionals as managers of any of the departments listed in Figure 1-3 or as staff professionals within departments. Supervisory or team leader responsibilities within a health information systems department are also fulfilling tasks.

As the health-care professional with knowledge of medical science, health data, medicolegal, and information technology, HIMs have an opportunity to expand their roles beyond those listed as the demand for data increases in the health-care environment. These expanding horizons offer job enrichment opportunities to HIM professionals while meeting the needs of organizations and communities.

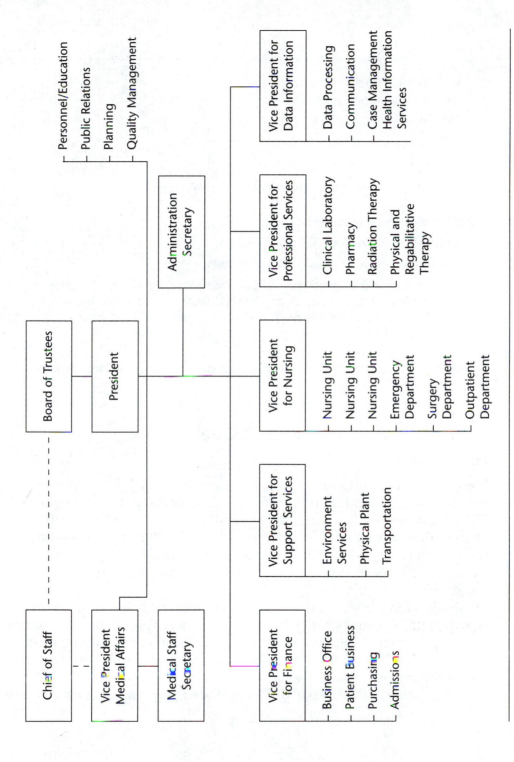

Figure 1-2. Organizational Model, Community Hospital

1. With advanced degrees:

   Hospital administrators

   Chief information officers (CIOs)

   Chief financial officers (CFOs)

   Vice presidents of operations

   Attorneys (salaried or under contract)

2. With or without advanced degrees:

   Quality improvement (QI) coordinators

   Diagnosis-related group (DRG) specialists

   Assistant vice presidents with responsibility for several departments such as health information services, admissions/patient registration, finance services, utilization management, risk management, information systems, or medical staff

Figure 1-3. Possible Positions for HIM Professionals in Acute-Care Facilities

Customers of Health Information in Acute-Care Facilities

Physician Customers

Networking within the organization, especially with the medical staff, brings opportunities for HIM professionals to participate as contributors. Physicians use the services of the HIM department with greater frequency than any other group of customers. By sharing information on new regulations, computer enhancements, work redesign, and other changes, HIM professionals can become valuable resources for physicians.

By listening and encouraging physicians to become involved in change, HIM managers can gather new ideas to improve the information flow to and from physicians. When individuals feel ownership for an idea, they are willing to be advocates for needed changes. The idea can then permeate throughout the facility and a greater understanding of the advantages for change is disseminated. Thus are born the pressures for **paradigm shifts**.

Upper-Level Administration Customers

HIM professionals have information of value to share with upper-level management customers. As opportunities arise for demonstrating the value of specific information for strategic planning, for example, HIM managers can offer to demonstrate the advantages of using these captured data for strategic planning. Then, this first opportunity can be a catalyst for offering additional creative uses of information.

Nursing Customers

Another major group of customers is nurses. HIM managers can initiate discussions of information needs and concerns with nursing professionals. Again, listening skills are crucial as nursing professionals verbalize their ideas for the flow of clinical information. Through communication, enhanced clinical information systems that assure a process where data are entered efficiently and accurately can be envisioned. As brokers of information, HIM managers have the expertise to customize reports for meeting specific nursing needs, thus promoting the concept of analyzed data as useful information, not merely data elements.

Patient Finance Accounts Customers

Another example of HIM customers is the patient financial accounts staff. By communicating with these people and assisting in their understanding of the body of information available for customized reports to meet their needs, HIM brokers are true advocates. Results of this networking can be improved relationships and improved workflow. By encouraging the patient accounts staff to think of additional information of value to them, HIM brokers have the opportunity to massage the database and customize appropriate reports.

Thus, intrapreneurs who are entrepreneurs within the facility will flourish and create ways of helping others do their tasks through the burgeoning of new methods, technology, and concepts. Managers in other departments have information needs also. By networking, HIM managers can gain knowledge of their activities and then offer appropriate information. The HIM manager's value as a team player will grow as a result of the efficient and effective systems created through the new roles of change agent and broker of health-care information.

Customers external to acute-care facilities, such as health-care planning councils and government agencies, also use data maintained by HIM professionals. As appropriate information is shared with these external customers, the role of HIM managers will be enhanced.

Ambulatory Facilities

An expanding segment of health-care organizations involves the diverse group of facilities referred to as ambulatory-care settings. These settings include physician office practice centers, urgent care centers, wellness centers, surgicenters, dialysis centers, and other specialty centers. Home health care is discussed in a separate section to emphasize its special features. Employment opportunities for HIM professionals in ambulatory care are increasing. The skills of HIM professionals are needed in ambulatory-care organizations to create information systems that will meet a facility's specific needs. As longitudinal electronic patient records develop, community health information networks (CHIN) and regional networks are being created by integrating ambulatory-care information into the CPR. HIM professionals have the knowledge to be team players in this development.

HIM professionals may also contract as **consultants** in ambulatory-care settings. Consultants can provide expertise in state and federal regulations as they constantly monitor publications for the latest updates. This information is not all that is needed, however. They also monitor trends in health-care and accreditation standards and are ready to advise should possibilities for change occur. Strategic planning within ambulatory-care organizations is thus enhanced.

Currently the trend is for physician office practices to merge as specialty or multispecialty organizations or to become part of a larger health-care facility such as a hospital. These more complex settings offer employment opportunities for HIM professionals. An alternative to employment, consulting also affords opportunity in physician practice with a shorter-term commitment to planning and implementing office systems that will create efficiency and effectiveness within practice groups. HIM professionals have the knowledge to integrate the resulting information that can lead to enhanced health-care delivery and excellence in patient care. As **information superhighways** become reality, physician office settings will demand the expertise of brokers who can deliver timely, accurate, and comprehensive information through a longitudinal CPR that will extend beyond the CHIN into national database systems.

The trends just mentioned emphasize the importance of integrating patient health-care information into networks. This health-care information from database systems residing in ambulatory-care facilities, skilled nursing facilities, and acute-care organizations thus becomes available to caregivers. By serving as liaisons among acute-care facilities and other health-care settings, HIM professionals offer expertise in integrating and disseminating appropriate information.

Skilled-Care and Nursing Home Facilities for Long-Term Care

In addition to ambulatory-care settings, diverse patterns of organization exist for facilities with inpatient beds for patients not requiring the intensive services of acute-care units. The demand for long-term-care beds continues to increase throughout the United States. The organizational structure in these settings is less complex than in acute-care facilities and predictably there is a narrower range of services.

While the length of stay and level of care in long-term-care settings creates a somewhat different need for health-care information, the patient/ resident as a customer continues to be the focus in both long-term care and acute care. To meet customer needs, regardless of the setting, caregivers need timely, accurate, comprehensive information. Thus, basic HIM standards of practice remain the same and long-term care offers excellent opportunities for HIM professionals. Larger facilities may have the resources to hire full-time HIM professionals to manage their health information systems. Other facilities may utilize the services of HIM consultants.

Home Health Care

Home health care is unique and is a rapidly growing industry. A natural shift from acute-care settings to home health-care settings has occurred as new technologies make home health treatment increasingly feasible. Cost-containment pressures also demand that care, such as infusion therapy, be given in the least costly health-care setting. The expansion of home health-care settings is creating opportunities for HIM professionals within these home health businesses. As employees, HIM professionals assist in efficient capture of data from various caregivers and then analyze and integrate these data. This creates the information needed by the caregivers as well as the decision makers within the administrative level of the business. HIM professionals with appropriate backgrounds may find a career in managing home health-care businesses very rewarding. Another career possibility in home health-care settings is contracting as HIM consultants to assist in creating appropriate health information systems and maintaining them.

Maintaining health information systems and managing the flow of information for health-care needs such as advocacy, development, implementation of the CPR, and patient decision support systems will continue to challenge HIM professionals who choose a career involving home health-care settings. Unique needs within the home health-care settings include remote telecommunication and computer technologies. These can create significant cost savings for home health-care businesses as the CPR is developed and integrated into the community network. HIM professionals have the knowledge and skills to plan and implement these systems as management teams struggle to equip their organizations for efficiency and effectiveness in health care. Choosing appropriate hardware and software can be a difficult task; HIM professionals are prepared to assist in these decisions because of their knowledge of information systems and potential vendor applications.

Financial savings can also be realized when automated client-care documentation systems are implemented for home health-care uses. Well-planned and -documented policies and procedures are needed as systems are installed. HIM professionals are well positioned to meet their career goals while offering expertise within the home health-care setting.

Local, State, and National Government Agencies

Government agencies can be a part of any of the health-care delivery services mentioned in this chapter. Examples are found in the inner cities, Indian Health Service, and prison clinics and hospitals. Some of these have unique needs that merit special mention. Communication skills are especially crucial in settings with increased cultural diversity. Also, some facilities give high priority to hiring employees from the local community who may need special training.

These special needs offer HIM professionals an opportunity to be of service in these settings. Training employees in professional standards of practice such as confidentiality of patient information can be very rewarding. When patients are from among an employee's family or acquaintances, adequate training in confidentiality policies and procedures becomes imperative. Also, the wording of policies and procedures should be sensitive to the culture of the community.

As CHINs are developed, data will be captured from all the healthcare facilities and providers in the network. HIM professionals have an opportunity to advocate the need for standards, security, and decision support systems throughout this network. With the educational curriculum designed specifically to address these issues, the HIM professional is best qualified to perform these tasks and manage this information flow.

Emerging Opportunities for Health Information Managers

Every day all of us are affected in our professional and personal lives by information technology. With information and knowledge growing at an ever-increasing rate, HIM professionals face challenges and time constraints just monitoring the latest advances (Melbin, 1991). But this constraint carries with it opportunities to grow, to learn, to innovate, and to excite others as advocates for systems that will improve lives, lengthen lives, and enhance the public health of the nation.

Health-care managers can be proactive participants in the effort to review the present structure of patient care, the management of the systems, and the information flow. This effort can lead to paradigm shifts that may create major reorganizational possibilities.

One innovation being tried in a limited number of organizations is a move to **patient-focused centers** where the caregivers in the centers provide all of the care to the patients. The possibilities for assuring quality information as a contributing member of the health-care team are exciting. This multidisciplinary team can monitor risk management, utilization management, infection control, and documentation of the diagnosis, procedures, and code assignment. Through a **matrix organizational structure**, the HIM staff can be actively involved in patient-focused centers. The matrix structure is discussed in Chapter 6.

Emerging Opportunities in Reorganization

Rightsizing a health-care facility's management structure offers the opportunity to combine departments and create nontraditional alliances. Rightsizing may be synonymous with downsizing; the difference can be that downsizing means deleting services and employees. In contrast, rightsizing means reorganizing for efficiency and effectiveness in meeting customer needs.

In today's information/communication environment the pressure to combine departments and create nontraditional alliances can bring excellence to the workplace and enhance the quality of patient care. HIM managers who are willing to expand their area of control can assume responsibility for such areas as patient registration, business service department, quality management, tumor registry, risk management, medical staff liaison, and utilization management. Such changes will demand HIM professionals with the ability to form teams that can accomplish a combination of these responsibilities and develop a culture where each team member understands the role of the entire team. For teams that avoid turf battles, creativity, innovation, and efficient systems will result. For example, HIM professionals, nurses, and other team members in utilization management can expand their roles by monitoring risk issues, diagnosis issues, and coding details.

An alliance between health information services and business services or patient accounts services can effectively decrease accounts receivable days because of enhanced cooperative efforts. Constraints in such alliances may be due to the lack of knowledge and experience of the managers involved. By taking advantage of formal and informal education opportunities, managers can prepare themselves for expanding roles. Developing the skills necessary to create the cultural changes that alliances offer is crucial to successful alliances.

Innovations in Emergency Departments

Another area where creative managerial ideas can contain costs is data management in emergency departments. Medical-care documentation is increasingly important and HIMs who explore enhanced systems for emergency records find there are systems available that offer legal protocols, financial savings, and administrative efficiency. For example, by using flowcharting and computerized documentation applications in emergency departments, physician time devoted to paperwork can be lessened. These systems can also assist support personnel in their documentation efforts. Using a dictated discharge document for emergency departments can augment flowcharting for the physician and increase the likelihood that complete information on the patient will be included in the record. HIM professionals can network with the caregivers in emergency departments and expose them to opportunities for creating information and documentation systems best suited to their needs.

Emerging Opportunities in Ambulatory Care

A fast-growing ambulatory-care center may historically have given low priority to its health-care records. Eventually, the inability to have records available for patient care leads to a crisis among the health-care providers. Such an organization will find that it needs the expertise of a health information professional.

Planning and implementing appropriate systems for ambulatory-care centers can challenge the skills of HIM managers. However, the rewards of seeing effective and efficient systems in place for such diverse health-care settings are great.

Concerns continue to be expressed about the quality and effectiveness of information management systems within outpatient facilities. As managed-care practices increase and ambulatory health-care delivery grows, more emphasis is being placed on effective systems where data integration and networking can take place enterprise-wide and regionally (Gennusa, 1995).

Choosing employment or contracting as consultants with physician practice groups and other ambulatory settings will continue to attract HIM professionals who enjoy the challenges offered. Automated systems created specifically to enhance integrated delivery and continuum of care for ambulatory health-care settings will increase and provide opportunities for HIM managers.

Emerging Opportunities in Health-Related Settings

In addition to the opportunities described previously, innovative HIM professionals are enjoying nontraditional roles as emerging needs create new opportunities. These settings include insurance companies, contract research organizations, peer review organizations, recruiting firms, publishing firms focusing on health care, allied health practice firms, state health planning agencies, and pharmaceutical firms. Consulting opportunities are increasing in organizations such as certified public accountant (CPA) firms also. As the need for database management skills increases and regional health data repositories become commonplace, new opportunities for HIM professionals with these skills will emerge.

Workplace of the Future

How will HIM professionals and health-care facilities respond to the federal government's mandate for a CPR by the year 2001? Workplace of the Future suggests the role of HIM managers will take paradigm shifts with different functions, tasks, and roles emerging.

Health information services in the hypothetical Workplace of the Future will occupy less physical space; the large file room will be noticeably absent. All patient data will be captured via an information system—from demographic information scanned from the patient's health-care card to the plan of care individualized by a nursing professional. Handheld wireless computers will be in use by health-care professionals to assess patient needs and by HIM professionals to update utilization management information and broker this information appropriately.

Taking raw bits of data from the originators, HIM professionals will amass and organize data elements for analysis while maintaining accuracy of the data through monitoring of the data flow and interacting with the producers of the data. On the patient units, computer hardware serves as the data entry point for the clinical database. The creation of these EPR systems allows HIM professionals to manage health information activities through electronic pathways. As the EPR becomes an enterprise-wide information tool, HIM professionals will manage digital data, perform medical record completion functions, and integrate patient information into databases. With this integration of the EPR, financial data elements and other enterprise-wide data elements, decision support systems can be created.

Opportunities exist for HIM professionals to participate in developing protocols for clinical-care databases. These protocols may include Lawrence Weed's **knowledge couplers** or some **critical pathway** concepts (Weed, 1991; Hart and Musfeldt, 1992). The vendors developing such automated protocols for patient care have a huge task that can involve many hours of initial effort. Reviews and updates will be ongoing as the practice of medicine continues to change.

In this environment, health information managers will be key team players responsible for coherent information content, format, and interpretation of data. A close working relationship with the CIO will be desirable because of the demand for accurate, timely information for various facility needs, especially for **clinical management**, licensure, certification, strategic planning, and executive decision making. Organizationally, in large health-care facilities, information services appropriately reports to the CIO. In smaller organizations, health information services may report directly to the CEO since this office is where executive decision support systems reside.

With sophisticated distributed processing and workstation networks in place, data will flow efficiently as needed throughout the system. HIM professionals will assure that health information services teams have appropriate security systems in place for database information. This is especially crucial as data elements will flow to the CHINs network, creating a longitudinal CPR for community-wide use in patient care. National health-care networks or information superhighways may also have access to this longitudinal record database.

Efficiency and effectiveness will be evident as information from the CPR is used in the short term for billing, for ongoing patient care, for quality improvement activities, and in resource utilization. The long-term uses of data will occur as analysis and integration result in reports that will be generated for strategic planning at all levels, especially as decision support software is used by health-care professionals throughout the organization and by the upper-level management team in the executive information systems.

In the Workplace of the Future, CEOs will have become increasingly aware of the importance of structuring the organization around the flow of information (unique to each entity) within the facility. HIM brokers, with timely information, can influence decision makers throughout the health-care organization of the future.

Summary

Management is defined as a process of activities for creating objectives and for teaming with people to meet these objectives through efficient and effective use of resources. For the HIM professional, data and their management are the focus of the management process. The term *broker* is one way to describe the role HIM professionals play as disseminators of health-care information. Current knowledge is crucial for managing data and disseminating information. Reading, networking with other HIM professionals and other members of the health-care delivery teams, and attending professional meetings are excellent methods for enhancing this needed professional growth.

The priority given to health-care information in quality patient care throughout diverse settings is expected to increase as timely, accurate information is demanded. The federal government is expected to continue in its role as catalyst toward a true CPR. HIM professionals are well qualified to participate in developing and implementing this transition. Advocating quality patient care, confidentiality, security, effectiveness, and efficiency are also important roles for the future HIM professional. Being prepared for and accepting additional responsibilities within health-care organizations during the transition will ensure HIM managers a role in the Workplace of the Future.

The flow of information/communication networks will continue to be crucial to success within organizations, within CHINs, within regional health-care systems, and eventually within international health-care markets.

Review Questions

1. Explain why HIM managers of the future can increasingly describe themselves as health information brokers.

2. List three methods HIM professionals can use to keep their knowledge current, and discuss the benefits of each.

3. Contrast the terms *efficiency* and *effectiveness* in the framework of health information management.

4. Describe several major management skills that will be needed by HIM brokers of the future.

5. Offer three ways an affiliated acute-care organization differs from a freestanding ambulatory-care organization and three ways in which they are similar.

6. Choose one of the ambulatory-care settings and discuss present and future opportunities for HIM professionals in this setting.

References

Dick, R., & Steen, E. (eds.) (1991). *The computer-based patient record: An essential technology for health care.* Washington, DC: National Academy Press.

Gennusa, C. (1995). Outpatient HIM practices improve as managed care increases. *Advance for Health Information Professionals, 5* (10), 23.

Hart, R., & Musfeldt, C. (1992). MD-directed critical pathways: It's time. *Hospitals,* December 5, p. 56.

Melbin, J. (1991). Patient record 2000. *For the Record, 3* (25), 4, 5.

Weed, L. (1991). *Knowledge coupling.* New York: Springer-Verlag, p. xviii.

Suggested Readings

Bennett, P. (1993). Physicians' offices: The brightest spots in the healthcare universe. *Journal of AHIMA, 64* (10), 52–55.

Calvert, C., & Wickham, F. (1993). The health information manager in a residential treatment facility: An innovator, a change agent, an educator. *Journal of AHIMA, 64* (10), 48–50.

Campbell, M. (1995). Homeward bound: Growth in home care industry opens door for HIM professionals. *Journal of AHIMA, 66* (8), 54–58.

Cohen, K. (1995). Occupational health consulting: An open field for HIM professionals. *Journal of AHIMA, 66* (1), 57, 58.

Cummings, K., & Abell, R. (1993). Losing sight of the shore: How a future integrated American healthcare organization might look. *Health Care Management Review, 18* (2), 85–93.

Dowell, S. (1992). President's message: Form follows function. *Journal of AHIMA, 63* (7), 4.

Drucker, P. (1992). The new society of organizations. *Harvard Business Review,* September–October, pp. 95–105.

Dunn, R. (1994). Preparing for the future. *Journal of AHIMA, 65* (1), 4.

Gennusa, C. (1995). Outpatient HIM practices improve as managed care increases. *Advance for Health Information Professionals, 5* (10), 23.

Huffman, E. (1994). *Health information management* (10th ed.) (J. Cofer, ed.). Berwyn, IL: Physicians' Record Co.

Johns, M. (1995). Issuing the challenge: Creating leadership for health information management. *Topics in Health Information Management, 15* (3), 1–8.

Johnson, S. (1993). Health care's new frontier: Challenges abound. *Hospitals,* March 5, p. 50.

Kelly, C. (1993). Into the light: National conference illuminates role of health information management. *Advance for Health Information Professionals, 3* (21), 12, 13.

Kilchenstein, J. (1995). Using HIM skills in systems analysis. *Journal of AHIMA,* January, pp. 54, 55.

King, K. (1993) Professional challenges and opportunities in long term care. *Journal of AHIMA,* October, pp. 59–61.

McCaffrey, K. (1995). Managing health databases for California. *Journal of AHIMA, 66* (1), 55–57.

Miller, S. (1993). HIM professionals in home care: They must march to the beat of a different drummer. *Journal of AHIMA, 64* (10), 42–45.

Montrose, G., & Marcoux, K. (1991). Management by information: A new imperative. *Computers in Healthcare,* November, pp. 49–54.

Palmer, L. (1995). Expanding horizons—A growth in ambulatory care means new HIM opportunities. *Journal of AHIMA, 66* (9), 42–46.

Rudman, W. & Kearns, L. (1995). Hospital administrator perception of health information managers as future leaders in health care reform. *Topics in Health Information Management, 15* (3), 67–71.

Spath, P. (1993). Critical paths: A tool for clinical process management. *Journal of AHIMA, 64* (3), 48–58.

Staszel, K. (1993). Hospice: The final frontier. *Journal of AHIMA, 64* (10), 56–58.

Thomason, S. (1995). Database management: An emerging HIM role. *Journal of AHIMA, 66* (1), 53, 54.

Wang, C. (1994). *Techno vision: The executive's survival guide to understanding and managing information technology.* New York: McGraw-Hill, Inc.

Wear, P. (1993). HIM in healthcare reform and allied health. *Journal of AHIMA, 63* (11), 6–8.

Chapter 2

Management Theories for an Integrated Management Model

Learning Objectives

After completing this chapter, the learner should be able to:

1. Identify a significant management theory still in use today from each of the major approaches to management thought since 1900.
2. Distinguish the different characteristics of the process, systems, and contingency approaches to management.
3. Differentiate between a closed system and an open system as used in the process approach to management.
4. Give a reason for modifying the participative management style under the contingency management approach.
5. Identify four present management ideas that are specifically incorporated into the integrated management model.

Key Terms

Closed systems

Contingency approach

Empowerment

External environment

Human relations approach

Integrated model of management

Internal environment

Objectives

Open systems

Participative approach

Process approach   Stakeholder
Quantitative approach   Systems approach
Scientific approach

Introduction

A strong foundation upon which to build an integrated model of management is developed in this chapter. This foundation begins with the scientific management approach developed in the early 1900s and builds on theories proven valuable throughout the twentieth century. Blending the best of these past and present theories into an **integrated model of management** creates the principles developed in this text for HIM managerial success in today's information/communication society. To build the integrated model of management for HIM managerial success, the best of these past and present approaches are synthesized into a useful framework.

First the chapter prepares a foundation for integrated management concepts by briefly describing the major management approaches and then develops further selected past and present theories that contribute to an integrated management model.

General Management Theories

Figure 2-1 outlines selected management approaches and theories developed during the twentieth century. From these approaches useful theories are incorporated into an integrated model of management that is of value in managing HIM activities today.

As the body of management knowledge and practice outlined in Figure 2-1 continues to evolve, management theories will continue to build on the comprehensive knowledge already tested and in practice. At the same time, new theories are being developed as research continues and paradigm shifts occur. For example, HIM managers are facing a paradigm shift as traditional roles for HIM departments change to information/communication roles. In the past the departmental roles were largely involved in filing and retrieving medical records, coding, transcription, and release of information. These structured activities were best accomplished utilizing

Scientific Management Approach

- Relationships between people and their work:
  - Eliminate wasted motions or activities to increase productivity.
  - Use incentive pay for reaching standards.
  - Choose the employee best suited to a task to perform that task.
  - Use the correct tools or techniques for a task.
  - Schedule complex tasks through use of devices such as the Gantt chart.

Human Resources/Human Relations Approach

- Relationships between people and among groups of people:
  - Adopt acceptance view of authority—the willingness of subordinates to accept authority.
  - Focus on social behavior and satisfaction among employees.
  - Satisfy human needs in the workplace with development of an employee's full potential.
  - Motivate employees and thus increase productivity.
  - Use communication tools effectively.
  - Develop work groups for specific tasks.

Quantitative Approach Theories

- Apply statistical models to solving complex problems.
- Use computer simulation for decision making.

Process Management Approach

- Use functions of planning, organizing, leading, and controlling to describe management activities that integrate several previous theories.

Systems Approach Theories

- Recognize internal and external environments as important to decision making.
- Manage the input of labor, capital, and materials into the organization as they are transformed into finished products or services.
- Integrate various theories of management.

Contingency Approach Theories

- Use appropriate managerial approaches for different situations and conditions.
- Use participative management appropriately.
- Accept new ideas that fit the situation such as continuous quality improvement techniques.

Figure 2-1.   Selected Twentieth-Century Management Approaches

process and systems approaches to management. Technology, cost containment, and evolving expectations of upper-level management that HIM professionals have a broad range of valuable information create pressures for a paradigm shift in today's society. The challenge for HIM managers is to embrace those aspects of the new ideas that will continue the development of a professional management style, while retaining an open mind that invites future creative growth. An integrated model of management offers the opportunity for meeting these challenges successfully.

Each of the management approaches outlined in Figure 2-1 has points of validity that meld into the unifying view of management that creates a foundation for HIM professionals. The diversity of ideas so evident in current management texts is the result of past and current research and the testing of management concepts over time. Synthesizing this diversity into an integrated view of management for HIM managerial success in healthcare organizations is not only exciting but rewarding. Each of the management approaches is now briefly discussed.

A Scientific Approach

Early in the twentieth century modern management theory was born with the publication of books describing scientific management research theories. These **scientific approach** theories became widely accepted by managers. The emphasis of these researchers was on eliminating waste and inefficiency in manufacturing and other labor-intensive industries. As the relationship between people and their work became the guiding philosophy, standards were set for repetitive tasks. In each instance these standards were developed by management and researchers as the one best way of performing a task. Performance was then compared to these standards. Experiments in hand-and-body motions in laying bricks, for example, helped to eliminate wasted motions and thus increase productivity. (Robbins, 1994). Choosing the best tools and the right employee for a task resulted in significant increases in productivity.

During the early 1900s, Frederick Taylor, Frank and Lillian Gilbreth, and Henry Gantt became well known for their scientific management research. Frederick Taylor believed there was one best way to do a task and his research focused on giving workers the right tools for the task, training them in the one best way for doing the task, and motivating them through wage incentives. When manufacturing companies followed these scientific principles, they increased productivity (Donnelly, Gibson, and Ivancevich, 1987).

Frank and Lillian Gilbreth were inspired by the work of Taylor. Their research focused on reducing wasted hand-and-body motions. In labor-intensive jobs, the Gilbreths' research showed significant time savings, thus reducing cost (Terry and Franklin, 1982).

Henry Gantt suggested offering a bonus to the manufacturing foreman, as well as the workers, when the standard was met or exceeded. He also introduced management to a graphic bar chart for use as a scheduling device. The Gantt chart continues in use today for planning and controlling projects (Rue and Byars, 1986). Details on using Gantt charts are outlined in Chapter 5.

Modified management concepts based on scientific approach concepts continue in use today and have increased importance as efficiency and effectiveness are given priority in health-care organizations. The concepts from the scientific approach that are incorporated into the integrated management model are outlined in Figure 2-1.

Human Resources and Human Relations Approaches

The concepts that focused on human behavior and managing were partially developed and publicized during the same period as the scientific researchers were sharing their ideas. However, **human relations approach** enthusiasts focused on the social relationships in the workplace. They challenged the traditional view of authority—the view that authority comes from above. In its place these researchers presented an acceptance view of authority—the view that authority comes from the willingness of subordinates to accept it (Robbins, 1994).

These theories were further developed as group norms and behavior were studied during the 1920s to 1950s and results were published by different groups within the broad human resources approach. The growing human relations movement focused on behavior and employee satisfaction. Research showed that employees were positively influenced by group standards and security. The human relations movement emphasized a belief that a satisfied employee will be productive. Motivational behavior and productivity became the focus of many research studies. One example from the 1930s became famous as the Hawthorne studies. Although the initial focus of the studies involved productivity and change in the physical environment, the results showed that productivity increase occurred when supervisors developed effective human relations skills that included cooperative effort with employees (Robbins, 1994).

Abraham Maslow proposed a hierarchy of five human needs with the highest being self-actualization (Robbins, 1994). Managers who accepted the human relations approach attempted to develop organizations where employees could meet their needs and develop their full potential. Maslow's hierarchy of needs is discussed in greater detail in Chapter 13.

Modified human resource management concepts have a firm base of support in today's health-care organizations. Motivation, human relations, group behavior, and communication within organizations continue to gain managerial importance and are a part of the integrated model of management.

A Quantitative Approach

Quantitative approach solutions to management problems began during World War II and continue to be useful in decision making. Applications of statistical models, information models, and computer simulations make this approach valuable for complex problems that are measurable and well defined. In Chapter 5 specific quantitative management models are discussed as part of the integrated model of management.

A Process Approach

In the 1960s, Harold Koontz detailed a **process approach** that synthesized major theories into an integrated whole. Koontz defined the process approach as management performing the functions of planning, organizing, leading, and controlling. He interpreted these four functions as being circular and continuous (Robbins, 1994).

Several researchers took this process approach a step further into a modified process approach to management. They used the same four functions, although they gave them different names or divided them for greater detail. Thus began the integrated view of management theories that continues to be modified through research and new technology (Robbins, 1994).

The Systems Approach

The **systems approach** theory views an organization as a set of interrelated and interdependent parts. This management theory, developed in the mid-1960s, is a way of approaching the job of managing holistically. This approach views inputs and outputs for organizational activity in much the same manner as physiologists view the body in a state of equilibrium. The inputs would be material, labor, and capital. These are transformed in the process and become outputs or finished products and services. As in physiology, forces in the environment can place restraints on the organization (Drucker, 1990).

Open and closed systems are contrasted in this approach. The **closed system** is neither influenced by nor interacts with its environment. Since health-care organizations are dynamic systems that interact with and are influenced by their environment, they are referred to as open systems.

Stakeholder is a name given to any entity with a stake in the future of an organization. For health-care organizations, as **open systems**, input comes from several stakeholders—the community, employees, physicians, and researchers. Health-care organizations are significantly influenced by their environment. Much of this influence is in the form of constraints, such as mandates from government agencies. When the organization successfully ensures coordination of all its parts and meets the needs of stakeholders and the constraints of the environment, the output or service should meet customer expectations (Robbins, 1994).

The Contingency Management Approach

The **contingency approach** steps beyond the systems theories and recognizes that situational variables will arise that require managers to use different approaches to solving problems. For example, circumstances occur that demand immediate answers and leave no time to ask for employee participation in the decision-making process to solve a problem. The contingency approach encourages managers to meet such a demand appropriately, then honestly share the background circumstances and the decision with employees. Managers will then be committed to a **participative management** style but accept that it is not appropriate or possible in every situation (Robbins, 1994).

Because the contingency approach represents the value of using the best management theory to meet the circumstance a manager is facing, it encourages the paradigm shift facing HIM managers. As information/communication technology and cost containment become the focus of upper-level management, HIM departments need to be redesigned or perhaps even reengineered to meet the new demands. Thus, the emphasis becomes focused on the situation, on the **internal** and **external environments**, and ultimately on a creative solution that breaks with traditional roles.

The contingency approach to management predominates as theories are integrated into the management model. Interwoven into the fabric of this approach are quality improvement theories, innovation and change theories, participation and **empowerment** theories, and ethical standard theories. This integrated approach creates a unifying framework that allows managers to meet today's challenges and explore tomorrow's opportunities.

Summary

Figure 2-1 outlines major management approaches for the theories that have continuing usefulness for today. Productivity was a major thrust for many of the early management researchers. Productivity certainly remains important today as managers plan objectives that must be accomplished with limited resources.

The scientific management approach was developed early in the 1900s by researchers who focused on eliminating wasted activities, using incentive pay, and choosing the best employees and tools for a task. Human relationships in the workplace became important to researchers of the human resources approach, which developed an acceptance view of authority, focused on satisfying the needs of employees, motivating employees to improve productivity, and using communication tools and work groups effectively.

Quantitative approach theories focus on statistical models for solving complex problems and the use of computer simulations to enhance decision making. The four management functions of planning, organizing, leading, and controlling were developed by process management theorists for describing management activities that integrate selected theories to create a balanced view. Theorists of the systems approach to management emphasized the internal and external environments of organizations for inputs and outputs that resulted in finished products or services.

Advocates of the contingency approach to management use selected theories from previous approaches to appropriately meet managerial situations or conditions. Participative management grew in importance with work teams and quality improvement techniques.

An integrated approach to management for HIM professionals combines these major features from past and present approaches and includes quality improvement ideas, transition ideas, empowerment ideas, and ethical standard ideas. This framework offers HIM managers and brokers the tools for meeting the challenges of paradigm shifts as health-care organizations face the pressures of change.

Review Questions

1. Choose one major management theory and explain the value of it in building an integrated model of management.
2. Give four typical stakeholders who offer input into managing a health-care organization.
3. Explain why health-care organizations are considered open systems under the systems approach to management.
4. How does a participative management style fit into the contingency approach to management?
5. Discuss the role mentors can play in teaching both management theory and practice.

References

Donnelly, J., Gibson, J., & Ivancevich, J. (1987). *Fundamentals of management* (6th ed.). Plano, TX: Business Publications.

Drucker, P. (1990). *Managing for the future.* New York: Truman Talley Books.

Robbins, S. (1994). *Management* (4th ed.). Englewood Cliffs, NJ: Prentice Hall.

Rue, L., & Byars, L. (1986). *Management: Theory and application* (4th ed.). Homewood, IL: Richard D. Irwin.

Terry, G., & Franklin, S. (1982). *Principles of management* (8th ed.). Homewood, IL: Richard D. Irwin.

Suggested Readings

Berk, J., & Berk, S. (1993). *Total quality management.* New York: Sterling Publishing.

Donnelly, J., Gibson, J., & Ivancevich, J. (1987). *Fundamentals of management* (6th ed.). Plano, TX: Business Publications.

Kanter, R. (1992). The best of both worlds. *Harvard Business Review*, November–December, pp. 9, 10.

Longest, B. (1990). *Management practices for the health professional* (4th ed.). Norwalk, CT: Appleton & Lange.

Rakich, J., Longest, B., & Darr, K. (1992). *Managing health services organizations* (3rd ed.). Baltimore: Health Professions Press.

Robbins, S. (1994). *Management* (4th ed.). Englewood Cliffs, NJ: Prentice Hall.

Rue, L., & Byars, L. (1986). *Management: Theory and application* (4th ed.). Homewood, IL: Richard D. Irwin.

Terry, G., & Franklin, S. (1982). *Principles of management* (8th ed.). Homewood, IL: Richard D. Irwin.

Chapter *3*

The Art of Decision Making and Problem Solving

Learning Objectives

After completing this chapter, the learner should be able to:

1. Explain differences between strategic planning decisions and day-to-day problem-solving decisions.
2. Describe problem seekers and ways they manage differently than problem avoiders.
3. Outline the steps in the decision-making process.
4. Differentiate conditions for certainty, risk, and uncertainty.
5. Describe the pressures facing decision makers in satisficing rather than using total rationality.
6. Illustrate well-structured problems and contrast these with ill-structured problems.
7. Explain how to create programmed decision-making tools for teams and contrast these with nonprogrammed decision-making methods.
8. Identify advantages and disadvantages of team decision making.

Key Terms

Certainty

Continuous quality improvement

Creativity

Decision-making process

Electronic meeting

Moderator

Nonprogrammed decisions

Problem avoider

Problem seeker

Problem-solving process

Programmed decisions

Quality improvement

Rational model in decision making

Risk

Rules

Satisficing decisions

Uncertainty

Introduction

Developing decision-making skills for meeting organizational needs now and for the future is a crucial component to managerial success. The art and science of decision making is a central element in the planning function of the integrated model of management, and these skills permeate the other managerial functions as well. Were HIM managers to record every decision made during just 1 week, they would discover a lengthy list. Encompassing much of the daily activities of managers is this pervading relationship of decision making and successful management.

This chapter emphasizes both of these phases in making decisions— daily activities decisions and strategic planning decisions. Appropriate decisions made during the strategic planning phase can lessen the stress during the daily activities decision phase. And, daily decisions made in anticipation of problems will lessen the need for crisis decision making and related stress. In reality, problems will arise regardless of the skill used during planning, so problem-solving expertise for these daily activities decisions is very much needed. Increasingly, the highest level of decision-making skills is needed for planning the future direction of the department and/or the organization.

Problem-solving steps that assist managers in making the best possible decisions are outlined in this chapter. Also, the types of problems faced by managers are contrasted. Suggestions for different approaches to decision making for each type of problem give insight into ideas managers can use. To summarize, the chapter discusses how using a participative management style for solving problems can have lasting advantages.

Decision Making in Planning and Daily Problems

The paradigm shifts occurring in today's health-care environment make the **problem-solving process** during the strategic planning phase particularly important. As managers face growing unsolved problems in the health information management workplace, the dichotomy between actual and desirable situations creates pressure for changing a present paradigm. The manager who can forecast and generate ideas for shifting to a new paradigm is helping to create the exciting health-care environment of the future. This task is hard work. Peter Drucker (1990) emphasized the work involved in his timely book, *Managing Non-profit Organizations*.

Strategic planning in itself is also hard work, with commitment needed to take the plan through to a satisfactory decision. **Problem seekers** are found to have a higher level of commitment to strategic planning. Problem seekers who actively look for opportunities to plan, anticipate, and solve possible problems before they occur have the potential for becoming exceptional managers.

At the other extreme are **problem avoiders**, who may ignore signals of possible problem eruption. Several causes for this avoidance may be valid. They may include (1) time constraints, (2) delegation of responsibility to others who are also too busy, or (3) a perception that upper-level management will avoid the problem also. Once problem avoiders recognize the value of a team approach to finding solutions, they can share the responsibility. By actively sharing the challenges of planning by creating a participative culture, they can expect better alternatives and earlier solutions to problems (Drucker, 1990).

In the daily work environment, crises occur and problems erupt when reality fails to equal the desired situations. In other words, there is a difference between what is and what should be. An example in a health information department is when the manager finds the work flow suddenly faltering in one section due to excess absenteeism. Action to bring the actual and desired situation back in balance can be taken by the manager and, ideally, with the participation of the team within that section. The solution may include asking that budget funds be allocated for hiring a temporary employee through the human resource department. This example shows that few problem-solving decisions are truly made in isolation. Here the manager, the team, the human resource department, and the person to whom the department reports may all be involved in solving this problem.

The absenteeism problem may have been entirely unanticipated. However, a crisis need not occur if the manager plans ahead with the human resource department for budget allocation to use an on-call resource person in such situations. Some managers use on-call professionally trained resource persons to meet such emergencies. When professionals prefer only part-time employment, this can be a viable short-term solution to obtaining well-trained employees to solve an absenteeism problem.

The Process of Decision Making

Several steps are included in the **decision-making process**. While decision making is defined as making a choice between two or more alternatives, a more complete description includes the whole process as shown in Figure 3-1. The process is shown in seven steps. In actuality, the decision process encompasses the first five steps; the last two steps can be considered actions taken as the result of the decision. They are included because action following the intellectual work is crucial to the success of the decision.

Abbreviated versions of the process may be adequate for a personal decision, such as when plans begin for enjoying a 2-week vacation. Looking at alternative vacation spots may be the major decision-making step taken. In contrast, managers need to immerse themselves in all seven steps outlined when choosing among alternatives for all but the simple problems. As these steps are discussed in detail, decisions appear to be made in isolation. This, of course, is not true. Managers deal with an interrelated network of problems and solving one problem may have implications that

---

1. Define the real problem, after awareness of the symptoms.
2. Set criteria for making the decision while analyzing available information.
3. Generate relevant alternative solutions to the problem.
4. Analyze and evaluate these alternatives.
5. Select the best alternative for a solution.
6. Implement the chosen alternative.
7. Monitor and evaluate the decision's effectiveness.

Figure 3-1. The Decision-Making Process (Robbins, 1994)

impact others. The busy professional must keep a broad and integrative perspective as decisions are made.

■ *Practice Example*

As each of the steps is explored in detail, a practice example problem is used to create a climate for discussing decision-making skills. This example problem discusses the response to a budgetary committee mandate that the HIM department plan a budget with three fewer full-time equivalent (FTEs) employees than the present year. The management team begins strategic planning to rightsize the HIM department for the coming year. The focus will be on increased efficient and effective work-flow systems throughout the department. The team, at its first meeting, plans the strategy for beginning the seven-step decision-making process.

1. *Define the real problem following awareness of the symptoms.* The organization's problem in the example is a facility-wide budget constraint while the focused problem for the HIM management team is preparing a plan with a budget showing three fewer FTEs. The actual problem to be faced, however, is inefficient or ineffective work methods where redesign for cost containment is possible. In this example, problem awareness of the symptoms came with a falling patient census, then crystallized with the budget committee action to rightsize the facility. At this awareness phase, the HIM management team develops sensitivity to facility and departmental events that show discrepancies between actual and desired situations. Perceptual skills enable the manager to collect and interpret cues from these events for beginning identification of the problem. At this step a decision may be made that no further action is needed. In the example, of course, this is not a viable alternative.

As details of the problem are defined, these are documented by the team. It is also helpful at this point to begin listing objectives for returning to the desired situation, which may actually be a revised desired situation, as mandated in the problem.

A management team approach is being used in the example as one way to solve problems. Certainly managers make decisions by themselves in many instances. However, using a team approach when applicable has several advantages that are discussed later in the chapter. The use of a team keeps the decision making at the lowest level in the organization possible—where the activity takes place.

2. *Set criteria for making the decision while analyzing available information.* Using a team approach to solve the problem, the managers next empower employees in each section to review the department's philosophy and objectives and then set priorities for action. For example, having staff available from 7 A.M. to 11 A.M. to assist physicians in record completion activities may be a priority activity that is not negotiable.

3. *Generate relevant alternative solutions to the problem.* At the next management team meeting there is a concensus that section meetings should be encouraged and the team managers of each section plan to meet and generate ideas. Reviewing present systems critically can open windows of opportunity. Listening to experiences of others, reading journals for ideas, talking to vendors—these activities will assist the team in generating alternatives. **Creativity** is crucial in this step as the final solution can only be as good as the quality of the alternatives chosen for review. Looking at creative alternatives opens doors and expands the possibilities for a workable solution.

Every employee has creative abilities when empowered to work in an atmosphere of trust, freedom, and security. Certainly for some people creative ideas appear to come as a "bolt from the blue," but creativity mostly incubates as a person becomes saturated with information. By choosing to organize the concepts into new and meaningful relationships, creative ideas surface.

Since every system in the HIM department is involved in this example, step 3 is a time-consuming activity. The section teams generate ideas for more efficient and effective systems. These ideas are analyzed by the management team.

4. *Analyze and evaluate these alternatives.* Some alternatives may require capital funds; some may involve other departments; some may suggest reengineering the work flow completely. This step is also time-consuming as the managers network and further develop ideas for possible solutions. Alternatives to consider further are those that have the greatest number of desired results possible and the fewest undesirable consequences.

Three conditions are present as this analysis is undertaken: **certainty**, **risk**, and **uncertainty**. Ideally, all decisions would be made with certainty;

unfortunately, that is not the norm. Estimations of how likely it is that certain events will occur and then acting on those estimates in a risk environment is much more likely. At the far extreme is uncertainty, where the decision maker has several variables lacking certainty. It is then very difficult to estimate the positive or negative impact of alternatives. Decisions on the alternatives may be influenced more by the personality of the manager. An optimist is more likely to choose an alternative that will maximize the benefits, with the uncertainty factors of less weight. Risk factors associated with alternatives can have probabilities assigned to them, which allow managers to use computer software to assist in the decision-making process. Further discussion of computer-assisted decisions is found in Chapter 5. In the example, the management team analyzes the alternative brought forward by the sections.

5. *Select the best alternative for a solution.* In this step of the process, the decision maker should ask four questions as outlined in Figure 3-2. The first question regards no choice, which is always a possibility: Is the best choice one of doing nothing? This choice may be taken if it is perceived that no action will provide the most desirable result. Should this alternative be rejected, then the remaining three questions are relevant. Doing nothing is not a viable solution in the example since the budget committee has mandated change.

The second question asked is whether and to what extent each alternative will contribute to achieving the objectives that were documented in step 1. Again the responses to this question should be expressed in terms of possible results. In the example, the management team continues to encourage section teams to participate during this analysis phase.

---

1. Is the best choice one of doing nothing?

2. To what extent will each alternative contribute to achieving the objectives documented in step 1?

3. To what extent will each alternative contribute to economic effectiveness by maximizing use of available resources?

4. To what extent is expertise available to implement the alternative with the highest positive factors?

Figure 3-2.   Questions to Ask in Selecting the Best Alternative

Economic effectiveness is considered in the third question. Not all decisions relate to maximizing the use of available resources, so this may not be a criterion for every decision. Since some team efforts are interdepartmental, it is important to ask the fourth question as team members may be unaware of the resources available in another department.

The last question seeks in very practical terms the feasibility of implementing an alternative that appears to have the highest positive factors. Should an alternative pass the test posed in question 3 regarding economic resources, this fourth question can focus on available expertise. A decision to automate aspects of the HIM department work-flow systems to reduce labor may be one alternative considered by the teams in the example, but could fail if the expertise for implementing such a program is unavailable.

Asking and seeking answers for these four questions increases the chances that a good decision among the appropriate alternatives will be made. Involving all those affected by the forthcoming changes as decisions are made at this step will ease the transition into step 6.

6. *Implement the chosen alternative.* In our example, employees were actually lost through attrition rather than by outright layoffs. And, the alternative chosen was to reorganize the record analysis section. First, the teams worked with the medical staff to decrease the number of elements looked for in a discharged record. Guidelines developed by the American Health Information Association (AHIMA) (DeVitt et al., 1991) were used to acquaint the medical staff and the department staff with acceptable practice. By networking and through journal review, the team generated ideas for streamlining discharged record procedures. By implementing these ideas, cost savings were achieved.

Nursing representatives were invited to share their expertise on the team and joined in the cost-saving effort by accepting specific record completion tasks at the point of patient care. The coding section staff also suggested ideas for shared responsibility during concurrent coding and accepted these completion tasks. Using these combined efforts, the rightsizing task was accomplished and the team eliminated the three FTE positions within the time frame requested by the budget committee.

The change was implemented when one record analysis team member moved away and two others were retrained for other positions in the department as employees left. The team planned biweekly meetings for two months to discuss any implementation difficulties that might arise.

Frequent team meetings during this transition period kept the managers aware of potential problems that could retard successful implementation.

7. *Monitor and evaluate the decision's effectiveness.* Through a **continuous quality improvement** program, this step can be incorporated into each section's regular monitoring activities. The loop becomes complete as any problems that develop are taken back to step 1 for solution. Chapter 15 describes the manager's role in quality improvement. ■

Rationality in Decision Making

The busy manager is expected to behave rationally, objectively, and logically when following the seven steps in decision making. But, is it realistic to assume that managers know all the alternatives available and all the consequences each alternative might bring to the situation? The **rational model in decision making** expects managers to maximize every choice in decision making. This model fails the test of reality since, in a manager's real world, time constraints may not allow for full development of all possible alternatives with analysis of the consequences of each alternative, if implemented. Other factors may also create blocks to total rationality and are discussed below (Robbins, 1994).

Managers may have a combination of reasons for deviating from the path of total rationality. For instance, their values, backgrounds, past experiences, and interests all work to influence perceptions as alternatives are explored. Expectations of others and the organizational culture can create distortions and encourage maintaining the status quo. Another possibility is that a past decision and its results may be a component of the current problem. This situation may escalate a manager's commitment toward one of the alternatives in an effort to demonstrate that an earlier decision was correct. Using a team approach to solving problems can minimize these constraints to some extent.

When a manager or team uses the seven-step model in theory, but takes shortcuts because of limitations outlined above, the result is more likely to be a **satisficing decision** rather than one that maximizes all available information. The satisficing alternative is thus considered "good enough" given the constraints (Rue and Byars, 1986).

Contingency Approach to Decision Making

The contingency approach to management is outlined in Figure 2-1. Additional aspects of the contingency approach to planning are discussed in Chapter 4. For this discussion, a description of some of the unique features of contingency management that relate to making decisions is helpful. First, the type of problem and decision a manager faces can determine the reaction to it. Some decisions can be made that efficiently solve well-structured problems with a minimum of effort. However, there are ill-structured problems that demand time-consuming additional knowledge. These factors show the value of contingency theory, where the approach to a problem is contingent on the type of problem.

For example, when managers perceive there are new opportunities for growth in computer technology that would enhance managerial decisions, they get excited. But, then they find new computer purchases are contingent on other decisions to be made by upper-level management. Extra time and effort may be required to develop viable alternatives when so many other factors are involved. This is especially true when managers are involved in exploring a new technology such as an electronic patient record (EPR).

Two types of problems arise in this situation. The decisions for problem solutions can be separated into two categories. First are **routine** or **programmed decisions** for handling well-structured problems. The second category of decisions can be described as **nonprogrammed decisions**, where contingency management approaches are especially useful. Here the problems tend to be unique and nonrecurring. Each of these types is discussed in further detail (Robbins, 1994).

Programmed Decisions

An example will give focus to this type of decision. An annoyed attorney telephones a release-of-information team member to complain that a record he needs for court the next morning has not yet been delivered. Because this situation has occurred in the past, the section team has created a procedure for solving this problem. There is no need to review the seven-step process with the developing of alternatives. Team members need only follow the step-by-step procedure, first by accessing the database to find when the request was received. Then they can check whether the release of confidential information was included with the request, and when the information was sent. Armed with this information, the team member can respond to the attorney and then meet the attorney's needs—following the procedure. The decision for this team member is a routine programmed one.

As procedures are documented for programmed decisions, they include **rules**. The procedure mentioned in the situation above would include a rule that sets parameters on what is a valid release form. Rules explicitly state what can and cannot be done. Programmed decisions can be made with efficiency and effectiveness when procedures are in place to guide in the resolution with explicit rules.

Policy statements are also used in developing procedures. A policy sets parameters for making a decision, thus allowing the technician to use judgment. In contrast, a rule allows for very little interpretation. For example, a rule regarding the patient's signature on a release form before sharing health record information leaves little room for judgment. However, a policy stating that, "Every attorney is treated courteously and promptly," gives the technician direction and guidelines while allowing opportunity for discretion in that treatment.

Nonprogrammed Decisions

Managers need skill in handling unique and nonrecurring problems that require a custom-made solution, contingent on the situation. HIM managers find opportunities to develop these skills as new technologies create system capabilities unheard of before the 1990s. When unsolved problems are occurring with the present dictation system, for example, an opportunity for a nonprogrammed decision is created. Certainly all seven steps in the decision-making process are utilized as the managers empower the transcription team to join in developing a strategy for purchasing the latest in dictation technology for the best price and service available in the area.

In reality, most problems faced by managers fall between fully programmed and nonprogrammed decisions. A measure of individual judgment is needed, even in programmed decisions, while components of nonprogrammed decisions make use of structured procedures that could be considered a programmed approach. Upper-level management bears responsibility for the majority of decisions involving unique and nonrecurring problems. At the lower level in the organization are the teams responsible for sections where the more routine decisions are made. Only the difficult decisions are passed up to the managers.

As the examples show, standardized procedures facilitate organizational efficiency; managers and the section teams appreciate them for this reason. They allow decisions to be made at the lowest level possible within an organization. This process is cost-effective and creates an environment where employees feel empowered and in control of their activities.

A Team Approach in Decision Making

Teams have been mentioned frequently in this chapter as participating in making decisions. These teams or groups may be called task forces, section teams, multidisciplinary teams, study groups, work groups, or committees. This team approach brings advantages into the decision-making process. The axiom that two heads are better than one holds true here. A first step is reaching out to the team performing the activity in question. This puts the manager in touch with the best perspective as the discussion begins. Increasing the possibilities for diversity of opinion in this way strengthens the process and also brings the true problem into focus. Typically a wider range of alternatives results from this diversity of ideas, with increased opportunity for creatively solving the problem.

In addition to the section team, other teams can be formally assigned specific tasks. To include professionals from other specialties on these teams may be crucial to the success of the project. This multidisciplinary group can bring valuable insights from different perspectives into the problem-solving process. Shared understanding of the problem leads to creative solutions. Another benefit of the multidisciplinary team approach is the mutual understanding of the challenges and opportunities facing the various specialty groups as they work together. And, this democratic model can be perceived by the employees as more legitimate, thus increasing acceptance of the eventual solution and facilitating a smooth implementation phase.

Used appropriately, teams can successfully tackle many problems. But, there are some drawbacks to group decision making that must be considered. First is the increased time factor and the cost of each employee's time to attend meetings. Also, busy professionals may feel there is no time for another committee. Managers must plan these team meetings carefully and ensure that they move at a brisk pace. An experienced **moderator** can decrease negatives by seeing that vocal individuals do not dominate the meetings and that social pressures to conform are minimized.

One last drawback is that group responsibility for the final decision releases any single individual from that burden. Again, the moderator can reinforce team/individual responsibility for the decision.

The **electronic meeting** is a recent innovation that can give anonymity, honesty, and speed to the decision-making process. This technique and others for group meetings are discussed in detail in Chapter 18.

Summary

Decision making is described as choosing between two or more alternatives. Decisions are needed when an actual situation fails to match the desired situation. Managers make critical choices when planning effectively, but decision making also permeates all the other functions of management. Committees or teams meet for strategic planning sessions where the future direction of the department or organization is decided. Philosophies and objectives result and future decisions are made based on these strategic plans.

In contrast, day-to-day decisions are made in shorter time frames. These decisions complement those made during the planning function. As unsolved problems surface during day-to-day activities, pressure mounts to make a paradigm shift that creates the need for further strategic planning decisions.

Problem seekers generate opportunities for solving problems before crises arise; whereas problem avoiders tend to ignore signals that problems are surfacing. Problem avoiders may be overworked and under pressure. By using a team approach, problems can be solved at the lowest level of the organization possible, thus freeing the management team for other pressing tasks. Seven steps that assist managers in making decisions are outlined and discussed. This process then becomes a loop that can lead to awareness of problems before they become crises.

As alternatives are analyzed and evaluated, those favored have the greatest number of desired results and the fewest undesirable consequences. Managers weigh the alternatives in an environment of risk, since few decisions are made with the certainty that the desired results will follow. Uncertainty is the third condition to consider. Mathematical computer models can be used by assigning weights to these conditions. Use of these models when making quantitative decisions gives assurance that all factors are considered in the final decision.

In totally rational situations, managers make decisions that maximize the economic payoff, because all information in each alternative is available. In reality, the pressures faced by managers cause them to make decisions without full information; thus, they choose the alternative that is considered good enough at the time. This is called a satisficing solution.

Employees facing well-structured problems have procedures for solving them. These procedures include consideration of rules and policies and allow day-to-day problem solving at the lowest level possible. Problems that are ill structured require unique solutions and therefore demand the attention of managers. Decisions are made contingent on the variables surrounding the problem.

The day-to-day problems offer opportunity for managers to use a team approach in creating tools, such as procedures and manuals that will allow for programmed decisions when these problems are well structured. With ill-structured problems, use of nonprogrammed methods is more likely. Managers must monitor current and future technologies constantly for optimum use of appropriate new tools.

Empowering section teams with a voice in the decisions that affect their daily activities offers many advantages. Managers create an environment of openness and trust by respecting the ideas and concerns voiced by teams.

Review Questions

1. Why can the group decision-making process be both efficient and effective?

2. Give three reasons why top management in a health-care organization would encourage department managers to document a wide range of programmed decisions for their staff.

3. Interpret the meaning of the phrase "satisficing decision" and then describe a decision you have made recently that aligns with its assumptions.

4. Consider the steps of the decision-making process; identify one step, if any, that is more important than the others. Defend your answer.

5. Discuss the value of encouraging group members to share differing ideas as they explore alternative solutions to a problem.

6. State reasons why managers may not routinely anticipate difficulties before they become problems.

7. Explain the rationale for avoiding a difficult decision, hoping the problem will go away. Discuss advantages or disadvantages for tackling the problem immediately.

8. Think of several decisions you have made in the past week. Describe the conscious steps you took in the process of reaching the final decision for each.

9. Compare the use of rules and policies in managerial action; explain the difference between these tools.

Case Study

Complaints have come to the department manager regarding timeliness of requests for patient information and a decision must be made.

Three months ago, Community Hospital opened a 24-hour urgent-care center 10 miles away in a rapidly growing community. Kent Jones, the health information services manager, took part in the planning that included the use of a combined record and one patient identification number. The decision was made to use electronic sharing of patient records between the facilities; however, at present it is necessary to fax some portions of the record upon request. In the past month, Kent has received four complaints from the urgent-care center that records were not faxed in a timely manner.

There are 26 employees in health information services. Three full-time employees care for record activity during the day, with one employee devoted to record activity during the evening shift, when a team leader and four other employees are usually in the department. During the 11 P.M. to 7 A.M. shift, one employee cares for the department and picks up the discharged records from the patient-care units. This time away from the department averages 1 hour. Adding additional employees is not an option, since there is a hiring freeze in place.

Kent envisions an increase in the requests for record information as the patient load at the urgent-care center increases, and realizes the assumption of his management team that this activity could be absorbed without adjusting work schedules was in error.

Prepare to assist Kent in solving this problem, using the steps outlined in this chapter.

References

DeVitt, M., Haenk, B., Picukaric, J., Kerwin, J., Hettel, S., Cameron, M., Testa, F., Fainter, J., & Feste, L. (1991). Health record completion guidelines. *Journal of AHIMA, 62* (11), 26–44.

Drucker, P. (1990). *Managing non-profit organizations.* New York: Truman Talley Books.

Robbins, S. (1994). *Management* (4th ed.). Englewood Cliffs, NJ: Prentice Hall.

Rue, L., & Byars, L. (1986). *Management: Theory and application* (4th ed.). Homewood, IL: Richard D. Irwin.

Suggested Readings

Donnelly, J., Gibson, J., & Ivancevich, J. (1987). *Fundamentals of management* (6th ed.). Plano, TX: Business Publications.

Drucker, P. (1990). *Managing the non-profit organization.* New York: Truman Talley Books.

Drucker, P. (1992). *Managing for the future.* New York: Truman Talley Books.

Longest, B. (1990). *Management practices for the health professional* (4th ed.). Norwalk, CT: Appleton & Lange.

Robbins, S. (1994). *Management* (4th ed.). Englewood Cliffs, NJ: Prentice Hall.

Rue, L., & Byars, L. (1986). *Management: Theory and application* (4th ed.). Homewood, IL: Richard D. Irwin.

Terry, G., & Franklin S. (1982). *Principles of management* (8th ed.). Homewood, IL: Richard D. Irwin.

Planning to Meet the Information Needs of Health-Care Facilities

Chapter 4

Planning in the Health-Care Setting

Learning Objectives

After completing this chapter, the learner should be able to:

1. Define the management function of planning.
2. Explain differences between formal and informal planning.
3. Distinguish between strategic and operational planning.
4. Describe contingency planning and its advantages in health-care management.
5. Define organizational vision and its role in the mission statement.
6. Explain how departmental objectives flow from organizational mission statement, goals, and objectives.
7. Identify the four components of SWOT analysis and describe the steps in analyzing the environment.
8. Outline major steps in the planning process.
9. Define transitional planning.
10. Describe use of a business plan.

Key Terms

Business plan

Entrepreneur

Informal planning

Intrapreneur

Management by objectives (MBO)   SWOT analysis
Mission statement   Transitional planning
Operational plans   Vision
Span of control

Introduction

Planning is a crucial element to success in professional career choices and in personal growth. Planning is just naturally a part of daily activities. Think back to the decision-making process in making your career selection. You chose a college to meet that career goal and then planned details for reaching personal objectives. This planning may have involved formal planning concepts as long-range goals were documented on the road toward a chosen career path. This section on planning includes tools for increasing the certainty of success in meeting professional goals in the workplace, and personally.

This chapter first discusses the broad foundations of planning that give this management function the importance it deserves. The discussion outlines the different types of plans that managers use and various methods for using these planning tools appropriately. Next, strategic planning is described in detail as a part of the planning process. The transitional planning section focuses on the opportunity to redesign systems for a smooth transition through a paradigm shift. Lastly, developing a **business plan** as discussed in this section will be especially helpful to entrepreneurs and intrapreneurs.

Planning Defined

One reason for planning is to get from where we are to where we want to go. Knowing the goal, setting the objectives, developing the strategy, choosing methods for achievement—these are components of planning. Or, it could be said that planning is choosing the ends or what is to be done, as well as the means or how it is to be done. Thus, planning lays the foundation for organizational activity. The health-care organization may be a consulting firm; it may be a new home health-care facility; or it may be a large inpatient facility. HIM professionals can choose involvement in the planning associated with each of these three examples of health-care organizations.

Planning involves the six universal questions: Who? What? Where? When? Why? How? The managers and planning teams of an organization must answer these questions to achieve a coordinated effort toward the planned direction (McArdle, 1993).

Planning does not stay behind closed doors; it is a communicated, coordinated effort. When every person concerned knows where the organization is going and what they must contribute to reach the objective, they will become a part of the team effort. As Kevin McArdle states, "If the lowest person in the organization cannot tell you what the strategy of the organization is, you do not have a strategy" (McArdle, 1993).

Formal and Informal Planning

A manager carries around in her head some plans for the day's activities. Several are probably not written down anywhere and have no objectives formally tied to them. They are examples of **informal planning** that occur in every organization. Even an **entrepreneur** catching a **vision** of the future may not formally document that vision and the plan for getting there until after the company is established. This circumstance can also occur with **intrapreneurs** in HIM departments. They may not document ideas for creating a profit center within an HIM department until formal requests for space or capital equipment demand formal planning. Planning, as discussed here, refers to the formal type of planning with goals and specific objectives documented and shared.

Figure 4-1 shows how transforming the vision into the mission statement is the first step in the planning process. During the strategic planning phase, the mission statement is subject to revision (Robbins, 1994).

Strategic and Operational Plans

Strategic planning brings focus to the organization's vision and provides direction toward the goal. As long-range plans are developed, it is the strategy that will create this plan into action and eventual results. We can consider strategic planning as a bulldozer at a construction site, making the moves, converting the goals into accomplishments. In the health-care

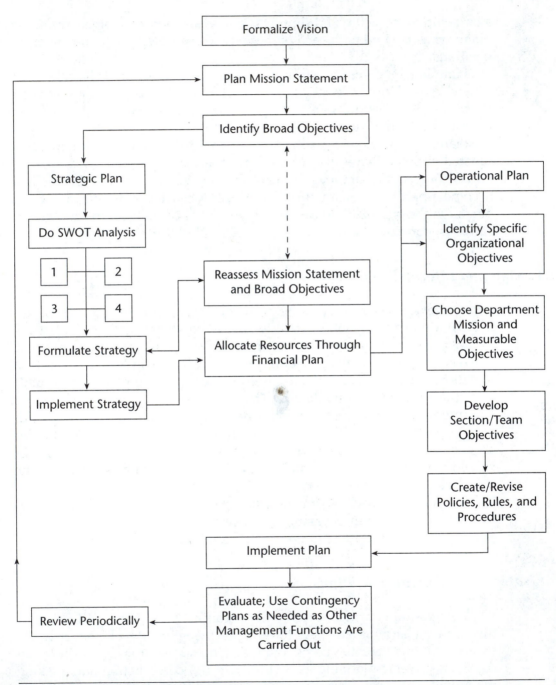

Figure 4-1.   The Planning Process

setting, where the product includes a variety of services, strategic planning will determine which services or products to offer. As these plans are shared, members of the organization are directed toward these goals.

In contrast, operational planning tends to be short term. This type of planning identifies specific details for achieving the objectives outlined during the strategy or long-term planning phase. For example, an HIM department's operational plans for the month may include specific objectives for maintaining the 3-day submission of patient information for billing despite the vacation plans of a coding technician.

Strategic planning is emphasized in this chapter and operational plans are covered in detail in Chapter 5.

Short-Term Versus Long-Term Planning

As the examples in the section above show, long-term plans are typically strategic and are usually documented for 5 years or more. In contrast, the time frame for short-term planning is 1 year or less. Plans that cover 1–5 years may be called intermediate plans. Despite these traditional time frames, managers should realize the value of flexibility. Should any internal or external environmental changes occur, appropriate adjustments may be needed in the plans. This is particularly true in the volatile health-care environment.

Contingency Approach to Planning

From the previous discussion, the value of a contingency approach that gives flexibility to formal planning can be observed. Just as Chapter 3 showed the value of developing contingencies in the decision-making process, so these examples show the advantages of adjusting to forces within and without the organization when planning for the future.

Strategic Planning

Developing a strategic plan for the organization begins with the **mission statement**. It is the strategy that transforms long-range objectives into action and reality. The mission statement and objectives are the good intentions, but these can lie dormant. The strategic plan is the bulldozer that turns the mission statement and objectives into accomplishments. One key to the bulldozer action is the leader who skillfully translates the mission and long-range objectives to the team. The team then joins the leader in converting these objectives into strategies and then into action at the department level. Each team member needs to feel a commitment for that goal in order to say, "I contributed to the goals of our department, our organization."

Strategic planning for the health information manager is exciting but demanding. A vision for the future may be glimpsed only by a manager. It may at first be an unclear vision to have innovative technology in the department for maximum productivity and effectiveness. As the vision becomes focused, the management and team will formalize the strategic plan by documenting the goals for enhancing productivity and effectiveness. Another goal may be to maintain the long-term prosperity of the department.

The organization and the department managers will plan the goals for flexibility because of possible health-care system changes in the external environment. The manager understands this dynamic environment and thus builds into the plan the flexibility to anticipate and act quickly. Networking, reading, listening, empowering teams for knowledgeable input—these activities will allow the manager to reflect on complex issues. Skillful, quick, appropriate, intuitive responses will be forthcoming as strategic plans are developed. Thus, for effective planning, goals must be clearly defined. The strategic plan will then blend with environmental pressures to create long-term effective results.

Developing Strategy from the Organization Mission Statement

A vision of the future has been mentioned several times as the starting point for a strategic plan. This vision, when documented in the formal planning process, is identified as a mission statement. From the mission statement, the objectives are developed. While the mission statement encompasses the broad vision at the organization level, the objectives flowing from it tend to become more specific. As can be seen in Figure 4-1, strategic planning flows from the mission statement, and when complete, requires reassessment of the mission statement.

In a health-care facility, planning strategically may begin with upper level management setting the tone for the process by asking department managers to assist in communicating the vision and developing the organization's mission statement. Department managers may then be asked to develop strategies that would be unique for their departments. The resulting mission statement lays the foundation not only for the facility but also for the objectives of the department. In other facilities, upper-level management may first develop the mission statement and then ask managers to plan specific departmental goals using this statement with their teams.

For the entrepreneur just starting a business, strategic planning may occur as the vision is formalized into a mission statement before the major objectives are developed for the new firm. From these beginnings the entrepreneur formulates the choices for future direction, setting the stage for action, forecasting the future. Through strategic planning, the risks can be minimized and the resources allocated for accomplishing these broad goals. It is most important that the strategic plan include the resources necessary for implementation.

Developing the Goals or Objectives from the Mission Statement

The next step in strategic planning is to assess the broad goals or objectives that managers will use to create operational plans. These terms—*goals* and *objectives*—can be used interchangeably. They refer to the outcomes expected and desired from the activities of the organization, from a specific area within the organization, or even from an individual. The proposed objectives will be reassessed and revised during analysis and development of the strategic plan.

As service organizations, health-care facilities have products that are intangible. Their mission statements frequently express a desire to heal the sick in a global setting. The domain of the organization is thus defined in very broad terms. This gives managers an opportunity to prepare goals or objectives that describe how areas of responsibility are a part of the mission of the facility. They should be designed by focusing on what the organization does best—that is, the areas of competence.

For example, Peter Drucker describes an emergency department struggling to create an overall goal that became, simply, "to give assurance to the afflicted" (Drucker, 1990). This is operational; it is a goal around which a culture can be created. Translating that goal into policies and procedures for team implementation changed the focus of every employee in the department. With the major focus on giving assurance, the team changed the flow of patient care, and when Drucker wrote his book, *Managing Non-Profit Organizations*, this emergency department had a qualified person seeing anyone who came through the door within 1 minute—that is the only way to give initial assurance in an emergency situation (Drucker, 1990).

This change to a customer-driven goal became a reality because upper-level management revised the mission of the hospital and then actively demonstrated their willingness to encourage departments to make cultural changes. They also empowered middle managers to set the pace for change within their **span of control**.

Because the mission statement tends to be a long-range vision, the more specific objectives can be long-, middle-, and short-range goals that have a tendency toward contingencies. Thus, they can be adapted as the environment changes. Certainly regulatory changes can create a need for revisions in an objective. By periodically reviewing the forces in the external environment, managers can anticipate regulatory or other changes and have contingency plans ready for intervention.

Leaders in health care today can expect to revise or completely change strategic plans as the environment in which they operate changes.

Analyzing the Environment

In order to answer the universal questions of who, what, why, when, where, and how, it is now necessary for managers to further develop a strategic framework by analyzing the environment. Knowing the opportunities and threats in the environment allows managers to align the organizational activities with that environment to enhance success. The framework includes an analysis of the strengths and weaknesses of the organization or department. This thinking process model is frequently called **SWOT analysis** because it puts together the strengths, weaknesses, opportunities, and threats to show how to best serve customer needs (Robbins, 1994). These four components are used to analyze the environment with the following two-step SWOT process:

Step 1. Strengths and weaknesses: By looking inside the organization, managers can answer the questions: Where are we now? What unique skills and tools do we have that will give us advantages in meeting our customers' needs? Where are the weak areas in our organization? Answering these questions, in concert with step 2—the opportunities and threats in the environment—gives insights into whether the organization's strengths can indeed meet the needs of the customers.

A strong organization culture can be a strength if its emphasis aligns with an environmental opportunity. For example, during expansion, a record-copying service may have a culture that embraces hospital department employee satisfaction. Thus, it would commit to equipment that would enhance relationships with these employees, possibly including having each copying service representative use computer software for tracking copies made for specific requestors and for making this information available to the department in a timely manner. This procedure could be a distinct advantage if analysis of the environment showed an opportunity in the expansion area because of past poor relationships with other copy services.

Included in exploration of strengths should be documentation of the core competencies. The objectives for the organization or department must be linked to the core activities that will accomplish the stated objectives. An organization or department is only as strong as its weakest core competency. A core competency can change suddenly, such as the changes in federal regulations in the 1980s, which suddenly changed coding expectations. Many HIM departments found they lacked competence in the coding accuracy demanded when the prospective payment system became a reality with billing linked to ICD-9-CM codes.

Step 2. Identifying opportunities and threats: Identifying opportunities and threats in the environment is the second step for health-care planners. However, this step is most effective when done in concert with step 1. It allows planners to focus on those strengths and weaknesses that will have the greatest impact on opportunities or threats in the environment. For example, the HIM department managers in a hospital where there is a large ambulatory-care department would want to define environmental opportunities and threats relative to the caregivers and patients in ambulatory care as a high priority.

Health-care managers will also identify opportunity and threat possibilities relative to legislative and regulation changes. Monitoring legislative activity and factoring in flexibility that can respond to sudden changes in the environment gives planners a strategic advantage.

Through professional organizations, HIM managers are offered the opportunity to monitor proposed legislation and to influence regulations through the activities of legislative affairs offices. Journals and newsletters from other health-care organizations also give the current status of such activities. These informational tools are very helpful to health-care planners performing SWOT analysis.

Formulating and Implementing Strategy

Once the SWOT analysis is documented and communicated, the management team can begin to plan the strategy that will allocate resources to accomplish the objectives that have been reassessed and revised in response to the analysis. The strategy is then transformed into operational plans where the action takes place.

Steps in the Planning Process

A review of Figure 4-1 shows the major steps in the planning process, from formalizing the vision of the organization down to the contingency planning involved during evaluation of the plan. As specific organization or department objectives are created, it is crucial that they be in measurable terms. The language should be clear and specific. It is helpful to compare each objective with one that is well stated, such as the choice of words used by President Kennedy in the 1960s: "man on the moon by the end of a decade." Or compare it to the mandate for nationwide automated records. Congressional leaders did not say, "We are going to be a world leader in health-care automated technology." They said, "We will have a computerized record in health-care by the year 2000" (Ball and Collen, 1992).

After the objectives are planned by each section/team, policies and rules will need review and revision. Again, professional organizations and other health-care organizations have information on changes in the environment that may need incorporating into these policies and rules. The procedures for the team members are revised to reflect an emphasis on the objectives that give direction for the future. Chapter 6 covers these aspects of planning.

As stated in Chapter 2, planning is a function managers do in their daily activities. In reality, planning covers all functions of management. As the strategic plan is implemented, the procedures that flow from the objectives become a part of the organizing, leading, and controlling functions.

As the plan is evaluated during the controlling function, contingency planning may be required as environmental forces change. Anticipating change and preparing contingency plans will assist busy managers in this step. As the planning process cycle is repeated, adjustments are made at each step to reflect the strengths, weaknesses, opportunities, and threats of the future. This cycle appropriately covers all the management functions during the process.

Managers Who Make a Difference

The mission statement of Tokos Medical Corporation (Tokos) includes serving the customers' real needs and creating a physical environment conducive to an efficient and effective workplace for valued employees. Managing high-risk mothers during pregnancy, at home, by nurses in regional centers throughout the country was the first objective of Tokos. Therapeutic medication to control premature contractions is a part of the home-care program. Developing systems to care for the resulting client records at the corporate offices was the task facing the health information services manager.

Mary Moody accepted this challenge, developed the systems, and organized the department to meet the special needs of the corporation. Team members were chosen carefully and nurtured. As Mary and the team explored the possibilities for the department, they became enthusiastic about the technology available to make their tasks more enjoyable and efficient. The first major strength of health information services was the quality and capabilities of the manager and employees.

A second strength of the department was the move to a larger physical environment where the open floor plan allowed adequate space for growth. Creative workstation arrangements allowed the team to function and communicate more effectively. Employees throughout the facility understand the culture of Tokos and their attitudes show a willingness to invest in innovation.

The third strength lay in the willingness of the team to embrace emerging technology. Because the records from the regional centers are stored at the corporate center, the volume of records increased dramatically as the company expanded. Mary and the team chose optical disk technology for retention and retrieval, after successfully preparing and presenting a strategic plan to upper-level management.

(continued)

Mary's presentation to upper-level management delineated the customers of health information services. She showed where the strategic plan flowed from the department's objectives that were developed from the company's mission statement. Meeting the needs of clients meant having accurate and accessible records for the nurses, for physicians, for reimbursement, and for research. She described the efforts to build a team that could not only meet and exceed the present department objectives but could also implement optical disk technology. Mary also emphasized the use of optical disk technology as a medium that would allow the compilation of paper-based and electronic patient records onto one medium.

The planning that Mary and the team developed for the presentation included a SWOT analysis as follows.

Planning Through a SWOT Analysis

Figure 4-2 outlines an analysis of the department's strengths, weaknesses, and environmental opportunities and threats for health information services at Tokos as the strategic planning process entered the analysis step. Note that in Figure 4-2, the "environment" is internal to Tokos but external to the department and external to Tokos. Mary and her team needed to assess both.

The well-planned presentation to upper-level management brought approval for the optical disk technology installation. Being a beta, or test site for the optical disk system saved a significant portion of the budget since the supplier charged less for installation and hardware. The success of Mary and the team is being rewarded on several fronts. These include:

1. Recognition by Tokos president and leadership team.
2. Recognition by peers, especially educators who feel fortunate that students can visit Tokos and become excited about this alternative setting.
3. The William Olsten Award for Excellence in Records Management in 1992 (Moody, 1992).

As an innovative HIM professional, Mary stretched her area of expertise into business record management and disaster recovery. She was encouraged in these efforts by upper-level management and was asked to add these responsibilities to her domain. With these additional responsibilities, Mary chose Rebecca Gomez, RRA, M.S., a dynamic HIM professional, to manage the day-to-day activities of the HIS department and install and maintain the optical disk system.

Health Information Services Strengths

Strong leadership

Record and technology expertise

Skilled employees

Open architecture

Health Information Services Weaknesses

Financial constraints

Lack of health information services expertise at regional centers

Nonstandardized forms used at various regional centers

Environmental Opportunities

Supportive management team

Willingness to innovate

Beta site for supplier

Environmental Threats

Resources from other departments

Opposition to change—regional centers

Legal and regulatory constraints

Technology still in developmental stages

Figure 4-2. A SWOT Analysis of the Environment for Tokos Corporation Health Information Services

Transitional Planning

Transitional planning is a process that offers a new paradigm for planning that will begin by designing a bridge to the future and to a new system for health care. This process stretches beyond strategic planning to meet the demands for changes in incentives and focus. HIM professionals have an exciting opportunity to participate in this transition to a health-care system that will emphasize full-continuum health care with priority given to preventive and health-oriented services. As this transition from inpatient, disease-oriented services to the new paradigm occurs, incentives will change. Information systems of the past that created data to assist strategic planners in assessing the environment for competitive advantage and marketing designs will need changing. Transitional planning will focus instead on information necessary for building cooperative regional health-care delivery systems (Philbin, 1993).

Involved in the planning for these new systems will be a broad base of stakeholders: health-care organizations, physicians, other health-care providers, payers, regional businesses, and the public. Sophisticated software systems will be needed to create the information base demanded by these regional planners.

Developing the Vision for a Transitional Planning Model

Transitional planning refocuses on a vision that asks health-care organization planners to place ethical issues on the discussion table as incentives change. A healthy population, well educated in preventive care, will have value over sophisticated advertising planned for repairing a disease-specific group. These ethical issues will be reflected in the mission statement. Visionaries will create regional networks with a focus on avoiding duplication of services. These networks can involve all the responsible parties in a commitment to an efficient and effective health-care delivery system. This participative process will create a framework that includes a redesigned health-care system, not just a piecemeal adaptation of an old system.

Assessing the Environment

During the transition phase the assessment of present delivery models, attitudes of responsible parties, internal operations, and external change will be ongoing and must be integrated into the plan for bridging to the new paradigm. As integrated regional networks are built, this assessment will reveal where the planners must focus energies to effect success.

Opportunities for HIM professionals will grow as network information systems become an increasingly crucial component of the new paradigm.

Transition Plan Creation

Priorities will be set, strategies planned, and objectives created toward the final phases of the assessment component. Commitment to new incentives, changed risks, and the new paradigm will require outstanding communication skills. Managers with organizational development skills and team-building skills will be highly valued during this period.

Patrick Philbin, from the Institute for Health Care Futures, cautions that resistance to change can disrupt the process at this point. He emphasizes the exciting though challenging opportunity in which health-care providers have to become involved for transitional planning to a paradigm of the future (Philbin, 1993).

Implementation Plan Creation

Building the infrastructure completely will depend on where the external environment has led. At this phase of the plan, the forces creating the change toward full-continuum health care should have most of the incentives in place. Implementation will inevitably lead to repeating the cycle of transitional planning toward the next paradigm shift.

Rural areas of the United States are leading in creating regional collaborative centers for expensive diagnostic and therapeutic equipment. This type of collaboration will increase the transitional demand for the electronic patient record (EPR) and timely regional record transfer to a total computer-based patient record (CPR) (Cerne, 1993). As the regional information/communication structures become operational, new ventures toward the national network will be created. This new paradigm will include participative planning groups with a broad community-based commitment to quality, timeliness, efficiency, and effectiveness.

Developing the Business Plan

Intrapreneurs and entrepreneurs alike need to develop business plans for their ventures. Business publications tell of the high failure rate among small business in the first 5 years of operation. Frequently the documented reason for failure is inability to implement good management processes. Taking time to write out a detailed business plan assists the entrepreneur in thinking through all of the details that lead to success. Although business failure may not be the issue for the intrapreneur, personal failure of a project in the organization can follow initial enthusiasm if the business plan for the project is not well documented for presentation to key decision makers (Craddock, 1992).

Developing a Business Plan Within the Organization

While the enthusiasm for an innovative idea is still bubbling, the first question intrapreneurs should ask is, "Is there a demonstrated need that will be met by developing this idea into a project?" Financial constraints in today's health-care environment demand that there be a substantial need. The plan must show that this substantial need can be met in a cost-effective manner. So, the next question is, "Will the project be cost-effective?" Should the intrapreneur have uncertainty as to how these two questions might be answered by upper-level management, now is the time to put out some feelers, ask questions, sow seeds, and emphasize the perceived problem. Empowering a team to brainstorm ideas will enrich the problem-solving aspects of the project and thus enhance the documentation.

A resounding "yes" to the two questions above is a green light for the project at this point. Figure 4-3 outlines basic steps in a business plan; these can be adapted for a project. The executive summary can be identified as the manager's summary or the team summary. This introduction or summary should identify the exact nature of the project. An innovative name for the plan could be chosen that will give team members a sense of identity and ownership.

Next the HIM professional leads in planning the mission statement for the project—the goals in broad perspective. Blending the ideal with the practical aspects of the project can inspire creation of a mission statement for employees, medical staff, and upper-level administration. Selling the project to the major stakeholders is one burden of the mission statement; it needs careful thought. From it comes the operational plan.

The project is described in step 3. Some aspects of the universal questions will need more or less detail, depending on the project. For example, a project involving information systems (IS) will emphasize the capture of data and brokering data dissemination to the stakeholders as information of value to them. In today's competitive health-care environment, step 4 is crucial. For instance, should the project involve offering transcription service to local medical office practices, a survey to determine present transcription activity, future needs, problems with present services, and legal constraints will be needed. Also, IS capabilities will need to be addressed.

The intrapreneur may wish to involve the chief financial officer (CFO) in developing strategy for step 5. The break-even chart will be closely scrutinized by the stakeholders. The real challenge may be to explore and document savings that may not be evident at first glance. For example, a department developing an automated chart-tracking system needs input

1. **Executive Summary (Manager's or Team's Summary):**
   Exact name of business or project, specific nature of the business.

2. **Mission Statement:**
   Planned accomplishments and goals.

3. **Description of the Business or Project:**
   Who will manage the business?
   What is the product or service offered; the risks involved?
   Where will the business be located?
   Why is the business unique; why can it succeed?
   When is startup? (business timetable of key events)
   How will funding occur; how will risks be addressed?
   How will legal or conflict-of-interest threats be met?

4. **Target Market, Sales, or Service Market Penetration:**
   Market survey to assess need, competition, changing needs, and/or constraints.

5. **Financial Plan and Projected Budget:**
   Operating budget for first year; projections for 5 years.
   Projection of savings, a break-even chart.
   Projected balance sheet; profit and loss statement.

6. **Evaluation Plan:**
   Tools for monitoring effectiveness and efficiency.

Figure 4-3. The Business Plan

from all the sections in the department for complete documentation of time and cost savings.

Employees want to know their extra effort is noticed: What better way than to set target dates for evaluation of the project? Let them choose rewards at these interim steps. Involve all the stakeholders with feedback and ideas for adjustments. Of course, the budget process is also an evaluative tool as projection figures are reviewed.

Developing Entrepreneurial Business Plans

Increasingly, HIM professionals are becoming entrepreneurs. For example, small consulting firms are being developed and are offering a variety of services through publicizing in the major HIM magazines and state newsletters. These entrepreneurs need professional expertise, inservice teaching ability, and business acumen to interest clients, employees, and investors. The business plan outlined in Figure 4-3 will enhance the probability of success in all three of these areas.

Managers Who Make a Difference

In 1988, E'Vette Zeitlow created her own company, Design Data Resources, because she found a market niche for HIM professionals. As an entrepreneur, E'Vette explored market opportunities in health care that would challenge and interest her. A market survey to assess needs, competition, and constraints helped in her decision. She became excited about the need for temporary professionals and in starting a business that would offer excellence in contracting services to health-care facilities. She envisioned a staff well trained to perform clerical functions, coding, abstracting, Diagnosis Related Groups (DRG) audits, quality assurance, tumor registry, and managerial consulting.

The many details outlined in the business plan were covered as E'Vette planned a solid base for success. This planning is outlined in Table 4-1, where the financial estimates that E'Vette drew up for starting the business are detailed. These estimates serve as an example of the careful planning entrepreneurs must undertake for success.

In developing the financial plan for step 5 of the business plan for the firm, E'Vette estimated the start-up costs as shown in Table 4-1. The expenses outlined for payroll and employee benefits project the hiring of four employees initially. These estimates are for the Southern California area.

In talking with other vendors for health-care facilities, E'Vette found that collecting accounts receivables typically takes 2 months after submission of an invoice. Thus, she projected the need to have funds available for payroll expenses right from the beginning.

E'Vette's entrepreneurial spirit, dynamic personality, attention to detail, and constant emphasis on excellence have all propelled her into success as a small business owner in the demanding health-care environment. Her firm continues to grow steadily and employees continue to be hired and trained with the attention for detail and demand for quality that are E'Vette's trademarks. By developing a realistic business plan, E'Vette enhanced her chances for success (Zeitlow, 1995).

Table 4-1. Financial Estimates for Business Start-Up

	Initial Cost Estimates
Legal Expenses	
Attorney's fees	$1,000
Incorporation costs	3,000
Licenses	100
Accountant Expenses	
Accountant's fees	1,000
Telephone Expenses	
Business telephone and fax	500
Answering service and voice mail	400
Office Expenses	
Office equipment (including computer)	6,000
Office space (deposit and first month)	3,000
Office supplies (stationery, cards)	1,000
Payroll and Employee Benefits	
3 month's payroll readily available	36,000
Payroll taxes (approx. 12 percent)	4,320
Health insurance (down payment)	1,000
Liability/workers' compensation insurance	2,000
Miscellaneous	
Promotionals/entertainment/advertising	2,500
Total	$61,820

Several optional items that can also be considered for a small business owner include:

Cellular telephone	$ 500
Pager	200
Dedicated modem line	100
Mac Powerbook or other laptop computer	1,500

Summary

Planning, in some form, is used by managers every day. The importance of the long-range planning function is evident in organizations of any complexity. In the dynamic health-care environment of today, the advantages of contingency plans are stressed. Maintaining flexibility as changes occur and paradigms shift will be increasingly necessary.

Strategic planning flows from the vision and mission statement of the organization to set the tone for the future. The objectives written in response to the strategy become increasingly specific down through the organization. When individual employees plan objectives and goals for the time period with the manager, these will be aligned with the broad objectives of the organization. Just as important, when the process is participative, employees will understand how individual objectives help accomplish those broad objectives. Strategic planning is cyclical; before the next budget period, the process is repeated.

Part of the planning process is an analysis of the strengths, weaknesses, opportunities, and threats facing the organization, referred to as a SWOT analysis. When the internal and external environments are analyzed frequently, planning is enhanced.

Transitional planning goes beyond traditional strategic planning to assist managers in paradigm shifting. In today's changing health-care scene, HIM professionals have the opportunity to participate in the transition by advocating information systems to meet new demands and by preparing to work with new tools and knowledge. Networking among all health-care givers should ensure a longitudinal patient record as the CPR is developed.

Business plans are structured documents to give focus to planners. Intrapreneurs anxious to bring about change by adopting a new system use business plans to formalize their requests. Entrepreneurs need detailed business plans for providing a directional map to future success.

Review Questions

1. Explain how an organization's mission statement, strategic plan, and overall objectives relate to one another.
2. Give examples for using informal planning in a manager's daily activities; then explain when formal planning would be more appropriate.

3. Describe the major steps in strategic planning and document reasons why each step is important.

4. Define the terms *objectives* and *goals*; then discuss their importance in strategic planning.

5. Your management team is giving priority to automating chart tracking during strategic planning meetings. Write out possible major objectives the team members should consider as they prepare for a presentation to top management.

6. Describe the steps in a SWOT analysis. Give examples that show the value of SWOT analysis in strategic planning.

7. Describe your nonverbal and verbal responses to the HIM manager who says, "Plan? I seldom have time to plan. I live from day to day just attempting survival."

8. What are the components of a detailed business plan?

Case Study

Jackie and Sandra began a long-term-care consulting firm 5 years ago in a retirement region. They now have six employees: 2 RRAs and 4 ARTs. They now have consulting contracts with 35 long-term-care facilities and have developed a reputation for excellence.

During a meeting with the employees, Jackie and Sandra commended them for the effort each had contributed to the success of the firm. In planning for the future, Jackie and Sandra then asked the employees to share with them ideas on expanding the business by revising the vision. One option they had discussed and now shared was that of expanding their geographic region into another state. This would mean actively marketing to long-term-care facilities beyond their present region and hiring additional staff.

Bryan said he had been listening to employee conversations at a nearby hospital and learned that there was a need for additional home health-care personnel and resources in the region. Hospital utilization management staff expressed concern with the difficulty of referring patients promptly to home health-care firms. Bryan thought developing and managing home health care as a separate cost center would fill this market niche and offer challenges to each of them.

(continued)

Ann shared an experience she had at one of the nursing homes. Two physicians were telling her how difficult it was to hire knowledgeable office staff and retain them. Ann suggested expanding their business into physician offices. She felt they had the expertise to manage practice offices and train competent staff. Ann further stated that when she mentioned this need to a physical therapist who recently joined a group of fellow therapists in opening an office, her friend responded that such a service would be welcomed by them also. Then he related the difficulty they were having finding competent office managers.

Jackie, Sandra, and their staff have three options to consider as they undertake strategic planning:

1. Develop a SWOT analysis for this consulting firm.
2. Make assumptions regarding the region and factors that relate to each of the three options.
3. Choose one of the options and prepare a business plan for the firm.

References

Ball, M., & Collen, M. (eds.) (1992). *Aspects of the computer-based patient record.* New York: Springer-Verlag.

Cerne, F. (1993). Joining forces. *Hospitals*, March 5, p. 26.

Craddock, M. (1992). Planning for success in the information management business. *Speakers' directory and handout book.* Chicago: American Health Information Management Association, pp. 67–70.

Drucker, P. 1990). *Managing non-profit organizations.* New York: Truman Talley Books.

McArdle, K. (1993). *Creating the future, building a strategic plan.* St. Louis Park, MN: McArdle Enterprises, p. 7.

Moody, M. (1992). Interview.

Philbin, P.W. (1993). Transition to a new future. *Hospitals*, March 5, p. 20.

Robbins, S. (1994). *Management* (4th ed.). Englewood Cliffs, NJ: Prentice Hall.

Zeitlow, E. (1995). Interview.

Suggested Readings

Donnelly, J., Gibson, J., & Ivancevich, J. (1987). *Fundamentals of management* (6th ed.). Plano, TX: Business Publications.

Drucker, P. (1992). *Managng for the furture.* New York: Truman Talley Books.

Fogelsonger, L. (1995). Information resource management strategic business planning. *Topics in Health Information Management, 16* (1) 1–10.

Longest, B. (1990). *Management practices for the health professional* (4th ed.). Norwalk, CT: Appleton & Lange.

Nazanec, C. (1993). Strategic planning. *Journal of AHIMA, 64* (1), 38, 39.

Meador, L., & Cofer, J. (1993). Management by planning: Essential to continuous quality improvement. *Journal of AHIMA, 64* (1), 58–60.

Rue, L., & Byars, L. (1986). *Management: Theory and application* (4th ed.). Homewood, IL: Richard D. Irwin.

Shoger, T. (1993). Performance improvement, a strategy for improving financial strengths and operational efficiency. *Journal of AHIMA, 64* (1), 40–44.

Terry, G., & Franklin, S. (1982). *Principles of management* (8th ed.). Homewood, IL: Richard D. Irwin.

Chapter 5

Planning in Health Care: Operational Plans and Tools for Planning

Learning Objectives

After completing this chapter, the learner should be able to:

1. Describe the scope of operational planning.
2. Explain the value of a budgeting process.
3. State the advantages of including team members in planning.
4. Identify major factors in planning operational objectives.
5. Outline major ingredients of the MBO system.
6. Contrast fixed budgeting versus variable budgeting.
7. Contrast incremental budgeting versus zero-based budgeting.
8. List the major factors for success in budgeting development.
9. Give several advantages for using Gantt charts and PERT networks.

Key Terms

Bottom-up budgeting process	Gantt chart
Fixed budget	Incremental budget
Flex time	Management by objectives (MBO)

PERT network	Top-down budgeting process
Results management	Variable budget
Section/team manager	Zero-based budgeting

Introduction

This chapter begins the next phase of the planning function, which is operational planning. Operational planning is concerned with short-term plans that specify details on how the strategic or transition plans, described in Chapter 4, will be implemented. During the strategic planning function, resources were allocated to meet the broad objectives chosen for the organization. Now the scope is narrowing and the management team develops specific plans for a department or cost center. These operational plans will focus on departmental objectives and then on resource allocation to meet the chosen objectives. Finances, personnel, and other resources are considered as these detailed plans materialize.

Managing the budget process, an important operational tool, is discussed next. Then other tools and techniques that assist in planning are described.

Preparing Operational Objectives

Creating specific and measurable departmental objectives in harmony with the organization's strategic goals and objectives may seem daunting to managers initially. But the HIM manager, who begins by learning all the steps in the process and then exerts mental effort toward visionary leadership, will be ready for the challenge. Including **section and team managers** in the process makes it a participative effort. Reinforcing the vision and goals of the organization and communicating priorities for the coming year are the manager's activities that build concensus and a sense of ownership by the management team. Since the operational objectives are subject to final approval by the budget committee, the HIM manager ensures that the team understands this limitation.

After the managers are familiar with the steps in the operational planning process and in setting organizational objectives, team members become involved in the planning. This is where the brainstorming ideas for the operational objectives begin. The sections within the department can meet as independent groups first and then bring their ideas to a larger group meeting. Here priorities are set and objectives are chosen for the budget committee.

Strategies for holding successful meetings are outlined in Chapter 18. By following these strategies, managers can defuse tensions that may begin to develop when one section or team appears to lose importance. As priorities change and rightsizing occurs, one section may necessarily be downsized and another given added responsibilities and financial gain. Figure 5-1 emphasizes the integrated process as the vision and mission of the organization are communicated to each level.

For example, coding/reimbursement sections grew in importance and staffing in most hospitals during the 1980s under the prospective payment system. In the 1990s, it might be necessary to cut staffing because of increased automation and streamlining of the functions performed. At the same time, additional staffing may be needed for concurrent record completion activities. When the department objectives show, in clear measurable terms, the rationale for such decisions, tensions can be defused. Managers can demonstrate a balanced perspective by verbally reinforcing the value of each section/team and of each individual employee to the total organization.

As this process occurs, documents created during the SWOT analysis described in Chapter 4 will assist in developing operational plans. First, the objectives or goals regarding the future are broken down into operational terms. Next, the list of factors or threats that could hinder implementation of the objectives are identified to keep the plans realistic. Contingencies that could create new opportunities need review and discussion. These ideas for the future may enthuse the teams to greater effort. As all of these factors are discussed and decisions are made for specific departmental objectives, they can periodically be compared with broad organizational objectives to ensure priorities are aligned.

As the teams sit down to plan specific objectives for the future, the HIM manager has an opportunity to lead the discussion toward innovative ideas. By encouraging brainstorming techniques, the HIM manager can set the tone for the meeting and guide the discussion into creative thought. These ideas are then developed into possible objectives that can lead the depart-

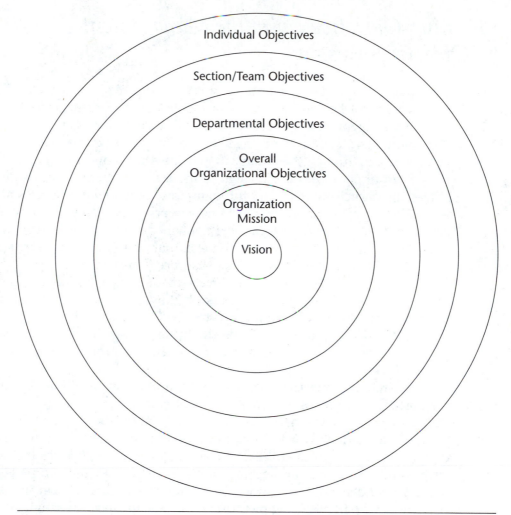

Figure 5-1.   Levels of Planning Objectives

ment into the future. By reviewing the forecasts in the external environment and the strengths within the department, new ideas can be generated. The ideas are then prioritized. Lastly, ideas are incorporated, where feasible, into the objectives for the department. Those ideas that are not feasible right now should be saved and brought into later discussions.

Planning Objectives with the Management by Objectives System

Objective setting is being emphasized throughout this chapter. Our discussion would not be complete without mentioning the management system termed **management by objectives** (MBO) or **results management**. This concept combines a cluster of management techniques to create objectives that cascade down through the organization. Figure 5-2 shows this flow of objectives from upper-level management to the individual employee. It demonstrates the participative activity throughout with overlapping circles at each level. The communication and feedback network shows the bottom-up aspect as well as the top-down aspect as objectives are planned. Originally named by Peter Drucker, MBO emphasized his belief that every individual should participate in planning the goals for the workplace (Longest, 1990).

As shown in Figure 5-2, the levels of the organization are meshed together as the setting of objectives flows downward through the communication network. The beginning of the cycle lies with the mission statement. The flow of upward feedback brings ideas from the individual employees clear up to the top of the organization for input as objectives are developed.

Research indicates that a commitment from all levels of management to the participative process enhances personal motivation for achieving results. Because of upper-level management communication, the mission of the organization flows downward as objectives become a link to the more specific departmental objectives at the next level. Figure 5-2 emphasizes the participative culture by overlapping the circles. In this way, each employee can share an understanding of the organizational mission. Thus, individual objectives are part of the big picture and become the focus of activity.

The plan of action calls for periodic review of the results, with performance evaluation at each level as feedback flows upward. Because employees know what to expect and have helped develop the plan for action and target dates, they are committed to striving for quality results. Their rewards can then be seen as fair and equitable.

A new cycle begins as results are fed upward and upper-level management reviews them and begins the next strategic planning process.

In summary, MBO takes selected management principles into a process that benefits an organization when all employees participate. The major principles involved are:

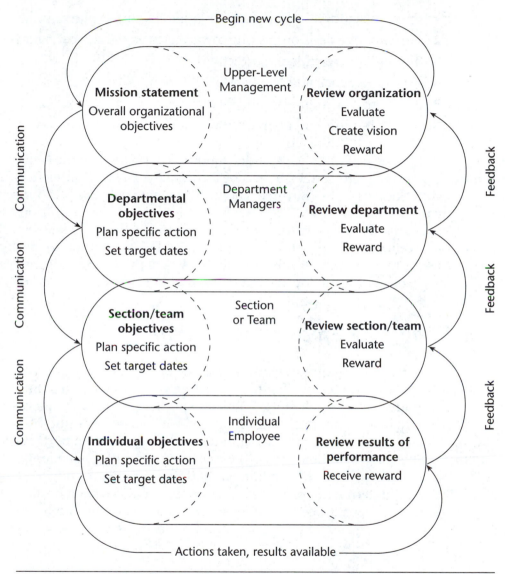

Figure 5-2. Flowchart of Management by Objectives (Results Management)

1. Specific objectives created at each organization level
2. Participative decision making toward creating and meeting goals
3. Target dates included in objectives
4. Communication and feedback at all levels
5. Performance evaluation and feedback
6. Rewards and recognition of results achieved (Robbins, 1994)

Having each employee understand and participate in the MBO process appears to increase the success of the system. The human element in the workplace must be nurtured and encouraged at all levels. Studies show that when individual employees have a high level of compulsion to complete a task within a specified time frame and with a personal expectation of excellence, success results (Robbins, 1994). One author suggested that results management or MBO should not be adopted unless an organization has been able to employ and develop a highly motivated staff (Terry, 1982).

The Budgeting Process and Planning

As shown in the entrepreneurial business plan section on "Managers Who Make a Difference" in Chapter 4, creating the objectives sets the stage for the budget process. Here the funds for specific activities are allocated. The HIM manager presents the proposed objectives and specific plans to the budget committee for inclusion in the master plan. Since budget committees perform their functions in a variety of ways, HIM managers will want to be assertive in becoming familiar with the steps their budget committee takes in determining priorities. This information can then be shared with the teams. Two processes are described that illustrate different levels of input into the budget by departments and teams within departments.

Bottom-Up Budgeting Process

Given the complexity of hospitals, the time span for completing the hospital budget process is typically several months and begins with a review of the mission statement, goals, and major objectives. In other health-care organizations, a shorter time frame may occur. Depending on the management style of upper-level management, this may be a **bottom-up budgeting process** where first-level and middle-level managers have the opportunity to share in setting priorities during the initial phase of planning and priority information gathering. With the opportunity to share their concerns and ideas in the early stages of the process, these managers embrace an ownership in the process. To avoid disappointment later, however, decision makers should use terms such as *concerns*, *ideas*, *suggestions*, and *input*. Negative feelings will follow if first-level managers and their teams perceive their specific goals and objectives are rejected outright. The first planning principle in Figure 5-3 emphasizes the need for this participative effort (Longest, 1990).

Top-Down Budgeting Process

A **top-down budgeting process** can also be effective when effort is taken to communicate the objectives and priorities of the organization for the budget year. Middle-level managers then have a greater responsibility for giving their teams a sense of ownership as the components of the departmental budget are planned. Many health-care organizations use a combination of these top-down and bottom-up budgeting processes. After the initial idea-generating phase, the broad priorities are set by upper-level planners. Each department can then negotiate for its share of the budget.

Future Budgets for Information/Communication Systems

HIM professionals have a special role in monitoring organizational objectives for any mention of information systems. Because of the importance of planning for newly integrated systems, HIM managers must be ready and

---

1. Make the budgeting process participative.
2. Use strategic plans in developing operational budgetary needs.
3. Keep budgets as flexible as possible.
4. Base budget figures on factual information.
5. Keep budgets easy to understand.
6. Tie budgets to desired performance results.

Figure 5-3.   Planning Principles for the Budgeting Process

participate in planning these capital expenditures. Correct decisions made during this process can mean success later. Capital expenditures refer to major purchases of buildings or equipment. The cost of an item determines whether it falls into this category. For example, items over $5,000 may need to go through the capital equipment budget process. As facilities transition toward information/communication commitments, budgets will reflect this commitment.

Once the focus for the budget period has been outlined, preparation for the numerical details begins. Traditionally HIM departments were labeled nonrevenue-producing departments. This is no longer true under the prospective payment system. HIM departments are now revenue departments. Managers can effectively show the impact their departments have on reimbursement and on cash flow. Also, departments with specific expertise, such as in transcription or record storage, may become revenue producing in another way—such as by offering a service to the medical office practice community.

Fixed Versus Variable Budgeting

The concept of a **fixed budget** assumes a fixed level of activity or volume over the period of the budget. Planners predict this fixed level as the budget is prepared. In contrast, the **variable budget** recognizes that a number of costs vary with the volume of activity, and flexibility is built into the budget. Thus, variable budgets represent flexible standards that can be realistic goals for managers as costs and activity are monitored periodically (Robbins, 1994).

Either of these types of budgets can be powerful management tools; during the planning function they keep the team focused on strategic goals, objectives, and priorities. During the controlling function budgets facilitate performance evaluations and results-oriented control. In a stable environment the fixed budget clearly outlines the resources that are allocated to a specific purpose and the controlling function can be very straightforward.

Fixed Budget Approach

Fixed budgets can be effectively applied in facilities such as a health maintenance organization (HMO) setting. Once the rates have been set and clients have been estimated for the budget period, the allocation of those resources must be carefully planned and controlled. Department managers need fairly accurate forecasts as they take careful short- and long-range views of departmental needs for the future. A balanced perspective of needs and alternatives for meeting these needs is best created with input from the team members. In this way visionary changes or anticipated regulatory requirements can be discussed and incorporated into the budgeting process. Having to go back and ask for additional funds when federal regulations require an additional piece of datum is a stressful experience. This is especially true when the proposed requirement was published in the *Federal Register* 6 months earlier, leading to an unwanted label—that of crisis manager.

Variable Budgeting Approach

When patient activity is unstable, a flexible or variable budget can lead to prompt action in keeping costs down when patient activity is decreased. Using a reliable temporary agency for the peak periods can keep the backlog to a minimum when patient activity peaks. Another alternative is to build **flex time** into the budget for special projects that must be accomplished. For example, a manager planning conversion to automated information systems technology can use the extra employee hours effectively if the slow time corresponds with the conversion time. A flexible budget is not an invitation to spend, however. The variables in the cost schedules are tied to the patient census or other revenue streams.

Chief financial officers usually have preferences for the type of budget the facility will complete. Organizational tradition is frequently another factor in the type of budgeting process used. Keeping detailed appropriate information from one budget period to the next assists the HIM manager in setting the stage for negotiating in the new budget period regardless of the type of budget used. Computer applications can make this task efficient. Team manager procedures should include tracking activities to capture data for information that is needed periodically for a variety of needs such as the budget. Monitoring and evaluation are the last components of the budget process.

Incremental Budgeting Versus Zero-Based Budgeting

Incremental Budget Approach

As the budget for a facility is developed, year after year, the majority of allocations become standardized. For instance, the new patient folders that will need to be ordered for the budget period are estimated and the manager does not question the need to include folder costs in the budget. The budget allocated for folders will not vary greatly from year to year and an inflation factor is just added each year. This is an example of an **incremental budget** where funds are allocated to departments based on the amount in the budget for the present period.

Thus, with the incremental or traditional budget, funds are allocated to the HIM department on the basis of what was budgeted the previous period and only incremental changes beyond an inflation factor are reviewed. Should the manager be seeking to identify inefficiency and waste in the department, budget data are not particularly helpful under this approach (Robbins, 1994).

Zero-Based Budget Approach

One company, in an effort to become more efficient, developed **zero-based budgeting (ZBB)**, which required managers to justify budget requests each budget period. This company, Texas Instruments, was successful in becoming efficient; however, a modification of ZBB became less costly for the company (Robbins, 1994). In its pure form, ZBB requires managers to justify all budget requests in detail each budget period. Allocations from the previous year are not considered. The burden is shifted to managers to justify all requests as the budget is developed. Requests are grouped into decision packages by the department managers and then planners rank them according to their value in meeting the goals of the organization.

A decision package may be quite detailed and include a breakdown showing effort levels and alternatives for reaching each level. For example, the team responsible for coding and reimbursement considers spending $30,000 during the current year in efforts to obtain physician final diagnoses promptly. The team's decision package for the new budget year might propose a second alternative—spending only $20,000. This reduction could be achieved by taking only three trips per week to physician offices. In contrast, the team might propose spending $40,000 by dedicating an additional technician for 2 hours every morning to ensure records are available for physicians to complete. The package would then estimate the average turnaround time for completion under each of these three alternatives.

At the first effort level, the cost would remain at the present level, $30,000; the turnaround time at present averages 36 hours. The second effort level, or alternative, has a cost of $20,000; the estimate for turnaround time might be 48 hours. The third effort level would cost $40,000 with a projected turnaround time of 24 hours. With this information the budget committee can make a decision based on the priority given to prompt completion of final diagnoses.

An adaptation of zero-based budgeting is most likely the budget process facing health-care managers. Here the budget committee plans the budget process and develops the adaptation chosen for use in the organization as budget planning time approaches. Rarely is the pure-form ZBB process seen in health-care organizations. Since the pure form of ZBB requires managers to justify each line item in their request, it is quite expensive in terms of time and detail. Certainly it imposes a rigorous approach as managers evaluate budget needs and prepare decision packages for upper-level management.

For these reasons an adapted version of zero-based budgeting is frequently used. This approach asks managers to justify specific line items where variables exist. The goal of management, especially in an era of rightsizing and financial restraint, is to use the budgeting process for allocating limited resources effectively and fairly.

While a modified ZBB has advantages over the traditional budget, there are drawbacks—it increases paperwork and preparation time. And, political concerns are not totally eradicated; managers can still inflate the benefits of their pet alternatives. However, its value in managing declining resources makes it especially popular with health-care managers today (Robbins, 1994).

A review of the principles outlined in Figure 4-1 reinforces the importance the budgeting process plays in the planning function. These principles are applicable for HIM managers in health-care facilities and for small business owners alike. Effective budgets are not viewed as just time-consuming paperwork, but as tools that turn strategic planning into action at every level of the organization.

Making the Plans Operational

Typically there is a time lag between submission of the budget proposal and final approval during which additional information may be requested quickly. Budget committees have hundreds of details to synthesize into one package and need all the facts at hand as decisions are made. Thus, managers should expect last-minute requests and allow time to give priority to them.

Once final approval has been received, the management team sets the tone for implementing any additional changes for the revised objectives and new budget. Every person involved in the changes must understand the plan and have the opportunity to become excited about it. When opportunity for change comes, resistance comes trailing along. As employees are involved in the planning, organizing, and implementing of the change at their level, they have the opportunity to commit to change, which can lower resistance. Of course, revising policies and procedures is a crucial component for success of the plan and the changes involved.

Revising Policies and Procedures in the Planning Process

Policies give working structure for internal goals and for regulations mandated by the external environment for health-care facilities. Policies also communicate broad guidelines to assist in making decisions and in taking action toward meeting the objectives of the department. When each manager in the organization uses the same set of policies for making decisions, the values of the organization are communicated and the unique culture for the department is given consistency. While policies are revised continually as information is received, review of all policies during the planning process helps managers correct inconsistencies and errors.

Procedures that flow from the plans give consistency in specific situations and they also need review. Since they give precise guidelines for daily employee activity, frequent revisions and accuracy are mandatory. Each employee should have a handbook with the latest revisions. Revisions are especially important in the transcription section and in the coding/reimbursement section where guidelines are mandated by new technology or federal and state regulations. The mechanics for planning and documenting policies and procedures are covered in Chapter 6.

Implementing and Monitoring the Plan

As discussed earlier, the last step in the process is evaluating the results as changes occur. Figure 4-1 emphasized the value of correlating the budget to desired performance results. A review of the evaluation tools for monitoring may show the need for revision also. The team members can assist in reviewing the present tools and suggesting new ones. Planning data capture at the time the task is done allows for efficiency in analyzing and integrating subsequent results. When automation is available for this step, timeliness can be a realistic goal and adjustments can be made promptly.

Tools and Techniques to Assist in Managerial Planning

Operational planning tools help managers to be more effective. Some of these tools and techniques may be used in strategic planning also. Two techniques to assist managers in scheduling are the **Gantt chart** and **PERT network**. Scheduling includes preparing a list of planned activities, the order of completion, who is to do each activity, and the time needed to complete each.

Other tools involve mathematical models that are often computerized. They assist managers in making complex decisions. These managerial tools are part of the quantitative approach to management mentioned in Chapter 2. Through sophisticated software, these models offer alternative solutions and then the computer program chooses the best alternative according to the information given.

Gantt Chart

Henry Gantt was an engineer at Bethlehem Steel during the early 1900s and worked with Frank and Lillian Gilbreth to increase worker efficiency. One of the tools Gantt developed during this scientific management era continues in use today, in modified form, for scheduling. Called the Gantt chart, it compares progress of a project at different points in time. Targeting these decision points in a project is most useful (Robbins, 1994). The Gantt chart can be reviewed at any point in the continuum as shown in Figure 5-4. This figure illustrates a simple example of how this scheduling tool assists a team in monitoring progress. It outlines the tasks for a team involved in a 3-month project to plan a reception for area physicians to publicize a home health-care unit opening.

The Gantt chart forces the team to address all facets of the project and to assess whether the timing of each task is on schedule. As the figure shows, at the 2-month team meeting, activities 1 and 2 have been completed on

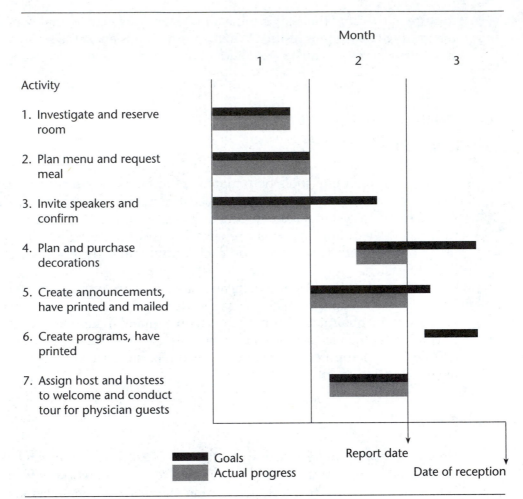

Month

1   **2**   **3**

Activity

1. Investigate and reserve room

2. Plan menu and request meal

3. Invite speakers and confirm

4. Plan and purchase decorations

5. Create announcements, have printed and mailed

6. Create programs, have printed

7. Assign host and hostess to welcome and conduct tour for physician guests

■ Goals
■ Actual progress

Report date

Date of reception

Figure 5-4.   Gantt Chart for Home Health-Care Reception. Reviewed at the End of 2 Months

time. However, one speaker had not yet been confirmed for activity 3. Activities 4 and 5 have been started and the team discussed a problem with the order for printed napkins. The coordinator was asked to monitor this order in 1 week. As planned, activity 6 will be completed during the third month. The chart shows that activity 7 was initiated by the host and hostess and confirmations were received.

PERT Network Analysis

When activities are relatively independent of one another and are few in number, the Gantt chart is helpful as a scheduling tool. When a project has many activities and they are interdependent, program evaluation and review technique (PERT) is preferable (Longest, 1990). Although a software program can be used to create a complex PERT model, the example in Figure 5-5 reviews the manual steps of creating a simple PERT model for understanding the process. The practice example gives details of PERT activities.

Practice Example

Installing a computerized incomplete record (CIR) system is used in this example. While there are many details to manage in such an installation, the PERT chart will be used to diagram major events and activities involved. In this way the manager and his staff can estimate when the new system can be operational and where major monitoring should occur.

In this example, simultaneous exploration of an automated system occurs involving the medical staff and the HIM department. At a medical staff meeting, several physicians suggested that the facility automate the incomplete record completion system. They described the experience of another facility, Children's Hospital, that has recently installed an automated system. About 40 percent of the medical staff is also on the staff at Children's Hospital and staff members are enthusiastic about the new system. Administrators stated they will meet with the HIM manager and discuss the possibility.

At the same time, the HIM manager has been networking with the manager at Children's Hospital and has visited the hospital to look at the system. The manager had prepared a proposal for inclusion of a computerized incomplete record system in the next capital expenditures budget.

This proposal would replace the current system in which incomplete records are filed by physician name on shelves in the work room. Four employees are on the physician record activity team, which is responsible for incomplete records. The team would need training in any new system and procedure changes involved. Technicians who are crosstrained to work in any area of the HIM department would also need training if the new CIR system were approved.

The initial meeting with administration produced a concensus to proceed with the proposal. Next, the HIM manager met with the physician record activity team and empowered them to assist in the planning. One request from this meeting was that temporary employees be hired to assist in the routine work flow while the team members were trained.

The team also emphasized the need for additional workstations in the work room. The decision was made to remodel the work room, take out the shelving, and add three additional workstations. The plant manager and physician record activity team were involved in the planning and implementation of the project. At this point, the HIM manager prepared the PERT network shown in Figure 5-5 for tracking activities.

As can be seen in Figure 5-5, events are outlined in the rectangles and the activity for reaching each event is identified with an arrow. Above each arrow is an estimated time, in weeks, for completion of the activity. For example, it is estimated that event E, to hire temporary employees, is needed 2 weeks before the employees will complete training. Should event F, installation of the training computers, be delayed, then event E should also be delayed to allow efficient use of the temporary staff.

Looking for the critical path on the PERT network is the next step. The critical path is the longest path in weeks to accomplish the activities. In this simple chart there are only three pathways, so each needs to be calculated as follows:

1. A-B-C-E-H-J-K equals 10 weeks.
2. A-B-C-F-H-J-K equals 13 weeks.
3. A-B-D-G-I-J-K equals 15 weeks.

The calculations show pathway 3, at 15 weeks, is the critical path, indicated in Figure 5-5 by heavy lines. Should any of the activities on this pathway be delayed, the project completion date will be delayed. However, should an activity in pathways 1 or 2 be delayed, the HIM manager can review the PERT network and determine whether there will be a delay. The slack time for pathway 1 is 5 weeks and for pathway 2 it is 2 weeks. Because of the interdependence of pathways 1 and 2, should the delay be between events B and C, both pathways are affected and would need review. ■

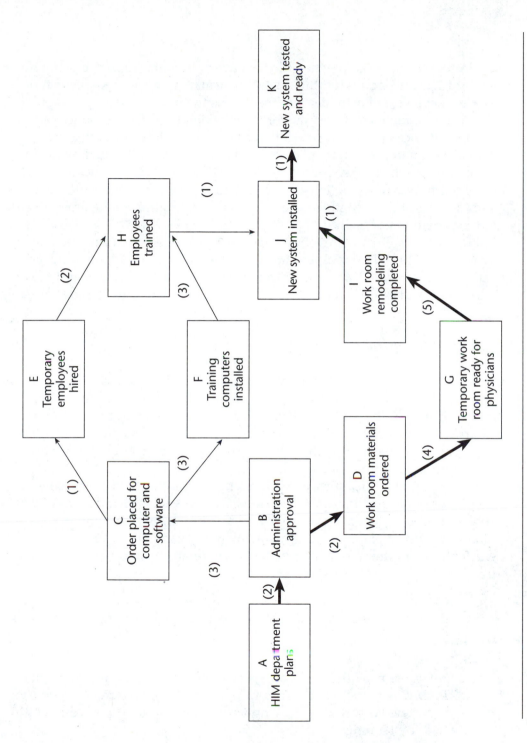

Figure 5-5. PERT Chart for Incomplete Record System Installation

In this simple example the HIM manager can make adjustments manually. Software programs for PERT networks can handle hundreds, even thousands, of events and activities and then adjustments are made by computer.

When estimations of the time for completion of activities are uncertain, a further enhancement can be used. By creating three different time estimates, managers can improve their planning skills. This is accomplished by having an optimistic, a most likely, and a pessimistic time for each activity. The shortest time length is called optimistic, the middle time length is called most likely, and the longest time length is called pessimistic. In Figure 5-5 the times given are considered most likely.

Delays in activity completion have been discussed; the opposite is also a possibility. Should it take less time to complete an activity along the critical path, then the HIM manager can review the PERT network and make adjustments that could mean completion of the project ahead of schedule.

Mathematical Models as Planning Tools

Other tools involve mathematical models that are often computerized. They assist managers in making complex decisions. These managerial tools are part of the quantitative approach to management mentioned in Chapter 2. Through sophisticated software, these models offer alternative solutions and then the computer program chooses the best alternative according to the information given.

As a part of the team involved in planning a project, one of these tools may be useful in arriving at the best decision. These tools include break-even analysis, queueing theory, probability theory, linear programming, and simulation. Complex planning tasks involving many variables can be completed efficiently using these quantitative tools. There are several books available that cover these topics in detail.

Summary

This chapter begins with a focus on operational planning at the department level. The concepts include short-term plans and the resources needed to fulfill the planned objectives. This implies that the budgeting process is intimately tied to planning.

Emphasis is given to participative management by involving the sections and teams in planning objectives that affect their work. At this level objectives are specific and measurable. Use of SWOT analysis keeps the teams' focus on priorities. Encouraging employees at all levels to share creative ideas and demonstrating the value of their ideas are important managerial concepts in this integrated planning model. Setting objectives at each level within the MBO system outlines a thrust of participative management that can lead to productive results.

Planning phases of the budget process shows how the department objectives become reality. Through a bottom-up budgeting process, managers at all levels convey their ideas upward, where the final decision makers set the priorities for the time period. In contrast, with top-down budgeting, the decisions lie with upper-level management and are disseminated down with little input from managers. A combination of these budgeting approaches is frequently used in health-care facilities.

A fixed budget has value in a stable environment such as a health maintenance organization where contracts control the income stream. However, a variable budget has advantages when the volume of client activity tends to fluctuate.

Incremental budgeting refers to stable budgets where increases may be only a percentage for the inflation factor. At the other end of the spectrum is the zero-based-budgeting approach that requires justification of all budget items. A modification of this last approach is used more frequently.

Success in budgeting is enhanced when six planning principles are followed: (1) use participation, (2) adhere to priorities set during strategic planning, (3) be flexible, (4) use factual information, (5) create understanding, and (6) tie budgets to performance standards.

Two quantitative planning tools, Gantt charts and PERT networks, examples of which were provided, are valuable tools for successfully planning and completing projects. Using software programs that assist in decision making when there are many variables involved in planning gives added value to these models.

Review Questions

1. Describe differences between a top-down approach to creating objectives versus a bottom-up approach.

2. Discuss potential conflicts between objectives being planned by financial services and those planned by HIM department managers in a large hospital.

3. Outline an operational plan for the transcription section of an HIM department.

4. Give several differences in the budget you would prepare for a consulting business plan and the budget an HIM department director would be creating in a hospital with 50 employees.

5. Interview an HIM professional involved in planning a project. Document the tools being used in planning this project and in carrying it into implementation.

6. List some items in a departmental budget that have flexibility, depending on patient activity.

7. Develop a Gantt chart for one of your class projects.

8. Compare incremental and zero-based budgets.

9. Explain why the critical path in a PERT network is so important.

10. Give two examples where automation would lend valuable assistance in solving managerial problems.

11. How would you respond to the statement, "It is impossible to plan when we do not know what we are going to be doing next month."

12. Explain the value of participative managerial concepts when coordinating a group effort.

13. Think of the person to whom you were responsible in your last position. Give some operational planning activities you observed that manager doing.

Case Study

The last JCAHO (Joint Commission on Accreditation of Healthcare Organizations) report for Community Hospital was unfavorable with regard to employee ongoing education. Top executives admitted they set other priorities and the managers concurred. Overall the report was very good and the managers were pleased, but determined to focus on education during the coming year.

With this mandate, upper-level management developed one corporate objective relating to education as the budget process for the coming year began. This corporate objective read:

Corporate objective III: To educate health-care professionals within the enterprise to meet the health-care needs of society and to define 5-year plans to meet educational needs for the several professional groups.

The corporate objectives were distributed and discussed at a meeting with middle managers. The responsibility for developing departmental objectives for the coming year was delegated to the managers. Community Hospital culture was participative in nature and the flowchart in Figure 5-1 describes the communication process as the managers shared the vision with the teams and the team leaders empowered individual employees to offer suggestions.

1. Develop ongoing educational objectives for health information services to meet corporate objective III for the coming year.
2. Develop ongoing educational objectives for the major teams in the department for the coming year.
3. Choose two professional employees that you know and develop educational objectives for each of them for the coming year.

References

Longest, B. (1990). *Management practices for the health professional* (4th ed.). Norwalk, CT: Appleton & Lange.

Robbins, S. (1994). *Management* (4th ed.). Englewood Cliffs, NJ: Prentice Hall.

Terry, G., & Franklin, S. (1982). *Principles of management* (8th ed.). Homewood, IL: Richard D. Irwin.

Suggested Readings

Cofer, J. (1992). Flextime programs recognize "the whole human." *Medical Records Briefing*, August, p. 6.

Donnelly, J., Gibson, J., & Ivancevich, J. (1987). *Fundamentals of management* (6th ed.). Plano, TX: Business Publications.

Drucker, P. (1990). *Managing the non-profit organization.* New York: Truman Talley Books.

Longest, B. (1990). *Management practices for the health professional* (4th ed.). Norwalk, CT: Appleton & Lange.

Meador, L., & Cofer, J. (1993). Management by planning: Essential to continuous quality improvement. *Journal of AHIMA, 64* (1), 58–59.

Powell, T. (1993). Planning a successful process improvement effort. *Journal of AHIMA, 64* (1), 36–39.

Robbins, S. (1994). *Management* (4th ed.). Englewood Cliffs, NJ: Prentice Hall.

Rue, L., & Byars, L. (1986). *Management: Theory and application* (4th ed.). Homewood, IL: Richard D. Irwin.

Shoger, T. (1993). Performance improvement: A strategy for improving financial strengths and operational efficiency. *Journal of AHIMA, 64* (1), 40–44.

Terry, G. & Franklin, S. (1982). *Principles of management* (8th ed.). Homewood, IL: Richard D. Irwin.

Chapter 6

Planning Policies and Procedures

Learning Objectives

After completing this chapter, the learner should be able to:

1. Explain the differences between rules and policies and how each relates to objectives.
2. Discuss the value of documenting procedures into manuals in the work environment.
3. Give several reasons for creating an open-mode environment for employees.
4. Outline guidelines for developing departmental rules and policies that will conform to organization-wide rules and policies.
5. Describe the steps for creating rules and policies to cover unique problems.
6. Identify the steps for successfully revising department procedures.
7. Defend managerial decisions that empower teams to revise their own procedures.
8. Give examples of alternative health-care settings where HIM consultants need skills in writing policies and procedures.
9. Describe the main features of the narrative format for writing procedures.

Key Terms

Manual   Single-use plan

Open-mode environment   Standing-use plan

Introduction

Some managers find creative enjoyment in outlining a plan of how a task is efficiently undertaken and then documenting each step. There are also those who are energized to creative effort while thinking through how a task is to be done, but lose the energy quickly when it comes to documenting the steps and putting policies and procedures into actual sentences. One management style is not necessarily preferable to the other, just as no one person can possess every managerial quality.

However, effective managers can honestly explore and accept their own strengths and weaknesses. They understand the need to complement their weak areas by hiring employees with strengths in those needed skills. This can be especially crucial when a manager has weak writing skills. By actively choosing assistants, supervisors, and/or team leaders who have strong skills in writing and documenting, strong management teams may be built.

Walk in any department and ask to review the procedures for a specific task in the departmental **manual**. You will quickly discover the importance given to this aspect of managing. Compare the procedure with related policies in the manual and then with actual tasks being performed by the team. When high priority is given to planning policies and procedures and keeping user-friendly manuals readily available to employees, this will be evident through observations.

Or, explore the documentation qualities of a consulting firm; ask to review the sample policies and procedures for a specific HIM task and the priority given to documentation will soon become evident. The writing expertise of consultants is frequently in demand because long-term-care and ambulatory-care facilities also need well-documented rules, policies, and procedures for accrediting and licensing purposes. An effective consultant also emphasizes the value of updated manuals for the day-to-day activities of the facility.

Developing Rules, Policies, and Procedures

The examples detailed in the Introduction show the value of documenting policies and procedures in various health-care settings. Developing concise steps for HIM departmental activities can increase productivity, efficiency, and effectiveness. Policy and procedure manuals will increase in value as automated systems replace manual activities, which is another excellent reason to devote time and effort to preparing them.

Managers have found several advantages for documenting rules, policies, and procedures and making them serve as useful tools in the workplace. These advantages are identified in Figure 6-1 and are referred to throughout the remainder of the chapter.

In Chapters 4 and 5, policies, rules, and procedures were mentioned as flowing from the objectives developed during strategic planning activities. Policies and rules thus allow for a consistent pattern of behavior within organizations as objectives are embraced. These strategic planning goals and objectives give direction to the operational goals and objectives within the department and subsequently to the procedures.

1. Encourage teamwork.
2. Promote clarity, consistency, and continuity of performance.
3. Provide excellent information for training programs.
4. Establish standards and expectations against which actual performance can be monitored.
5. Serve as a central database for adding, revising, or deleting rules, policies, or procedures.
6. Release managers, supervisors, and team leaders for departmental planning or other activities by saving time spent answering repetitive questions.
7. Serve as source documents for inspection by accrediting and licensing agencies.
8. Become working benchmark documents and thus serve as a warning signal for potential problems and quality improvement actions.

Figure 6-1. Reasons for Documenting Rules, Policies, and Procedures

Policies Defined

Policies are guides that establish parameters for making decisions. They allow for judgment and interpretation on the part of managers. For example, a human resource department policy stating that, "The HIM department wage scale shall be competitive with that in the community," leaves room for interpretation. Staying competitive with several other organizations in the beginning wage for medical record technicians, for example, does not require a manager to begin a new employee at a specific wage. It does insist that the manager review community wages and choose a beginning wage within the range discovered in this review. Parameters are thus set for managerial action.

Rules Defined

A rule differs from a policy in that it is written as an explicit statement that tells managers what they ought to do officially or outlines what they should not do. Rules limit specific actions. HIM managers find rules give direction to many facets of their work. For instance, the federal rules regarding ICD-9-CM codes that are to be used for specific surgeries or diagnoses leave no room for a coding technician to use personal judgment in assigning such codes. In addition, these specific rules allow vendors to develop coding software with precision. Such federal standards give consistency across the country in the development and use of coding rules and policies.

Procedures Defined

Once the rules and policies are developed to give substance to the objectives, then procedures are needed. Putting action into the plan, a procedure is a series of interrelated sequential steps that give the necessary details for meeting one aspect of an objective.

Empowering the teams assigned to perform specific tasks by encouraging them to document their role in meeting an objective increases the opportunity for complementing strength and weakness traits across the group. The team can assign a member with special writing skills the task of updating the policies and procedures for the manual. Using the strengths of this team member increases the effectiveness of the total team effort. At the same time, the team needs the organization's protocol for writing procedures and for making changes in policies and rules for incorporation into the manual.

Assuring that the team has the tools for performing tasks empowered to them is a responsibility of the manager. This includes having computers available for maintaining the procedure manual with timely updates. As rules and policies are disseminated or created by the team, procedures are developed or revised to give them action. Steps for data gathering to monitor effectiveness of the rule or policy should become a part of the procedures. Including this evaluation tool as rules, policies, and procedures are developed emphasizes the expectation that quality improvement techniques will increase the team's effectiveness.

In an HIM department there are activities that frequently overlap among teams. Communication is crucial as employees on different teams need access to updated procedures that affect their work. As coordination across the teams occurs, an added bonus is the interaction that encourages understanding of another team's tasks and pressures. This also promotes cohesiveness among the employees and enhances the team spirit as well as the total departmental spirit.

Manuals as Tools

Within a department or a firm, policies, rules, and procedures that affect all employees are gathered into a departmental or organizational manual. A copy of this manual is then made available to each employee. It may be called a handbook, a guidebook, or a manual. HIM managers grow accustomed to the term *manual* as regulatory agencies use manuals for disseminating information and accrediting agencies refer to manuals in their requests for information. One of the more technical teams in a department may prefer *data quality manual*. Having the team feel ownership of this instrument by naming it and updating it is more important than the name itself.

Creative Manual Writing

How do managers invite creativity into the work setting? Creative writing author, John Cleese, suggests managers create an **open-mode environment** for employees that encourages creativity and original thinking (Cleese, 1991). By contrast, well-defined tasks are typically performed in a closed mode of thought as little creativity is involved.

To create an atmosphere where an employee can move to an open mode of thought, Cleese suggests that managers:

1. Provide a specific work space away from the demands of the daily routine.
2. Set specific time periods for using this space.
3. Eliminate the fear of making a mistake.
4. Allow the employee freedom to express humor.

Cleese emphasizes that once the task has been completed and documentation submitted, the employee must return to a closed mode of thought to effectively carry out the new or revised procedure.

Writing Policies and Rules

As already noted, policies and rules are developed from the operational goals and objectives in the department. These were created or updated from the strategic plan of the organization. For example, the procedures for hiring new employees are developed from the objectives of the department. These objectives were developed from the organization's overall goals and objectives. Hiring high school graduates who have completed at least one applied computer course may be a goal of the organization. The department would, consequently, include this rule in the manual and in the position descriptions.

The example mentioned above shows how specific and explicit a rule can be. There is no leeway for the manager. Rules apply to specific situations. On the other hand, a policy is a guide that gives parameters for the decision-making process. The policy has a broader scope. Either policies or rules may derive from organizational culture, social, or ethical considerations. These facts are reinforced here to set the stage for getting them down in written form.

Sources of Information

HIM managers monitor a variety of sources for information that will assist in updating rules and policies within their area of responsibility. The human resources department publications are one important source. Some rules and policies can be considered programmed decisions or **standing-use plans**. They assist managers in repetitive and routine decisions where a problem is well structured and relatively simple. When a manager takes action in line with such a standing-use plan, she can be confident the decision treats employees equally. The format for writing these standing-use policies may come from the human resources department as well as from the revised policies.

Other sources for standing-use policies are those mandated by regulators or by standard professional practice. These policies must be updated when regulations or standard professional practice guidelines change. They are reviewed with employees periodically. In this way they assist in creating the culture of the department. When new or revised rules and policies are presented, time should be allowed for discussion about their unchanging nature. Empowering the teams to participate in formulating policies and rules when appropriate gives a sense of ownership to employees.

The new rule outlined above for hiring a high school graduate with an applied computer course is in response to an internal environmental change. An example of a revised rule necessitated by the internal environment would be when changes are made in data system configurations and rules or policies need revision as a result.

External environmental changes impact the workplace when federal regulators or professional organizations enact or publish changes that affect the role of HIM professionals. For example, Figure 6-2 gives a new rule that might be developed in response to the Patient Self-Determination Act passed in the early 1990s.

A copy of the information sheet, "Right of Patient to Make Decisions Regarding Medical Care," will be given by the admitting officer to each patient admitted for treatment in this facility as mandated by the Patient Self-Determination Act.

Figure 6-2. Rules for Advance Directives Information to All Patients

The rule in Figure 6-2 gives an explicit statement that specifies:

What: "Right of Patient to Make Decisions Regarding Medical Care"
When: On admission
Where: Admitting office
Why: Mandated
Who: Patient
How: Information sheet

Figure 6-3 outlines a policy that could be part of the HIM department's manual. This policy allows the manager to choose the type of in-service best suited to the needs of the department. Judgment is also allowed in how and when to present advance directives information to new employees. No specific time frame is given in this policy.

In another example, setting policies for scheduling vacation times throughout the year can be facilitated through team effort. The total department policy can be broad, with a statement such as, "Coverage of priority tasks during an employee's absence will be planned before final vacation approval is given." Within a specific team, such as record retrieval, a more specific rule can refer to having someone available to retrieve records during certain time periods.

Considerations for Writing Rules and Policies

Organizational rules and policies will become a major part of a department's manual. The guidelines in Figure 6-4 can assist in writing departmental policies and rules that will be in conformity with those of the organization.

One challenge for writing rules and policies lies with those infrequent problems that arise. Problems that require unique solutions, those with lit-

---

Employees of the HIM department will receive in-service education regarding advance directives and the Patient Self-Determination Act.

Figure 6-3.   Policy for In-Service Education on Advance Directives

1. Review any regulations that mandate specific wording of a rule or a policy as the result of required or prohibited courses of action.
2. Set boundaries for action that are as broad in scope as possible.
3. Construct rules and policies to reinforce goals and objectives, yet be flexible enough to accommodate a changing climate.
4. Include any applicable legal constraints that apply and document source of information.
5. Develop a strategy for handling conflicting accrediting and regulatory policies.
6. Show consistency throughout the manual in tone and format.
7. Review the manual periodically, especially for needed revisions because of accrediting body updates or other reasons.
8. Date the replacement pages for new or revised policies and rules; include the signature of the person approving the change.

Figure 6-4. Guidelines for Developing Rules and Policies

tle structure, or those where specifics change frequently need decisions that are nonprogrammed. The decision-making process outlined in Chapter 3 is needed for developing rules and policies to handle these problems. As mentioned earlier, a nonprogrammed decision is a synonym for a **single-use plan**. When possible, decisions made for unique problems should be documented. The documentation for these single-use rules and policies may be kept in the manager's manual only. For subsequent unique problems the manager may refer to these policies to gain insights into making a specific decision.

Writing Procedures

Specific, chronologic procedures flow from the policies and rules. Procedures outline how tasks will be accomplished by listing a series of related steps or tasks to achieve a specific purpose. First, the action must be described. Second, what must be done and under what circumstances should be explained. Not only is the person doing the procedure identified but other team members who contribute in some way are also included.

As mentioned earlier, for some procedures, interdepartmental personnel who contribute to the task are also included.

Procedures are valuable tools for managers as they standardize tasks that are repetitive. They give uniformity to tasks regardless of who performs them. Also, they are of value for giving confidence that personnel training is complete. Lastly, they facilitate performance appraisal and quality improvement efforts.

Revising Procedures

The need to revise procedures occurs with greater frequency than writing a totally new procedure. As tasks are performed and data are gathered that relate to their accomplishment for the performance of employees, problems inevitably surface. Through quality improvement techniques, managers and teams can focus on solving problems. When steps in a procedure are involved in the problem, updating the procedure once the decision is made assures that employees will have the best tools available for creating uniformity and excellence. And, of course, the updated procedures give documentation for later monitoring during the fourth management function—controlling. Concepts of quality improvement techniques are covered in Section V, where the controlling function of management is discussed.

Gathering information from every person involved in the procedure is the first step in revision. The data already available have typically shown the problem. Now the team can assist in solving the problem by focusing on the customer, the service, and the desire for excellence. Managers can listen to those ideas and assist in incorporating the chosen solutions into the revision. Lastly, the manager can give recognition to the team for creating excellence that results in better procedures and happier customers.

After the difficult task is completed, the manager can enjoy the satisfaction of accomplishment with the team. Rewards may be appropriate. For example, when physicians are the customers, visibility is important. This could be achieved by allowing the team to disseminate creative notices of any changes that impact physician patterns of practice. This action would enhance physicians' perception that the team truly desires to serve their needs. The manager can then encourage the physicians to verbalize their appreciation directly to the team members.

Writing New Procedures

Concurrent with any reengineering of department systems or installation of new systems is the demand for documenting the necessary steps to make the change useful. After the policies are developed or revised, the managers would use the decision-making steps outlined in Chapter 3 to incorporate the new tasks into the work setting. Alternatives are explored, always focusing on the customers who will use the information, the records, or whatever the new system produces.

Again the teams involved should make all the decisions appropriate for their level. An implementation team with members from several sections of the department may be used to assist in creating the process. As mentioned earlier in this chapter, by choosing the person with the best skills for documenting these procedures, successful implementation is enhanced.

It should be emphasized that when responsibility is given to a team member for this writing, recognition of the extra effort needed must be given. A team member can become discouraged very quickly if no release time is given from routine tasks. The value of the manual to the team and the department is such that the budget should reflect time allotted for preparing the new procedures and revising the manuals. When creative thought is needed, the employee should be given both time and space for an open-mode environment.

An alternative to the use of a team member is to assign the revision of manuals to a resource person. This person may be a professional who performs a broad range of activities when employees are ill or on vacation. Should such a resource person be chosen to perform procedure writing, the manager would include technical writing expertise in the skills section of the job description for that position. Job descriptions are discussed in Chapter 10.

It is possible the new system being implemented will alter the department functions so dramatically that even the mission of the department will need changing before the policies and procedures are developed. Enthusing employees to make such a major change is a challenge facing many department managers today as regulations mandate the use of computerized systems. By emphasizing that these changes can be opportunities for greater service to the department's customers, managers can gain the support of the team. HIM professionals can share their enthusiasm for the opportunities being created by changing health-care patterns.

HIM professionals who choose a career in consulting for long-term-care facilities, physician office practice, urgent centers, or surgery centers will find writing skills very important. Consultants meeting with the administrators of such facilities will likely be asked questions relating to procedure writing. In fact, administrators may ask to see samples of procedures prepared by the consultant. Not only are consultants involved in the training of health record employees for these settings and need procedures for this training, but they typically provide the manuals to assist these employees when the consultant is absent.

Format for the Procedures

In some organizations, standardized formats are already in place for writing procedures. If not, managers can explore different formats with the management team and then assist in choosing the most useful model for departmental procedures. Introducing the team to sample procedures with different formats can be helpful. A narrative sample format is shown in Figure 6-5. It shows selected portions of the procedure for a department receptionist.

As shown in Figure 6-5, the narrative style used is an outline form with action verbs beginning each statement and explanations or notes written in paragraphs. A narrative style is used most frequently for HIM department procedures.

Outline Format Using All Numeric Style

The outline format used in Figure 6-5 is an alphanumeric format. Some writers prefer to use an all-numeric format as shown below, in brief:

1.   Request . . .
1.1.   Show . . .
1.1.1. Pull . . .

Abbreviated Narrative Format

An abbreviated narrative form uses *key steps* and *key points* to emphasize the content of a procedure. This style is useful when detailed explanations are needed and the steps in the action are easily described in a few words.

Objective: The Health Information Department responds to customer requests courteously, professionally, and promptly while following rules and policies for confidentiality.

Date of Preparation _____

Revision Date _____

Person Responsible _____

Signature _____

I. Voice Mail

  A. Listen to voice-mail messages before 8:15 A.M. each workday.

    1. Document messages as needed for follow-up.

    2. Respond to messages appropriately and promptly.

      a. Refer to appropriate team for answers as needed.

      b. Retrieve information and return calls.

      c. Inform the supervisor or team leader of any messages containing potential problems.

  B. Check voice-mail messages periodically throughout the day and follow steps in **A** above as needed.

    Note: The dial tone on the telephone has a beep in it when there is a message waiting in voice mail. By checking for this beep at the end of the workday, all messages can be cleared before the counter is closed.

II. Telephone Calls

  A. Answer the telephone by the third ring.

    1. Identify yourself after stating, as appropriate, "Good morning or good afternoon, Health Information Department."

    2. Offer courteous assistance to the customer. If unsure of the answer, refer to supervisor/team leader; never say, "I don't know." Always offer to find an answer.

    3. Ask if there is anything else you can do for the customer before hanging up.

  B. Talk with any customer on hold at least once every 30 seconds.

(continued)

Figure 6-5. Procedure for Department Receptionist

III. Walk-in Customers

    A. Smile and offer help to the customer.

        1. Telephone the employee to come to the counter and meet the customer when the workstation is out of sight.

        Note: Customers are thus escorted while in the department so they are not wandering about.

        2. Offer a chair to the customer if there is a wait.

        3. Ask if you can do anything further for customers before they leave.

    B. Use a professional attitude at the reception counter at all times.

        1. Avoid gossip.

        2. Refer to employees respectfully.

        3. Maintain confidentiality policies.

Figure 6-5.   *(continued)*

It is especially valuable for training manuals. The rationale behind a step can be detailed under key points. The example below is just one step in a release-of-information procedure:

Key Step	*Key Points*
Open correspondence and sort.	Different types of requests for information are separated for efficient input into the computer—attorneys, insurance companies, other health-care givers.

Action Verbs

Action words give procedures vitality and meaning. Using the best action verb can challenge the writer. Below are some verbs that are frequently used for departmental procedures:

check	mail	destroy
verify	send	show
distribute	compute	gather

issue	obtain	use
place	read	pull
write	input	forward
provide	prepare	telephone
fax	request	record
decide	print	receive
open	stamp	flag
respond	refer	offer

Page Numbering

For ease in revising the manual, page numbering is best done by section, with each section identified by letter. Thus, the page numbers for Section A would begin with A-1, A-2, etc. An index is also helpful. Dividers can be used to separate the sections.

Advantages of using computer software and laser printers are evident in the finished product. Proofreading can be done using the computer and then special graphics can give a professional look to the manual. Loose-leaf binders that will survive constant use can be purchased. These allow for update insertions with minimal waste. Manuals should be user-friendly and readily available to everyone.

When these steps are followed, employees can feel ownership of their manuals. Managers and team leaders who keep a high awareness level of the need for procedure revisions can succeed in keeping manuals user-friendly and current. When employees see the manual as a baseline tool for quality improvement, they will want to incorporate the revisions into their day-to-day activities. Through these efforts, managers are focusing on outcomes-based management.

Summary

Documentation through the use of rules, policies, and procedures serves several needs for the HIM professional. These tools promote teamwork and consistency. They provide a base for training programs and serve as a standard for practice. They offer effective and efficient use of a manager's time and play a role in quality improvement.

Whereas policies are guides that set parameters for making decisions, rules are explicit statements that set the direction for action. Writing or revising rules, policies, and procedures can be a participative task where the manager or team member with technical writing skills is selected. Appropriate tools and an open-mode environment enhance the activity.

Policies and rules should be consistent with the goals and objectives of the organization as well as the more specific objectives of a department. And, in fact, the entire manual is best developed and written consistent with the culture of the organization.

Standing-use rules and policies assist in meeting well-structured problems with speed and efficiency. But they must be updated when changes occur in regulations or standard professional practice.

Nonprogrammed decisions have unique problems and require the decision maker to use the decision-making process. These single-use rules and policies should be documented in the manager's manual for reference.

Procedures flow from the rules and policies and give direction to daily activities. They need frequent updating as change occurs. Each team member performing the activities should be involved in the planned changes. By recognizing a team's efforts to maintain a user-friendly current manual, the manager enhances team spirit.

Writing skills are a strength for consultants, since ambulatory-care settings and long-term-care facilities need this expertise. The documentation also gives direction to employees in these settings when the consultant is absent.

A narrative format is useful for writing procedures. While procedures may necessarily follow organizational guidelines in their preparation, they should be user-friendly and effective. Action words, abbreviated sentences, and frequent updates give them value.

Computer software, printers, and loose-leaf binders give a professional look to documents. If computer capabilities are used appropriately, making revisions and subsequent dissemination of revised or additional pages will be efficient and effective.

Review Questions

1. List several of your attributes that you feel have contributed to creative ideas in your past experiences. Compare these with attributes you feel contribute to your skills in explaining activities in written form.

2. List eight advantages managers have when they choose to document rules, policies, and procedures.

3. Give several examples where standing-use plans would be valuable for a consulting firm that contracts with long-term-care facilities.

4. Define policies and explain how policies differ from rules.

5. Outline four steps managers can take to enhance an open-mode environment for creative writing.

6. Describe the narrative style of procedure writing and give an actual example of statements showing the flow of activity.

Field Practice Questions

1. Ask to review a manual in an HIM department and then document strengths and weaknesses of this manual using Figure 6-1 as a guide and standard.

2. Prepare a policy for use by the record activity team pulling and filing 500 records per day.

3. Be ready to discuss procedure revisions you have observed in HIM departments; enrich the discussion with actual participation in procedure revisions if you have had this experience.

References

Cleese, J. (1991). And now for something completely different. *Personnel*, April, p. 13.

Suggested Readings

Cleese, J. (1991). And now for something completely different. *Personnel*, April, p. 13.

Cofer, J. (ed.) (1992). Anti-dumping law calls for complete documentation. *Medical Records Briefing*, August, p. 7.

Cofer, J. (ed.) (1992). Auto-authentication policy is a winner. *Medical Records Briefing*, December, p. 7.

Donnelly, J., Gibson J., & Ivancevich, J. (1987). *Fundamentals of management* (6th ed.). Plano, TX: Business Publications.

Huffman, E. (1994). *Health information management* (10th ed.). Berwyn, IL: Physicians Record Co.

Longest, B. (1990). *Management practices for the health professional* (4th ed.). Norwalk, CT: Appleton & Lange.

Robbins, S. (1994). *Management* (4th ed.). Englewood Cliffs, NJ: Prentice Hall.

Terry, G., & Franklin S. (1982). *Principles of management* (8th ed.). Homewood, IL: Richard D. Irwin.

Chapter 7

Planning the Physical Environment

Learning Objectives

After completing this chapter, the learner should be able to:

1. Define the term *ergonomics* and give several reasons for applying ergonomic principles when designing or remodeling the HIM work environment.

2. State the reasons for implementing an ongoing inventory of equipment and furnishings in an HIM department.

3. List the specialists best prepared to participate in the design of a new department or a remodeling project; give ways the expertise of these specialists can be useful.

4. Outline the principles used to create a space model that can lead to success in planning the new environment.

5. Give examples of the tools used in planning a remodeling project or new construction and explain ways HIM managers would use these tools.

6. Present a space model for an HIM department, defend the placement of each section within the department, and describe how automated technology placement is considered.

7. Discuss the value esthetics play in the work environment and how the efforts of interior designers can impact the comfort and satisfaction of employees.

Key Terms

Ergonomics
Space modeling

Templates
Two-dimensional templates

Introduction

When customers enter a health-care facility's HIM department for the first time, what initially catches their attention? Is it the interior design? Is it the lighting? Is it the friendliness? Would a first-time customer immediately feel he would enjoy interacting with the staff again? Should not customers leave the department with a desire to return again and again for service? What steps can managers take to create an attractive positive atmosphere?

Department managers can set the tone of friendliness and helpfulness by their own attitudes, thus permeating the culture of the whole department. This positive tone should then become evident to all who enter. But, the tone of friendliness and helpfulness can be jeopardized by the physical appearance of the department, and customers may leave with mixed feelings about the service. The physical appearance of the work environment is discussed in this chapter as ideas for creating a pleasant work environment are suggested. With appropriate planning, managers can design workplace settings that will enthuse employees and create goodwill in customers.

First, the current trends in the work environment and the factors to consider when change becomes a possibility are discussed. Considerations include an assessment of the present department design and an inventory of furniture and equipment. Concerns employees may feel about the anticipated change and how their work environment may be affected are discussed.

In the next section, ergonomics, an applied discipline, is offered as an important component in planning for either remodeling or new construction. Assessing the present department design is the next phase of the redesign project and the major assessment features are outlined. The formal planning begins with a discussion of the appropriate participants and the setting of priorities.

The next section includes a plan of action for undertaking the project and **space modeling** for the new department design is roughed out for discussion. Fourteen principles for planning the layout are detailed. Next the tools needed for creating and sharing the documentation are discussed.

These include graph paper, templates, computer software programs, and architectural symbols. Details on their use are explained.

As the space model or layout is shared with the planning committee, possible constraints to the project are likely to become an issue, so this probability is documented. Creating the space model itself, using the tools and ergonomic principles, is then detailed. Working and reworking the layout as ideas are introduced makes this part of the project a challenging one. The concepts discussed here for creating a floor plan in an acute-care HIM department can transfer to designing a new one in any alternative setting.

Current Trends in Physical Environment Design

Two major regulatory agencies impacting the design of work environments for HIM professionals are the Americans with Disabilities Act (ADA) and the Occupational Safety and Health Administration (OSHA). Creating a safe workplace for each employee must be a major consideration when remodeling or new construction is contemplated. The concern is also that customers entering the department have a safe environment with accessibility, when caring for their health information needs. As priorities are developed, HIM managers will want to work closely with the human resources department as plans take shape—reviewing and revising details for compliance with current regulations.

Specialists in **ergonomics** are being hired in increasing numbers for their expertise in human factor engineering. Ergonomics is an applied science that is defined as the "design of products, processes, and systems to meet the requirements and capacities of those people who use them" (Foster, 1988). By combining relevant engineering, psychological, and anthropological concepts, ergonomics introduces the relationship of people to their work environment in today's complex society. Using computers and other high-technology equipment causes stress on the human body with resulting workplace injuries. To avoid or minimize these problems, managers take advantage of the expertise ergonomists have to offer when planning to remodel a department or install new equipment.

Researchers are finding that the consideration given to human factor influences in today's technologically intensive environments can increase the financial savings later (Layman, Heaps, and Bell, 1992). As professionals interface with computers and other automated equipment, in a technologically intensive environment, attention must be given to layout design and work methods at the same time new equipment is planned, or lower productivity may result. "Working smarter" is a phrase that managers use as the teams reengineer patterns of activity for the new environment.

Sensitivity to the needs of customers during the planning phase of remodeling can give managers creative ideas. Physicians and other stakeholders may request, for example, that patient-care information be at their fingertips—on the first floor of the facility. Entrance doors into the department take on new importance with such requests. Physicians wish quick access to their records, reviewers and auditors wish to interface with the records in a convenient setting, and patients desire ease in finding the department to request information. Other demands for first-floor space can make it difficult to place a large HIM department in such a treasured location. In some facilities the solution is to divide the department so sections interacting with these customers are placed on the first floor and other sections, such as transcription and birth certificate completion, are elsewhere.

Attention to individual employee needs is another trend that is gaining importance. Today departments are frequently open 24 hours a day with different shift employees sharing workstations. When they have different physical needs, difficulties arise that managers must resolve. For example, flexible lighting arrangements will allow employees on any shift to work in individualized settings that meet their needs. Flexible workstation heights can also enhance the morale of employees when they share the same environment and have different needs.

While lighting and height adjustments are very important, the chair is probably the workplace item that deserves the most attention. Sharing a chair that does not adjust creates serious problems, even injuries. It may be necessary to purchase individualized chairs for some employees. When the height differences of employees ranges from under 5 feet to over 6 feet, adjustable chairs and workstations are mandatory (Kelly, 1993).

With these trends in mind, ergonomic principles are now outlined. These principles apply whether a department is being remodeled or construction of a new department is undertaken. These principles can also be adapted to alternative health-care settings.

Ergonomic Principles

Ultimately, the goal of ergonomics is to increase productivity by creating the best office design for the purpose and for the people. When appropriately designed, there can be job satisfaction and employee comfort. By studying the relationship of people to their work environment, ergonomists match peoples' capabilities and their individual requirements with the equipment and other environmental factors in the workplace. Thus, ergonomics is concerned with the following:

- Noise control
- High-technology equipment
- Lighting
- Heating, ventilation, and air conditioning
- Esthetics
- Furniture

Job design includes all of these ergonomic factors. Recommendations are then made to ensure the new design will decrease impediments to high productivity while creating a technologically intensive attractive environment.

Monetary compensation is found to be only one of several motivating factors in employee satisfaction. Therefore, to enhance satisfaction, attention must be given to other factors such as a pleasant work environment and an improved quality of work life. To meld these employee factors into a cost-conscious health-care environment, ergonomic principles are increasingly utilized. Seven general principles, outlined by Michael Foster, are listed in Figure 7-1. These principles for the workplace guide the ergonomists as they make recommendations.

---

1. Select the best worker for the task.
2. Train workers in human factor habits and practices.
3. Analyze and design jobs in order to produce interest, efficiency, and safety.
4. Design equipment that fits human anatomy and physiology.
5. Eliminate stressors that reduce productivity and quality.
6. Design organizational systems that support and involve workers.
7. Build effective organizational communication systems.

Figure 7-1. General Principles of Ergonomics

Ergonomists use these general principles as a basis for their study when changes are planned. Managers, using the expertise of ergonomists during the planning phase of remodeling, can create a space model for increasing employee satisfaction, comfort, and productivity.

Redesign: Assessing the Present Department

Once approval is given to proceed with the plans, assessing the present department design is the first step. Appropriate team members in each section should be involved as this evaluation of their present tasks and workstations takes place. The procedures will show the tasks and work flow for each section or team, so these need to be updated first.

Interviews and questionnaires can also be used to involve team members. While these interviews and questionnaires combine with procedures to show the work flow, volume of work, bottleneck areas, and interaction with other teams, another aspect should also be assessed. Questions relating to reasons for job satisfaction or dissatisfaction should be asked. Responses relating to ergonomic principles can then be addressed during the assessment.

The Task Itself

With the varied tasks in an HIM department, evaluation of the tasks and the work flow becomes rather complicated. Time must be allowed for a thorough assessment at this point in the planning process.

Next, the physical forces impacting the body and the frequency of each of these tasks is assessed and documented. Carpal tunnel syndrome, musculoskeletal pain, and eye strain can be related to repetitive tasks. These injuries often have a cumulative effect. In fact, the Bureau of Labor Statistics reports the fastest-growing occupational illnesses are cumulative trauma disorders (CTDs) (Layman, Heaps, and Bell, 1992). Professionals showing the greatest number of CTDs in the report are employed in telecommunication and journalism. Clearly, increased use of computers is a major culprit. And, as automated technologies are installed in increasing numbers in HIM departments, the profession is at risk also.

The Employees

During the hiring phase, managers may include ergonomic factors when selecting the best applicant for the tasks within a job description. Technologic requirements for performing the tasks and the individual needs of the applicant can then be compared, reviewed, and assessed. This same type of assessment is needed when remodeling and new equipment installation takes place. The resistance to change is lessened when employees feel their individual needs are being considered in the redesign of their jobs.

The new employee and the employees facing installation of new equipment need effective training. This means more than a quick demonstration of ergonomic principles during orientation. Effective training covers posture, relaxation techniques, rest period spacings, and exercises. As a part of the monitoring activities in the department, monthly reviews of ergonomic practices should be scheduled. The assessment covers documentation of such monitoring activities (Wear, 1992).

Workstations

The physical area where an employee spends his time is now assessed. The design of the present section/team area first needs review and then recommendations can be made for the remodeled or new workstation. This assessment focuses on ergonomic principles involving the height of the workstation, the lighting, present equipment location, assessibility to reference materials, availability of storage space, and the noise factor.

Figures 7-2 and 7-3 contrast the use of a chair with ergonomic enhancements and one that results in poor posture. Using an adjustable chair with the correct height for the employee and with support for the lower back creates an environment where employees can give optimum effort. Footrests should be available for employees who choose to use them, as shown in Figure 7-2.

The PowerDesk workstation shown in Figure 7-4 allows the employee to move right into the work area and rest arms and wrists on the work surface. Strain on the arms and wrists can be lessened with use of this workstation.

Each video display terminal (VDT) will receive special attention during this phase of planning. The position of the VDT in relation to the employee is assessed. VDTs have been the focus of research for possible connection

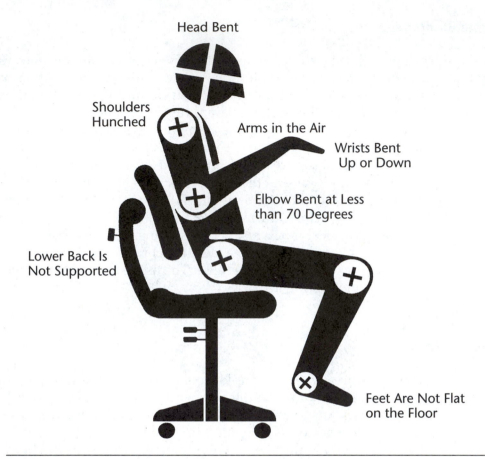

Head Bent

Shoulders Hunched

Arms in the Air

Wrists Bent Up or Down

Elbow Bent at Less than 70 Degrees

Lower Back Is Not Supported

Feet Are Not Flat on the Floor

Figure 7-2. An Example of Poor Posture. This Chair Lacks Ergonomic Enhancement (Courtesy of Fox Bay Industries, Inc.)

with physical problems such as miscarriages, cancer, headaches, cataracts, and eyestrain. Researchers look for problems relating to the cathode-ray tube that generates extremely low emissions or very low emissions of radiation. These emissions come from the back and sides of the monitor cabinet. Monitors with very low emissions are now available from some companies. Also, some companies will install metal strips inside existing monitors to deflect these emissions. There are other items that can be purchased to block unwanted radiation. The assessment includes a review of existing equipment that will continue in use after remodeling for possible needed

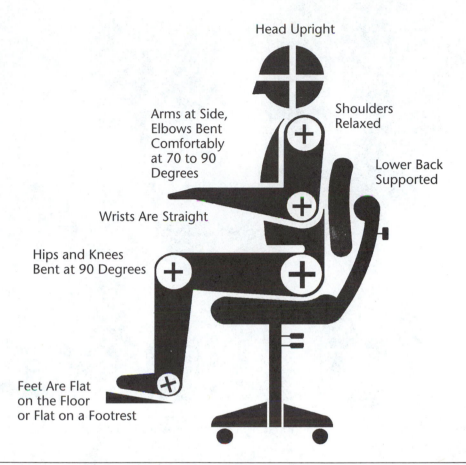

Head Upright

Shoulders Relaxed

Arms at Side, Elbows Bent Comfortably at 70 to 90 Degrees

Lower Back Supported

Wrists Are Straight

Hips and Knees Bent at 90 Degrees

Feet Are Flat on the Floor or Flat on a Footrest

Figure 7-3.   An Example of Good Posture. This Chair Is Ergonomically Enhanced (Courtesy of Fox Bay Industries, Inc.)

changes. Separating workstations appropriately is another way to reduce exposure. Keeping employees at least two arm lengths in distance from the side or back of a terminal is considered best (Kelly, 1993).

Environmental factors at the workstation may result in eyestrain. These will also be noted during the assessment; recommendations may include a VDT screen with higher resolution and frequent rest periods.

Examples of team leader workstations are depicted in Figures 7-5 and 7-6. Figure 7-5 shows an open environment while Figure 7-6 offers more privacy.

Figure 7-4. An Ergonomically Designed Team Workstation (Courtesy of Edwin Lockridge, Inventor)

The Department

Physical factors of the total department are also assessed. Factors that are reviewed include the architecture, the work flow through the layout of the department, the humidity and heating, the esthetics, and the lighting. Documentation will include any other factors that relate to effectiveness and employee safety. As noted earlier, policies and procedures are reviewed.

An inventory of furniture and equipment can be prepared by each team and then combined into one document. Knowing just what is presently in the department is very useful to the manager in negotiations. By emphasizing the need for flexibility in designing workstations that are adjustable for individual comfort, managers can clearly show why specific items of present

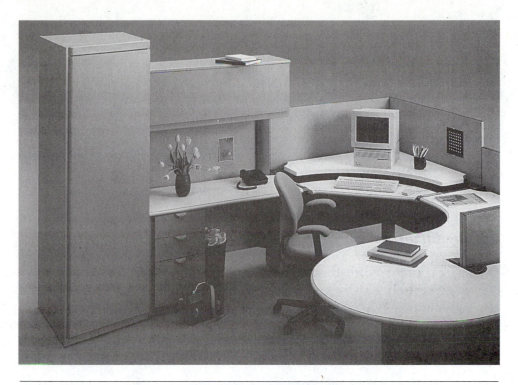

Figure 7-5. An Open Environment Team Leader Workstation (Courtesy of Steelcase)

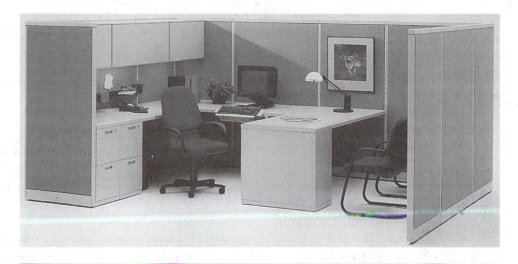

Figure 7-6. A Team Leader Workstation, Privacy-Enhanced Environment (Courtesy of Steelcase)

furniture and equipment will not meet this priority. Just as important is a manager's willingness to use items on hand that can be adapted to the new environment and an inventory reveals these as well.

An automated spreadsheet is effective for documenting the inventory. By including relevant information regarding items such as date of purchase, the spreadsheet can be a very useful document. By updating the inventory as the change progresses, the manager is ready for questions regarding just one piece of equipment or all of the department's furnishings.

The Organization

Corporate culture and its impact on worker health is assessed. The priority given to health and safety, the use of ergonomic devices, and the communication systems are reviewed and documented. The entire assessment is now gathered into a document from which decisions regarding the future can be made.

Planning for the New Department Design

When the assessment outlined above has been completed with care, any departmental difficulties should be evident. As planning for change gets under way, solutions to the documented difficulties should be worked into the planning.

Planning Participants

Ensuring that the project team includes the best participants may not be a task of the department manager, but it should be a concern. The need for an ergonomist has already been mentioned. This expert could come from the human resources department, as one of the experts from a health-care consulting firm, or from a firm specializing solely in ergonomics. An architect brings a wealth of helpful information to a project; even a small remodeling project can benefit from such expertise. Health-care facilities frequently have an architectural firm they use for remodeling projects. This gives continuity to the planning as a component of the total facility. Or, the architect may come from the same health-care consulting firm as the ergonomist. Similarly, an interior design firm may have a contract for planning the design of the entire facility.

Physical plant engineers can bring a wealth of information as planning gets under way. They can answer questions that arise. For example, Can the floor bear the weight of file shelving and thousands of patient records? This could be a constraint on the location of the files. They will also supply the architectural drawings and blueprints upon which the remodeling will depend.

Other participants in planning the physical environment include upper-level administration, other department managers who may be impacted by any changes, and the department employees. For large projects, work groups may be selected from among these participants to find recommended solutions to specific problems. As concerns are raised, they can be addressed and solutions documented for all participants. An ongoing challenge is updating each participant as adjustments in the plan occur.

Setting Priorities for Planning the Design

The previous paragraph mentions "adjustments." It is inevitable that some excellent ideas for the department will necessarily be deleted because of scarce resources or other constraints. HIM managers can be ready to negotiate for items on the department's wish list by prioritizing the list, by documenting how each item fits into the total plan, and by preparing valid rationale. This rationale can delineate why an item is essential for:

1. Information systems planning for the facility.
2. Quality patient care.
3. Esthetic reasons.
4. Other departmental objectives for the future.

As priorities are set, the mission statement and overall objectives of the facility as well as the department must be reviewed so the planning complements these long-range directional plans. For example, if a facility should plan a shift to increased ambulatory-care customers for the next budget period, equipment that will meet the information needs of ambulatory-care patients will have high priority.

Functional/Product Flow-Lines Pattern

Now that decisions have been made for the redesign of the department or the design of a totally new department, a functional or product flow line is created. First, the present work flow is visualized and then decisions for new work-flow patterns are addressed. Blueprints can be copied and used as these decisions are made. Figure 7-7 shows the present work-flow pattern and then a revised example with use of an electronic patient record (EPR) eliminating the need for paper records.

Principles for Planning Revised Work-Flow Patterns

Copies of the blueprint can first be distributed to all section/teams with instructions for visualizing their present work-flow pattern. Documentation already completed during the assessment can be utilized for this task. Architectural and flowchart symbols should be used to standardize the blueprints. The managers can then combine the section/team blueprints to create one functional work-flow pattern for the department.

Should reengineering of the department be planned, consideration can be given to restructuring around product flow lines. For example, the major products and customers of the department could be considered as:

1. Patient information (patient record) to medical staff and professional staff.
2. Statistical patient information from database to business services and other requestors.
3. Aggregated statistical information to upper-level management and other requestors.
4. Patient information released to attorneys, patients, and other requestors.

Using these four product lines in planning the product flow-lines pattern forces the managers to consider customers first and thus impact the final blueprint pattern.

As the planning committee reviews the functional/product flow-lines blueprint pattern, consideration must be given to new equipment constraints or engineering constraints that could change the placement of a section. When concensus is reached on the pattern, creation of the space model can begin.

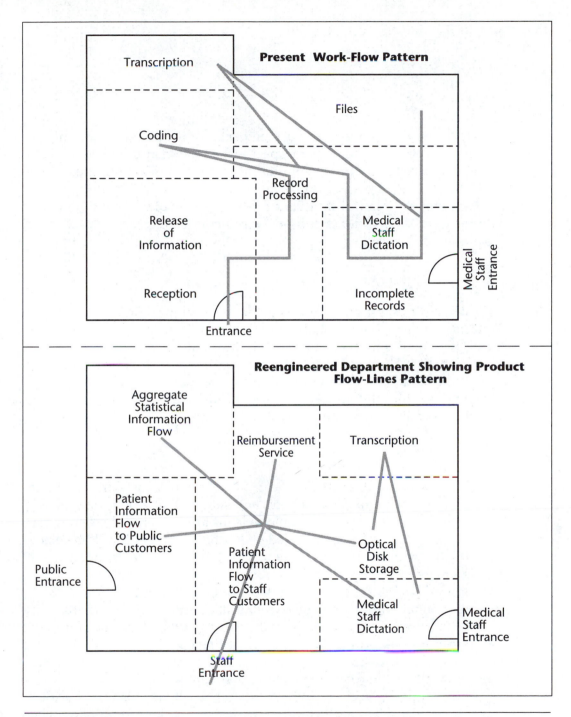

Figure 7-7. Functional/Product Flow-Line Pattern

The Space Model

Principles for Design

The space model or layout brings together all of the planning committee's work and represents the physical space in actual miniaturized detail. Fourteen principles to guide in preparing the space model are outlined in Figure 7-8.

Many of the principles in Figure 7-8 are self-explanatory; others need comment. Additional comments on the principles are given as space model details are discussed.

Principle 1

This principle asks managers to consider space allocation carefully. Facility designers may have already chosen a manufacturer for furniture purchases and managers need to know this information well in advance of the purchase date. This knowledge will enable them to negotiate for appropriate workstations should the manufacturer be unable to supply adequate workstations for HIM use. Modular furniture with privacy panels offers advantages for efficient use of space.

Principle 2

When new systems are installed, teams may need brainstorming sessions to explore the full range of new tools and storage that will be needed. Visits to other facilities can be valuable as ideas are gathered. Decisions such as how many fax machines are needed or where printers should be placed need to be finalized before placement of the equipment and storage of needed materials can be planned.

Planning for storage of present tools can be overlooked since employees are familiar with them. One facility found, after remodeling was completed, that lack of an area to park the rolling carts when not in use was creating problems. In the old department the aisles at the end of the file room had been wide enough to allow space for unused carts. Without that space in the new file room, there was a problem.

One way some facilities handle cart storage is to install a countertop at a height for standing use; then carts can be stored under the counter when they are not in use.

1. Look for equipment vendors who offer efficient use of space for workstations when floor space is at a premium.

2. Place storage and tools for the convenience of employees who will be using them.

3. Arrange the section/team areas in a work-flow pattern that minimizes backtracking of record movement and/or team movement.

4. Use present entrance doors or create new ones that will allow customers access to appropriate work areas.

5. Place teams who must share equipment close together, but purchase additional equipment should this principle violate principle 3.

6. Arrange workstations in groups that allow for easy access; where open-area desks are planned, have them facing the same direction.

7. Place team leaders or section managers where employees will be in front of them.

8. Allow natural light to come over the shoulder or the back of the employee, not directly in the face.

9. Ensure adequate ventilation and light when private offices or partially enclosed workstations are created.

10. Provide flexibility at all workstations that will allow for individual adjustments of VDTs, desk height, footrest level, and chairs.

11. Provide individual controls for lighting, both for direction of the light and for intensity of the light.

12. Design access to workstations and to the department for accommodating the physically challenged.

13. Provide privacy and record security for customers—patients, families, auditors, reviewers, and, of course, the medical staff.

14. Use L-shaped workstations for employees having to use several materials or resources simultaneously in their activities. Purchase mobile pedestals that can be pushed under workstations when not in use.

Figure 7-8.   Principles for Designing the Space Model (Bennett, 1990)

Principle 4

This principle suggests separate doors for customers of the department. It is typical to have a separate entrance into the physicians' work room. However, other customers may be using the same door as employees. Why not have a public entrance separate from a hospital staff entrance? This configuration can give release-of-information teams better control in handling requests. Having a staff entrance also gives employees a less congested reception area for entering and leaving the department, and the reception area can better serve customers.

Another entrance directly into the file room for movement of carts also has advantages. Since carts can damage walls, doors, and furniture, this separate entrance adds to the esthetic look of the other entrances. This file room entrance can have protective covering placed on the walls and door.

These separate entrances have another advantage. The doors for employees and physicians can have keypads installed for authorized entrance only.

Principle 9

Adequate ventilation at each workstation is most important. The architect and engineers need to know the workstation configuration as plans are being developed. Since computers and other equipment generate heat, reviewing this aspect of the layout with these specialists may avoid later problems.

For example, one manager reviewed the ventilation, heating, and air conditioning drawings with the engineers when remodeling a transcription area where additional computer terminals and printers were being placed. The manager outlined for the engineers the need for extra ventilation and air conditioning because of the heat generated by the equipment. Despite these precautions by the manager, the engineers did not make the adjustments. As a result, after a grand opening with enthusiastic transcriptionists ready to enjoy their new setting, a heat problem soon became evident. In fact, before the end of the second day, the temperature stood at 88 degrees! The engineers had to scramble to adjust the airflow to keep the area usable and then make the permanent changes needed.

Principle 12

Accommodating customers with disabilities is a mandate by federal regulation. The concern in this chapter is for the physical layout. Aisle width in the public reception area must accommodate wheelchairs. Since the typical request is to review a record, table height is important. With little added expense, a folding table of wheelchair height can be stored in the reception area, ready for use.

Principle 14

As computers become the major source of information and data flow, the size of workstations can hopefully decrease. This principle holds for departments relying on paper records for the majority of the data flow. Assembly and analysis teams will continue to need significant desk space with paper records. Tasks where references are frequently used also need desktop space. Coders have traditionally needed space for records, code books, and reference materials. With encoding capabilities there is less space needed, but code books may still be used for complex issues. By allowing the coding team to assess their needs for the future and recommend their own space needs, managers can be assured these technicians have a satisfactory work environment. The use of mobile pedestals that can be pulled out and positioned whenever extra desktop space is needed is one solution used to alleviate space problems in some facilities.

Tools for Layout Design

Templates, **two-dimensional templates**, ruled layout paper, rulers, tape measures, and architectural symbols are all tools managers will need during project planning. Office layout templates can be purchased in different scales. One-fourth inch to a foot is a typical scale for a template and ruled layout paper. It is possible to purchase layout paper that is ruled for one-third-inch scale. This size should be avoided, since templates typically come in one-fourth-inch scale.

Templates representing office furniture can also be purchased or cut from card stock. These two-dimensional templates can then be moved around on the space model during brainstorming sessions. They may be backed with an adhesive material that will hold them in place temporarily. It may be helpful to color code these templates by section/team workstations for easy identification. Adhesive tape to represent walls and partitions can also be purchased to save time when creating the layout.

Architectural Symbols

Working with architects will open a new world of terminology, and learning some of the symbols and terms will be valuable for this interaction. Managers responsible for determining where to place electrical outlets and database access on the layout will want to understand and use these symbols appropriately. The architect or the physical plant engineer can assist HIM managers and the planning team in using symbols effectively. Also, some additional terminology will be heard frequently from architects and engineers as details on spatial requirements are documented. Becoming familiar with this technical language assists HIM managers and teams in making the best decisions.

Vendors can also be valuable resources as space modeling gets underway. They can share success stories from other facilities and share the names of managers who have installed their systems. Networking with these managers and other peers will broaden the scope of ideas for managers and the work groups. Hearing about things that went wrong is just as important to success, so listen to the horror stories as well.

Architectural computer software programs are also used to perform space modeling. Because parameters are integrated into the modeling, managers can test many options without concern that parameters such as aisle width are being violated. Becoming involved with such a computer program can offer managers insight into how other professionals use automated technology.

Eventually the strenuous effort comes together and the space model is in its final form. A simple space model is shown in Figure 7-9 with the major features of one department on the first floor of a facility. This space model does not show the transcription section and birth certificate area. These activities take place elsewhere.

In this plan, the HIM manager has three section managers reporting to him. With the flattening of the organization levels over the past year, the assistant manager position was eliminated. Now the day-to-day operation of the department lies with the section managers and the team leaders. Frequent meetings of the management team keep all managers involved in the daily activities, and communication takes place by voice mail, electronic mail (E-mail), and written memos. The open-environment setting pictured in Figure 7-10 offers managers room for two-person conferences. In the space model, a conference room is available for larger team meetings.

Two evening team leaders serve as managers for the teams working until midnight. They use the hospital staff reception counter and the record activity team leader's desk during their shift. Management team meetings are held in the conference room at least once a week in the late afternoon and include these two team leaders.

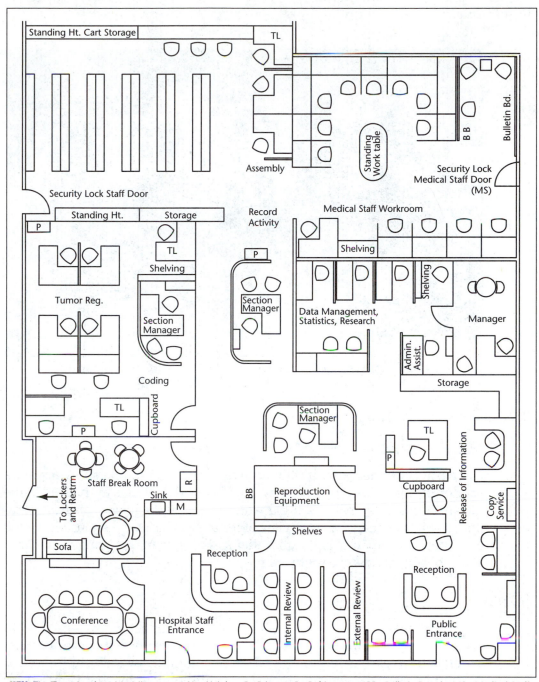

KEY: TL - Team Leader • M - Microwave • Ht - Height • P - Printer • R - Refrigerator • BB - Bulletin Board • MS - Medical Staff

Figure 7-9. Redesigned Space Model

Figure 7-10.   Managerial Open Environment (Courtesy of Steelcase)

Record Activity Section

Record Activity Section Manager

Glass privacy panels around the top area of the workstation allow the manager of record activity to have privacy. The workstation is at the side of the file area, with assembly and filing workstations at the back. This configuration gives the manager an overview of the area. He is also responsible for the physician work room. One team leader assists in managing this section and is responsible for the file room team.

File Room

Since this redesign depicts a department where paper records are still in use, a file room continues to be necessary. This area has open shelves that are eight shelves in height. Work tables run along two walls with chairs for the employees. On each side there is a length of counter that is raised for standing height and carts are stored below these counters. A closed storage area is near the assembly workstations. The workstation for the team leader is at the end of one work counter. There is an entrance near the back of the files for bringing carts of records into the department. Closed shelving is placed above the counters on both sides of the room for storage.

Assembly Workstations

These large L-shaped workstations have the desktop surface necessary for assembly of records. There are adequate covered storage shelves above each workstation. These workstations are adjustable as is the lighting just above each desktop. The chairs are adjustable also. The second-shift team assembles outpatient records, so the workstations are in use for two shifts.

Coding/Tumor Registry Section

This area is away from much of the noise of the department and is close to the conference room for the many meetings involving team members. When remodeling plans were taking place, the coders chose smaller desks with pull-out mobile pedestals. However, the tumor registry team chose the larger L-shaped desks because they still need a second computer for some of their tasks. There are two printers in this section. The section manager workstation is conveniently located and has glass panels for visibility and privacy. The workstations pictured in Figure 7-11 are an ideal environment for coding.

One team is performing concurrent coding and analysis on the patient units with workstations there. Since most of the analysis is performed on the patient units, larger desks were not needed in the department for this specific function. Coders check for missing reports and physician signature on the face sheet, and typed reports.

In addition to the team leader responsible for concurrent coding and analysis, there is a team leader responsible for tumor registry activities. There is also a team leader in charge during the evening hours. Team members in this section can work flexible shifts and share workstations. The workstation and lighting components are adjustable to meet the needs of all the team members.

A close relationship exists between concurrent review, quality improvement, utilization review, and social work teams. A physician advisor is available to answer questions from any of these teams during the afternoon.

Figure 7-11. Coding/Tumor Registry Team Workstations (Courtesy of Steelcase)

A conference room for this purpose is available in the medical staff offices across the hall from the department.

Reception/Release-of-Information Section

This section cares for all customers with the exception of physicians entering their work room. The manager's workstation has glass panels and is in the center at the back of the work area. Two large reception counters dominate the area; at least one team member is scheduled for each counter during the day when the public and hospital staff entrance doors are open. During the evening and on weekends, the hospital staff doors are entered by keypad access and one team member staffs this area. Figure 7-12 shows an appropriate work counter for the public reception area, and Figure 7-13 pictures a work counter for the staff reception area.

A team leader is in charge of the release-of-information and public reception area. Responsibility includes ensuring confidentiality and privacy

Figure 7-12.   A Public Reception Area

Figure 7-13.   A Staff Reception Area

for the patients and their families. Two private carrels are provided for them to review records. Auditors, reviewers, and in-house researchers use an audit room between the two reception areas. However, copy service representatives perform their tasks in a separate work area near the team leader's workstation. A cupboard in the audit room holds standard forms frequently needed by auditors and reviewers. In this room a large work table is provided for internal reviewers working together on a project.

Confidentiality is enhanced with the location of the VDT at each workstation, thus preventing customers from viewing the screen during a database search. Ample seating arrangement for customers allows team members to encourage customers to wait in appropriate areas.

Responsibility for the reproduction equipment room also lies with this section. There is a high-speed copier, a fax machine, and a central printer located here. Space is also planned in this room for future telecommunication technology. A small printer is available for the correspondence software program near the team leader workstation. There is modem capability in this area also.

Any concerns relating to the conference room, lounge, rest rooms, and locker areas come to this section. There are lunch facilities within the lounge. Adequate lockers for all employees are beyond the lounge. Three lockers are designated for HIM student use, since administration and the managers are committed to providing learning experiences for students in HIM educational programs. Another rest room is located in the main hallway outside the department.

Supplies for this section and some general supplies for the remainder of the department are kept in a large storage area at the back of this section. Supplies for the lounge area are stored under the counter there.

Data Management, Statistics, and Research

The team involved in data management, statistics, and research is in the same area as the manager of the department. The team is directly responsible to him. There is also an administrative assistant in this area who cares for the coordinating activities of the department and scheduling of the float technicians. Being available to assist the manager as needed is also a part of the job description.

There is a printer in this area and a work table for research projects.

Esthetics of the Department

With this floor plan the department design enhances the services and information offered. The visual image of the department creates an ambiance of efficiency and competency. The open office landscape minimizes territoriality that is sometimes defined by fixed walls. Thus, employees feel an ownership in the total work environment. By allowing the teams to interact with the interior designer as the esthetic atmosphere was being planned, managers encouraged a sense of ownership.

Maintaining the Team's Environment

Team members who are allowed to plan the decor within the guidelines of the interior designer tend to increase their commitment to their work space. Wall hangings and plant choices can be a joint effort of the team. Since sharing the workstation environment is a fact of life for many teams, the decor within a workstation may have to be quite mobile. Taking down family photos and other personal items at the end of a workday may need to be done routinely so the next person can individualize the workstation for his preference. By encouraging open communication and team effort regarding esthetics in the workstation, managers can increase morale and the satisfaction of each team member.

Maintaining a Clean and Neat Environment

Even though the HIM department is cleaned routinely, there is still a need to encourage employees to keep their work area neat and clean. The team spends a good part of the day in this environment, and when it is kept neat and clean, their self-image is enhanced. The file room is a good example of an area that can look like a battlefield very quickly. Paper may no longer be usable but left scattered, and carts may be left standing where they were last used. Managers can set an expectation of neatness and cleanliness and then walk the talk by keeping their own area orderly.

One way of showing the priority given to esthetics, neatness, and cleanliness is to plan an in-service education on this topic periodically. Another way is to create a bulletin board display on this subject every now and then. This extra effort helps set the tone for the department.

Looking Forward to Change

Plans are now in place for the actual construction work. At this point, the perception of every employee should be assessed. Any concerns about the changes will need to be addressed. Also, the long-term positive effect of this more technologically intensive environment can be discussed and, hopefully, fears diminished.

When managers verbally reinforce the time and effort taken by the planning committee to see that the workstations are user-friendly and user-created, commitment to the project can be solidified. As the plans are reviewed, the teams can see that these workstations demonstrate that managers respect the emotional and physical needs of employees. Increased interface between professionals and computers can be seen as a challenge for growth. During this transition period, managers will want to be sensitive to these concerns among employees and respond to them.

Changes that will undoubtedly demand new uses for the space just allocated to specific teams are inevitable, but with an open landscape and flexible workstations, changes can be made with minimal expense. Employees are thus encouraged to embrace change by HIM managers who are committed to creating an environment where change is an accepted experience. Teams that see this construction as a step to future changes can be led to think creatively toward those future possibilities.

Summary

Providing satisfaction and comfort to employees while increasing productivity of services and information to customers bring challenges to managers. When remodeling is planned for an HIM department, it is inevitable that change will increase the technologically intensive environment in which employees perform their tasks. By careful planning for this new environment, managers can steer the project toward success.

Ergonomics is an applied science that combines engineering, psychological, and anthropologic concepts to create a work environment for today's complex society. Seven general principles of ergonomics are used by ergonomists when assessing the present work-flow tasks. Any repetitive activities performed by an employee are especially noted. Changes are then recommended for the remodeled environment.

Managers and teams prepare an inventory of the present furnishings during the next planning phase. An automated spreadsheet is an excellent vehicle for this task. The inventory can be used later for multiple purposes as it should be updated periodically.

Planning for the remodeling can now be accomplished using the information gathered during the assessment. The design participants should be from a wide spectrum of specialists: ergonomists, architects, interior designers, physical plant engineers, top administrators, other department managers, and department employees. When all information has been gathered, the functional/product flow-line patterns can be created and space modeling begins. Fiscal constraints may require adjustments, so priorities need to be set by the teams to ensure changes take place in a coordinated fashion.

Principles that can assist the participants in creating an efficient and effective workplace are incorporated in the plan. Many of these are related to employee satisfaction and comfort. These principles include (1)using equipment vendors specializing in efficient use of space; (2) arranging workstations and tools for convenience and a smooth work flow; (3) creating privacy, security, and noise reduction for the records, the customers, and the employees; (4) allowing appropriate access through entrance doors into workstations and customer areas for all employees and customers including the physically challenged; and (5) providing appropriate ventilation, lighting, and work space with the flexibility to give multiple users satisfaction and comfort.

Templates, layout paper, rulers, tape measures, and architectural symbols are some of the tools needed as planning is undertaken. Managers who learn to use these tools find increased confidence and effectiveness as they work with the planning participants. When architectural computer software is available, it is also an excellent tool for creating the model.

As the model is finalized, esthetics of the department are considered. Options for individualized work settings may be limited, but by allowing the teams to take advantage of all possible options, managers can increase morale and satisfaction.

During this planning phase, managers can gradually instill the sense of continuous transitional planning among the employees. Because of the changes taking place in the health-care environment, HIM professionals who willingly embrace change and make it a part of the culture within their sphere of influence will be ready for future transitions.

Review Questions

1. List several factors you would bring into a remodeling project to give satisfaction and comfort to the team that is facing a change from a manual record-tracking system to an automated system.

2. Define the term *ergonomic principles*.

3. Delineate six factors in job design that concern ergonomists.

4. What does the term *space modeling* mean and how is it used in a remodeling project?

5. Create a list of several steps a manager would appropriately take in preparing and maintaining an inventory of furnishings and equipment for an HIM department.

6. Explain the role vendors can take in planning the physical layout of an HIM department.

7. What steps would you take in preparing an in-service education for the employees on maintaining a clean, safe, and attractive work setting? Outline your major topics.

Field Practice Questions

1. Choose an HIM work setting and assess its present environment using the seven general principles of ergonomics. Recommend any major changes you would make to improve the work setting for the employees.

2. Create a simple space model of an HIM department with which you are familiar and show how the work flows through the department. Include the entrance doors on the model and defend your assertion that they are well placed or poorly placed for efficiency and effectiveness.

3. Prepare two-dimensional templates of workstations for one section of an HIM department and present at least two layout alternative plans that could be used effectively and efficiently for this section.

References

Bennett, A. (1990). Methods improvement in hospitals. *Topics in Medical Record Management*, pp. 20–24.

Foster, M. (1988). Ergonomics and the physiotherapist. *Physiotherapy*, September, p. 484.

Kelly, C. (1993). No uncertain terms: Medical transcriptionist manager enhances workplace through CPRI, ergonomics. *Advance for Health Information Professionals*, 3 (6), 7, 8.

Layman, E., Heaps, T., & Bell, B. (1992). The human factor: Ergonomics and the coding function. *Journal of AHIMA*, 63 (8), 78.

Wear, P. (1992). Pam's packet: Patient advocacy and health information management. *Journal of AHIMA*, 63 (3), 8-11.

Suggested Readings

Cofer, J. (ed.) (1991). Department's renovation makes room for every type of review. *Medical Records Briefing*, November, pp. 6, 7.

Donnelly, J., Gibson, J., & Ivancevich, J. (1987). *Fundamentals of management* (6th ed.). Plano, TX: Business Publications.

Longest, B. (1990). *Management practices for the health professional* (4th ed.). Norwalk, CT: Appleton & Lange.

Muther, R., & Wheeler, J. (1985). *Simplified layout planning*. Kansas City: Management and Industrial Research Publications.

Robbins, S. (1994). *Management* (4th ed.). Englewood Cliffs, NJ: Prentice Hall.

Rue, L., & Byars, L. (1986). *Management: Theory and application* (4th ed.). Homewood, IL: Richard D. Irwin.

Slade, D., Foley, M., & Cohen, S. (1994). Reengineering along departmental product flowlines. *Topics in Health Information Management*, February, pp. 37–42.

Organizing to Meet Information Needs of Health-Care Facilities

Chapter 8

The Process of Organizing Health Information Services

Learning Objectives

After completing this chapter, the learner should be able to:

1. Define the management function of organizing.
2. Describe the three main parts of the basic model for organizational structure.
3. Give the advantages and disadvantages of dividing labor into discrete parts.
4. Demonstrate ways that rules and policies are used in creating a formalized organizational structure.
5. Contrast managerial power with managerial authority.
6. Identify differences between line and staff relationships.
7. List reasons why the span of control varies from one manager to another.
8. Give the four departmentalized organizational structures and an example of each for health-care facilities.
9. Explain the advantages of using a contingency management approach in organizing.

Key Terms

Authority	Span of control
Centralization of authority	Span of management
Departmentalization	Specialization of labor
Division of labor	Staff authority
Formalization	Unity of command
Power	

Introduction

Health-care professionals who provide care for the human body become knowledgeable about the anatomical structural design of the body and use that knowledge for making treatment decisions. Just as this anatomical structure is a major feature of the body in defining the shape and frame, so an organization has structure that defines its shape. In fact, the root term for organizing is *organism*, meaning an entity with parts so integrated that their relation to one another is governed by their relation to the whole. In this section on the organizing function of management, the integrating role of HIM managers for meeting the organizational objectives is explained.

Dissecting various organizational structures will lead to an understanding of the importance of the organizing function in their success. The inner workings of organizational structure are covered in this chapter and lead to an appreciation of organizational structure and design complexity.

The impact of emerging technologies on managerial planning is mentioned in Section II, during the discussion of SWOT analysis. This impact is also emphasized in Section III on organizing as changes in organizational structure become necessary. In fact, Chapter 11 is devoted to organizing for emerging technologies. Reengineering or redesign of the organizational structure of HIM departments can be an effective response to these changes.

Since the HIM profession is committed to accepting responsibility for quality information throughout health-care systems, organizing to best meet this objective, regardless of the setting, is the professional's goal. The basic organizational structure outlined in this chapter can be adapted for use in each of the various health-care settings described in Chapter 1.

The need for a contingency approach to organizing HIM departments as change occurs is also discussed. Later chapters in this section examine traditional organizational designs and explore several new designs for organizational structure. By the end of Section III, the foundations of planning and organizing will have form and structure, giving guidance toward the remaining management functions: leading and controlling.

Organizing Defined

The definition of the organizing function of management is stated as "the management function that determines what tasks are to be done, who shall do them, the reporting structure, and at what level decisions will be made" (Robbins, 1994). This definition lends credence to the crucial role upper-level management has in creating the organizational structure. It is upper-level management that chooses the reporting structure and the level at which decisions affecting the organization will be made. Once these choices are made and responsibility is allocated, managers can organize within designated parameters to meet specific organizational objectives.

As paradigm shifts occur in health-care facilities, the board of trustees and the medical staff are given increasing responsibility for assuring stakeholders that an appropriate organizational structure is in place. The board of trustees delegates authority for this assurance to upper-level management. However, perceived community health-care needs at present and future projected needs are rightly the concern of board members, mandating that they take an active interest in the structure that will meet the mission and objectives of the facility. Medical staff members are in a unique position to assist in shaping the structure of a facility; they are stakeholders sharing responsibility for success with the board of trustees while making decisions that affect many activities within the organization.

As the decision-making process moves downward, authority is delegated to department managers; thus, HIM professionals organize the department according to the structure outlined by upper-level administration. As the structure takes shape, managers have the opportunity to create levels of decision making within the department that are best suited to the structure and to the activities involved for meeting the objectives.

Organizing Terms Defined

Before turning to a closer look at organizational structure, several terms used as organizing tools must be defined.

Differentiation, Degree of Regulations, and Concentration of Authority

The basic model for organizational structure has three main parts. As each part is dissected and defined, the anatomy of the structure will emerge. These three main parts are:

1. *Differentiation*—one end of the spectrum is simplicity; at the other end is complexity.
2. *Degree of regulations*—with formalization at one end of the spectrum and an informal structure at the other end.
3. *Concentration of authority*—one end of the spectrum is centralization, at the other end is decentralization (Robbins, 1994).

Each of these major parts will be brought into later discussions; here definitions, synonyms, and related terms are provided as a foundation to the content.

Differentiation

Differentiation means the **specialization of labor** where each employee specializes in skilled tasks. These tasks may be grouped into a unit for efficiency. Another term for this managerial activity is **division of labor**. When the tasks are few and are quickly learned, they are considered simple. Because of the complex activities inherent in health-care settings, differentiation of tasks is found throughout the organization. A wide array of professionals have specific specialties, making the complex specialization of labor crucial to the whole organization. Coordination of the complex activities delegated to the HIM departments within this environment is the exciting task of the HIM managers.

Degree of Regulations

As outlined in Section II, when organizations become larger and more complex, the rules, policies, and regulations increase. Upper-level management then formalizes the structure to standardize activities. This process is called **departmentalization**. Here, employees are grouped together according to their specialized activities. Thus, the HIM department employees perform activities related to health information management to accomplish departmental objectives.

Breaking this **formalization** down further, within the department there may be groups clustered according to specialized tasks. For example, transcription specialists are typically grouped together as a section/team.

To standardize regulations, the rules, policies, and regulations are documented and guide the behavior of employees. In addition to government and accrediting body regulations and policies, each of the various professional associations, whose members are a part of the health-care teams, have rules and policies to guide behavior. As a result, employees behave according to their own specialty expectations as well. This creates a formal structure for employees of the health-care organization and very little effort may be required by managers in setting policies for those specific behaviors. An example of these expectations is the set of position statements available from the American Health Information Management Association (AHIMA) that covers a wide range of HIM subjects. For instance, several of them relate to appropriate behavior for HIM professionals who are delegated responsibility for release of patient information and related confidentiality issues (Roberts, 1994; Brandt, 1993).

There are many examples of government regulations that create formalized behavior for HIM functions. A major set of these government regulations are those mandating specific activities for coding and case-mix management. These regulations lead to a more formalized information structure as managers seek to standardize the activities of the coding section.

Concentration of Authority

Concentration of authority concerns decision making and problem solving. When problems are routinely sent to upper-level management for resolution, there is a high degree of **centralization of authority**. In health-care organizations activities relating to professional specialties are typically decentralized while the organization may be structured toward centralization for other types of authority and decisions. This is additional evidence of the complexity of health-care facilities.

Given this complexity within health-care organizations and the differences among them, assessing the total structure and gaining a true picture of how these three main parts of the organizational structure operate within a health-care organization can be difficult. However, for the HIM functions, there is opportunity to dissect the structure and determine the degree to which each of these parts is scaled.

Chapter 9 gives detail on creating organizational change by mixing and matching these three structural parts for effectiveness and efficiency in meeting the objectives. Since change is expected to continue in health-care organizations, in health-care professions, in health-care regulations, and in health-care modalities, managers must become comfortable with creating change as opportunities arise and creating appropriate organizational structures through an integrated model of management.

Managerial Power and Authority

As discussed in Chapter 2, the classical view of managerial thought was that **authority** refers to the rights inherent in the position. For example, an HIM manager has the authority to organize the department and delegate tasks for meeting the objectives. This authority does not relate to the personal characteristics of the manager; it relates to the position (Robbins, 1994).

Later management approaches recognized that authority is a subset of the larger concept of **power**. While authority is a right, power refers to an individual's capacity to influence the decision-making process. It is seen that authority is formal power and may be just one avenue by which an individual affects decisions. However, one may have power without formal authority (Robbins, 1994).

For example, the administrative secretary has a central position within the department and may exert power as the gatekeeper of the department managers. Within the organizational structure, however, the administrative secretary position may lack delegated authority.

Several types of power are used to describe this concept. In contemporary organizations, the following sources of power can be observed in managers and nonmanagers: coercive power, reward power, legitimate power, expert power, and referent power. Each of these sources of power deserves attention.

Coercive Power

Coercive power is dependent on fear—fear that negative results could occur from failure to comply. Managers have the authority to suspend employees, assign them to tasks they may find unpleasant, or dismiss them. Nonmanagers also possess coercive power; for example, a subordinate may choose to embarrass her manager in public. When nonmanagers use this threat successfully to gain advantage, coercive power is evident.

Reward Power

Managers can give rewards that employees value and thus hold power over them. These rewards may be promotions, favorable performance appraisals, enjoyable tasks, requested work shifts, or money. Again, nonmanagers also have reward power such as acceptance, praise, friendliness, and gifts. By comparing these rewards with the coercive power threats listed above, the contrast is obvious. Power to remove something of value is the opposite of giving something of value.

Legitimate Power

This power is synonymous with authority and represents power based on position in the formal organizational structure. Legitimate power still requires acceptance of the manager on the part of others. Acceptance must come from subordinates as well as other members of the organization.

Expert Power

Experts in their specialty areas are an increasing power source in health-care facilities. An example is in technical knowledge. As expertise in health information for the information superhighway becomes increasingly sought after, expert power in this area will become very visible. This expertise will gain importance to the degree the users of the information lack the knowledge to access it. Data capture, analysis, integration, and dissemination are critical power bases for the HIM profession.

Referent Power

The base of referent power lies in a desire for resources or personal traits that are attractive. Charismatic managers have influence because others are attracted to them, and their behavior and attitudes are modeled. Nonmanagers may also have traits that give them referent power to influence their peers, their superiors, and others in the organization (Robbins, 1994).

Resources

In this discussion on power, little mention has been made of the value of resources. However, there are several reasons why resources can relate to a manager's power. Certainly information is one reason—the expert with information valued by others has power. Another reason relates to resources that may be available only through a staff person. For example, final approval for expansion of an HIM department into an adjoining space may depend on the feasibility study prepared by an administrative assistant who holds a staff position in the organization.

Unity of Command

Management theories describe the **unity of command** principle when outlining the concepts of the division of labor. This principle states that an employee has one and only one immediate manager. This clear separation was considered crucial to a smooth work flow with the absence of conflicting priorities. It is further stated that when this principle of unity of command must be broken, a clear separation of activities and responsibilities should be documented. This principle complements the granting of authority principle described above. When carried to the extreme, the concept leads to a chain of command where each action must painfully progress through each link of the chain. To make this unwieldy activity reasonable, management experts state that, when there is confidence and loyalty among the organization members, shortcuts are appropriate. The key is that the shortcuts are not done in a deceitful or secretive manner (Rue and Byars, 1986).

As the authority and responsibility delegated to managers are detailed, this organizational structure can be shown visually as an organizational model. A traditional model is shown in Figure 8-1. It depicts a visual description of the chain of command for an HIM department in a community hospital, and demonstrates the unit of command principle. It shows line authority flowing from the HIM manager down to the supervisors of the sections and then to the team members. Line authority is authority delegated to managers, entitling them to direct the work of subordinates.

In Figure 8-1, the position of secretary is shown as a separate line box. This position is one of **staff authority** where the secretary supports, assists, and enables managers in line authority to perform their tasks. Other

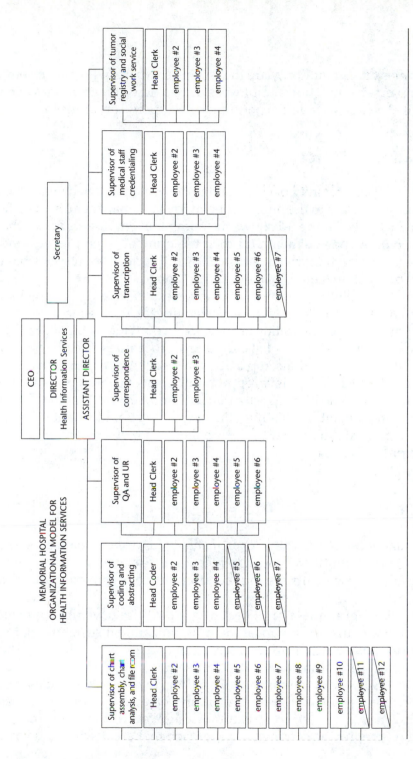

MEMORIAL HOSPITAL
ORGANIZATIONAL MODEL FOR
HEALTH INFORMATION SERVICES

CEO

DIRECTOR
Health Information Services

Secretary

ASSISTANT DIRECTOR

Supervisor of chart assembly, chart analysis, and file room

Head Clerk
employee #2
employee #3
employee #4
employee #5
employee #6
employee #7
employee #8
employee #9
employee #10
employee #11
employee #12

Supervisor of coding and abstracting

Head Coder
employee #2
employee #3
employee #4
employee #5
employee #6
employee #7

Supervisor of QA and UR

Head Clerk
employee #2
employee #3
employee #4
employee #5
employee #6

Supervisor of correspondence

Head Clerk
employee #2
employee #3

Supervisor of transcription

Head Clerk
employee #2
employee #3
employee #4
employee #5
employee #6
employee #7

Supervisor of medical staff credentialing

Head Clerk
employee #2
employee #3
employee #4

Supervisor of tumor registry and social work service

Head Clerk
employee #2
employee #3
employee #4

Figure 8-1. A Traditional Organizational Model

examples of staff authority are the technical experts who may be employed to implement and train employees when new information systems are installed. These technical experts have no supervisory duties.

Span of Control

Closely related to unity of command is the principle called **span of control**. This phrase refers to the number of employees a manager directs efficiently and effectively. Figure 8-1 shows the number of employees under the director's **span of management** and then the number of employees under the span of control for each supervisor. Several factors are responsible for the appropriate managerial span of control (Longest, 1990).

For example, the number of employees changes as contingency variables change. Managers with responsibility for professionals with experience and advanced education are able to have a wider span of control. Other variables include the use of standardized procedures, the physical proximity of the team, and the complexity and variability of the tasks being performed. A crucial factor in an appropriate span of control is the information system available to managers for quality improvement. Another factor is the organizational culture that may dictate status quo. In Chapter 9 several of these factors are discussed further as the design of a matrix organizational structure is discussed.

Organizational Structure

Organizations are typically departmentalized to allow managers to coordinate a subset of tasks that lead to meeting the overall organizational goals. Typically, departments are formed around one of the structures shown in Figure 8-2.

As these examples show, health-care facilities have the opportunity to use a combination of groups in their organizational structure. Some organizations have redesigned their structure and are now following the trend toward process or customer departmentalization. This trend is likely to increase as needs of the customers continue to be emphasized as the strategic planning process envisions goals and objectives. This trend leads to a contingency approach in structural design. And, there are other trends that favor using the contingency approach that are discussed below.

1. *Functional departmentalization:* Activities are grouped into like functions such as admitting, accounting, or health information services.

2. *Customer departmentalization:* Customers with common problems are grouped to allow activities for meeting their needs effectively. Intensive care is an example where like customers are grouped together for treatment.

3. *Product departmentalization:* Similar products are grouped into departments where activities relating to them can be accomplished efficiently. In health-care facilities radiation therapy and clinical laboratory departments each have similar activities.

4. *Process departmentalization:* Grouping of activities is based on the flow of the product or service to meet the needs of customers. Insurance validation and other steps in the admission process may be grouped in a facility to enhance the flow of patient admissions.

Figure 8-2.   Department Structures

Work Team Structures

As health-care facilities seek to become more efficient, they cannot overlook the advantages offered by flexible, self-disciplined, multiskilled work teams given responsibility for performing services. These services may involve all of the work processes, such as the teams created to manage the patient-focused care unit. The multiskilled work teams created for patient-focused care units are grouped for process departmentalization. Under this concept, the admissions, utilization review, testing, therapy, nursing care, concurrent review, and coding are the responsibility of the team. This creates a matrix organization structure that is detailed in Chapter 9.

Self-Directed Teams

Permanent self-directed work teams have unique features, but several characteristics are typical; these are outlined in Figure 8-3.

Shared Leadership Teams

Shared leadership teams can also be created that enable managers to empower employees and give a sense of ownership and control in the workplace. The shared leadership teams may be empowered to perform many of

1. *Empowerment:* authority and responsibility to share in managerial functions.
2. *Goals and objectives:* a vision created for the team within the overall goals and objectives of the facility.
3. *Budget resources:* sharing in the budgeting process that allocates resources for meeting the objectives.
4. *Materials:* ordering supplies and approved equipment.
5. *Planning:* organizing the work processes and creating team schedules.
6. *Training and in-service:* coordinating and implementing training and in-service needs.
7. *Hiring:* sharing in hiring decisions.
8. *Quality improvement:* monitoring the quality of services and initiating improvements.
9. *Discipline:* taking responsibility for disciplinary action.
10. *Performance appraisal:* completing periodic appraisals and recommending wage adjustments.
11. *Leadership:* rotating the team leader or choosing a permanent one to act as spokesperson, internal facilitator, and to perform other managing functions.

Figure 8-3.   Self-Directed Work Team Characteristics (Wellins, 1991)

the activities listed in Figure 8-3; those typically not assigned to the team are discipline, budgeting, and performance appraisals. Within HIM departments the shared leadership team concept is found frequently, but there is no "common" team concept. The empowerment continuum differs depending on the unique circumstances. HIM managers can develop the organizational structure that will best meet the needs of the department and the organization.

Temporary Work Teams

Temporary work teams are created to meet specific needs and may utilize multiskilled employees. An example of a temporary work team is the work group gathered to plan and implement an information system. The members of a temporary work team may be assigned to the team for a specific number of hours per week and continue performing other activities during the remainder of the week. Empowerment varies and typically authority and responsibility rest mainly with the technical aspects of the task assigned to the team.

Other aspects of work teams are discussed in Section IV, where the leading function of management emphasizes the changing role of managers.

Informal Organizational Structure

The planned organizational structure of an HIM department outlined in Figure 8-1 shows a deliberate process of patterned relationships for accomplishing activities. The model emphasizes line and staff authority positions. Within all departments there is a second structure that emphasizes people and their relationships. This informal organization is not under the control of managers, but must be recognized by them. Several factors relating to informal organizations are outlined in Figure 8-4.

Since formal authority is not bestowed on informal groups, the leader exerts power over the group through one or more of the types of power already discussed. Referent power is frequently seen as charismatic employees naturally take the leadership role in informal groups. However, expert, reward, and coercive power is also seen.

Not all members of an informal group have similar needs. One person may become a member of the group to satisfy social needs, another person may be seeking advancement, and a third person may want to obtain information. The group members change frequently and may include employees outside the department.

---

1. *Small groups:* Small groups come into being to satisfy individual needs that cannot be fully met by the formal organizational structure.

2. *Leaders:* Members choose leaders they perceive as important for satisfying their needs.

3. *Informal groups:* Informal groups are inevitable within HIM departments.

4. *Positive aspects:* Informal groups can complement the formal organizations and provide stability to work teams.

5. *Negative aspects:* Role conflicts can occur when goals of the groups are not compatible with the goals and objectives of the formal organization.

Figure 8-4.   Informal Organizational Factors

Managers can take advantage of the informal organization when they understand it. As an additional channel of information, the group can be given information by managers who can then determine employee feelings and attitudes about issues. Being sensitive to these feelings and attitudes allows managers to integrate the interests of informal groups into those of the formal organization. This provides strength and stability toward the accomplishment of department objectives.

Role of Contingency Approaches in Organizing

The trend to group services according to process departmentalization results in the formation of teams where the members cross traditional departmental groupings. As facilities search for effective and efficient use of scarce resources, the use of teams that combine the skills of various health-care professionals on the patient-care units is expected to increase. As mentioned earlier, this new structure is called patient-centered care units or patient-focused care units, when the change involves direct patient care. As these trends show, organizational structure changes in response to the vision of upper-level management as the strategic planning process takes place. The changes are likely to be in response to planning function activities such as a SWOT analysis.

The size of an organization also affects its structure in a variety of ways that demand a contingency approach. A community home health-care agency, for example, will have an organization structured around a high degree of collaboration and adaptation among the team members. This contrasts with a large hospital where there will tend to be high formalization and structured activities. As the home health-care agency experiences growth, however, its structure will naturally increase in formalization. Again the managers will benefit from use of contingency approaches as decisions are made.

During the strategic planning process, health-care organizations may choose an objective that will increase information technology capabilities. This objective will then be embraced by the HIM department and a contingency approach to structural changes must be addressed. With appropriate adjustments, the department can keep pace with data capture capabilities that can result in reduced managerial and staff time and effort to meet customer needs. In this dynamic environment HIM managers who react to changes in a timely manner but are also proactive in suggesting changes will become increasingly important. As the planning function creates a foundation for change, HIM managers have an opportunity to review the contingencies confronting them, seize the momentum, and organize accordingly.

HIM managers frequently find themselves managing departments with systems that include a mix of high-technology capabilities and antiquated processes. Organizing the work flow and teams for efficient and effective effort is frequently a challenge they face. The following practice example illustrates this circumstance and demonstrates how managers use contingency approaches in organizing.

Practice Example

The hospital in this example is unusual in that a clinical information system was installed in the 1970s to support physicians, nurses, and allied health professionals in patient care. In that time period, it was typical for the first automated systems to support the billing process. In contrast with that early start toward an EPR, however, several health information services are still performed manually. Figure 8-5 details the automated systems and the manual systems in the department at present.

A review of the systems that are still manual indicates record management is still very much a paperwork environment. The record-tracking card system for incomplete records and other record activity require intensive employee time and commitment by each employee to maintain record locations. Because of this commitment, the system works well and there are few lost records. Incomplete records are not allowed out of the department except for patient-care purposes; this facilitates the process.

The department is organized into work teams with extensive crosstraining. The work teams are led by team leaders; the teams choose whether they prefer permanent team leaders or rotating ones. A temporary work team has been involved in developing the automated systems for the EPR, leading to regional longitudinal health records, and this team will continue this effort for at least another 10 months. This multidisciplinary team has three health information services members; they devote 50 percent of their time to this responsibility and the remainder to their routine activi-

Automated Systems

1. *Record storage:* Longitudinal health records are in the developmental stage with patient information stored on the computer indefinitely; portions of the records remain on hard copy, however. This requires dual-storage systems—automated and paper. At present the longitudinal health record covers patient care within the network of medical staff offices and ambulatory-care settings only.

2. *Transcription:* Delivered directly to PCs from outside transcription; can be printed out in hard copy as needed. Transcription services within the department are not yet linked to the longitudinal record, requiring hard copy for those reports.

3. *Network:* Fiber-optic network links workstations, working toward total linkage to the clinical system.

4. *Coding and DRG assignment:* Computerized billing information flows directly to billing services.

5. *Release of information:* PC software is specifically designed for correspondence with attorneys, insurance companies, and other customers.

6. *Statistical information:* Integration of clinical systems data allows for dissemination of aggregate statistics, some medical staff activity, and decision-support systems.

7. *Completion of automated portion of the health record:* Medical staff and nursing staff have responsibility for completing the clinical record with the exception of dictated reports; these are tracked by health information services staff.

Manual Systems

1. *Record storage:* Open-shelf filing, until recently the computerized portion of the records were printed out totally for hard-copy storage. Now both hard copy and computerized portions of the longitudinal record exist.

2. *Record tracking:* 3-by-5-inch index cards are used.

3. *Analysis and incomplete record activity:* Analysis has been streamlined; however, cards are used to track completion and manual counting for delinquent records. Physician notification is manual.

4. *In-house transcription:* Transcriptionists use computers, but reports are printed out on hard copy, not linked to the longitudinal record.

5. *Departmental continuous-quality improvement:* Data capture and monitoring are possible for some of the work teams; manual tracking continues for other teams.

Figure 8-5. Automated and Manual Systems in Health Information Services

ties. Part-time staffers were hired and trained to keep the work current while these team members are out of the department.

The teams are responsible for ensuring that each team member is familiar with computer capabilities within their work environment and for training when new systems are installed. They are also responsible for quality improvement. The monitoring tools vary, depending on whether the task is automated, with data capture for review or whether the task is manual, with handwritten tallies.

Organizing efficiently and effectively for dual systems in the department has challenged the management team, and reorganizing takes place periodically as additional automated capabilities come online. The department's 5-year strategic plan includes the following:

1. Totally automated for the incomplete record system.
2. Automated record tracking for all hard-copy record activity.
3. Transcription reports linked to the electronic patient record.
4. Quality improvement activities increasingly automated as systems are installed that offer monitoring capabilities.
5. Record storage as a dual system. Facility-wide strategic plan includes electronic storage and use of hard-copy records for the next 5 years. One reason is that state law requires patient authorization in hard copy.

As these objectives are realized, organizational change will continue to occur. The managers are committed to a contingency approach to organizing and will perform periodic SWOT analysis. For example, should state laws change, the managers can develop a revised objective to accommodate the change. The teams are becoming comfortable with redesign of their activities, since the gradual implementation of the EPR began in the mid-1970s. Because of the gradual process, the HIM managers anticipate the changes will not require a total reengineering of the work process.

Anticipating skills that will be needed as automation progresses and future systems that can best meet the needs of the department are objectives of managers that can lead to organizing efficiencies in an effective manner (Watson, 1994). ■

Summary

This chapter begins a discussion of the management function called organizing. Organizing is described as the function that determines what tasks are to be done, who shall do them, the reporting structure, and at what level decisions will be made. Upper-level management creates the reporting structure and then managers organize within the delegated parameters.

An organizing structure has three main parts: (1) differentiation leading from simplicity to complexity; (2) degree of regulation leading from the informal to the formal; and (3) concentration of authority leading from centralization to decentralization. Specialization or division of labor is frequently seen in health-care facilities where differentiation is commonplace because of professional specialties.

Managerial power refers to an individual's capacity to influence the decision-making process with authority inherent in the position, not the personal characteristics of a manager. Employees may have power without formal authority. Coercive power depends on fear, reward power is giving something of value, and legitimate power is synonymous with authority. Expert power is frequently evident in health-care and will become increasingly important as the information superhighway is developed. Charismatic managers have influence called referent power.

The unity of command principle holds that an employee has one and only one immediate manager. A traditional organization model demonstrates this principle and shows line and staff positions.

Organizations must choose the best structure for coordinating the tasks that meet their goals. Four departmentalization structures are functional, customer, product, and process. A combination of these structures is seen in complex health-care organizations. A contingency management approach assists managers in creating an organizational structure best suited to their needs.

Review Questions

1. Describe the organizing function and give several reasons for organizing.
2. Relate how a manager integrates the planning process into the organizing function.

3. How is power and authority given to an HIM department manager?

4. Describe several aspects of an informal organization that differ from those of a formal organization.

5. What is the organizing phrase used to describe the structure when the coding specialists are organized into a team that works independently, making most of the decisions regarding coding activities?

6. Give examples of the five types of power you have seen while interacting with employees in a health-care setting.

7. Show how automating several record tasks can lead to a change in the span of control for the managers.

8. Which of the four departmentalizations would be used to best advantage in an HIM department? Defend your answer.

References

Brandt, M. (1993). Position statement: Disclosure of health information relating to adoption. *Journal of AHIMA, 64* (12), insert.

Longest, B. (1990). *Management practices for the health professional* (4th ed.). Norwalk, CT: Appleton & Lange.

Robbins, S. (1994). *Management* (4th ed.). Englewood Cliffs, NJ: Prentice Hall.

Roberts, C. (1994). Position statement: Documentation timeliness. *Journal of AHIMA, 65* (5), insert.

Rue, L., & Byars, L. (1986). *Management: Theory and application* (4th ed.). Homewood, IL: Richard D. Irwin.

Watson, L. (1994). She helps to plan for the computerized future of HI. *Advance for Health Information Professionals, 4* (2), 5.

Wellins, R. (1991). *Empowered teams.* San Francisco: Jossey-Bass.

Suggested Readings

Donnelly, J., Gibson, J., & Ivancevich, J. (1987). *Fundamentals of management* (6th ed.). Plano, TX: Business Publications.

Foerster, R. (1994). Electronic data interchange (EDI): An enabler of financial business process reengineering. *Journal of AHIMA, 65* (4), 38–42.

Fox, L. (1994). Organizational change: Reengineering the workflow. *Journal of AHIMA, 65* (4), 35, 36.

Lavelle, F. (1994). Looking ahead to the year 2010: Future applications of the electronic information highway. *Journal of AHIMA, 65* (8), 44–46.

Longest, B., (1990). *Management practices for the health professional* (4th ed.). Norwalk, CT: Appleton & Lange.

Mastrangelo, R. (1991). Health information managers must adopt "global" skills. *Advance for Health Information Professionals, 1* (25), 5.

Murphy, G., & Anderson, E. (1994). An organizational model for data access and management—Work in progress. *Journal of AHIMA, 65* (8), 50–54.

Nardonne, L., & Bliss, A. (1994). From retrospective to concurrent. *For the Record, 6* (7), 4, 5.

Robbins, S. (1994). *Management* (4th ed.). Englewood Cliffs, NJ: Prentice Hall.

Rue, L., & Byars, L. (1986). *Management: Theory and application* (4th ed.). Homewood, IL: Richard D. Irwin.

Torie, C., & Houston, S. (1994). Reengineering—Impact on organizational culture. *Journal of AHIMA, 65* (4), 46–48.

Wanerus, P. (1994). Managing the health information department through a merger. *Journal of AHIMA, 65* (4), 55–58.

Watson, L. (1994). She helps to plan for the computerized future of HI. *Advance for Health Information Professionals, 4* (2), 5.

Wellins, R. (1991). *Empowered teams.* San Francisco: Jossey-Bass.

Chapter 9

The Organizational Model

Learning Objectives

After completing this chapter, the learner should be able to:

1. Describe mechanistic structural design and state how functional departmentalization becomes a part of this design.
2. Explain several advantages of an organic structural design and list several health-care settings where this design is appropriate.
3. Outline the basic parts of a matrix structure model.
4. Define network structure and describe when it is used advantageously in health-care firms.
5. Describe critical factors involved as health-care facilities choose reengineering the organizational structure in an effort to solve problems.
6. Give examples of reengineering activities that can appropriately belong to HIM professionals.
7. Explain the major features involved in the three phases of reengineering.

Key Terms

Adhocracy

Committee structure

Functional departmentalization

Matrix structure

Mechanistic structural design

Multiskilled health professional

Network structure   Reengineering
Organic structural design   Task force
Process innovation

Introduction

Chapter 8 discusses the background for developing organizational models to document the structure of health-care firms. From the mission statement and objectives for new organizations come the ideas that translate into decisions regarding the three main parts of the organizational structure and the type of structure to be created. The objective-setting process begins with the strategic planning process, which results from the vision of the planners.

As typical organizational models are developed in this chapter, size of the firm is an important variable. Examples of models for complex hospital HIM departments are discussed as are entrepreneurial firms that begin with a flat organizational structure. Since smaller organizations, such as local transcription firms, home health-care centers, urgent-care centers, and consulting firms, have diverse models, examples from these organizations give insights into their structural design. A major feature of these smaller organizational models is the flat or simple structure where task responsibilities can be quite straightforward. Formal communication flows easily in such a model.

On the other hand, many HIM managers work in complex facilities where organizational models are large and the formal lines of communication tend to traverse upward through several layers. Preparing organizational models for HIM departments in this setting offers creative options. Managers can transform a traditional department structure into a contemporary model by using the steps already outlined for the management functions of planning and organizing. Contemporary examples are:

- Team approaches
- Matrix structure
- Network structure

Each of these structures offers opportunities for HIM professionals to create change. In this chapter, these models are examined and examples are documented.

First, the two major structural designs—mechanistic and organic—are discussed and several additional organizing terms are defined.

Mechanistic Structural Designs

When speaking of **mechanistic design**, organizers are referring to a bureaucracy. In this design the structure is highly complex and formalized, with authority remaining centralized. The larger an organization, the greater the tendency toward a mechanistic structural design (Robbins, 1994). In healthcare facilities tending toward a mechanistic design, **functional departmentalization** predominates over other departmentalization options. As described in Chapter 8, functional departmentalization refers to organizing groups of similar or related occupational specialties into departments. Departmental examples are physical therapy, radiation therapy, and health information management.

Traditionally, this structure was seen as enhancing the organization's economies of scale. For example, when all of the coding specialists are responsible to one manager, scheduling for efficiency is possible. Also, the cost of resources is minimized since sharing is feasible. Another advantage in functional departmentalization is that employees are comfortable and satisfied working with peers who "speak the same language." Figure 9-1 depicts an HIM department design using traditional functional departmentalization.

■ Practice Example

The complex HIM department shown in Figure 9-1 has a mix of supervisory responsibilities with two locations. Three assistant directors care for the operations of the departments with supervisors and charge technicians serving in managerial positions. The assistant director at the satellite is responsible for managing the department, meeting with upper-level management, and solving routine problems interdepartmentally. Frequent meetings of the managers keep the two departments functioning smoothly.

The transcription department resides at the satellite facility with one transcriptionist at the main location to receive online reports and resolve difficulties. The evening transcriptionists are supervised by the second-

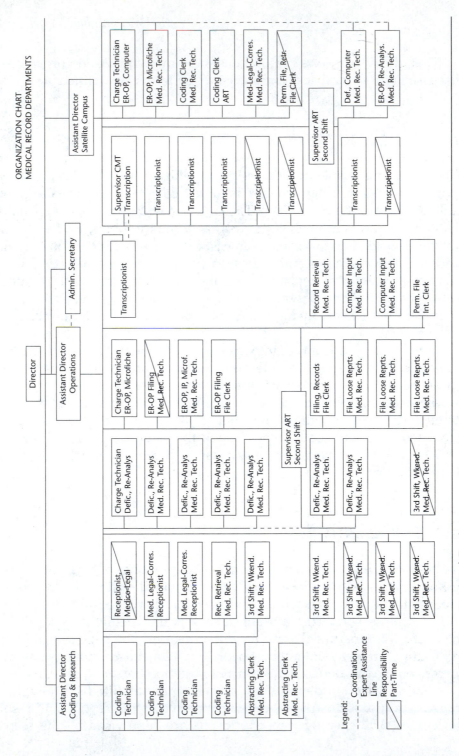

Figure 9-1. Departmental Design

shift supervisor with a broken line showing the coordination by the transcription supervisor.

Because the coding technicians are unable to transfer billing information directly, second-shift technicians abstract the information. The strategic plan includes a new information system that links the facilities and enhances the work flow. Efficiencies in the process can be realized when the capability to transfer coding and DRG assignment directly becomes a reality with this system. Coding technicians can then efficiently abstract information from the record that is not already online in the new system. The managers are planning organizational change and **reengineering** of the work flow as installation of the new system occurs.

Analysis or deficiency checking and reanalysis activities involve seven technicians under the assistant director for operations. Traditionally this facility has performed detailed deficiency checking at the request of the medical staff. The managers have discussed the possibility of streamlining this activity. With less time devoted to record analysis, the technicians will have additional time to assist in medical staff activities that have been a limited part of their responsibility. Positions could also be eliminated or changed during reengineering. ■

As the example indicates, technicians such as coding specialists are insulated from the activities of other employees. Record activity technicians performing deficiency review or reanalysis activities may have a limited understanding of the tasks performed by the legal correspondence team. In such an environment, can the technicians lose sight of the objectives of the total department? Of the facility? "Yes," is the response from an increasing number of organizational experts who turn to an **organic design** for appropriate parts of the organizational structure in health-care facilities (Hyde and Fottler, 1992). HIM professionals can redesign the work flow and create a more organic design where possible. This change can not only enhance efficiency and effectiveness in the workplace but also create a team environment where job enrichment can be translated to job satisfaction.

Organic Structural Designs

In contrast to the mechanistic design, an **organic structure** is an **adhocracy** where complexity is low, formalized design is low, and there is decentralized authority. In this adaptive structure a facility or a department within a facility can change more easily when operating in a dynamic and uncertain environment. Several options are available when designing organic structures. These include the simple, matrix, network, task force, and committee structures. A review of each of these shows how they may be a desirable option for appropriate applications within health care (Robbins, 1994).

The Simple Structure

The size of an organization is a major determining factor in whether a simple organizational structure is feasible. The simple structural option minimizes organizational complexity. Managers of smaller health-care organizations will find advantages in using this simple structure, including organizations started by HIM entrepreneurs for the purpose of contracting specialized services.

With this simple structure, there is a flat organization with authority centralized in a single person with two or three vertical levels. Typically, the decision-making authority is centralized in the owner/entrepreneur. The strength of this design lies in its flexibility and low maintenance cost. In Figure 9-2 the simple structure created by an entrepreneur of a new transcription firm is shown.

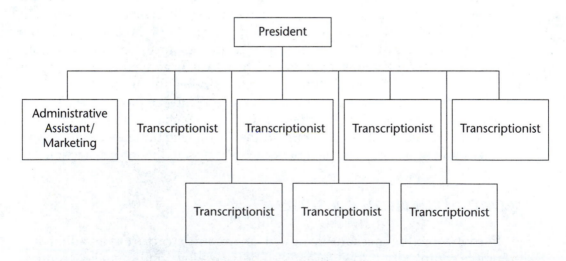

Figure 9-2.   Organizational Model: Simple Structure

One major weakness of the simple structure becomes evident when the size of the organization increases to the point where decision making becomes too slow for effectiveness. Of course, a second weakness is that everything depends on just one person. A major illness can literally destroy the organization at the center (Robbins, 1994).

The Modified Simple Structure

While the complexity of acute-care facilities usually demands a mechanistic structural design, departments within a facility can develop a modified simple design where the levels of management are kept to a minimum. The modified simple structure includes the team concept where the position of assistant director is deleted and team leaders and team members themselves are empowered with managerial responsibilities.

The Matrix Structure

The **matrix structure** has the advantage of assigning various professionals to work teams to care for patients or customers in a product-oriented manner. It combines the advantages of functional specialization with the focus and accountability of product departmentalization since professionals from various functional departments are assigned to work together on a specific project, or in a patient-focused care center. By creating this structure, managers transform the traditional unity of command principle into a shared responsibility. However, the advantages of the matrix structure can be seen to outweigh the disadvantage of a dual chain of command in more and more health-care facilities today (Bennett-Woods, 1994). The organizational model in Figure 9-3 shows the matrix design of a work team.

Unique projects of a specified duration may have professionals from several specialties organized with a project coordinator to whom they are responsible for the duration. This situation can occur when major information systems are being created and installed and the expertise of various professions is demanded. This is the more common form of matrix design (Robbins, 1994).

With the trend toward patient-focused care centers, where all activities and care are rendered to patients in the center, matrix configurations will take form in various ways. Such a change demands reengineering efforts, which are discussed later in this chapter. A major difference is that in the

Patient-Focused Care Centers

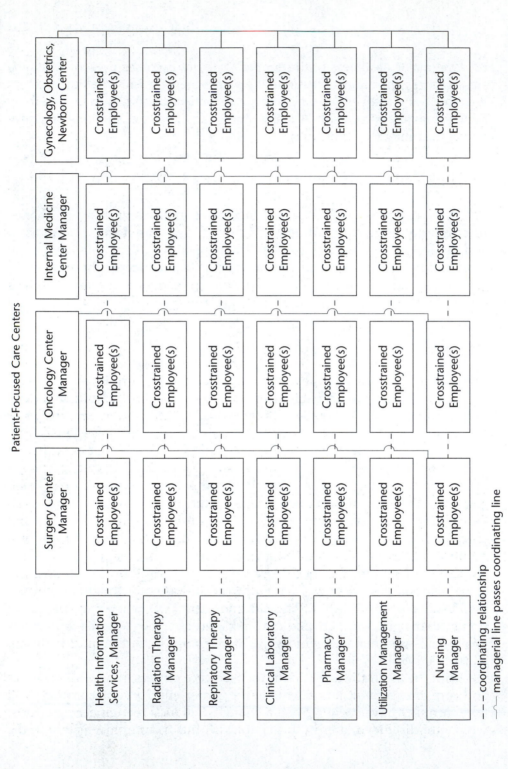

Figure 9-3. Organizational Model: Matrix Structure

patient-focused care centers, the matrix structure is permanent. Having this matrix design for customer services increases the complexity of the organization, so special effort must be made for effective communication across teams and departments.

To increase the complexity of the design for patient-focused care centers even further, the team members are crosstrained and become **multi-skilled health professionals**. For example, team members are trained in laboratory services such as specimen collection and cardiac testing. HIM professionals are crosstrained to ensure that information systems are flowing properly and to perform administrative functions such as utilization management (Hyde and Fottler, 1992). Futurists predict an increase in this dual chain of command structure (Hyde and Fottler, 1992).

As already mentioned, the unity of command principle is broken with the matrix design. This demands that authority and responsibility be clearly defined and understood by the managers and team members. Quality improvement techniques that include periodic evaluations need careful construction, especially when promotion and pay scale are involved.

Periodic analysis of the design needs to be undertaken to assure there is no confusion or ambiguity. These disadvantages of the matrix structure can result in power struggles.

The Network Structure

The **network structure** is designed to take advantage of the expertise another organization has, rather than build that expertise within one's own organization. This structure is typically seen in small centralized organizations that choose to rely on other organizations to perform a part of the business functions on a contract basis (Robbins, 1994). In Figure 9-4 a network structure illustrates the growth of the transcription firm previously depicted in Figure 9-2.

HIM professionals use network structure when they share expertise by performing contract functions for organizations such as physician practice offices. Also, entrepreneurial professionals may choose to outsource the financial aspects or the human resource management aspects of their businesses. Another example of a network design in health-care is the urgent-care center that contracts with a group of emergency medicine professionals to serve its customers.

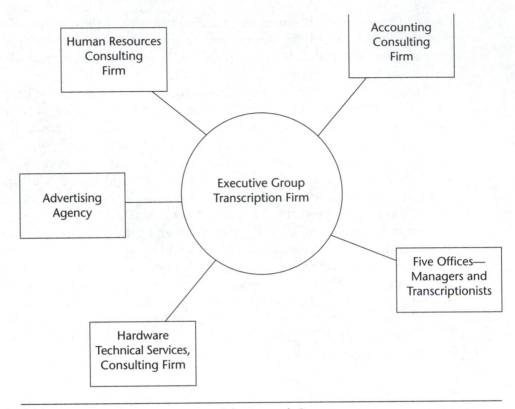

Figure 9-4.   Organizational Model: Network Structure

Task Forces and Committees

A **task force** is a temporary structure created to perform specific, well-defined, usually complex tasks using professionals from various organizational departments. In contrast, a **committee structure** brings together individuals from various departments to solve problems. Effective use of committees is detailed in Chapter 18.

Reengineering and Contemporary Model Structure

As HIM managers choose innovative approaches to organizing departments for processing information, reengineering the work flow may be required. Reengineering is defined as the search for implementation of radical change in business processes to achieve breakthrough results and dramatic improvements in contemporary measures of performance (Torie and Houston, 1994). Some organizers prefer to use **process innovation** to describe this activity. A business process is considered a group of related activities that produce a result of value to the patient/customer (Foerster, 1994). When reengineering is done well, it can "provide extraordinary gains in speed, productivity, and profitability," according to Peter F. Drucker, as emphasized by Torie and Houston (1994).

Since process innovation or reengineering is a radical change for the organization, all levels of management are involved. New management structures are considered as the work flow is reviewed for the best approaches to serve the customers. The need for a paradigm shift grows as managers search for solutions to solve information work flow difficulties. These solutions must control and reduce health-care costs associated with the processing of data into useful information in a timely, accurate manner. Through team brainstorming activities, solutions are found for discarding outdated policies and breaking with tradition. Thus, managers and their teams can bring innovative organizational change through process innovation.

Thomas Webb and Barbara Mountford of Applied Management Systems emphasize the need for reengineering systems and processes that are critical to the delivery of patient care. Their past efforts in reengineering show a 20 to 30 percent reduction in operation costs. At the same time, the facilities involved in this reengineering increased direct care to the customers by 60 percent (Webb and Mountford, 1994). Webb and Mountford lead facilities toward a goal of transforming the organization into a high-performance hospital that meets or exceeds the expectations of its stakeholders. This transformation goal is led by "a vision that reflects both a responsiveness to the market and a commitment to operational excellence" (Webb and Mountford, 1994).

In their consulting activities, Webb and Mountford (1994) have found that the framework for the reengineering process of restructuring health-care facilities must include the following:

1. Upper-level managers define the new organizational culture and lead in its implementation.
2. Department managers commit key staff time and resources to the process.

3. Department managers and team members commit to becoming knowledgeable by reading, by thinking, and by performing research into the reengineering process.

4. Upper-level and department managers develop an awareness of the "culture shock" that the facility will experience during this process.

Figure 9-5 identifies the three phases involved in reengineering: the discovery phase, the vision phase, and the actual reengineering process phase.

Reengineering requires a dedicated project coordinator devoting full-time effort to the process. By creating an environment that nurtures staff, entrusts the teams with patient care, and provides them with necessary resources, the project coordinator successfully leads the task forces in redesign of the systems.

During reengineering of the department, HIM managers will expend extra effort in communication and reassurance. Positions will change, informal relationships will be broken, and stress becomes evident. The opportunities to create a new work environment, focusing on the customers, can enthuse employees. As managers emphasize the need for change and these opportunities, employees are encouraged to grow, to learn, to become valued team members for the department, and to bring reality to the facility's vision.

Practice Example

Darice Grzybowski, director of Health Information Management at Hinsdale Hospital in the Chicago area, has undertaken a series of steps in reorganizing the department. Working with her managers, Darice developed a transitional organizational model in 1988. Figure 9-6 is the model that was in use prior to 1989. A major concern was that employees at several pay-scale levels were reporting directly to Darice.

In an effort to flatten the organization and lessen the direct supervisory responsibilities demanded of Darice, the managers developed a simple structure as shown in Figure 9-7. This model served the department for 5 years, a period of growth for the facility. This growth increased the number of employees in the department, which increased the need for training and performance improvement activities. In addition, Darice was involved in plan-

Phase 1—Discovery

The first phase, discovery, finds employees and physicians frustrated and customers unsatis-fied and leads to a problem-solving search for solutions. HIM managers can take an active role in this discovery phase. As part of the task force, they can ask three fundamental questions that are to be answered for the facility as a whole and for each department individually:

1. Why do we do what we do?
2. Why do we do it the way we do it?
3. Why do we do it where we do it?

Phase 2—Vision

Formulating the vision for the delivery system of the future is phase 2. This vision could include one or all of the following:

1. Outcomes that reach the optimum in health care.
2. Health care that is affordable and cost-effective.
3. Dedicated hospital staff and physicians.
4. Health care that is reliable and maintains quality.

Phase 3—The Reengineering Process

Multidisciplinary task forces are created for the process phase. This phase focuses on sys-tems and processes to meet patient needs and uses information to support outcome-oriented care. The data are gathered and analyzed by the task forces, who then develop revised processes to improve throughput and eliminate nonvalue-added steps to produce better outcomes. As members of the task forces, HIM professionals will develop systems to provide information for these tasks. Shifting from the traditional functional organizational structure to a patient-focused care system involves six organizational principles:

1. *Reaggregation:* Group patients in centers to develop distinct service lines.
2. *Redeployment:* Functional departments are dismembered and regrouped as follows: Patient Care Team, Unit Care Team, and Administrative Team. HIM professionals will be a part of the Unit Care Team performing continuous quality improvement (CQI) and utilization review tasks. They will also be a part of the Administrative Team that admits patients, performs discharge planning, reservations, record assembly and completion, and financial services. Through crosstraining, the teams will become multiskilled and self-directed.
3. *Simplification:* Nonvalue-added steps in procedures are reduced or eliminated. Automation of information enhances this simplification. The steps toward increased automation can be led by HIM managers.
4. *Flexible, crosstrained jobs:* Daily patient care is given by fewer employees, increasing patient satisfaction.
5. *Self-directed teams:* Through training, team members make decisions on activities such as discipline, budgeting, and compensation.
6. *Organizational architecture:* Structure, culture, style, and communication are redesigned to support the new patient-focused system (Webb and Mountford, 1994).

Figure 9-5. Reengineering Phases (Webb and Mountford, 1994)

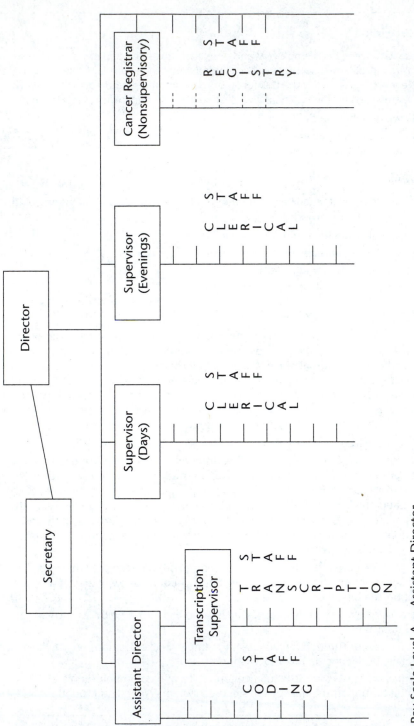

Figure 9-6. Organizational Model: Hinsdale Hospital Medical Record Department, Pre-1988

Pay Scale Level A— Assistant Director
Pay Scale Level B— Evening Supervisor
Pay Scale Level C— Day Supervisor
Pay Scale Level D— Cancer Registrar
Pay Scale Level E— Transcription Supervisor

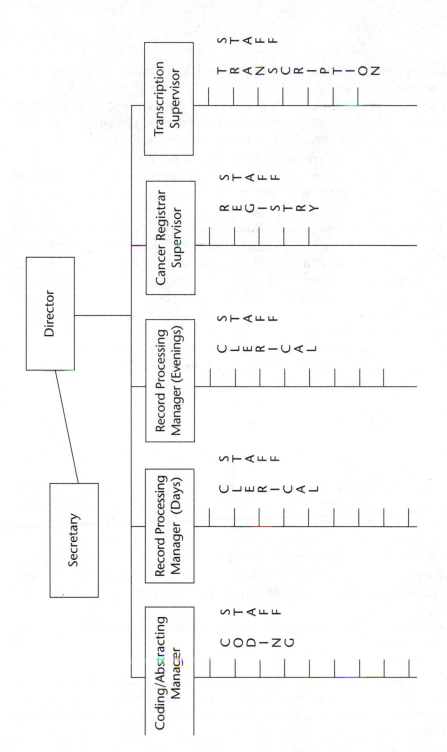

Figure 9-7. Organizational Model: Hinsdale Hospital Medical Record Services, Transitional Model, 1989–1994

Pay Scale Level A— Assistant Manager
Pay Scale Level B— Supervisor, Cancer Registry
Pay Scale Level C— Supervisor, Transcription

ning a facility-wide computer system and this installation promised additional changes.

As management team members discussed the coming changes, they chose to be proactive and reorganize the department. The proposed organizational model is described in Figure 9-8 and clearly shows the emphasis on automated technology with a manager and three teams devoted to clinical data. Coordinators lead the teams in planning and implementing work-flow activities. Other supervisory functions remain managerial responsibility.

As shown, the managers now number four rather than five and the record-processing areas will continue to take less FTEs (full-time employees) as implementation of automated functions continues.

With increased emphasis on performance improvement and training, the managers plan to include a coordinator of QI (quality improvement) and training. This coordinator is crosstrained to assist in training for team activities and as a facilitator of QI initiatives.

As technology advances make it possible for the department to implement a true EPR, Darice and the teams will continue to find organizational challenges in reorganizing for the future.   ■

Summary

Mechanistic structural designs are complex and formalized. They resemble a bureaucracy. Functional departmentalization around occupational specialties is typically seen in health-care facilities with mechanistic design. Economies of scale is an advantage of this design.

In organic structural design the complexity and formalization are low. Redesign can be accomplished with relative speed in a dynamic environment. Structures in organic design include simple, matrix, network, task force, and committee.

Entrepreneurs typically organize using a simple structure with two or three vertical levels. The simple structure must be abandoned when growth brings a halt to effective decision making.

Matrix structure breaks the unity of command principle and consequently demands careful organizing. Matrix structures can be used permanently for bringing various professionals together in work teams or temporarily for special projects.

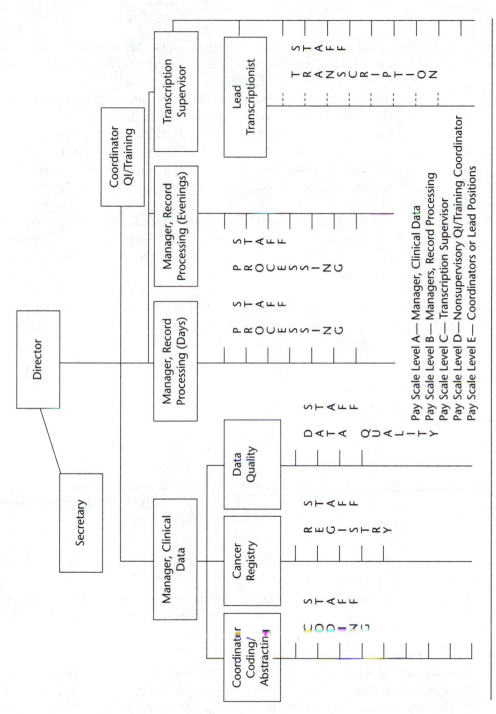

Figure 9-8. Organizational Model: Hinsdale Hospital, Health Information Management, 1995–

Pay Scale Level A— Manager, Clinical Data
Pay Scale Level B— Managers, Record Processing
Pay Scale Level C— Transcription Supervisor
Pay Scale Level D— Nonsupervisory QI/Training Coordinator
Pay Scale Level E— Coordinators or Lead Positions

Network structures build on the expertise of organizations outside the facility. By contracting with a firm offering expert services, an organization can organize for efficiency and effectiveness.

Reengineering or process innovation is occurring with increased frequency in health-care facilities as the search to contain costs and increase productivity continues. Reengineering is a radical departure for organizations and requires a commitment from all levels of the organization. By integrating data into information for decision making, HIM professionals play a key role in reengineering as task forces are developed for the process phase of the effort.

The framework for reengineering includes four factors: (1) upper-level management defines and leads the process, (2) commitment of key staff time and resources, (3) individual commitment to learning on their own, and (4) awareness that culture shock will be experienced.

The three phases of reengineering are discovery, vision, and the process itself. A project coordinator is needed to lead the task forces in process innovation and into a new structure where patient-focused care centers and attention to stakeholders' needs predominate.

Review Questions

1. Obtain an organization model presently in use at a HIM department and review it before answering the following questions:
   a. Does the model tend toward a mechanistic or organic structure?
   b. Are the sections within the department organized by functional, customer, product, or process departmentalization?
   c. Are the line relationships clearly drawn?

   Now create a revised model that uses one or more organic structural designs after making assumptions about reengineering the work flow.

2. As an HIM department manager, choose to use a network structure to meet departmental objectives by contracting with several firms for departmental services. List several types of firms you would choose for this and the expertise you would expect from each of them.

3. You have made a decision that immediately after graduation you will find employment, for 6 to 9 months, as a transcriptionist. During that time you will explore opportunities for starting a transcription service

in an underserved area. Develop an organizational model for use during the first 3 years your new company is in operation; then redesign it for an expanded business beginning in the fourth year.

Case Study

Community Hospital is licensed for 200 beds and has a medical staff of 45. The health information services is responsible to the CFO, and the department manager has the following employees:

1. QI specialist involved in projects and medical staff meetings
2. Team leader for transcription with three full-time transcriptionists, two part-time transcriptionists, and one part-time courier
3. Team leader for reimbursement (coding, case management) with four full-time coders, one part-time case management statistician, one full-time tumor registry specialist, and two part-time on-call coders
4. Team leader for record activity with one full-time second-shift team leader, two full-time record activity team members, two part-time record activity team members, and one full-time physician liaison
5. Team leader for customer services, which includes information management, two full-time receptionists/legal correspondence team members, one full-time correspondence team member
6. One part-time resource registered record administrator crosstrained to perform many tasks; performs orientation and training activities.

The department is open from 7 A.M. to 11 P.M.

1. Develop an organizational design for the health information services using one of the designs discussed in this chapter.
2. Use an organizational design software package, if possible.

References

Bennett-Woods, D. (1994). Patient-focused laboratory and pharmacy services. *Advance for Health Information Professionals, 4* (17), 24.

Foerster, R. (1994). Electronic data interchange (EDI): An enabler of financial business process reengineering. *Journal of AHIMA, 65* (4), 38–42.

Hyde, J., & Fottler, M. (1992). Application of the multiskilled staffing innovation to the health information management professional. *Journal of AHIMA, 63* (11), 54–60.

Robbins, S. (1994). *Management* (4th ed.). Englewood Cliffs, NJ: Prentice Hall.

Torie, C., & Houston, S. (1994). Reengineering—Impact on organizational culture. *Journal of AHIMA, 65* (4), 46–48.

Webb, T., & Mountford, B. (1994). *Organizational model for re-engineering healthcare.* Burlington, MA: Applied Management Systems.

Suggested Readings

Bennett-Woods, D. (1994). Patient-focused laboratory and pharmacy services. *Advance for Health Information Professionals, 4* (17), 24.

Dixon, C. (1995). Assessing allied health data needs. *Journal of AHIMA, 66* (4), 44–46.

Donnelly, J., Gibson, J., & Ivancevich, J. (1987). *Fundamentals of management* (6th ed.). Plano, TX: Business Publications.

Flejter, J. (1995). Seizing the opportunity for a paperless record. *Journal of AHIMA, 66* (3), 30–36.

Foerster, R. (1994). Electronic data interchange (EDI): An enabler of financial business process reengineering. *Journal of AHIMA, 65* (4), 38–42.

Hyde, J., & Fottler, M. (1992). Application of the multiskilled staffing innovation to the health information management professional. *Journal of AHIMA, 63* (11), 54–60.

Longest, B., (1990). *Management practices for the health professional* (4th ed.). Norwalk, CT: Appleton & Lange.

Mahoney, M., & Doupnik, A. (1993). Health information department reorganization resulting from the implementation of optical imaging. *Journal of AHIMA, 64* (4), 56–58.

Palmer, L. (1995). Reengineering healthcare: The future awaits us all. *Journal of AHIMA, 66* (2), 32–35.

Robbins, S. (1994). *Management* (4th ed.). Englewood Cliffs, NJ: Prentice Hall.

Torie, C., & Houston, S. (1994). Reengineering—Impact on organizational culture. *Journal of AHIMA, 65* (4), 46–48.

Webb, T., & Mountford, B. (1994). *Organizational model for re-engineering healthcare.* Burlington, MA: Applied Management Systems.

Chapter 10

Organizing Position Designs for Employees

Learning Objectives

After completing this chapter, the learner should be able to:

1. Give a historical description of job design and explain how specialization has been especially important in health-care organizations.
2. Explain the value of position analysis and methods used in this analysis.
3. Outline the major components of position descriptions.
4. Identify advantages of job rotation; then give possible drawbacks to its use in health-care settings.
5. Contrast job enlargement with job enrichment.
6. Describe the use of work teams and how self-managed teams can increase employee productivity and morale.
7. Summarize the advantages of flexible work schedules.

Key Terms

Compressed work week	Job design
Job characteristics model	Job scope
Job description	Job splitting

Position depth

Position description

Position design

Position enlargement

Position enrichment

Position rotation

Position specification

Work sharing

Introduction

Once the design of the organization is envisioned through strategic planning efforts, department managers begin the task of organizing to achieve specific objectives. The organizing function plays a key role in the integrated model of management. As new organizations are created and planned, the HIM department managers have an opportunity to plan, organize, and purchase the latest technology and equipment. At this point, it is possible to begin an analysis of each position needed to accomplish the objectives. In this ideal environment, when the new organization begins operation, the HIM information systems in place can make it possible to operate efficiently and effectively. This ideal department will be, in reality, possible for only a few HIM managers.

More typically, the challenge is to redesign or reengineer an existing department to provide timely and accurate access to health-care information as organizations become involved in reengineering efforts. And, these changes must occur while the rush of everyday activities continues. These routine activities are performed by employees hired for specific tasks to accomplish objectives. As redesign of a department begins, the tasks performed by each employee and the skills needed to accomplish them will also need review and revision.

Whether managers are grouping activities to organize a new department or reviewing activities during the redesign or reengineering of a department, the activities and skills needed must be documented. This activity is defined as **position design** or **job design** and leads to full-time position allotments by separating specific tasks, methods, and organizational relationships. The resulting documentation for each is called a **position description** or **job description**. A position description is a written statement that identifies the activities, skills, and performance requirements for a position (Layman, 1993).

In this chapter, key components of position descriptions are identified and analyzed. Steps in documentation are discussed and options to the design offer variety. Self-directed teams may rotate leadership positions; therefore, documenting position descriptions for teams is discussed separately. Examples of position descriptions are brought into the discussion.

Analysis and Design of Position Descriptions

Analysis of position descriptions begins with the documented activities that have been identified and grouped. When redesign or reengineering is occurring, all employees will ideally be involved in documenting the activities. Empowering employees to share in developing documentation of the activities that will be a part of the position design gives them a sense of ownership.

Managers will find it helpful to network with the human resources department during the analysis process. Copies of position descriptions are ultimately utilized by the human resources staff for hiring and for assigning wage scales to each position. Managers will want to create documents that clearly show the knowledge and skills needed for each position and then use them as tools for defending the requested level of salary.

Figure 10-1 outlines specific items that are typically a part of position descriptions, regardless of the activities to be performed. These details need to be considered during analysis so decisions can be made as the design is developed. Position descriptions are then created following this analysis position design. These should clarify the responsibilities, authority, relationships, and accountability expected for the position.

During the analysis and design or redesign of positions, most of the effort will be expended on items 6 and 7 from Figure 10-1. Item 6 includes the major responsibilities designed for the position and documents the decisions of how activities are grouped. Technical positions, especially, should have measurable expectations for the responsibilities. These expectations give managers interviewing prospective employees an opportunity to bring expectations, knowledge, skills, and experience together.

Item 7 in the position description can be broadly defined as a **position specification**, which includes the human qualifications needed to perform the activities: abilities, skills, education, work experience, traits, judgment, and physical attributes. The position specification is valuable for choosing applicants to interview when positions are available (Rue and Byars, 1986).

1. Title of the position
2. Name of the department, position number for human resources use, salary range (optional)
3. Title of the person to whom this position is accountable
4. Status—that is, permanent/temporary, work hours, flextime option
5. Position purpose or mission, may be titled the position summary
6. Major responsibilities of the position—these should be specific to the point that performance can be measured
7. Specifications or minimum knowledge, skills, experience, and abilities required; credentials, if required
8. Working conditions
9. Approvals, dates, revision dates

Figure 10-1.   Position Description Content (Robbins, 1994)

A detailed position specification from Hinsdale Hospital for use in hiring the manager of clinical data is shown in Figure 10-2.

Other elements of the position description that need mention are the signature of the manager with responsibility for the position and the date of latest revision. Because of the multiple uses for position descriptions, accountability for the content is needed.

Once these elements are in place, a position description will provide a complete understanding of the responsibilities of each position in the department and the qualities best suited in the applicant for each position. Further, they describe relationships, authority, and accountability. Each position on the organizational model developed in Chapter 9 will have a position description that corresponds with the graphic relationship.

Documenting Position Descriptions

Once the design or redesign and analysis is completed, the formal documentation of each position description can begin. First, it is helpful to list the multiple uses of a position description to emphasize the importance of keeping them current and accurate. These uses are shown in Figure 10-3.

HINSDALE HOSPITAL

JOB SPECIFICATIONS

TITLE: Manager, Clinical Data

OCC # TRD

DEPARTMENT: Health Information Management

REPORTS TO: Director

F.I.S.A. Exempt

Skills & Experience:

Minimum 4 years experience in health information management or related field required. 1 year management experience required. Microsystems experience required. Ability to read, write, speak and understand English.

Education:

B.S. degree in Health Information Management or related field required. R.R.A. or A.R.T. required. Master's degree in business administration or information preferred. Certified tumor registrar (CTR) preferred.

Scope of Authority:

Position carries direct responsibility for other members of the health-care team. The individual has the authority to carry out the duties as defined in the job description.

Judgment:

Day-to-day responsibilities require good use of judgment regarding timely and appropriate communication with the hospital staff.

Work Relationships:

Must recognize the need for teamwork and function accordingly. Will be expected to work as part of a multidisciplinary team.

Job Relationships:

Workers Supervised: HIM Technicians, clinical data analyst, cancer registry technicians, lead coder/abstractor, cancer registry coordinator.

Promotion from: Not defined.

Promotion to: Not defined

(continued)

Figure 10-2.   Job Specifications for Manager of Clinical Data (Courtesy of Hinsdale Hospital, Darice Grzybowski, RRA)

Responsibility for Resources:

Responsible for proper use and operation of supplies and equipment. Improper care or use of supplies and equipment could result in damage and added expense to the hospital. Delay in processing can result in financial loss to the hospital or loss of accreditation by various agencies. Inaccurate data can result in inappropriate patient treatment, breach of confidentiality, or invalid statistical data.

Responsibility for Safety of Others:

Complies with department safety policies and procedures. Responsible to help ensure that the safety and physical well-being of patients, family members, visitors, and co-workers are maintained.

Physical/Mental Requirements:

The physical effort is moderate, requiring mobility. Ability to cope with stressful situations and respond quickly and appropriately.

	Frequency	*Effort*	*Duration*
Standing/Walking	Occasional	N/A	Up to 1 hour
Sitting	Constant	N/A	Up to 7 hours
Stooping/Bending	Occasional	N/A	Up to 20 minutes
Lifting	Occasional	10 lbs+	Up to 20 minutes

Job Conditions and Hazards:

Works indoors under standard office working conditions where the individual experiences minimal discomfort due to noise, dust, or severe temperature fluctuations.

Machines, Tools, Equipment, and Work Aids:

The following is a partial list of equipment that may be necessary to perform the job duties:

Communication equipment	Data processing equipment
General office supplies	Information systems and related software

_____   _____

Department Head   Date

_____   _____

Vice President   Date

_____   _____

Vice President for Human Resources   Date

Figure 10-2.   *(continued)*

1. Assist in clarifying relationships between jobs and teams, avoiding overlaps or gaps in responsibility.
2. Enable managers to prepare position orientation materials and procedures.
3. Establish the basis for a just and fair salary within the compensation structure.
4. Create one tool for use in performance appraisals.
5. Establish a base for position analysis and further redesign in the future.
6. Assist manager in position interviews with prospective employees.
7. Create base for benchmark comparison with positions in other health-care facilities and with regional compensation reports.
8. Help with strategic planning and budget review.

Figure 10-3. Position Description Uses

Figure 10-4 shows the position description for a health information analyst in the department at Lakeland Regional Medical System. This example includes a summary of the position and offers detailed duties and responsibilities. The knowledge and skills needed demonstrate the crosstraining aspects of the department.

This position description shows the analyst is responsible to the manager of the department and has no supervisory responsibilities. To assure that applicants chosen for this position have the aptitudes necessary, note the several references to the expectation of skills for interacting with physicians.

Performance standards are given under "responsibilities." These would be repeated in the procedures for the position. Should the department choose to adjust performance standards, changes must be made in all documents, including the position descriptions filed with the human resources department.

The responsibilities include computer usage, so this is reflected in the knowledge and skills section. This section requires statistical knowledge also, since the duties include maintaining statistics and disseminating them periodically.

When retrieving records manually demands much physical exertion, this should be made a part of the position description. By documenting this specification in the description, managers protect themselves from discrimination problems in this area.

LAKELAND REGIONAL MEDICAL SYSTEM

TITLE: Health Information Analyst   FLSA: Non-Exempt
DEPARTMENT: Health Information Management

GENERAL SUMMARY: Enables compliance with medical staff and regulatory guidelines for medical record completion. Answers requests for health information following organizational and regulatory guidelines.

PRINCIPAL DUTIES AND RESPONSIBILITIES:

1. Reports, monitors and makes judgments relative to physician's delinquent/incomplete records. Sends notices to physicians regarding the number of delinquent/incomplete records. Reminds the physicians of upcoming delinquency dates. Notifies appropriate personnel of physician delinquency.

2. Analyzes records for completion of documentation utilizing regulatory guidelines. Assigns deficiencies to the appropriate physician on the computerized deficiency system. Reponsible for the accuracy of the data in the deficiency system. Ensures that the records are placed in the correct physician's incomplete box.

3. Maintains statistics on the number of delinquent/incomplete records, the number of records not coded, and the dollar amount of unbilled accounts for use by department managers and senior management of the hospital.

4. Analyzes all information thoroughly concerning requests prior to releasing health information. Prepares and copies medical records for release in a timely and accurate manner. Responds to all correspondence concerning lawsuits and keeps appropriate personnel (i.e., legal counsel, physicians, management) informed of all potential and active legal liability. Assists in preparing court certificates, notarized affidavits and other documents.

5. Performs focused chart audits as necessary.

6. Performs all other duties as assigned.

KNOWLEDGE AND SKILLS:

1. Must have working knowledge of confidentiality rules and regulations regarding the release of health information, including alcohol and substance abuse, and areas relating to mental health.

2. Must have working knowledge of medical terminology.

3. Must possess the ability to read, comprehend and follow complicated verbal instructions, and the ability to perform basic arithmetic, writing, and spelling in order to perform the tasks described above. This level of education is normally associated with the completion of 12th grade.

4. Must be able to pay attention to detail of work with less than one percent error rate.

5. Must possess interpersonal skills sufficient to interact effectively with attorneys, physicians, co-workers, patients/families and other internal and external contacts.

6. Must be able to work with frequent interruptions and must be able to prioritize a wide spectrum of duties in an environment where changing priorities are ongoing.

Figure 10-4.   A Position Description of a Health Information Analyst (Courtesy of Shereen Martin, RRA)

7. Must possess the ability to read and maintain statistics, percentages and graphs.
8. Must be motivated, goal oriented, have initiative to accomplish goals, the ability to work independently, handle stressful situations, be cooperative, and handle inappropriate behavior in a professional manner. Must have assertive characteristics.
9. Must possess analytical skills to identify problem issues and must be able to problem solve, to assemble and analyze incomplete records as required by established guidelines and the preferences of individuals physicians.
10. Meets established productivity standards with less that a one percent error rate.
11. Must be able to operate related business office equipment. Knowledge of computer keyboard necessary.

REPORTING RELATIONSHIPS:
Reports to the Manager of Health Information Mangement.

WORKING CONDITIONS:
Normal office environment where there is no discomfort due to temperature, noise, dust and the like.

APPROVALS:

NAME	TITLE	DATE

NAME _____   TITLE _SR VP-Qual. Mgl._   DATE _7/11/9√_

NAME _____   TITLE _____   DATE _____

THE ABOVE STATEMENTS ARE INTENDED TO DESCRIBE THE GENERAL NATURE OR LEVEL OF WORK BEING PERFORMED BY PEOPLE ASSIGNED TO THE CLASSIFICATION. THEY ARE NOT INTENDED TO BE CONSTRUED AS AN EXHAUSTIVE LIST OF ALL RESPONSIBILITIES, SKILLS AND ABILITIES REQUIRED OF PERSONNEL SO CLASSIFIED.

REVISED: 7/8/94

HIAJOBD.DOC

Figure 10-4.   (continued)

Position Description Options

This section explores several opportunities managers have to be innovative as they organize for change. During times of change, the challenge of creating an environment that provides motivation for employees and increases job satisfaction becomes even greater. Empowering employees to be a part of the decision-making team has already been mentioned and Chapter 13 offers broad motivational theories. Special mention of motivation as a part of organizing is made here to provide continuity.

Job Characteristics Model

One approach to position description redesign options is found in the **job characteristics model**. This is a framework for analyzing and designing jobs around five major qualities and their impact on outcome variables. Figure 10-5 identifies these five core dimensions and defines them (Robbins, 1994).

As individual tasks are grouped together to form positions within a team, within a section, and then for the total HIM services, managers become aware of the complexity facing them. Some groupings have tasks that are quite standardized and repetitive; at the other end of the spectrum are indi-

---

1. *Skill variety*—the degree to which a position requires a variety of activities, enabling the employee to use a number of different skills and talents.
2. *Task identity*—the degree to which a position requires completion of a whole and identifiable task.
3. *Task significance*—the degree to which a position has a substantial impact on the lives or work of people.
4. *Autonomy*—the degree to which a position offers substantial freedom, independence, and discretion to the employee for scheduling the tasks and determining the procedures for accomplishing them.
5. *Feedback*—the degree to which accomplishing the tasks results in the employee obtaining direct and clear information on the effectiveness of the performance.

Figure 10-5. Job Characteristics Model

vidualized tasks that may be most effective when performed independently. Awareness of this diversity is one key to organizing success for HIM managers. Each position developed is crucial to the success of the organization, so as employees are hired and trained, whether within a team or independently, the departmental culture plays a major role in having employees accept their place within the department. And, the managers create the culture for this acceptance.

Exploring the advantages of various position designs brings an awareness of the need to guard against overspecialization of tasks. As the division of labor became popular in the early 1900s, tasks were separated into minute divisions with repetitive work done day after day by employees. As discussed earlier, this can lead to boredom and frustration. The designs outlined next recognize this problem and offer solutions.

Job Design Options

As the multitude of tasks under the responsibility of HIM managers are grouped for team effort, options to meet specific department demands and employee needs are available. This section describes several that can create a cost-effective design for the department. These options include the following:

- Position enrichment
- Position enlargement
- Position rotation
- Work sharing
- Compressed work week

Position Enrichment

As tasks are grouped, managers can effectively look for opportunities to enrich positions by expanding the positions vertically. Two areas typically added are planning and evaluating responsibilities, thus giving **position enrichment**. A component of this enrichment is an increase in **position depth** where the employees are given an increased degree of control over their work.

The team involved in utilization management, for example, can be trained to prepare the computer-enhanced reports of their activities. Each team member could have responsibility for presenting the results to a facility committee and working directly with the committee members on concerns and suggestions. This procedure gives HIM professionals increased control over their monthly activities and adds planning for the reports as an enriched opportunity. Lastly, evaluation activities could be the result of computer reports, committee member comments, or other performance standards where employees can have increased input in their position design.

Position Enlargement

While position enrichment gives vertical expansion, **position enlargement** offers a horizontal expansion of activities and an increase in job scope. As might be expected, employees can easily feel that enlargement really means additional tasks to complete every day. Because of this effect, managers should combine enlargement with automation or other enhancement that gives added value to the tasks. **Job scope** relates to the number of different tasks required in a position and the frequency with which the task cycle is repeated. As there is an increase in the different tasks to be performed, the cycle may be lengthened if the way in which the tasks are performed stays approximately the same.

For example, as HIM services revise discharge analysis tasks to keep pace with AHIMA professional standards of practice recommendations, the hours allotted to analysis will be lessened. Employees can be given the opportunity to enlarge their positions with other tasks added; thus, the cycle for discharge analysis is shortened while the position is enlarged with other tasks. With specialized tasks, such as record analysis, other task cycles can be added toward the end of the week, when discharge activities are current.

Position Rotation

Position rotation, as an organizing design option, can be effective in reducing the monotony or boredom associated with repetitive tasks. By scheduling employees to rotate among different tasks every two to three months, managers broaden each employee's knowledge and increase skills and flexibility in addition to reducing boredom or monotony. Teams organized around position rotation increase individual responsibility among the group and thus offer team members a greater sense of ownership.

Training time can be increased with position rotation, however, since each employee is being taught a variety of tasks. Another possible negative is that productivity may fall as rotation occurs and the learning curve slumps until employees are back to full productivity again. The complexity of the tasks must be a factor when considering this organization option.

Rotating activities is best utilized on a voluntary basis since some employees, who are typically highly motivated, may resent forced task change. Within a team's assigned activities there are typically some tasks that are perceived as undesirable. By suggesting position rotation in a fair and consistent manner as a voluntary option, team leaders can increase satisfaction and overall productivity. Also, the advantages of employees who maintain their skills with such cross-training can maintain productivity when absenteeism occurs. Lastly, position rotation option is most effective in a stable environment where employees are not facing change pressures from other sources.

Job Sharing

Health-care professionals such as physicians and nurses are accustomed to job sharing where commitment and continuity are a given. Physicians with family responsibilities may choose specific office hours that are less than a full-time schedule and share the office workload in this way. The 24-hour patient-care setting in hospitals demands that nurses share in caring for patients, regardless of the hours they work. Communication, verbal and written, is vital to the success of job sharing for health-care professionals and patient records reflect the written communication.

When HIM services are available during second and third shifts, continuity of information and work flow are also important to quality patient care. By organizing the change of responsibilities and dissemination of information as team members come and go, managers can maintain effective communication networks for continuity. Position descriptions will reflect this continuity by emphasizing excellent communication skills. This type of job sharing is commonplace.

However, when two employees ask to share one full-time position, this design creates challenges. Jeannette Schein (1993) relates the experience of Stephanie Stine, RRA, with job sharing in *For the Record*. With small children at home, Stephanie considered a change to part-time employment, but wanted the security of a permanent position and the satisfaction she found in her present position. She and another mother with the same desire for part-time employment organized a plan for job sharing and presented it to the department manager. It included having each of them work two and a half days per week and receive benefits as part-time employees. Figure 10-6 gives advantages and disadvantages the employees and the management team discovered as they implemented and evaluated job sharing.

As reported, Stine was enthusiastic about job sharing and pointed out that it could be "the wave of the future" (Schein, 1993). To lend credence to her belief, Stine conducted a survey to determine how department managers perceived the job-sharing concept. The study revealed that managers would be comfortable offering job sharing to employees in technical positions, but not in managerial positions.

Advantages

1. Skilled HIM professionals can continue as valuable employees in a department.
2. Flexible scheduling is possible since two people share the same position. Time management is enhanced as team members cover for one another during vacations or illnesses.
3. Permanent employment as a part-time employee is possible because the full-time position is permanent.
4. Professionals can maintain their current status in health information management.
5. Quality and quantity of work increase, stress and fatigue decrease.

Disadvantages

1. Part-time benefits may not meet the needs of both employees.
2. There is an increase in administrative paperwork, which is more expensive. Position design may require two descriptions.
3. Communication breakdown creates loss of continuity.
4. Perception may develop that part-time employees have a lower commitment to the organization.

Figure 10-6.   Advantages and Disadvantages of Job Sharing

The study further showed that having two employees with equal skills desiring to share one position may not be an option and the managers suggested that **job splitting** could also be of value. Job splitting is when one full-time position is divided with the lower-level tasks performed by a part-time employee with a lower-level job category and the remaining tasks performed by an employee with higher-level skills (Stine, 1993).

Other Design Options

Several other position designs deserve mention. One is the **compressed work week** where employees may work four 10-hour days. This concept is fairly common among other health-care professionals and shows mixed results. Initially, employees maintain productivity and enjoy the option; however, studies show that over time, fatigue can become a negative factor. Also, over time, employees with families tend to have increased stress. Specific employees may enjoy this option, but the recommendation is that it remain an option, not a mandate (Stine, 1993; Schein, 1993).

When faced with the need to downsize or rightsize departments, managers may choose to offer employees the option of **work sharing**. This option can avoid layoffs since work sharing means that employees temporarily reduce work hours and/or salary. The priority tasks are shared as redesign of the work flow occurs. Position descriptions are temporarily revised during this period. An advantage is that the work force can be reduced through attrition, thus avoiding layoffs, when the change becomes permanent.

The advantages of the flextime option have already been mentioned. When flextime is routinely used in a department, managers may wish to document the possibility of flextime in specific position descriptions. When flextime is a popular option in an organization, prospective employees should be aware of those positions where flextime is not an option.

Summary

The first step in designing position descriptions or redesigning them is to analyze the position. Employees performing the activities should ideally be empowered to share in the analysis and resulting documentation.

Content of position descriptions varies, depending on the facility. Major components of position descriptions include the following:

- Title of the position
- Department name
- Person to whom the position is responsible
- Position summary
- Major responsibilities of the position
- Specification requirements
- Space for approvals and revision dates

This documentation is then reviewed and revised periodically for multiple users.

Current position descriptions are useful for clarifying relationships among team members and within the department, for preparing orientation and procedure documentation, for assessing compensation structure and performance appraisals, and in position interviews.

A job characteristics model is useful in designing HIM department positions where education and skills vary from position to position. This model identifies five core dimensions:

1. Skill variety
2. Task identity
3. Task significance
4. Autonomy
5. Feedback

Using these characteristics, managers can give value to each task and the team member performing it.

Position enrichment is used effectively to expand employee positions vertically. Position depth can be increased at the same time, giving the team members additional control over their activities.

Position enlargement offers horizontal expansion of responsibilities and increases job scope. When position enlargement is coupled with new tools such as automated systems, employees are accepting of the added tasks.

Job sharing is seen frequently in health care and is becoming useful in HIM departments where professionals wish to work part-time in responsible positions. Disadvantages are that communication breakdowns can create difficulties and administrative paperwork will likely increase. However, the time management advantages, such as coverage for vacations or illnesses, can offset the disadvantages when valuable employees are retained through this option.

Work sharing is one option when rightsizing occurs. By reducing work hours temporarily, layoffs are avoided and the work force can be reduced gradually through attrition.

Review Questions

1. Describe the two major components in the content of a position description.
2. Briefly explain the major uses of position descriptions.
3. Explain how the job characteristics model assists managers in redesigning position descriptions.
4. Give five options to traditional job designs that assist managers in better meeting employee needs.

Field Practice Questions

1. Interview an HIM professional and document major responsibilities. Develop a position description for the professional.
2. Redesign the work schedules for an HIM department staff of 16 where rightsizing plans call for an FTE budget for 14. Choose among the position design options.
3. Create position descriptions for two employees who share one full-time position—that of team leader for the coding and reimbursement team.

References

Layman, E. (1993). Preparing for the future: Job redesign. *Journal of AHIMA, 64* (9), 96.

Robbins, S. (1994). *Management* (4th ed.). Englewood Cliffs, NJ: Prentice Hall.

Rue, L., & Byars, L. (1986). *Management: Theory and application* (4th ed.). Homewood, IL: Richard C. Irwin.

Schein, J. (1993). Saying "I do" to job sharing. *For the Record, 5* (7), 9.

Stine, S. (1993). Take this job and share it. *For the Record, 5* (7), 6.

Suggested Readings

DeVitt, M., et al. (1991). Health record completion guidelines. *Journal of AHIMA, 62* (11), 26–44.

Dick, R., & Steen, E. (eds.) (1991). *The computer-based patient record: An essential technology for health care.* Washington, DC: National Academy Press.

Donnelly, J., Gibson, J. & Ivancevich, J. (1987). *Fundamentals of management* (6th ed.). Plano, TX: Business Publications.

Dunn, R. (1993). Performance standards for coding professionals. *For the Record, 5* (23), 4–6.

Layman, E. (1993). Preparing for the future: Job redesign. *Journal of AHIMA, 64* (9), 96–98.

Longest, B. (1990). *Management practices for the health professional* (4th ed.). Norwalk, CT: Appleton & Lange.

Robbins, S. (1994). Management (4th ed.). Englewood Cliffs, NJ: Prentice Hall.

Rue, L., & Byars, L. (1986). *Management: Theory and application* (4th ed.). Homewood, IL: Richard D. Irwin.

Schein, J. (1993). Saying "I do" to job sharing. *For the Record, 5* (7), 9, 10.

Stine, S. (1993). Take this job and share it. *For the Record, 5* (7), 6, 7.

Terry, G., & Franklin, S. (1982). *Principles of management* (8th ed.). Homewood, IL: Richard D. Irwin.

Chapter 11

The Role of New Technologies in Organizing

After completing this chapter, the learner should be able to:

1. Identify situations where HIM managers may choose to develop interim organizational models.
2. List several techniques HIM professionals can use for self-education in managing new and emerging technologies.
3. List five major components of an effective clinical decision support system.
4. Define executive information systems and identify the role health information brokers have in its application for health care.
5. Describe community health information networks and relate methods for developing such integrated networks and the role they will have in a national database.

Key Terms

Clinical decision support systems

Community health information network (CHIN)

Electronic data interchange (EDI)

Executive information systems (EIS)

Interim organizational models

Introduction

As this chapter unfolds, a vision of how HIM professionals will continue to plan, organize, redesign, and reengineer for the future demands attention. Before this vision becomes focused, there must be a critical look at present organizational design. By creatively exploring alternative design structures, managers can open new vistas for organizing models and embrace new technologies that will focus on meeting the information needs of various customers. By melding new technologies and organizational change, HIM professionals can offer information and services of value in all health-care settings. These two factors—new technologies and organizational change—will continue to challenge and excite HIM professionals during the 1990s.

Examples of present and emerging technologies that generate the impetus toward a paradigm shift are included in this chapter. Organizational changes can then lead to opportunities for redesigning the structure or for a complete reengineering of the department. As defined in Chapter 9, reengineering involves radical change in business processes to achieve breakthrough results that increase productivity and decrease costs. The examples where reengineering is appropriate will contrast with examples where redesign is adequate for changing the organizational structure and will provide efficiency and effectiveness. Redesign is less radical than reengineering and practice examples give redesign options that are appropriate for some new technology applications.

Since the focus of this section is on the organizing function in the integrated model of management, the emphasis in this chapter continues to be on structural redesign and reengineering as new technologies are embraced. The behavioral aspects of change and meeting the challenges of managing these aspects are explored in Chapter 20.

Organizational Problems with New Technologies

As new technologies are incorporated into the strategic plan of facilities, one goal may be to solve specific problems. However, at the same time, other unfocused problems may be left unresolved. Or, in other situations, funds may be allocated for only partial solutions to problems and thus new sets of problems can arise, such as when one new automated system is planned for an HIM department, but other systems remain manual.

Interim Organizational Models

Managers are faced with designing interim workable organizational design structures within the constraints mentioned above. Solutions that involve flexible planning for **interim organizational models** must then be designed and implemented.

Installing automated applications that will coexist with manual systems in an HIM department creates opportunities for organizational change. For example, a department has just installed the computers and software application for a record-tracking system and connected transcription data to this new system. Bar-code technology is an integral component of the new system. This automated application creates an environment for organizational redesign. Figure 11-1 lists factors that will impact the structure and shows the new tools available to the managers and the teams under section A-1. Next it describes the interaction managers can engage in prior to organizational redesign. The third section gives major areas for redesign focus. The fourth section suggests several possibilities for change.

With the installation of record deficiency processing, several applications that offer further efficiencies in medical staff functions are now possible. By integrating a digital transcription system with the other application, it becomes possible to automate record deficiencies by having data transfer to the deficiency system with frequent updates. This will allow timely response to physician requests for incomplete records. At the same time, the record-tracking system creates an environment for making records available in a timely manner.

As section C in Figure 11-1 shows, by integrating the transcription system, record completion information is available automatically. The record activity team is free for job enrichment in other activities. Figure 11-1 emphasizes job enrichment and process innovation work groups or teams for employees displaced by organizational redesign. Another possibility must be mentioned—rightsizing of the department could involve loss of FTE (full-time equivalent) positions also.

A. Automation of Record Tracking

1. *New tools:* Computers, printers, bar code wands and strips, new forms and statistics.

2. *Interaction:* Teams within department, other departments receiving records and using wands.

3. *Redesign:* Focus on record-filing area. Now with fewer missing records, record processing is less time-consuming, there is prompt delivery of records, records search time is shortened. These factors result in fewer telephone calls regarding records; eliminate calls regarding transfers done at point of use where wands are available.

4. *Possibilities:* Enrich team positions by adding additional responsibilities. Reassign employees to other teams. Change productivity standards or structure. Explore reengineering that includes crossing department lines to be involved in process innovation work groups.

B. Automation of Medical Staff Record Deficiencies

1. *New tools:* Additional computers, printer, new forms for notices and statistics.

2. *Interaction:* Teams within the department, medical staff and medical staff relations, and upper-level administration sharing deficiency information and resulting statistics.

3. *Redesign:* Focus on incomplete record area and medical staff. Now possible to file all records together and eliminate separate incomplete records file area. Eliminate manual tracking of deficient and incomplete records so less team time required. Prompt completion of records results in fewer telephone calls and interaction with medical staff regarding problems. Calculations and notices are generated by computer.

4. *Possibilities:* Enrich team positions by adding other responsibilities. Reassign employees to other teams. Focus on better meeting the needs of the medical staff. Explore reengineering that includes crossing department lines to be involved in process innovation work groups.

C. Integration of Transcription Data with Other Medical Record Systems

1. *New tools:* None; seamless integration flow of data to other systems.

2. *Interaction:* Teams within the department, medical staff, patient-care units with automatic transfer of information.

3. *Redesign:* Focus on data transfer to other systems. Automate deficiencies.

4. *Possibilities:* Dissemination of information to various customers using their printers, thus freeing employees for other activities.

Figure 11-1.   Impact of Automation on Organizational Design

The complexity of redesign as new technologies are installed is envisioned. The following practice example further demonstrates this through the creation of interim organizational models to meet changing needs.

Practice Example

A medium-sized acute-care facility developed a strategic plan that included automating health information services functions over time. Betty is the department manager, Holly is the assistant manager, Loren is the supervisor for record activity, and Ann is the coding and reimbursement supervisor. As redesign begins, Ann is the only manager with automated functions; her section has encoding and abstracting capabilities.

Betty became involved in automated applications as a member of the administrative task force planning the hospital's vision of the future. The task force recommended to upper-level management that automated applications be prioritized throughout the facility, that the needs of all departments be included in the plan, and that each year's budget over the next 5 years include information systems/computer applications. Once approval for this strategic plan was assured, Betty organized a planning team within health information services to set priorities for automating the department. Holly, Loren, and Ann were members of the planning team and each chose key employees to join in this effort.

As the planning team members reviewed the present organizational model, talked with other facility HIM managers, and read material on information systems, they documented the positive and negative factors for choosing installation of major computer applications in a viable pattern. They also requested input from vendors. The team followed the decision-making steps outlined in Chapter 3 for choosing the information systems/computer application priority schedule. Prioritizing decisions were made by the team and the master patient index (MPI) was chosen as the initial automated purchase. This decision had the enthusiastic support of the employees.

The first modification in the organizational model, as the MPI installation was being planned, was an education facilitator to implement a training program. Since the MPI is used by all employees, initial training was planned as a time-consuming task and additional resource employee hours were planned in the budget. Not only must the position of education facilitator be funded for a period of time, but the resource hours and some overtime hours are also needed to keep the department activities current while employees are in training.

The second modification to the organizational model was for temporary employees, supervised by Loren, to begin the database for the new system. A date was chosen for implementing the system and all admissions from that date forward were included.

The emphasis on education and adequate training gave the employees confidence and the implementation phase occurred with only minor problems. At this point, Betty and her managers began team-building meetings to brainstorm a redesign of the department as additional automated systems were purchased over the next 5 years. This process kept employees involved in planning the change options.

Record tracking was chosen as the second computer application, with the record activity technicians excited about the opportunity to assist in choosing the system and then learning to use new tools for improving their tasks. Facility-wide budget constraints limited the total purchase of this application. The bar-coding component of record tracking was postponed for purchase. Bar coding was planned for use throughout the hospital for inventory tracking, nursing applications, and other purposes. Unfortunately, during the interim period, other departments in the hospital would not have computers available to transfer records automatically. Continuing communication problems resulted—the telephone would continue to be used extensively for record transfers. Figure 11-2 depicts the bar code attached to a patient record for scanning.

During this interim, health information services chose to begin the record-tracking system using computers, and training began. Again, the organizational model was revised to show an education facilitator and temporary technicians to keep the activities current. Because bar coding was postponed, employee hours would not be decreased as soon as planned.

At this point, the planning team began a proposed organization design that would create teams, team leaders, and team members in a process-focused environment. Terminology using supervisors and technicians would no longer be seen in the model.

As the planning team began discussing the redesign, each member shared informally with other employees; then Betty planned an in-service program where a manager from another facility and a consultant were invited to share their success stories about implementing the team concept. Employees were encouraged to ask questions.

Figure 11-2.   A Bar Code on a Patient Record Used for Scanning (Courtesy of U.S. Department of Veterans Affairs)

Loren reported problems with errors as the record-tracking system became operational. His quality improvement review found that keying six-digit record numbers into the computer gave opportunity for transposing numbers. It became necessary to recheck every number for accuracy. Employees became discouraged because this new application was not freeing time for other activities as planned. The planning team discussed recommendations from the record activity section that full implementation of bar coding be accomplished as soon as possible. The planning team prepared a position paper for upper-level management. As Betty shared the position paper and the problems of partial implementation with the administrative council, the concensus was that budget monies must be found to implement bar coding as planned, as soon as possible, throughout the hospital. Monies were allocated, and the bar-code system was installed throughout the hospital.

As bar coding was implemented and employees became proficient with the new system, Loren found that accuracy increased to an acceptable level as did the timeliness of record availability. Employee morale rose as well.

The organization of health information services for these major changes was discussed by the planning team. Success gave increased confidence. The decision was made to move forward with organizational redesign, using the team concept to better meet customer needs.

Over this 2-year period, health information services implemented an automated master patient index and a record-tracking system, and then redesigned the department. Cost-effectiveness resulted, with an increase in productivity, accuracy, and timeliness in meeting customer needs. Betty found Holly, Loren, and Ann receptive to change as the redesign occurred. Holly became the team leader for the information dissemination team, Loren for the record movement team, and Ann for the coding and reimbursement team. As future information systems and automated technology applications become a part of the strategic plan, they will continue to bring challenges and create further opportunities for organizational change. ■

During the turbulent period involved in implementing new technologies over time, as demonstrated, HIM managers who share the vision of the overall objectives of the institution with employees can maintain morale and stability within the department teams. Temporary setbacks occur when crises arise, but they are defused through participative management efforts and renewed focus on the facility's strategic imperative. This vision can then continue to guide in the redesign of the department's organizational structures during the transition period and into the future.

Self-Education During Transition to New Technologies

Pick up the current journal for the profession, flip through the pages for advertisements, and there are several attractive pages detailing how automated applications will benefit health information services. For example, several vendors offer optical disk technology. After reading the material from each vendor, it becomes clear that the hardware and software developed by the vendors have different features. Managers face the challenge of educating themselves and their teams in these major features that will offer their unique setting the best system. Outside their own departments,

HIM professionals must take a proactive role in demonstrating the value of new technology to their peers and upper-level management as well.

Through self-education, HIM managers become familiar with hardware and software capabilities and can then guide in the selection process. As the different systems are explored, educated HIM managers have the confidence to raise valid questions pertaining to the features of each system and ensure they have prepared themselves to be key players in new technology purchases. For example, knowledgeable managers ask about open architecture, capabilities for multimedia input, and establishing minimum connectivity requirements.

Transition to Information Brokers

HIM managers involved in self-education become valued brokers of information; they need not simply react to the strategic plans that bring new technologies into the facility. Educating themselves by interacting with vendors, by reading current journals and books, and by networking with others, HIM managers prepare themselves for a role in the decision-making process. During the planning and organizing functions, innovative organizational change can occur as ideas are generated, leading to acceptance of an organizational design that is then translated into action. Managers who offer the ideas and take an active role in promoting these ideas into action are the innovators; they are not just reacting to internal or external forces.

As innovators, HIM brokers can combine the planning for new technologies with the planning for appropriate organizational redesign that will create efficiency and cost-effectiveness over time. By organizing for efficient and effective capture, storage, retrieval, integration, and management of facility data, managers and their teams create change that will lead them into the fully automated environment of the future.

As automation increases in the facility, HIM professionals move into true data manager and information broker roles. But HIM managers cannot expect these roles to fall naturally to them—they must ask questions, determine what other managers need to make effective decisions, and then help them understand the data captured within the facility's information systems and how these data can be transformed into decision-making information for them. This analysis of the needs may take different forms, but it is essential that appropriate data be captured, analyzed, and disseminated to everyone with a need for information to best accomplish their tasks for customers.

New graduates may be challenged with organizational change in their first positions in a health-care setting. Some may find the need for self-education, focusing on the first stages of moving from HIM manual systems to automated applications. Organizational change will follow, and interim models may be required. Or, at the other end of the spectrum, new graduates may find automated applications already in place for the majority of HIM systems and processes. The education process toward information broker will be quite different from one situation to the next. The situation demands flexibility as one key to a new graduate's successful integration into the new environment.

Organizational Design for a Computerized Patient Record System

Nationally, the need for computerized longitudinal patient records that reside in an integrated database can become a reality—eventually. In the meantime, HIM professionals can prepare, within their sphere of influence, the tools and systems compatible with electronic patient record (EPR) efforts. As emerging technologies move health-care applications toward increased use of the electronic medium for health records, HIM professionals can be prepared to accept the challenges these technologies bring with them.

Clinical Decision Support Systems

As discussed earlier, the definition of a computer-based patient record (CPR) includes **clinical decision support systems** as a crucial component. This section discusses the CPR from a clinical perspective. HIM professionals have the background in medical science and information systems for a major role in the development of decision support systems involved in patient care. Indeed, as brokers of information, HIM professionals are employed as members of the staff developing systems within the vendor community.

By taking an active role in choosing clinical support systems, HIM managers can encourage the purchase and/or development of systems that include the following crucial features:

1. Open systems architecture that will integrate with other applications and be compatible with prevailing standards for exchange of health-care information.

2. Instant transfer of information using integrated networks. Clinicians, nurses, health-care professionals, and support staff have different needs and desires for accessing and keying in healthcare information. Automated tools include: pen computers, palmtop computers, bedside computers, personal terminals, electronic clipboards, and laptop computers. These tools allow for efficient point-of-service input.

3. Longitudinal patient records, from birth to death documentation, are being created that will be compatible with the community health information network.

4. Digital information is stored to the extent possible.

5. Confidentiality of patient-identifiable information is maintained (Currie and Stevens, 1993).

Figures 11-3 and 11-4 show direct patient caregivers using computers at point of service. In Figure 11-3, the computer resides at the patient's bedside and is used as care is given. Figure 11-4 shows a clinician using a pen-based portable computer as patient care is given. Ambulatory caregivers can also use point-of-service portable tools effectively.

Leslie Fox, president of Care Communications, Inc., a Chicago-based consulting firm, stresses the need for HIM professionals to take an active part in the strategic planning process. She also envisions a mandate for organizational and professional change as the CPR is developed. Looking at the CPR as a concept, a system of information processing, is a third point made by Ms. Fox (1994).

Putting this advice into practice as clinical decision support systems are developed and integrated into the CPR, creates exciting opportunities. Crossing department lines into process innovation and organizational redesign is one option for HIM professionals, as emphasized earlier. Involvement in choosing and developing clinical decision support systems will give HIM managers insight into how departmental teams can be a part of such a matrix organization.

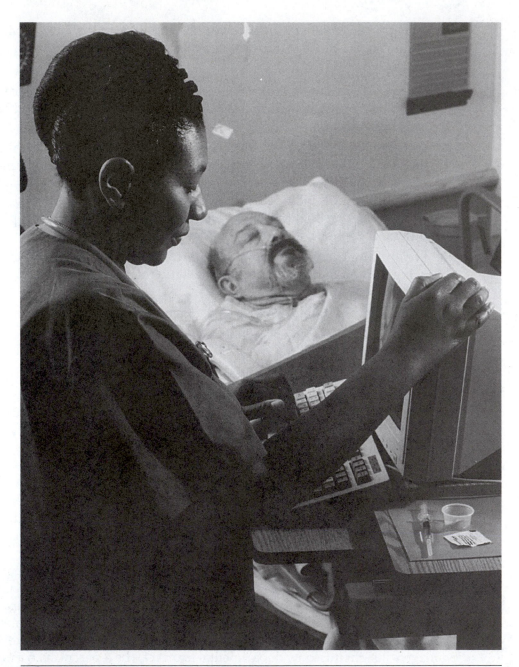

Figure 11-3. A Bedside Terminal Used for Point-of-Service Documentation
(Courtesy of U.S. Department of Veterans Affairs)

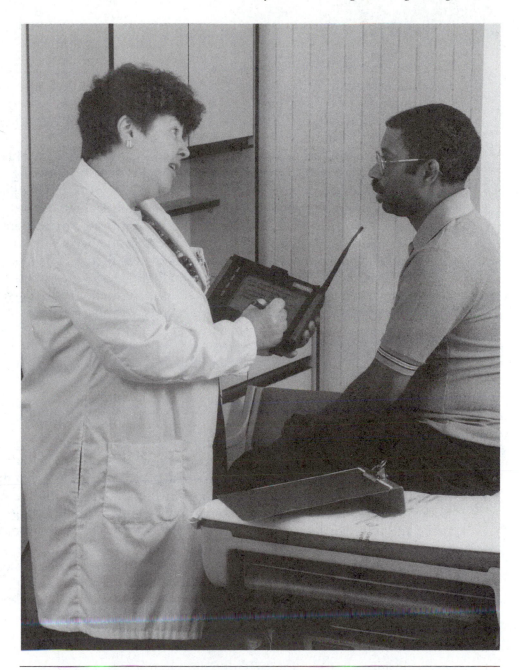

Figure 11-4. Point-of-Service Documentation in Ambulatory Care (Courtesy of U.S. Department of Veterans Affairs)

■ *Practice Example*

Jim is the director of the HIM department in a large facility. His management team redesigned their organizational model for a team approach 2 years ago and continues to explore emerging technologies to meet customer needs, while decreasing costs and increasing productivity. Six team leaders function under Jim and are moving toward self-directed team concept.

The focus in this example is to review emerging technologies for Jim and his teams as they create an organizational design for the future. Micrographic technology was incorporated for record storage many years ago and optical disk imaging technology was installed last year. Jim has asked the task force that planned for the optical disk system to continue listing applications that will enhance the department's thrust toward an EPR and eventually the CPR. At the last meeting of the task force, the list shown in Figure 11-5 emerged.

By prioritizing the list of technologies in Figure 11-5, Jim and his teams can monitor them and choose those that show promise for the department. Through self-education and in-service meetings, Jim and the teams will be prepared for a proactive commitment to change and organizational reengineering as a paradigm shift emerges. ■

Executive Information System

HIM professionals have the opportunity to be involved in the implementation and management of **executive information systems (EIS)** that assist upper-level management in making strategic planning decisions in a timely fashion. Since HIM departments manage much of the information required to develop a valid system for executives, health information brokers who make the effort to learn about this computer-based tool for upper-level management, are in a position of influence.

Three components typically create an executive information system:

1. Master database
2. Executive information system "engine"
3. "Briefing book" or ad hoc query tools (Dowell and Zieserl, 1992)

The system typically resides in the health-care facility's mainframe or as part of a local-area network (LAN). Integration of databases from various

1. Develop enhancements to optical disk imaging.
   a. Increase connectivity to PC-based hospital applications to increase data flow and decrease scanning. This integrates present minicomputer applications and technology with the PCs.
   b. Create uses for bar-code technology to index optical disk scanning process.
   c. Develop use of mark sense recognition (MSR) to electronically export paper-based information to a relational database. This allows patient-focused care centers to mark bubble sheets for scanning by HIM department.
   d. Continue storage of x-ray films on the system.
   e. Increase storage of fetal heart monitoring information on the system.
   f. Storage of surgical procedure videos is to be maintained electronically for physician review on computer screen.
   g. Work-flow processing software is used for record ordering, deficiency analysis, and correspondence.
2. Increase connectivity and integration.
   a. Deficiency record automatically updated as physician dictates a report.
   b. Deficiency record automatically updated as transcription is completed.
   c. Transcription documents uploaded to information system and available immediately for physicians and other caregivers.
   d. Electronic physician signatures; also flagging by physicians to make changes in a report.
   e. Increase PC networks with an open system platform, including connectivity to medical staff offices.
   f. Virtual record development with index that shows location of all parts of the record—electronic or paper—by increasing capability of present bar-coding system.
3. Create a long-term plan for using micrographics and optical disk storage cooperatively. Recommend keeping micrographics for archival purposes for inactive records.
4. Create a hospital-wide task force that will ensure accessibility of patient information while monitoring present policies and setting guidelines for confidentiality.
5. Continue efforts toward the EPR and CPR; work across departmental lines to format the data and their flow so they can be used effectively in clinical management.

Figure 11-5. Future Applications Leading to an Electronic Record (Hamilton, 1992; Kelly, 1993; Collins, 1993; Little, 1993)

sources is one key to the successful use of this tool. To effectively address issues of cost, quality, and outcomes, there must be uniform definitions for each data element used. And, once the standards are in place, the quality of data needs to be assessed periodically. Health information brokers have the expertise for this critical component (Dowell and Zieserl, 1992).

Applications for the Executive Information System

Senior executives with integrated data at their fingertips from various sources, can develop graphs, charts, tables, or on-screen comparisons using current information. Figure 11-6 summarizes the typical applications.

Organizing the data flow to provide timely, quality information to "run" the engine of an executive information system will challenge the health information broker. As a key player in disseminating information to customers, the broker can unlock the data sources and bring quality, cost, and outcome issues into the decision-making arena (Dowell and Zieserl, 1992).

Community Health Information Network

Health care's information highway becomes a reality as integration of community and then regional health-care networks occurs. As commitment and funding for **electronic data interchange (EDI)** become available in communities and regions across the country, linkages will occur. For example, in Illinois, health-care providers are developing a **community health information network (CHIN)** with financial assistance from telecommunication and information processing corporations. Hospitals are the major participants initially, but eventually alternative sites such as home health care, long-term care, and physician practices will be integrated. This large CHIN is positioned to grow into a regional health information network that will eventually link with a national health-care information highway (*For the Record*, 1994).

The Greater Dayton Area Hospital Association in Ohio is another example of provider-driven development of a CHIN. The association has created an information network in collaboration with telecommunication and information processing corporations. The goals are to improve the quality of patient care and to reduce health-care costs while sharing sub-

1. *Patient-care application:* Analyzes the following:
   a. Patient-care activity
   b. Service level
   c. Diagnosis patterns and episode of care
   d. Trends in patient population
   e. Utilization review patterns
2. *Medical staff application:* Creates profiles, such as:
   a. Financial and quality profiles
   b. Trends in practice patterns by individual physician, physician groups, and physician specialties
3. *Financial application:* Provides the following:
   a. Income statement and balance sheet information with key ratios, revenue, and expenses
   b. Trends in profit and loss
   c. Break-even analysis
4. *Quality application:* Organizes and tracks the following:
   a. Quality of care data
   b. Compliance with external accreditation requirements
   c. Compliance with review requirements
5. *Human resources application:* Presents the profile on each employee with productivity information and performance statistics
6. *Products and services activity:* Provides volume and statistical information with relationship information on products and services
7. *Payer application:* Furnishes insights into the following:
   a. Sources of operating revenue by payer classes
   b. Payment trends and profitability by payer type
8. *Market application:* Provides information on the source of patients, market demographics, and market share

Figure 11-6. Applications for Executive Information Systems (Dowell and Ziegerl, 1992)

sets of patient information through electronic data transfer (*Advance for Health Information Professionals*, 1994).

In the mid-1990s, about 50 CHIN initiatives were in various stages across the nation. While the CHINs in Illinois and Ohio have been initiated by providers, the majority of others are vendor driven. HIM managers participating in the organization of CHINs in their community can contribute significantly by offering their expertise in software appraisal and EDI solutions. They can assist in documenting the vision and objectives of the CHIN, and then assess the ability of vendors to offer cost-effective solutions that will meet these objectives.

Summary

As manual health information systems are dismantled and automated applications are installed, organizational challenges face HIM professionals. When systems are changed over time, it can be necessary to create interim organizational models.

Self-education will keep HIM managers aware of new and emerging technologies that can solve health information problems and lead to a paradigm shift. During the transition to automated information systems, managers can truly become health information brokers and be valued change agents.

With new technologies available for electronic storage, the CPR will become a reality and lead to a national database for longitudinal records. Clinical decision support systems will be a major component of the CPR.

Upper-level management will find that executive information systems lead to timely decision making. HIM departments and services manage the majority of data used in this process, giving health information brokers an opportunity to be key players in disseminating information of value.

Review Questions

1. Choose an automated application for HIM services and explain its impact on organizational design.

2. Identify three avenues that HIM professionals can use in becoming knowledgeable about new technologies.

3. Describe how HIM professionals can enhance strategic planning decisions within an organization.

Field Practice Questions

1. Using an organizational model from an acute-care setting, create an interim organization model that would be in use following installation of an automated HIM system.

2. Review several health information or computer journals and list the emerging technologies you find in the articles.

References

Collins, S. (1993). Micrographics and electronic imaging: Working partners. *Advance for Health Information Professionals*, 3 (26), 24.

Community health information network (1994). *For the Record*, 6 (3), 23.

Currie, R., & Stevens, D. (1993). The integration of existing specialized clinical information systems into a computer-based patient record. *Journal of AHIMA*, 64 (9), 62, 63.

Dowell, S., & Zieserl, R. (1992). Executive information systems technology and the health information management professional. *Journal of AHIMA*, 63 (8), 62–64.

Fox, L. (1994). Organizational change: Reengineering the workflow. *Journal of AHIMA*, 65 (4), 35.

Hamilton, M. (1992). Cutting edge technologies lead HI to paperless future. *Advance for Health Information Professionals*, 2 (26), 6, 7.

Innovative health information network (1994). *Advance for Health Information Professionals*, 4 (6), 23.

Kelly, J. (1993). Scanning for simplicity. *For the Record*, 5 (23), 13.

Little, E. (1993). Starting up an imaging system: Lessons learned. *Journal of AHIMA*, 64 (4), 60, 61.

Suggested Readings

Bolling, R., Jr. (1993). When choosing an optical imaging system. *Advance for Health Information Professionals, 3* (12), 13.

Brandt, M. (1994). Clinical practice guidelines and critical paths—Roadmaps to quality, cost-effective care (Part 1). *Journal of AHIMA, 65* (1), 51–54.

Brandt, M. (1995). Making the CPR vision a reality: Where should you start? *Journal of AHIMA, 66* (3), 26–30.

Collins, S. (1993). Micrographics and electronic imaging: Working partners. *Advance for Health Information Professionals, 3* (26), 24.

Dowell, S., & Zieserl, R. (1992). Executive information systems technology and the health information management professional. *Journal of AHIMA, 63* (8), 62–65.

Fenton, S. (1995). Making the computer-based patient record usable and user friendly. *Journal of AHIMA, 66* (1), 60–62.

Freeman, T., & Southern, B. (1994). Telemedicine and CHINS: Interviews with two experts. *Journal of AHIMA, 65* (8), 40–43.

Frey, L. & Bloomrosen, M. (1995). Impact of enterprisewide data. *Topics in Health Information Management, 15* (4), 31–43.

Hamilton, M. (1992). Cutting edge technologies lead HI to paperless future. *Advance for Health Information Professionals, 2* (26), 6, 7.

Image processing: Can it answer your records needs? (1992). *Healthcare Informatics*, April, pp. 14, 15.

Keele, L., Gilbert, D., & Smith, D. (1995). Modeling shared health and social care information. *Topics in Health Information Management, 16* (2), 40–49.

Kelly, J. (1993). Scanning for simplicity. *For the Record, 5* (23), 12, 13, 23.

Lytle, J. S., & Lytle, B. (1992). Getting back to healthcare: The new automation strategy. *Journal of AHIMA, 63* (10), 66–72.

Mahoney, M., & Doupnik, A. (1993). Health information department reorganization resulting from the implementation of optical imaging. *Journal of AHIMA, 64* (4), 56–58.

Mancilla, D. (1995). The electronic patient record maze: Where is the beginning—And is there an end? *Journal of AHIMA, 66* (3), 48–50.

Marsh, G., Guanciale, T., & Simon, M. (1995). Operations improvement and reengineering at Ohio State University Medical Center. *Topics in Health Information Management, 16* (1), 41–46.

McBrierty, L. (1995). Reengineering: A step beyond CPR. *Journal of AHIMA, 66* (2), 46–48.

McCollegan, E., Samuell, R., Jones, W., Moon, W., Pretnar, S., & Johns, M. (1995). An internet health care information resources server as a component of statewide medical information network. *Topics in Health Information Management*, *16* (1), 11–19.

Melbin, J. (1991). Patient record 2000. *For the Record*, *3* (24), 1, 6, 7, 9.

Merski, P. (1993) Optical imaging the "right" way. *Journal of AHIMA*, *64* (5), 69–72.

Miller, C. (1993). The electronic record. *Topics in Health Information Management*, *13* (3), 20–29.

Palmer, L. (1995). In practice. *Journal of AHIMA*, *66* (2), 54, 55.

Pomerance, W. (1994). Optical imaging systems: Who needs them immediately? *Advance for Health Information Professionals*, *4* (2), 9.

Robbins, S. (1994). *Management* (4th ed.). Englewood Cliffs, NJ: Prentice Hall.

Rollins, P. (1993). Converting to an optical disk system. *Topics in Health Information Management*, *13* (3), 30–38.

Shihadeh, S., & Rooks, C. (1994). The basics of EDI: A pathway to the information highway. *Journal of AHIMA*, *65* (8), 24–29.

Tashiro, R. (1994). The information highway to a healthcare utopia: Dream or possibility? *Journal of AHIMA*, *65* (8), 34–36.

Leading to Meet the Information Needs of Health-Care Facilities

Chapter 12

Leading: The Interpersonal Aspects of Management

Learning Objectives

After completing this chapter, the learner should be able to:

1. List synonyms for the term *leading* and state how their meanings differ in emphasis.
2. Describe how leaders use power within organizations to accomplish objectives.
3. Contrast the traits of leaders with the traits of managers.
4. Give the three components of attitudes and state how attitudes can predict employee behavior.
5. Describe how HIM managers can identify appropriate personality traits for specific positions in a hospital HIM department.
6. Define formal and informal groups within the organization and the role HIM managers have in each.
7. Give advantages of using the team approach for accomplishing objectives in the HIM workplace.
8. Define followership and outline the role managers have as followers.

Key Terms

Actuating	Informal leader
Attitudes	Leadership
Authoritarianism	Locus of control
Cognitive dissonance	Machiavellianism
Consistency perception	Perception
Directing	Self-esteem
Followership	Self-monitoring
Formal leader	

Introduction

It could be said that the management functions of planning and organizing are a preparation that sets the stage for the interpersonal aspect of management—leading. The leading function takes a manager into what may be considered the most complex aspect of management. And, with the demands on HIM managers to increase efficiency and effectiveness, leading the teams that perform the multifaceted activities encompassing the entire HIM field, gives added meaning to the term complex.

Again, it is important to emphasize the interwoven nature of the management functions. None is undertaken in isolation. There is rarely an opportunity to complete the planning cycle, create the department's organizational design, and then say, "Now it is time to begin hiring and leading the teams who are performing the activities outlined in planning and delegated in organizing." Hence, the complexity increases as the planning vision becomes ongoing reality through the leading function.

Leading Defined

Leading is defined as "the management function involved in motivating employees, directing others, resolving conflicts, and selecting effective communication channels" (Robbins, 1994). These interpersonal facets of leading are evidence of the crucial nature of this management function.

The purpose of leading is, of course, to accomplish the objectives of the facility through the teams delegated to perform specific activities. This chapter begins by defining terms frequently used in Section IV.

This third function of management is sometimes called **actuating**, which emphasizes the responsibility of managers to get all members of the team to want and to strive to achieve the team's objectives (Terry and Franklin, 1982).

Also, at times, authors choose the term *directing* to describe the leading function. Leading gives emphasis to the manager's role in setting the tone for the department and in encouraging the teams by example. In contrast, **directing** refers to the giving of assignments and instructions, the guidance of employees, and the overseeing of those activities (Longest, 1990). Leading and directing are used interchangeably in this text, depending on whether the topic is discussing the interpersonal aspects of an activity or the functional component of an activity.

The interpersonal aspects of managing require HIM professionals to address the need for an understanding of why humans behave as they do within their teams and with others in the organization. Section IV explores human behavior in the workplace and includes examples of individual behavioral response. There is no such thing as an "average" employee. Each one has individual differences. This chapter focuses on individual and group behavior. Chapter 13 explores the motivational aspects of leading and has a section on conflict and its effects. At times conflict is seen as the result of faulty communication. Communicating with skill in the workplace is the topic of Chapter 14.

Leadership Power and Authority

Leadership is the ability to inspire and influence others and, as such, is the process of influencing the behavior of group members in accomplishing the planned objectives. Thus, the leader is the person who has a central role in group activity. By this definition there can be two types of leaders: the formal or appointed leader and the **informal leader** chosen by the group. The HIM department manager is the **formal leader** of the department, appointed by upper-level management, and thus has the leadership authority. But, does this mean the manager is automatically the informal leader? Since the group chooses the informal leader, the manager may or may not have ownership of both roles (Rue and Byars, 1986). Is this situation a deterrent to the successful performance of the tasks to meet departmental objectives? The section on group behavior offers some conclusions to this question.

In Chapter 8 the discussion on power and authority showed how appointed authority is a subset of power as the formal lines of organization are drawn. Mature, self-controlled leaders will use this appointed authority wisely for influencing teams. The power inherent in their position can be used positively. This power is necessary, not for personal aggrandizement, but to accomplish the goals and thus enhance quality patient care. Effective leaders use the right combination of power and authority appropriate for their group of employees. As stated earlier, there is no "average" employee; the managerial challenge is to know the employees, know their strengths and weaknesses, and then utilize the most effective methods for accomplishing the delegated tasks.

Using Leadership Power Appropriately

Although there can be negative connotations to the different types of power discussed in Chapter 8, there are some positive aspects of power for HIM leaders. When positive power such as that outlined in Figure 12-1 is used wisely, it commands respect and gives stature to the professional.

Leaders Versus Managers

Abraham Zaleznik, writing in the *Harvard Business Review* (1992), explains that managers and leaders typically have different personalities, attitudes toward goals, perceptions about work, and relationships with others. These different characteristics lead to situational differences where leaders prefer to make improvements in even successful policies. Managers, on the other hand, tend to be guided by rationality, control, and an impersonal approach toward goals. This tendency may lead to avoidance behavior when making changes in policies that are presently effective.

Reviewing these major differences, it could be concluded that an HIM professional, who tends toward leadership personality traits, will be monitoring trends for the future and then planning possible changes toward a total computer-based patient record (CPR) as technology advances. Accord-

1. *Information:* As data are captured and analyzed by HIM teams, managers who wisely disseminate this information have ability to influence others.

2. *Experience and knowledge:* Theoretical knowledge gives a professional the edge in influencing others. However, high-quality work experience gives wisdom that others perceive of value also. These aspects are especially influential when change is occurring in an HIM department.

3. *Procedural control:* Not everyone enjoys developing procedures and training the team in implementing changes. HIM professionals who lead in creating or revising procedures have power by governing the actions of the team and thus enhancing the quality of work.

4. *Rewards:* This aspect of power can be easily misused. Used rightly, for tangible and intangible rewards, it gives managers stature and respect from their employees and peers.

Figure 12-1.   Positive Aspects of Leadership Power (Rue and Byars, 1986)

ing to John Byrne (1992) in *Business Week,* managers with these leader personality traits will be replacing managers that tend toward rationality and control. In the continuum between these personality traits, however, lies a broad range of characteristics with ample room for variation in managerial styles. Successful professionals are those who acknowledge their personality traits, develop those they desire, and with enthusiasm perform well into the twenty-first century.

Almost as crucial to success is the environment in which a leader operates. Successful leadership is also dependent on the followers—the teams within the department—and on the goals and objectives planned for the department and for the total organization. The conclusion is that the successful manager is not a blind adherent to any one particular leadership style, but rather chooses the style considered most appropriate for a given situation (Robbins, 1994).

Leadership traits can be learned, and effective managers have learned to develop the skills they desire through effort and practice. By giving diligence and constant attention to the practices outlined in Figure 12-2, new managers can become enthusiastic leaders.

By keeping this list of leadership practices for frequent review, new managers can be diligent in honing their leading skills, conquering their

1. *Empower and motivate others:* Consciously involve those performing the tasks in the planning, when possible. Enlist their assistance and support in creating change and improving the workplace. Get to know strengths and weaknesses of the team members and build on their strengths. Delegate and then ensure they have the tools to accomplish the tasks.

2. *Recognize valuable ideas:* Give ideas a try even though it means challenging tradition. Empower the teams to offer ideas; give them authority to implement the feasible ones. Challenge them to become part of solutions. Give encouragement, feedback, and praise when appropriate.

3. *Serve as a symbol of the work group's identity:* Have a winning philosophy that includes professional ethics and a value system.

4. *Create a vision:* Take time to plan for the long-range future of the department; share the planning and the goals; share the overarching vision; explain the facility mission; be passionate, intense, and inspirational as the vision takes shape. As new issues arise and policies are developed, communicate and negotiate.

5. *Renew the tangible (including people) and intangible resources:* Manage them for the future well-being of the facility.

6. *Network externally to promote data/information dissemination to customers:* Show a willingness to negotiate.

7. *Demonstrate credibility to maintain trust:* Credibility encompasses candor, integrity, self-control, professional ethics, and moral conviction.

8. *Listen, listen, and listen:* Keep in touch internally and externally; the best method for developing a sensitivity to employees' needs is to listen. Understand their dreams, their sense of values, what rewards them. Let them know you care. But, be willing to take a courageous stand on an issue when necessary.

9. *Maintain a standard of excellence:* Expect excellence, reward excellence, live excellence.

Figure 12-2. Leadership Practices

fears, understanding their strengths and weaknesses, and becoming the visionary, competent leaders desired. By taking a long-term view of strategic planning and creating a clear and abiding mission within the organizational structure, leaders guide the team in selecting desirable outcomes and then focus on the goals for success.

Attitudes as Predictors of Behavior

Attitudes are evaluative statements that reflect how an individual feels about something. Obviously the concern here relates to job attitudes and how to explain or predict behavior that is in response to one or more of the three components of attitude:

1. *Cognitive attitude component:* This component covers the knowledge, opinions, and belief system held by the employee. "Refusing to code diagnoses based on the highest reimbursement," illustrates a cognition.

2. *Affective attitude component:* Emotions and feelings are addressed in this component. "I feel uncomfortable surrounded with this bright new wall color at my workstation," reflects the affective component of attitudes.

3. *Behavior attitude component:* Action takes place with this component. Repainting the wall because of negative feelings about it puts action into the attitude.

Typically, when an employee attitude is mentioned, the reference is to the affective component, since awareness of feelings is usually most evident. Awareness of attitudes in the HIM workplace is crucial to managerial success, especially as change occurs. One useful managerial goal is to strive for employee job satisfaction and ongoing commitment to the department. When teams participate in planning and organizing their own activities, as emphasized in Figure 12-2, each member can identify with the team goals and increase job satisfaction. As a result, the attitudes of the team members should reflect this involvement. Researchers find that people seek consistency between their attitudes and behavior. When the team members feel the planned change is good for them and for the department, their behavior will reflect this positive attitude and result in **consistency perception** (Robbins, 1994).

Cognitive dissonance is the opposite of consistency perception. Incompatibility between the hope an employee has and the behavior that leads toward realization of that hope creates cognitive dissonance. When team members exhibit a positive behavior toward planned changes, for example, and then become frustrated with some aspects of implementation, their affective component is inconsistent with their behavior and leads to a sense of discomfort. Researchers have shown that employees will seek to reduce this dissonance and thus the discomfort.

For example, a team leader who has just given an in-service program on the importance of accurate data in quality reviews, and then is told that the figures released yesterday to a medical staff committee are incorrect, will have dissonance. This will lead her to (1) admit the mistake and submit corrected figures or (2) convince herself that the figures are not so far off and really not that important. Thus, by reducing the dissonance, she has reduced the discomfort and is back to consistency perception (Robbins, 1994).

With this knowledge of attitudes, managers can listen, observe, and take steps to reduce dissonance in the work setting. This may involve something as simple as making sure team members are aware of why change is taking place, why tasks are performed in a specific way, how they can assist in making decisions about tasks, or how external pressures affect their tasks. In the example given above, the manager has the opportunity to use several of the leadership practices in Figure 12-2.

Personality Traits as Predictors of Behavior

Personality traits were mentioned in the previous section as they relate to managerial styles. Knowing the major traits that are predictors of employee behavior is also useful. Stephen Robbins (1994) reports on research findings that describe several major personality traits appearing to affect behavior in organizations. Some of these traits have a strong relationship to various cultures and, with our increasingly multicultural work force, an understanding of how these traits affect employee behavior enhances managerial insight.

1. *Authoritarianism:* Persons with high authoritarian personalities perform well in structured jobs where rigid rules and policies define work parameters. **Authoritarianism** is a measure of a person's belief in status and power differences among people in organizations. When assigning tasks, team members should be chosen carefully for the type of position needed and the interaction involved. When the position demands sensitivity, tact, and adaptation, applicants with low authoritarianism should be chosen.

2. *Machiavellianism:* This trait is named after the sixteenth-century writer who articulated how to manipulate and gain power. **Machiavellianism** is a measure of the degree to which people believe that ends can justify means. Persons high in this trait do well in positions that require

bargaining skills. They should not be chosen for positions where ethical implications are high or for those lacking well-documented standards of performance.

3. *Self-esteem:* **Self-esteem** is defined as an individual's degree of like or dislike for himself or herself. Research has shown that people with high self-esteem are more willing to take unpopular stands and are willing to take risks. Also, it is found that employees who tend toward high self-esteem have greater job satisfaction.

4. *Locus of control:* This trait has two components. The first is internal, where people believe they control their own fate. The second is external, where the belief is that people are pawns of fate. It has been demonstrated that employees with high externality are less satisfied with their jobs. In addition, they tend to blame others for problems such as blaming their team leader for a poor performance evaluation. Employees who believe in internal **locus of control**, on the other hand, tend to explain events in terms of their own actions (Robbins, 1994).

Robbins mentions another personality trait that has recently been acknowledged for study. Called **self-monitoring**, it refers to an individual's ability to adjust behavior to situational factors. Initial studies show employees with a high degree of self-monitoring are capable of presenting themselves differently, depending on the situation. In other words, they have different faces depending on the audience. One characteristic of high self-monitoring useful for HIM managers is that employees with this trait tend to observe the behavior of others and adapt accordingly. When hiring employees who will be working with the patients and their families, this trait could be a strength (Robbins, 1994).

The effort to match personalities and attitudes with the work environment for effective behavioral response is an ongoing challenge for HIM managers. When consideration can be given to matching personality types with compatible work environments, the result offers efficient performance, greater job satisfaction, and effective teams.

Perceptions as Predictors of Behavior

The discussion of attitudes and personality traits as behavior predictors may give the impression that HIM managers can conduct several applicant interviews, assess the strengths and weaknesses of each applicant, and choose the one with the best match of traits for the work environment. Of course, it is not that simple. Education and experience are also considerations. Another consideration is **perception**, which is the process of organizing and interpreting sensory impressions so as to give meaning to the environment. Research gives credence to the axiom that individuals looking at the same thing perceive it quite differently (Robbins, 1994). The practice example illustrates this point.

Practice Example

Jeanne, the record-processing team leader verbalizes in a management meeting that she is finding it difficult to obtain timely data she needs from Gwen, a disorganized medical staff relations coordinator. In negative terms, Jeanne states that, when data are not available on the due date, Gwen explains to her that because the information must be verified before release, it is often not ready by the tenth of the month. By asking if other team leaders are having difficulty working with the medical staff relations coordinator, Jim, the manager, opens the floor for discussion. "I find Gwen very easy to work with," responds the statistical specialist, Hal. "I am aware the monthly data are reviewed and verified by the medical director and, because of the thoughtful, deliberate actions of Gwen in verifying and releasing accurate data, I never have to question the validity of the information."

In this illustration there are several factors that operate to shape or distort perception. One factor is the perceiver. Both Jeanne and Hal are perceivers. Their personal characteristics influence the interpretation they make of the target being perceived—the medical staff relations coordinator, Gwen. These personal characteristics include attitudes, personality, motives, expectations, and past experiences. Here it appears that expectation plays a major role in the perceptions. Jim asked questions of Jeanne and Hal and thus discovered the underlying problem. Jeanne needs the data from Gwen by the tenth of the month, whereas Hal can allow Gwen two additional days because his data are due on the twelfth of the month. By asking questions and unearthing the expectation differences, Jim is using problem-solving steps for changing interpersonal perceptions.

To solve the problem, Jim changes the deadlines for submission of the data from Gwen. Thus, the medical staff information is now needed at the same time by both the team leader and the statistics specialist. But, will Jeanne continue to perceive Gwen as disorganized? This perception is not likely to change immediately. Jim can take every opportunity to offer positive reinforcement to Gwen when the data are submitted on time and do this in the presence of Jeanne and Hal. It is likely that a series of interactions where Jeanne perceives Gwen in a positive light will need to take place in order for that negative perception to diminish significantly. ■

How Managers Can Shape Behavior

In the practice example, the actions taken by the HIM manager are an attempt to mold or shape future attitudes and behavior. This shaping in successive steps toward behavior that benefits the total department is a managerial tool for learning. As positive reinforcement in this fashion results in learning, so appropriate negative reinforcement shapes behavior also. For example, during meetings, managers may ignore employees who tend to frequently raise their hands and speak. In response to this negative reinforcement, these employees will tend to weaken the hand-raising behavior until it falls to acceptable levels.

Another reinforcement tool is punishment, which can result in a different type of learning. It too weakens behavior, but over time other problems may surface. HIM professionals can best use punishment as a reinforcement tool with caution.

Leadership and Group Behavior

Employees, in most instances, are assigned to some type of group activity in HIM departments. This predominantly interpersonal activity increases the need for leaders to understand how personality traits and attitudes affect employee behavior. This section looks at how managers use the leadership skills already discussed to effectively lead teams in reaching their objectives. Formal sections or teams are organized to perform specific tasks within the HIM department and are detailed in the organizational design model. Not listed on the model, however, are the informal groupings. Many employees join informal groups because they find informal groups meet their social needs for security, status, and self-esteem. These informal groups within the HIM department create nonstructured social alliances that affect the attitudes, behavior, and even the productivity of the sections and their individual members (Robbins, 1994).

A third grouping of employees consists of voluntary members who typically work together solving specific problems. These groups may be called quality circles or task forces.

Formal Group Structure

Formal groups are created by managers to perform tasks that lead to the accomplishment of departmental goals. HIM departments may have several formal groups or sections performing the major assigned activities. These groupings typically revolve around similar tasks such as transcription, coding and reimbursement, record processing, and confidentiality and release of information. Cross-functional teams, focusing on process innovation, formed within the department or across departmental lines, are becoming more common.

A department's organizational design details each team and the tasks of the members. Relationships across the teams can also be detailed but may be more easily seen from the procedures that show interactions among team members. As the groups perform the manager-assigned tasks, they develop team objectives compatible with the strategic plan for the department. While these details are performed at the department level, the cultural change process is the responsibility of upper-level management. Planning teams should involve people at all levels of the organization with education and information sharing major priorities. Enthusiasm and commitment for a self-directed work environment, with opportunity to participate in decisions and learn other job skills, can be the result of well-planned empowerment. Employees can then share a sense of job ownership and can feel that they are a valuable part of the organization (Wellins, 1991).

Education begins first with the managers. Self-directed teams demand mentors, facilitators, coaches, visionaries, and communicators. Leaders must develop the skill to assist others in leading themselves. As responsibilities change, leaders need new roles, and role-clarity sessions assist in communicating details.

Since some teams become more productive and successful than others, an understanding of formal group behavior assists managers in creating a team environment that builds on the strengths of each team member (Wellins, 1991).

To illustrate how perceptions affect group behavior, the interactions within a transcription section are examined. The section has six transcriptionists working the first shift and five working the evening shift. With this organization, the section will typically have a transcription supervisor and an evening lead transcriptionist. There may also be a secretary, depending on the level of automation. Each member of the section brings a valuable resource to the group—his or her ability to perform medical language specialist activities effectively. Members also bring their personality traits, attitudes, and perceptions. When these tend to be positive, there is a positive influence working within the section, resulting in job satisfaction and high productivity. When negative forces predominate, dissatisfaction results and lower productivity follows.

During organizational change, turning this transcription section into two effective teams may be just a change in terms, but when a name change combines with a change in leadership style, it can also build esprit de corps through cooperation and morale enhancement. As change was initiated, the transcription section was empowered to reorganize and chose to form two teams—one for the day shift and one for the evening shift. Team leaders were then chosen by the team members themselves. Empowering these teams to solve problems, develop work schedules, choose in-service topics, and be a part of the decision making in choosing new equipment requires leadership skills from the HIM manager.

HIM managers, who can build successful teams as they lead them through goal setting and team building, may choose to employ a facilitator skilled in reengineering to ensure all the tools necessary for this effort are in place. Chapter 8 discusses work teams and details the major characteristics of effective teams in Figure 8-3. Figure 12-3 lists the behavioral advantages of work teams.

Once a pattern of behavior is established within a team, it is called a norm. The norm is an agreement among the team members as to what constitutes appropriate behavior. Once a norm is in place, the team may pressure members to conform. A team member with low self-esteem is more likely to conform than one with high self-esteem. As team leaders are taught group behavior concepts, they will find that norms can enhance team effectiveness.

The team-building steps lead managers to:

1. Understand employees and know the strengths and weaknesses of each.
2. Manage by negotiation and dialogue with a mentoring stance.
3. Build a sense of ownership that leads to continuous quality improvement.
4. Flatten the organizational structure and reduce costs.
5. Develop department teams that become self-directed groups, operating efficiently in the absence of the manager.

Figure 12-3.   Behavioral Advantages of Team Building

Dynamic Teams: Quality Improvement and Quality Circles

The evolution toward the team concept has been enhanced by QI concepts. Empowering employees within a team toward decision making and independent activity has led to a strengthening of the team concept. Chapter 16 details quality improvement concepts for HIM managers. With continued emphasis on quality improvement in the JCAHO (Joint Commission on Accreditation of Healthcare Organizations) standards, this trend toward excellence will only increase.

Quality Circles

The value of quality circles in solving problems lies in the commitment of each member of the work group to solve the problem at hand. Work group members meet regularly to discuss problems within their area of responsibility, select those problems appropriate for the quality circle, and recommend a solution. Although some quality circle problems can be solved at the team level, those that cannot are referred to the department managers for further review. Team members typically rotate membership in the quality circle work group (Robbins, 1994).

Leadership and Informal Groups

Embedded within formal organizations are informal groups, created by employees to meet their needs for personal security, recognition, and other needs that cannot be met by the formal structure. Participants in informal groups typically share similar values and enjoy social interaction. Members value the communication channel or grapevine afforded by the informal group. The informal setting also offers leadership possibilities and some may join for this reason.

While informal groups are not officially recognized, they offer opportunities for HIM leaders to build stronger departments through cooperative efforts. Destructive informal groups also exist and cannot be ignored. Some positive aspects of informal groups deserve consideration first.

Positive Informal Group Elements

HIM professionals have an opportunity to turn informal groups into a positive force within the workplace. Figure 12-4 lists several positive factors available to managers.

Negative Informal Group Elements

It is inevitable that informal groups will at times work at cross purposes to the objectives of the formal organization. What is best for employees is not always in the best interest of the facility. A role conflict results. Since orga-

---

1. *Simplifies management's role:* When managers understand the informal organization groups within the department and know the leaders of the informal groups, delegating tasks and initiating change can be instituted in a way that is complemented by the informal group values.

2. *Complements the formal structure:* Generates flexibility and spontaneity that cuts across formal barriers to accomplish activities.

3. *Provides social stability:* Employees gain a sense of belonging and self-worth as part of an informal group; the group meets human needs and offers acceptance.

4. *Offers a channel of communication:* Experience can give managers the ability to use the informal grapevine to determine feelings and attitudes of employees on specific issues; informal leaders communicate information shared by the managers and offer feedback when positive controls are present.

Figure 12-4.   Positive Informal Group Factors

nizational change may be viewed as a threat to informal groups, managers can approach change with the informal group values and interests in mind. Although some role conflict assists in generating creative ideas, managers can defuse these possible aspects of negativism in advance of major change initiatives (Longest, 1990).

By integrating the interests of the informal groups with those of the formal departmental objectives, HIM managers can maintain a strong leadership role where understanding and acceptance are valued.

Leadership and Followership

Robert Kelley has authored a book on the flip side of leadership: *Followership-Leadership-Partnership* (1992). Dr. Kelley brings to our attention the total picture of one's role in a work setting. Explore the activities of several managers for a week and it quickly becomes evident that more time is spent being a follower of leaders up the organization than in leading those down the organization. Dr. Kelley suggests that more attention be paid to this **followership** role. He outlines six areas of outstanding skills exemplary followers have developed:

1. Attending to self-management
2. Caring and commitment
3. Building confidence
4. Learning how to contribute
5. Building credibility
6. Having a courageous conscience

Followers with these exemplary skills consider themselves as just having a different role than their leaders, not as inferiors. At the other end of the spectrum are people who are alienated as followers. They lack the team spirit that leads to developing the exemplary skills outlined above.

In the middle of the spectrum are the majority of followers, according to Dr. Kelley. These followers tend to let others do the thinking and planning for them. They also prefer to figure out which way the wind is blowing and then react accordingly.

Leaders, who have developed the leadership practices outlined earlier and have developed exemplary followership skills, will gain an understanding of their employees and predict their behavior. With this knowledge, they are positioned to encourage the exemplary followers, develop the mainstream and alienated followers, and motivate followers toward reaching full potential. Motivation is the focus of Chapter 13.

Summary

Leading is defined as the management function involved in motivating employees, directing others, resolving conflicts, and selecting effective communication channels. Understanding why humans behave as they do assists managers in this effort.

Leadership power is delegated by upper-level management. Through appropriate use of this power, HIM managers lead employees as they develop their personality traits through effort and practice.

The major predictors of behavior are attitudes, personality traits, and perceptions. Managers shape behavior by understanding these predictors and shaping behavior appropriately.

The team approach to organization design results in group behavior that is enhanced by empowerment and increased responsibility. Informal groups also exhibit behavior in the workplace with positive or negative elements.

Followership skills help managers understand employees and predict their behavior. As exemplary followers, HIM managers can assist employees in reaching their full potential.

Review Questions

1. Develop a profile of personality traits that an HIM professional beginning her own transcription firm would value.
2. Assess the attitudes of employees you have observed recently and categorize them into three attitudes as predictions of behavior.
3. Relate a personal experience with cognitive dissonance and the action you took to return to consistency perception.
4. Document the informal groups to which you belong and state the value you find in membership.
5. Identify three reinforcement tools of value to managers.

6. Describe how formal groups are structured in the workplace and how they differ from informal groups.

7. Give five behavioral steps in team building.

Field Practice Questions

1. Using the personality traits identified in this chapter, develop a list of the traits best adapted for various positions in an HIM work setting.

2. Interview two HIM professionals by asking questions about their skills in followership. Be prepared to discuss the results of this survey in class.

Case Study

Ann is employed as a file clerk in the health information services department at William Medical Center, an inner-city, unionized facility. Ann has worked as a file clerk in the department for several years. Prior to joining the record activity team, Ann had worked in several other departments of the hospital over the past 10 years. Ruth, Ann's mother, is a member of the board of trustees at William Medical Center.

The personnel file containing Ann's records includes a long history of disciplinary actions taken against her for issues including poor work performance, attendance irregularities, and unacceptable conduct. The informal grapevine reported previous supervisors of Ann had been subject to physical threats including telephone calls and being followed by a car filled with young men.

Because the disciplinary actions had failed to motivate Ann to improve her work performance, her team leader chose to ignore the problem and allow Ann to do whatever she liked. The team leader then left the department.

Marilyn was hired as team leader of the record activity team. As Marilyn reviewed the activities of the team members, she found that Ann's daily duties included pulling medical records for audits, filing records, and filing loose reports. Ann was also responsible for answering the telephone in the team's work area. During Marilyn's orientation to the department and her duties, Ann was on leave for a supposed back injury. This was one of her many workers' compensation leaves.

Marilyn and the team joined in an effort to develop performance standards for their team, and when Ann returned to work, the plan for production standards was explained to her and included the completion of a daily work log. Ann failed to submit the work log each day and Marilyn reviewed the plan with her again and specifically asked that the work log be submitted daily. As Marilyn reviewed Ann's work performance, several problems became evident:

1. The work log showed that records and loose reports had been filed; yet, several days later these items would be found hidden somewhere in the department.
2. Patient accounts complained that requested copies of records were not received; Ann stated she had sent them. They were not found and insurance reimbursement was in jeopardy.
3. Abuse of the telephone occurred frequently. Ann had many friends in and outside the hospital and used the team phone and phones outside the department during work time. One day a pizza delivery came for her when she was not scheduled for lunch or a break.
4. Responses to Marilyn's questions about an issue were verbalized in a loud voice that everyone in the department could hear. Ann stated she was given more work than anyone else in the department and did not think it was fair. She said that Marilyn and the department manager were singling her out.

The next step Marilyn chose was to interact with Ann at the beginning of the workday, try to motivate her, and verbally give her daily work assignments and review priorities. And, Marilyn asked that she continue completing the work log on a daily basis. In addition, Marilyn checked periodically on Ann's progress with her daily work assignment. Using leadership skills, Marilyn attempted to coach Ann toward increasing her productivity through positive reinforcement.

When the trial period for verbal daily assignments ended, Marilyn had to admit it failed to motivate Ann and her next step was to give Ann daily written work assignments. Marilyn retained a copy of the assignment sheet and monitored Ann's progress. Even this close monitoring and documentation was unsuccessful. For example, Ann neglected to copy records for patient accounts during a 1-week period, resulting in the billing loss of approximately $40,000. Each time errors were found, Marilyn documented the incident and forwarded a copy to Jim, the department manager.

(continued)

Documentation of these incidents was forwarded to hospital administration, who discussed the issue with Jim. Jim and Marilyn were asked at this point to tread lightly as Ann and Ruth, her mother, might cause trouble for the facility. Ruth had already visited top administration and voiced her opinion that Ann was being treated unfairly and threatened to sue the hospital. Ruth asked the administration to talk with Ann and made an appointment for her to do so.

Meanwhile, the human resources department offered limited support because of fear of repercussions from Ruth. Ann had already been suspended twice and a third suspension for another offense would result in dismissal.

Additionally, Marilyn began sensing dissatisfaction from the other team members because they were having to perform Ann's work when crises occurred. Some team members admitted they were thinking of transferring to another area of the hospital because of the problem (Courtesy of Robbyn Lessig).

1. Outline a plan of action for Marilyn and the team members that would change this team into a cohesive group.
2. Document theoretical reasons for your plan of action.

References

Byrne, J. (1992). Paradigms for postmodern managers: The accent is on adaptability. *Business Week*, October 23, p. 62.

Kelley, R. (1992). *Followership-leadership-partnership.* New York, N.Y.: Doubleday.

Longest, B. (1990). *Management practices for the health professional* (4th ed.). Norwalk, CT: Appleton & Lange.

Robbins, S. (1994). *Management* (4th ed.). Englewood Cliffs, NJ: Prentice Hall.

Rue, L., & Byars, L. (1986). *Management: Theory and application* (4th ed.). Homewood, IL: Richard D. Irwin.

Terry, G., & Franklin, S. (1982). *Principles of management* (8th ed.). Homewood, IL: Richard D. Irwin.

Wellins, R. (1991). *Empowered teams.* San Francisco: Jossey-Bass.

Zaleznik, A. (1992). Managers and leaders: Are they different? *Harvard Business Review*, March–April.

Suggested Readings

Donnelly, J., Gibson, J., & Ivancevich, J. (1987). *Fundamentals of management* (6th ed.). Plano, TX: Business Publications.

Dowell, S. (1992). President's message: Leadership logic. *Journal of AHIMA, 63* (3), 5.

Drucker, P. (1990). *Managing non-profit organizations.* New York: Truman Talley Books.

Easton, R. (1992). Reengineering health information management: The first steps. *Journal of AHIMA, 63* (6), 50–53.

Longest, B. *Management practices for the health professional* (4th ed.). Norwalk, CT: Appleton & Lange.

Martin, W. (1986). Are you a manager or a leader? *Journal of AMRA, 57* (6), 41–43.

Peters, T. (1991). *Thriving on chaos.* New York, N.Y.: Harper Collins.

Robbins, S. (1994). *Management* (4th ed.). Englewood Cliffs, NJ: Prentice Hall.

Rue, L., & Byars, L. (1986). *Management: Theory and application* (4th ed.). Homewood, IL: Richard D. Irwin.

Soltis, C. (1992). Managing by letting go . . . a team approach. *Journal of CHIA*, July, pp. 5–7.

Terry, G., & Franklin, S. (1982). *Principles of management* (8th ed.). Homewood, IL: Richard D. Irwin.

Wellins, R. (1991). *Empowered teams.* San Francisco: Jossey-Bass.

Chapter 13

Motivating for Leadership in the Health-Care Environment

Learning Objectives

After completing this chapter, the learner should be able to:

1. Compare Maslow's hierarchy of needs theory with Herzberg's two-factor theory by stating the major differences and similarities.
2. Give examples of the role that perception plays in motivating employees.
3. List motivating factors HIM managers can use for increasing productivity and morale in the workplace.
4. Describe the three major views of conflict and the differences among them.
5. Explain the role of the HIM manager in conflict resolution when self-directed teams perform departmental activities.
6. Suggest strategies for motivating difficult employees.
7. Define stress and suggest methods HIM managers can use to keep stressors from disrupting departmental activities.

Key Terms

Conflict	Motivation
Conflict resolution	Stress

Introduction

"Walk your talk" is not just a witty phrase for managerial inspiration. It can become a motivator for the manager who chooses to remind himself daily of the need to present a style that matches his beliefs (see Childs, 1993). Childs tells of a chief information officer (CIO) he has known, observed, and admired for some time. He comments on the AQ of his friend, the CIO. Yes, his AQ, or attitude quotient, not his IQ, or intelligence quotient.

Mr. Childs likened managerial attitude to the single-minded attitude of a runner. Just as a runner's attitude is crucial to winning a race, so commitment to a positive attitude shares no space with second thoughts or misgivings for managers. The CIO stated, "There are only two kinds of employees in this world: those that are for you and the goals of the business, and those that are against you or the project" (Childs, 1993).

The followers who are middle-of-the-roaders are unacceptable to this CIO also. He motivates them to become exemplary or weeds them out along with those who are against the goals. And, Mr. Childs states, this CIO walks his talk; he has successfully completed projects with three organizations and received nice promotions. He presents a superb attitude that attracts the best employees for his teams.

As Bill Childs's story suggests, the motivational task of leading is not easy; it takes racing energy. HIM professionals are challenged to create an environment that encourages effort while performing effectively. First, *motivation* is defined as the willingness to exert effort toward meeting goals to satisfy an individual need (Robbins, 1994). As this definition demonstrates, an unsatisfied need begins the drive toward the behavior—the effort—that will satisfy the need. The goals referred to here relate to the organizational goals of the work setting and an employee's need to satisfy these goals.

HIM leaders who develop motivational strategies and apply them consistently can see increased productivity, higher levels of quality, and creative solutions to team problems. This chapter explains how leaders can utilize motivational theories in developing strategies that will make a difference.

The last section of this chapter leads into a discussion of conflict and stress—factors that can thwart the best manager's efforts toward motivating the teams. Professional and highly skilled employees in health care are particularly susceptible to stressors that detract from goal attainment.

Motivational Content Theories

Since the early 1900s, when Frederick W. Taylor, considered the father of scientific management, increased productivity and earnings at Bethlehem Steel, researchers have explored motivational theories in the workplace. The findings have only emphasized the complexity of **motivational factors** facing leaders regardless of the activities. There is concensus that motivated behavior is goal directed. Taylor showed that the goal of increased earnings changed behavior (Robbins, 1994).

Later researchers focused on *what* motivates employees (content theories) and *how* the process takes place (process theories). To summarize their findings, the best motivator is a challenging position that offers advancement, growth, a feeling of achievement and responsibility, and earned recognition (Longest, 1990).

Maslow's Hierarchy of Needs Theory

Abraham Maslow's hierarchy of needs theory is among the best known of the motivation theories. He believed that within every human being needs exist in a hierarchical fashion. His pyramid of needs is as follows: (1) physiological, (2) safety, (3) social, (4) esteem, and (5) self-actualization. He stressed that the higher needs become dominant after the lower needs are satisfied (Longest, 1990). A graphic depiction of this hierarchy of needs is found in Figure 13-1.

The two major premises to Maslow's theory emphasize that (1) needs not yet fulfilled will motivate behavior, and (2) when one need is fulfilled, another emerges to be fulfilled. In truth, the needs in Maslow's hierarchy interact together within an individual and the lower needs recur again and again. Within this interaction it is found that people are motivated by what they seek more than by what they already possess. Also, a person's needs are not fully satisfied; new needs are generated through life's experiences (Robbins, 1994).

Developing situations in the HIM department that permit employees to satisfy their needs is the ongoing challenge for managers. To further complicate the picture, an action that may meet one employee's needs may not meet another's needs. This situation can lead to frustration for the employees and for the manager. Even more crucial, what will motivate the team as a whole may frustrate one or more of the team members. The fol-

Figure 13-1. Maslow's Hierarchy of Needs (From R. Edge, *Ethics of Health Care: A Guide for Clinical Practice.* Albany, NY: Delmar Publishers, 1994)

lowing practice example shares the experience of a leader facing such a frustration.

Practice Example

Pam, the HIM manager, had enjoyed the networking involved in developing a matrix team for the patient-focused unit reorganized recently. Two employees from the coding and reimbursement team were reassigned to the matrix team and spent most of their time on the unit. They were joined by an employee from admissions who had a coding background. The three of them were assigned responsibility for admissions, reimbursement screening, concurrent record completion, and coding. At the second meeting of the team with their managers, nursing team members suggested that care on the unit would be enhanced if the three team members rotated work hours so the early evening hours were covered. Since physicians are often on the unit during the late afternoon and evening, completing records and solving coding questions could be efficiently and effectively cared for by them. The three voiced negative feelings about a schedule change, so the HIM manager suggested that the proposal be put on hold until the next meeting, while those involved explored the various alternatives.

The cross-functional team and its success can be considered the "big picture" here. Pam and the admissions manager met to discuss the best approach for their upcoming meeting with the three team members. First, they reviewed their knowledge of the employees and discussed what would motivate them and satisfy their needs. They developed several options to offer at the meeting. Next, they made a decision to hold their options until the team members offered a plan.

At the meeting several team members presented a plan for rotating the schedule to ensure that a team member was on the unit with knowledge in record completion and coding during the evening hours. One of the team members offered to be crosstrained for these tasks and wanted evening hours twice weekly. It was a win-win situation since the other three employees were happy to rotate their work hours for the remaining shifts. The managers withheld their recommendations and commended the team for developing a resolution.   ■

Herzberg's Two-Factor Theory

The two-factor theory by Frederick Herzberg has been used frequently to explain job satisfaction and motivation. Despite criticisms of Herzberg's research methodology, his theories on job enrichment have been used widely. (Longest, 1990). According to Herzberg, the factors that lead employees toward job satisfaction are distinct from those leading to job dissatisfaction. He explained that employers who work toward eliminating the dissatisfactory *maintenance* factors may end dissatisfaction, but not necessarily motivate employees. Herzberg suggests emphasizing motivating factors. Figure 13-2 lists the maintenance and motivating factors promoted by Herzberg and his followers (Longest, 1990).

A review of the differences between the two sets of factors reveals that the maintenance factors tend to be related to the external environment of work whereas the motivating factors relate directly to the job itself and the person's performance. When compared to Maslow's hierarchy of needs, the two-factor theory shows similarities. A major difference is that Herzberg carried motivation into more detail, showing that it derives mostly from the work itself (Longest, 1990).

Maintenance Factors

1. Company policy and administration
2. Technical supervision
3. Interpersonal relations with supervisor
4. Interpersonal relations with peers
5. Interpersonal relations with subordinates
6. Salary
7. Job security
8. Personal life
9. Work conditions
10. Status

Motivational Factors

1. Achievement
2. Recognition
3. Advancement
4. The work itself
5. The possibility of personal growth
6. Responsibility

Figure 13-2. Herzberg's Maintenance and Motivating Factors (Robbins, 1994; Longest, 1990)

Now consider the process theories of motivation and how they can assist HIM managers in their motivational efforts. First is expectancy theory, developed by Victor Vroom. It states that an individual will exert effort at a certain level to achieve the performance that will result in attractive rewards. Three primary variables surface as follows:

1. *Choice:* the degree to which an employee perceives he or she can select from different performance behaviors; the individual has freedom.
2. *Expectancy:* the degree to which an employee believes that a particular behavior will lead to success.
3. *Preferences:* the value or importance an employee attaches to potential outcomes or rewards (Donnelly, Gibson, and Ivancevich, 1987).

The vital role that perception plays in motivating employees is emphasized in expectancy theory. The importance of perceptual differences among employees is emphasized in this theory, which then gives importance to selecting employees with not only skills and abilities for specific activities but also motivational factors. Of course, once the team is in place, the manager has the opportunity to offer leadership support and encouragement by utilizing the leadership practices outlined in Chapter 12.

Since people do not work in a vacuum, equity theories have been developed to address motivation in terms of whether an employee perceives the reward he is receiving for his effort is fair. Three referents are suggested by J. Stacey Adams. He suggests employees compare their reward with others, with the system, and with their own past experiences (Longest, 1990).

To illustrate, an HIM professional has exerted great effort in leading his employees toward thinking of data and information as resources the department makes available to its customers. A new software system was installed that required extra effort from an employee, who perceived his programming skills were of value in fine-tuning the system. Suddenly, he surprised the HIM professional and his fellow employees when he angrily announced his resignation. The catalyst? He discovered the programmers in the information systems department were making significantly more than his salary.

Seldom, however, is the equity theory seen in isolation. The motivation theories discussed in this chapter cannot be viewed independently. The underlying ideas are complementary, and only by integrating them together does the full picture emerge. HIM managers can have the insight to use the very best option for the specific situation. To review, predicting employee behavior assists HIM leaders in reaching objectives; thus, taking an active role in motivating that behavior is important. By integrating motivation theories into a knowledge base and by reviewing new research studies on motivation as they come into print, HIM professionals can take advantage of the benefits offered by motivation theories.

Integrating Motivation Theories

By now, the high priority that needs to be given to the human side of management should be evident. And, motivation strategy is the catalyst leading to results. Over time, satisfied, productive employees cannot be legislated, manipulated, mandated, or ordered. Each individual has unique, specific motivators operating within her value system. Managers can unlock this potential by following the leadership practices discussed in Chapter 12, especially those relating to participative management, such as self-directed teams and motivational theories. Some specific contemporary recommendations for motivating employees are listed in Figure 13-3.

It is risky for managers to suppose their personal work motivators can be transferred to employees and will predict productive behavior on the part of the total team. Each team member has strengths, weaknesses, and behavior patterns that influence motivation factors. Only by asking questions and listening can managers become acquainted with these factors. By encouraging employees to visualize the benefits and rewards of a productive team, the desire to achieve will grow. So too will the satisfaction when success follows the participative effort and the benefits are realized.

---

1. Offer challenging positions that lead to a feeling of achievement. Employees must perceive the position is challenging.
2. Outline in clear language the objectives and purposes for the task. Be sure your understanding is clear before sharing with employees.
3. Match the needs and wants of the employee with the interests of the department and assign work accordingly. Empathize with employees, especially during the training period.
4. Ensure that objectives are perceived as attainable and that increased efforts will lead to rewards.
5. Remove any obstacles between the employee and the task; see that equipment and other tools are workable; ensure adequate work area; ensure adequate training period.
6. Individualize rewards and link them to performance.
7. Use communication techniques, especially the listening skills. Share the "big picture" frequently.
8. Develop each team member's potential while coordinating teamwork among the group. Plan growth for individual employees, but only when it is in the best interest of the entire team.
9. Check for equity in the system periodically. Adding this task to the budget process ensures it is updated on a schedule.

Figure 13-3.   Recommendations for Motivating Employees

The majority of people continue to enjoy opportunities to be creative and imaginative. When tangible and measurable benefits are also derived, the motivation level increases. There is an impetus toward greater interest in continuing and accelerating the process even further. An added benefit is the carryover of enthusiasm to other employees and departments. The groundwork is then laid to increase the momentum of enthusiasm and motivation.

Managing Conflict and Stress

Managing **conflict** is one of the most important skills that leaders can possess. Results of research studies by John Graves (1989) showed that the leadership skill most positively related to managerial success was that of handling conflict. Conflict is defined as the perceived incompatible differences between parties that result in interference or opposition (Robbins, 1994). The term *perceived* is used to emphasize that whether or not the differences are real is irrelevant; the manager must respond to the conflict.

Figure 13-4 explains three differing views of conflict in organizations that have evolved over time. Because of the complexity of health-care orga-

---

1. *Traditional view:* Conflict is destructive and managers should work toward eliminating conflict from the organization.

2. *Human relations view:* Conflict is inevitable and a natural consequence of human interaction in organizations. Humanist philosophers observed that conflict can be a positive force for organizational performance.

3. *Interactionist view:* Some conflict is necessary for survival of organizations. Lack of conflict can result in inadequate decisions and stagnant thinking. This current view encourages a minimum level of conflict to keep teams viable and self-critical. Creativity is perceived as a response to conflict.

    a. *Functional conflict:* conflicts that are constructive and support the goals of an organization.

    b. *Dysfunctional conflict:* conflicts that result in destructive behavior and prevent organizations from achieving goals.

Figure 13-4.   Views of Conflict (Longest, 1990)

nizations, and the diversity of the employees and staff, conflict is fairly high and sometimes breaks over into public view through news media (Longest, 1990). HIM managers find the skills for conflict resolution are among the most valuable assets they can possess.

Functional and Dysfunctional Conflict

As difficulties arise in interpersonal relationships, HIM managers are challenged with deciding whether a conflict falls into the functional or dysfunctional category. A healthy disagreement over the objectives being prioritized for a team can lead to discussions that offer additional alternatives in the decision-making process. In this way, conflict can be a positive force in the department. On the other hand, if the team members have an underlying personal conflict that has erupted during objective-setting meetings, the destructive forces could delay action (Robbins, 1994).

A functional conflict may arise when the coding technicians from the clinical data management team are under pressure to have records coded within 3 days of discharge and the patient-focused care center team desires to hold discharged records an extra 24 hours for a project. This conflict is relatively independent of the individuals involved, so personal conflict can be at a minimum. This allows the managers to focus on the conflict and its resolution rather than on personality differences.

Conflict Resolution

Managers respond to conflicts by assessing the situation first, determining whether to intervene, and then taking appropriate steps for conflict resolution. Not every conflict situation can be resolved effectively, but, by following the steps outlined in Figure 13-5, HIM managers can develop effective conflict resolution skills.

Guidelines that are helpful during **conflict resolution** include (1) avoidance of personal attacks or sarcastic comments, (2) no interrupting other participants, and (3) use of specific examples. It is the manager who sets the tone of the meeting, builds rapport, and establishes an atmosphere of respect and willingness to compromise. As a facilitator or mediator, the manager assures that all participants have shared their feelings and understand the issues. By emphasizing areas of agreement first, the manager can gradually lead into the difficult issues and work toward a win-win situation when feasible (Cecil, 1994).

1. Take time to review the issue and past actions before making the decision to intervene. Understand the participants, their values, personalities, and resources. Assess the true source of the conflict, categorized as follows:

   a. *Communication differences:* Misunderstandings and cultural differences can create communication difficulties. However, personalities and value system differences may be creating the communication problem.

   b. *Structural differences:* Conflict over objectives, alternatives in procedures, and performance criteria are rooted in the structure of the organization itself. The root problem could be ambiguous policies, position descriptions, and procedures.

   c. *Personal differences:* Chemistry between the participants can cause conflict.

2. Understand your preferred style for conflict resolution. Contingency management calls for action in response to the review in step 1 and may call for changing your preferred style in a specific situation.

3. Choose whether to intervene and to what extent. Delegating discipline to self-directed teams can lead managers to serve as referees and not interfere with the team's responsibility to resolve the conflict. By keeping the participants focused on the issues, the manager acts as the facilitator in conflict resolution.

4. Know conflict-resolution options and choose among them, either as a direct participant or as a facilitator.

   a. *Accommodation:* Encourage participants to place another individual's concerns and needs above their own.

   b. *Force:* Use when quick action is demanded; one participant's needs are satisfied at the expense of the other.

   c. *Compromise:* Encourage each participant to relinquish something of value. This is effective when a temporary solution is needed while the problem is reviewed for a permanent solution.

   d. *Collaboration:* Win-win solution where all participants gain advantage; time-consuming resolution as alternatives are reviewed.

   e. *Avoidance:* Conflict may be trivial or emotions are high and a cooling-off period is needed; also of value when insufficient information makes open discussion of minimal value. Future date for discussion should be scheduled.

Figure 13-5.   Steps toward Conflict Resolution (Robbins, 1994; Cecil, 1994)

Managing Difficult People Amid Conflicts

Personality conflicts seem to follow some employees, and managers skilled in conflict resolution understand the need to evaluate situations involving these employees and take action. Negative team members can erode morale and disrupt the effectiveness of the team. Connie Podesta, of Communicare in Mandeville, Louisiana, offers several suggestions for managers of these difficult people:

1. Be assertive and positive. Use short answers in response to negative comments or questions.

2. Give choices; ask them to be part of the team and perform their tasks. Complaining is not a choice.

3. Refuse to listen to gossip—from the negative employees or others; bring the individual who is the subject of the gossip into the discussion of the problem.

4. Empower the team and challenge negative team members with job enrichment activities.

5. Use an anonymous questionnaire to solicit information from each team member.

6. Take a tough line with difficult people; do not allow them to dominate the team. Be a tough facilitator in conflict resolution (Scott, 1993).

Managers may need to document unacceptable behavior for the personnel file, which can help employees recognize how disturbing negative behavior is to the team and the department. Specific examples of the behavior need to be a part of the documentation.

Jill Sherer (1994) writes of the broader use that managers are making of the conflict resolution and negotiation skills, which can combat complex contemporary problems. Examples included are in dealing with vendors, third-party payers, and customer complaints (Sherer, 1994).

Managing Stress

Stress has both positive and negative aspects in an organization and can contribute to productivity of the teams and the HIM department as a whole. A formal definition of stress can be stated as a dynamic condition in which an individual is confronted with opportunities, constraints, or demands related to something desirable but perceived as unattainable (Robbins, 1994).

Employees who have a desire to earn a promotion will have stress before a performance review. However, when employees have the abilities outlined in a position description, are capable of performing well, and have a high level of self-esteem, the stress is lessened.

Another stress factor is the personality trait of employees. Studies show that type A personalities have higher levels of stress under the same conditions compared to type B personalities. Type A personalities have a sense of urgency and strong competitive drive. In contrast, type B personalities tend to be relaxed and noncompetitive. Understanding these differences in personalities helps HIM managers respond to symptoms of stress (Robbins, 1994).

Employee counseling through the human resources department is one alternative when employees exhibit dysfunctional symptoms of stress. Biofeedback, exercise, proper diet, and relaxation techniques are strategies for reducing stress and avoiding burnout.

In *Working Woman*, Kathryn Stechert (1988) offers several suggestions for lowering stress to acceptable levels:

1. Avoid work overload—this includes too much work, too little time to perform tasks, having necessary skills for the position, and having the tools to perform effectively.

2. Make it possible for people to succeed and then let them know they are doing a good job.

3. Give employees a sense of involvement and control by empowering them in decision making.

4. Offer employees information and feedback. Let them know what is happening in the department and the facility. Let them know how they are performing on a routine basis.

5. Admit mistakes honestly and grow from them.

In a study of health information management directors as reported in the *Journal of AMRA* in 1989, role overload was discovered to create the highest levels of stress. Role overload means that the directors had the skill and capability of performing the responsibilities given them, but the sheer volume of the demands and the limited time frame for accomplishing the tasks created stress (Floreani and Burke, 1989).

Summary

Motivation content theories include Maslow's hierarchy of needs and Herzberg's two-factor theory. These theories emphasize the complex nature of motivation.

Victor Vroom developed a process theory called expectancy. This theory states employees are motivated by choice, expectancy, and preferences. Each of these relates to the perception employees have about the work environment.

Recommendations for motivating HIM department employees include (1) challenging positions with clear objectives, (2) matching needs and wants of employees with the tasks, (3) ensuring that objectives are attainable and rewards are given for increased effort, (4) removing obstacles to success in performance and checking for equity in the system, (5) communicating effectively, and (6) developing employees to their potential in a coordinated team effort.

Managing conflict is a major leader's task. The current view of conflict is interactionist, where conflict is considered necessary and to be encouraged at a minimum level to keep teams viable and self-critical. Functional conflict occurs when teams have conflicting priorities and may be resolved without the personal chemistry difference prevalent in dysfunctional conflicts.

Stress is a dynamic condition that confronts employees when opportunities, constraints, or demands related to something desirable are perceived as unattainable. HIM managers can reduce their stress and the stress in the workplace by avoiding work overload and allowing people to succeed with a sense of involvement and control. In the complex health-care environment, managers of health information may have role overload from the sheer volume of demands placed upon them.

Review Questions

1. Identify two major motivational theories and contrast their premises.
2. Choose two contemporary motivating factors that especially appeal to you and give reasons for their value in the workplace.
3. Explain how managers respond to functional conflicts versus dysfunctional conflicts.

4. List four steps that lead to conflict resolution.

5. Offer five options managers have for lowering stress in their activities.

Field Practice Questions

1. Read through the following list of 16 factors people have indicated are motivators for them. Now go back through them and choose 5 that are the very best motivators for you personally. Check them off and then share your list with a small group in class. Choose a spokesperson and a recorder for your group. List the number of motivators used by members of your group and then defend why those you choose take priority for you over others. When class reconvenes, have the spokesperson summarize the findings of the group with the entire class.

   What motivates you?
   a. Opportunity for promotion
   b. Pay increase for increased effort
   c. Job security
   d. Respect for me and my ideas
   e. Work with a competent manager
   f. Excellent job benefits
   g. Good working conditions
   h. Responsibility and a degree of independence in how my work is accomplished
   i. Compliments from managers when work is good
   j. Knowledge of what is going on in the facility
   k. Opportunity for personal growth
   l. A sense that the work I perform has value to managers and the facility
   m. Work under close supervision
   n. Opportunity to perform interesting tasks
   o. Opportunity to know that my pay is the same as others doing comparable work, both in the facility and in the community
   p. Getting along with fellow team members and others in the facility

2. Document the negative activities you have observed in a health-care setting and then offer suggestions for setting behavioral limits and creating a positive atmosphere.

3. Give examples in your experience where perceptions about another person were unfounded.

References

Childs, B. (1993). AQs and racing to win. *Healthcare Informatics*, January, p. 6.

Cecil, C. (1994). Talking through trouble. *Advance for Health Information Professionals*, 4 (9), 10.

Donnelly, J., Gibson, J., & Ivancevich, J. (1987). *Fundamentals of management* (6th ed.). Plano, TX: Business Publications.

Floreani, W., & Burke, G., III (1989). Role stress and job satisfaction among directors of medical record departments. *Journal of AMRA*, 60 (1), 37.

Graves, J. (1989). Successful management and organizational mugging. *New Directions in Human Resource Management*. Englewood Cliffs, NJ: Prentice Hall.

Longest, B. (1990). *Management practices for the health professional* (4th ed.). Norwalk, CT: Appleton & Lange.

Robbins, S. (1994). *Management* (4th ed.). Englewood Cliffs, NJ: Prentice Hall.

Scott, F. (1993). Empowerment: The secret to staff motivation. *Advance for Health Information Professionals*, 3 (21), 22.

Sherer, J. (1994). Resolving conflict (the right way). *Hospitals and Health Networks*, April 20, p. 55.

Stechert, K. (1988). Your best defense against office stress. *Working Woman*, August, pp. 61–64.

Suggested Readings

Bassett, L. (1992). How motivation defines productivity. *Topics in Health Record Management*, 13 (2), 65.

Cecil, C. (1994). Talking through trouble. *Advance for Health Information Professionals*, 4 (9), 10.

Childs, B. (1993). AQs and racing to win. *Healthcare Informatics*, January, p. 6.

Davidhizar, R. (1994). Every department has a Cliff Clavin. *Advance for Health Information Professionals*, 4 (17), 25.

Davidhizar, R. (1994). A negative attitude can be deadly. *Advance for Health Information Professionals*, 4 (14), 27.

Donnelly, J., Gibson, J., & Ivancevich, J. (1987). *Fundamentals of management* (6th ed.). Plano, TX: Business Publications.

Drucker, P. (1990). *Managing non-profit organizations.* New York: Truman Talley Books.

Edge, R. (1994). *Ethics of health care: A guide for clinical practice.* Albany, NY: Delmar Publshers.

Floreani, W., & Burke, G., III. (1989). Role stress and job satisfaction among directors of medical record departments. *Journal of AMRA, 60* (1), 34–39.

Longest, B. (1990). *Management practices for the health professional* (4th ed.). Norwalk, CT: Appleton & Lange.

Rees, R. (1995). The new work of management or is it coaching, facilitating, or mentoring? *Journal of AHIMA, 66* (7), 50–51.

Robbins, S. (1994). *Management* (4th ed.). Englewood Cliffs, NJ: Prentice Hall.

Rue, L., & Byars, L. (1986). *Management: Theory and application* (4th ed.). Homewood, IL: Richard D. Irwin.

Scott, F. (1993). Empowerment: The secret to staff motivation. *Advance for Health Information Professionals, 3* (21), 22.

Sherer, J. (1994). Resolving conflict (the right way). *Hospitals and Health Networks,* April 20, pp. 52–55.

Soltis, C. (1992). Managing by letting go . . . a team approach. *Journal of CHIA,* July, pp. 5–7.

Stechert, K. (1988). Your best defense against office stress. *Working Woman,* August, pp. 60–68.

Terry, G., & Franklin, S. (1982). *Principles of management* (8th ed.). Homewood, IL: Richard D. Irwin.

To solve staff conflict, ferret out the causes and aim for prevention (1992). *Medical Office Manager,* December, pp. 11, 12.

Chapter 14

Communicating in the Health-Care Environment

Learning Objectives

After completing this chapter, the learner should be able to:

1. Describe the process of communication as the message flows from the sender to the receiver.
2. List several barriers to effective communication and steps managers can take to reduce these barriers.
3. Create the outline for a training session involving a new process in the HIM department.
4. Develop and document a speech for an in-service education meeting.
5. Suggest positive uses for the grapevine communication network.
6. Describe the use of communication skills when interacting with HIM department customers.

Key Terms

Channel	Feedback
Communication	Grapevine
Decoding	Message
Encoding	Noise

Introduction

Ideas, policies, reports, requests, visions—these managerial items are communicated up, down, and across a facility's channels as necessary communicating functions of leaders. It is too often assumed that senders of information and receivers of that information understand one another through these **communications**. Since understanding is the key to communicating, its definition can best be stated as the transferring and understanding of meanings (Robbins, 1994).

Communicating involves the mental, psychological, and emotional characteristics of both individuals. Further, communicating is undertaken in various mediums and the technical characteristics of the medium used is also involved in the process.

The process of communicating is the first focus of this chapter; then, since the leading function is especially dependent on communication, group dynamics and leading are discussed. Communicating with the customers using HIM information is covered in the final section. Practice examples showing effective communication are included as are those where barriers prevented communication from flowing freely.

The Process of Communication

Managers use several media or channels for communicating. These include oral interaction, written communications, nonverbal communications, and electronic media. In the process, the purpose for the communication or the **message** passes from the sender to the receiver. It is converted to symbolic form called **encoding**. Figure 14-1 traces the path of the message through the medium or **channel**, through decoding, to the receiver. Thus, an HIM manager conveys her message through this process.

As Figure 14-1 depicts, the employee sends a message by feedback to the manager. But, throughout the process, lightning bolts depict the **noise** that can create barriers to effective communication. These barriers may be illegible writing, garbled speech, telephone static, inattention, cultural differences, attitudes, or knowledge. Nonverbal communication such as tone of voice and body language also creates barriers (Robbins, 1994).

Figure 14-2 describes the communication process steps in greater detail.

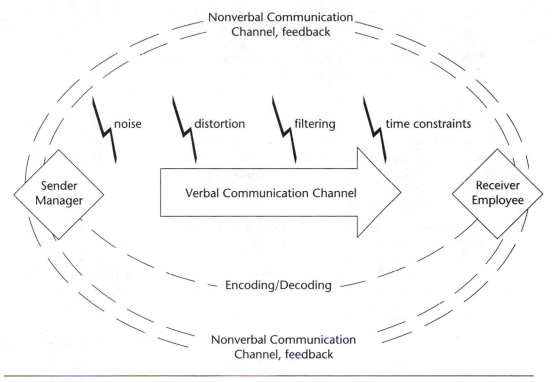

Figure 14-1.   Communication Model

Barriers in the Communication Process

Distortion is possible at any step of the communication process through the noise factors that occur. But, there are other barriers as well, such as filters, selective perception, time constraints, language, emotions, and nonverbal cues.

Filtering

By manipulating information, the sender can make the message appear more favorable to the receiver. This may be more common as information flows upward in an organization, but can also occur when upper-level management sends a message downward through several levels. Organizational culture can discourage filtering by rewarding openness (Robbins, 1994).

Step 1: Source or sender

Managers, nonmanagers, and nonpersonal entities such as the department or the facility itself are all sources of communication.

Step 2: Encoding

The communicator or sender chooses the medium for transmitting the information. The encoding is the mental wrapping of the message. The sender's goal is to select the best medium for the receiver. When the message is sent to multiple receivers, with differing noise levels, complexity increases.

Step 3: Message and channel

The physical transmission of the conceptualized message takes place. The message is what the sender hopes to communicate. The carrier of the message can be face-to-face communications, written communications, telephone, group meetings, electronic mail, policy statements, or memos. Also, there can be nonverbal media such as facial expressions, tone of voice, and body language.

Step 4: Decoding process

Decoding is a technical term relating to the thought processes of the receiver, or the interpretation of the encoded message.

Step 5: Receiver

The sender has the receiver in mind when the message is sent; communication is receiver oriented.

Step 6: Feedback

The feedback loop is important in the communication process. One-way communication has the potential for distortion. **Feedback** may be direct, such as face-to-face response, or indirect, such as increased absenteeism. And, noise can be a barrier to feedback communication.

Figure 14-2.   Steps in the Communication Process (Terry and Franklin, 1982)

Selective Perception

Past experiences, expectations, motivations, and other personal characteristics distort the perception of messages. For example, an HIM team leader interviewing a prospective coder may expect the person to put family problems ahead of work responsibilities when the prospective coder begins discussing her husband's health problems. The team leader has this expectation, having recently reprimanded a coder who was habitually late because of family illness (Donnelly, Gibson, and Ivancevich, 1987).

Time Constraints

Short circuiting occurs when time pressures do not allow every team member to be a part of the communication process. Time pressures also cause distorted perceptions when the receiver rushes through the decoding process (Donnelly, Gibson, and Ivancevich, 1987).

Language

Differences in word meanings create major barriers to communication, especially when age, education, and cultural differences are present. In health-care settings, technical jargon is commonplace and can distort communication because the sender may not be aware of modifications made to word meanings by the receiver (Robbins, 1994).

Emotions

Feelings enter into how an individual receives a message; managers can avoid some distortions by considering how employees, in general, feel at certain times, such as during the afternoon hours at the end of the work-week, or the week before a major holiday.

Nonverbal Cues

When nonverbal cues are inconsistent with oral communication, confusion results and the intent of the message becomes distorted. For example, when the HIM manager invites a team leader to have a chair while explaining a changed procedure, and then goes through the day's mail while listening, inconsistency reigns (Robbins, 1994).

Overcoming Barriers in Communication

The list of barriers to communication seem formidable, but the following steps can make the process effective: utilize feedback skills, empathy, listening skills, and language simplification.

Feedback Skills

By asking questions relating to the communication, managers can lessen misunderstandings. The questions should include more than "yes" and "no" answers and should be specific to the intended communication (Robbins, 1994).

Empathy Skills

By becoming receiver oriented, managers can anticipate how a message is likely to be decoded and respond accordingly. When the education or culture gap is great, empathy is a very important tool for effective communication (Donnelly, Gibson, and Ivancevich, 1987).

Listening Skills

Listening is difficult, but managers who develop active listening skills enhance their communication ability. Active listening is defined as listening for full meaning without making premature judgments or interpretations (Robbins, 1994).

Language Simplification

Using appropriate language for the receiver is one way managers can facilitate understanding. Jargon is acceptable when the audience understands the meaning. Regardless of the channel used for communicating, the language used should be clear and concise (Robbins, 1994).

Dru Scott, of Dru Scott Associates based in San Francisco, encourages managers to review the language they use and determine whether it could be perceived as cold and callous. Scott reports that managers sometimes fail because of how they say things. There is a "language of teamwork" that involves phrasing sentences toward consideration, conscientiousness, and positive requests. By making subtle changes in the spoken language and by showing empathy through body language, Dr. Scott reports finding increased cooperation and productivity (Breske, 1993).

Managers Who Make a Difference

Communicating effectively throughout the hospital when planned changes could impact departments outside health information services challenged Karen Darnell at Redlands Community Hospital in California. As manager of the department, Karen had developed, with her management team, the plans for remodeling their physical environment. Once the remodeling plan was developed, approved, and the time line for each major step in the process completed, Karen informed departments in close proximity to Health Information Services about the construction that would take place and the dates involved in specific activities.

Just when Karen and the management team were commending themselves for the planning that was right on schedule, an unexpected noise factor erupted. The noise factor did not relate to barriers in communicating, for Karen had communicated the plans very well. Rather, the noise was a jackhammer tearing up a cement slab under the old filing system. Up in the newborn intensive-care unit, was a baby whose blood pressure went up as the noise and vibration of the jackhammer reached into departments in the vicinity. The director of the unit (DOU) communicated with Karen and a problem-solving meeting was called while the jackhammers were silenced. The decision? Construction was put on hold, team leaders encouraged the employees to perform tasks with inconvenience for a longer time than planned, and the construction team went to work elsewhere.

The baby stabilized in a week, then it took another week to reschedule the construction team, and the perfect plans were back on track after a 2-week delay. Karen again communicated to everyone affected that remodeling was again under way.

Another noise factor problem erupted. The DOU of an adult unit called Karen to say that the jackhammer was bothering one of their patients. Karen again interacted with the direct patient caregivers and found that the noise was loudest in this patient's room. The solution this time was to transfer the patient to a room where the noise was not a factor. The construction continued and was completed without further incident.

In a critique session of the remodeling project, the question was raised, "Is the health or convenience of any single patient more important than completing a project?" Karen responded, "The jackhammer caused a significant risk to the health of the baby and so the project was halted. We did not believe that the noise caused risk to the adult patient and so arranged for a move, which made the patient happy and the work continued."

(continued)

In a final communication to other departments at the end of the project, Karen and her team expressed appreciation for their patience and flexibility during the construction. The note then invited them to an open house to visually enjoy the changes and share in the enthusiasm expressed by the employees.

Group Dynamics and Leading

Attending and participating in meetings is one of the responsibilities HIM managers have in health-care facilities. For some managers, the hours in meetings take their toll and this drain provides the impetus for creating meetings where agendas are prepared and distributed beforehand, and other steps are taken to keep meetings short. Committee meeting agendas, minutes, and steps that increase the likelihood of effective meetings are discussed in Chapter 18. This section focuses on meetings held for training sessions and in-service seminars.

Training Sessions and In-Service Seminars

Planning a training session to introduce new techniques or processes in the department gives HIM managers an opportunity to develop meetings with a specific focus. Because of the specific focus and the interest of the team members in learning how to perform new tasks, training sessions are among the easiest types of meetings to plan. However, even though the training materials seem straightforward and the participants will be interested, leaders should prepare the presentation with care, document what they hope to accomplish, and follow public speaking guidelines.

In-service seminar planning needs the same attention to details; however, guest speakers can be invited to speak on topics of interest. Encouraging the employees to offer ideas for in-service seminars can create interest in a current topic. LaNelle Walters, assistant director of medical records at Wadley Regional Medical Center in Texarkana, Texas, reported in *Medical Records Briefing* on her success with this shared responsibility.

When asked to participate, the employees chose motivation as a topic of interest. Walters reports a consultant was invited to come and speak. The employees planned for two back-to-back sessions so everyone could attend (Cofer, 1992).

Both training sessions and in-service seminars need to be held periodically and documented for accrediting or licensing agencies. Making them interesting and informative for the participants gives HIM professionals experience in planning meetings and in public speaking. Chapter 18 discusses communicating effectively through committee meetings and department meetings.

Budget allocations for training and in-service education can reach significant proportions. Barb Jamnick suggested in *Advance for Health Information Professionals* that the cost can reach 20 percent of the department's budget (Jamnick, 1993). Creative ways can be used to keep the costs reasonable. For example, employees can be invited to suggest health-care professionals within the facility or community as guest speakers. Suggestions could include:

1. Physical therapist to discuss proper lifting techniques and back injury prevention.
2. Telecommunications specialist to speak on courtesy and etiquette in telephone communications.
3. Vendor representatives with information to share on an emerging technology.
4. HIM professionals in the community with expertise in a specialty.
5. Physicians with specialty knowledge; a shared seminar with other departments may be more efficient, because of time constraints for most physicians.

Teleconferences and videos are also excellent tools for sharing up-to-date information. As employees become involved in the planning of seminars, they can become enthusiastic about learning new ideas, new technologies, and medical science. Another benefit is that change becomes a pattern of thought as team members visualize possibilities that are open to them.

Grapevine Communications

Informal social groups have a communication network that is referred to as the **grapevine**. Even the health-care facility that boasts excellent communication tools through formal structural lines is unable to disclose all the information that is available on the grapevine. Managers can use the grapevine to advantage, as already mentioned; however, distortions can lead to false conclusions and bad decisions, so care must be taken. The grapevine is best used as a barometer of opinions, attitudes, and concerns. Managers must develop a formal strategy for effectively communicating with teams on a continuing basis, for "communication is an ongoing process, not a one-time campaign" admonishes George Pozgar of Smithtown, New York in *The Health Care Supervisor* (Pozgar, 1986).

Pozgar encourages health-care managers to keep policies, job descriptions, and employee handbooks up to date and available. Further, he promotes disseminating information in periodic departmental meetings, in newsletters, payroll inserts, and bulletin boards in a timely manner. He is also concerned that new employees receive a detailed orientation to the facility and that training programs be held frequently. Through these efforts, both the informal and formal lines of communication can work effectively, carrying information suitable for each (Pozgar, 1986).

Communicating with Customers

The customers of HIM departments expect excellence in service as their information needs are met. These expectations are enhanced when effective communication is practiced by managers and team members.

Theresa Evans of Fishermen's Hospital in Marathon, Florida, reached out in an effort to increase dialogue with medical staff office managers. She developed quarterly luncheons where face-to-face communication could occur, and found that through this effort conflicts were resolved. By stretching her communication skills in facilitating meetings and then in public speaking, Evans created an environment of openness and trust between her department and the medical staff office managers (Evans, 1994).

Summary

The process of communicating effectively offers managers opportunity for success. The process travels in steps from the sender, where encoding takes place and selection of the channel or medium for transmission is made. The channel may be face-to-face communications, written communications, telephone, group meetings, or electronic mail. Nonverbal media also communicates. As the message reaches the receiver, it is decoded or interpreted and then feedback completes the loop.

Noise such as filters, selective perception, time constraints, language, and emotions can be barriers to effective communication. Managers can overcome these barriers by being aware of them and utilizing feedback, empathy, listening skills, and language simplification.

Managers communicate through leading in training sessions and in-service seminars. Through careful planning, HIM professionals can enthuse employees and assist in their learning process through periodic meetings.

The grapevine is a communication network involving informal social groups. This network cannot be eradicated and managers can use it to advantage for communication. There are frequent distortions in messages on the grapevine, which must be expected. By keeping documentation updated and using effective communication skills, HIM leaders can employ both formal and informal lines of communication to advantage.

Being of service to HIM customers includes excellence in communication skills. Conflict resolution takes place as communication is increased. Teams within the department also benefit from effective communication when their activities are dependent on one another.

Review Questions

1. Answer "yes" or "no" to the following communication questions; be prepared to discuss them in class.
   a. I choose to use face-to-face communication when talking with a friend about a sensitive topic.
   b. My writing is clear, reasonably concise, and free of cliches.
   c. When I am talking with other people, I am an active listener by keeping their points of view in mind without being judgmental.

      d. When I am talking with others about problems or opinions, I listen and ask questions, rather than offer lectures.

      e. I keep alert for nonverbal communication when interacting with others.

      f. I ask my friends for feedback on my communication skills.

      g. I keep my eyes on the speaker as much as I can.

      h. I use open-ended questions that encourage another person to share more freely.

      i. I let the other person finish her own sentence, even when pauses seem quite lengthy.

2. Outline six steps in communicating and describe each step briefly.

3. Explain how the communication process can be distorted by barriers.

4. What are the major disadvantages to grapevine communications?

Field Practice Question

1. Prepare an outline for an in-service education talk on a topic of your choice.

References

Breske, S. (1993). Communication is key to being a good supervisor. *Advance for Health Information Professionals*, 3 (25), 10.

Cofer, J. (1992). Motivational speaker adds spark to monthly inservices. *Medical Records Briefing*, December, p. 12.

Donnelly, J., Gibson, J., & Ivancevich, J. (1987). *Fundamentals of management* (6th ed.). Plano, TX: Business Publications.

Evans, T. (1994). Solving a locum tenens credentialing problem. *For the Record*, 6 (11), 9.

Jamnick, B. (1993). 52 ways to educate your employees in 1993. *Advance for Health Information Professionals*, 3 (1), 6.

Pozgar, G. (1986). On the grapevine. *Health Care Supervisor*, January, pp. 40, 41.

Robbins, S. (1994). *Management* (4th ed.). Englewood Cliffs, NJ: Prentice Hall.

Terry, G., & Franklin, S. (1982). *Principles of management* (8th ed.). Homewood, IL: Richard D. Irwin.

Suggested Readings

Breske, S. (1993). Communication is key to being a good supervisor. *Advance for Health Information Professionals, 3* (25), 10.

Donnelly, J., Gibson, J. & Ivancevich, J., (1987). *Fundamentals of management* (6th ed.). Plano, TX: Business Publications.

Hamlin, S. (1990). *How to talk so people listen: The real key to job success.* New York: Harper and Row.

Jamnick, B. (1993). 52 ways to educate your employees in 1993. *Advance for Health Information Professionals, 3* (1), 6.

Longest, B. (1990). *Management practices for the health professional* (4th ed.). Norwalk, CT: Appleton & Lange.

Miller, C. (1992). Physicians need your help. *Journal of AHIMA, 63* (9), 37, 38.

Robbins, S. (1994) *Management* (4th ed.). Englewood Cliffs, NJ: Prentice Hall.

Rue, L., & Byars, L. (1986). *Management: Theory and application* (4th ed.). Homewood, IL: Richard D. Irwin.

Terry, G., & Franklin, S. (1982) *Principles of management* (8th ed.). Homewood, IL: Richard D. Irwin.

Controlling to Meet the Information Needs of Health-Care Facilities

Chapter 15

The Focus of Control in Health Information Management

Learning Objectives

After completing this chapter, the learner should be able to:

1. Define controlling and explain the relationship to the other management functions.
2. Describe ways management information systems (MIS) assist HIM managers in quality improvement (QI) activities.
3. List the four major steps involved in the control process.
4. Give several methods managers can use to obtain subjective monitoring information.
5. Identify steps that will ensure integrated information systems for obtaining valid monitoring data.

Key Terms

Integrated systems
Monitoring
Performance improvement (PI)
Total quality management (TQM)
Work transformation

Introduction

The controlling function of management is the final link in the managerial chain. Not isolated, it is a valuable link in the continuous chain of the integrated model of management. HIM managers delegate processing activities to employees and empower them to perform these activities, which then require monitoring and modification. This chapter begins with a discussion of the controlling function within an integrated management approach. Chapter 16 emphasizes quality improvement (QI) concepts and the growing importance that continuous monitoring for improvement is having in service industries throughout the country, and specifically in health-care facilities.

Monitoring and improving quality using QI concepts and tools creates the need for management information systems (MIS) that collect raw data, analyze the data, and integrate these data into information that can be assessed and disseminated. Creating systems that offer needed information to all departments in the facility as computer hardware and software enhancement purchases are made is crucial to obtaining reliable data for implementing quality improvement. HIM professionals must have input into the purchase decisions to ensure the data captured in MIS will meet internal customer needs for strategic information in controlling and making decisions that best serve the facility and its customers.

QI concepts are gradually finding a role in the management functions of service industries. By the year 2000, some authors project, possibly 70 percent of service firms in the United States with more than 500 employees will have formal quality initiatives (Bissen, 1993). In Bissen's article, health-care facilities are mentioned as a major segment of these service firms. Quality management appears to be a factor in the long-term health of institutions.

In Chapter 17, specific controlling tools for measuring productivity are detailed. They include work sampling and the work standards that are given broad measurable identities in the planning and organizing functions of management. The last chapter in this section is devoted to several human resource management aspects of controlling.

Controlling Defined

Controlling has traditionally been the fourth function of managers in the process approach continuum. In this traditional sense, controlling ensures that plans are accomplished through monitoring employee activities and then through remedial action to correct significant variations (Robbins, 1994). Once plans are approved in accordance with the vision/mission of the facility, and organization of the department's resources is in place, the activities performed are evaluated for efficiency and effectiveness. In today's health-care environment it is essential that departments monitor and document processing factors of production through controlling activities.

There is no need to think of controlling as a sinister activity involving surveillance, correction, or even reproach. Rather, it can be normal, positive, future oriented, and dynamic. Through automated, continuous monitoring of processes and activities, managers are able to focus objectively on problem avoidance or correction. Improving the systems to better meet the needs of customers then becomes the focus of the controlling function.

Setting Standards and Monitoring Performance

Continuing with an integrative theory of management, this section melds systems, behavioral approaches, and contingency approaches in a cohesive pattern to give controlling the continuity of a total process approach. Integrating the best of these approaches seems particularly applicable with the QI model where the customers' changing needs, wants, and expectations are a major focus. Using MIS to meet increasing information demands helps HIM managers to refashion department functions to meet the opportunities of the future.

Of course, health-care facilities across the country are not increasing their MIS capabilities in a uniform manner. Flexible management approaches are needed by HIM managers as their personal vision may be quite divergent from the vision of any particular health-care facility. As the HIM manager attends meetings, reads the literature, and enthusiastically endorses and shares knowledge about effective and efficient methods for quality improvement through new technologies, all levels of management can join in and "catch the spirit" that quality health-care comes through quality information. However, the HIM manager may need to actively promote change and encourage the need for tools that can offer continuous monitoring and, as a result, continuous improvement.

For example, knowing that JCAHO (Joint Commission on Accreditation of Healthcare Organizations) is planning an agenda for change that includes a performance improvement focus, or awareness that the Health Care Financing Administration has published an intent to require additional billing data, gives the HIM manager powerful motivation to promote change. Negotiating for the budget necessary to capture and analyze the data is also enhanced with this knowledge.

As upper-level management commits to implementation of performance improvement (PI) initiatives and the cultural changes involved, the HIM manager is positioned to be a leader in improving the interrelated processes that support the revised mission of the facility. By taking the initiative in PI tools and techniques in problem-solving situations, the HIM manager will be ready to share success stories throughout the facility.

Through preparation, the HIM manager is also ready should the facility choose to move into a major **work transformation** or reengineering effort which, in reality, may focus on the human side of health care. The long-range objectives for reengineering, productivity standard setting, redesigning of systems, or PI must include a stable, financially sound organization that emphasizes quality for the customers and enhances employee work life.

Setting Standards

One of the recommendations from the 1990 Institute of Medicine study is that information in the computer-based patient record (CPR) be designed to "manage and evaluate quality and cost of the data within the system" (IOM, 1991). Data in the CPR and related information will also assist in evaluating quality improvement activities. The HIM manager can be an information innovator and can participate in the development of a management information system (MIS) that will access required data across the network for use in making these quality improvement decisions for measuring and modifying processes in the pursuit of excellence.

Looking for valid monitoring data within the department's present systems is one of the challenges of the management team as quality improvement tools are first used. With increasing capabilities of management information systems, the capture of meaningful data can frequently be incorporated into the routine activities for setting performance standards with minimal extra cost.

Reviewing the literature, visiting with vendors, and interacting with peers are excellent activities for keeping managers aware of capabilities and enhancements to management information systems and for monitoring productivity. Sharing this knowledge with the department managers and team members will assist in discussions of the most useful applications for continuous monitoring of specific HIM activities.

Tools for Standard Setting

Section II emphasized the role of the manager in establishing standards for the total department and for each section. In this chapter, these standards are explored in greater detail. Four steps are typically involved:

1. Capturing data to measure actual activity
2. Analyzing the data into integrated information for comparison with the standard
3. Determining whether variations are significant
4. Taking team and managerial action

Just as objectives prepared during planning are to be measurable, so the systems implemented to monitor activities must be measurable. Not all relevant data can best be captured electronically; managers and teams can expect to use more subjective methods also. Questionnaires, survey forms, or work sheets can be used effectively. Each has particular strengths and weaknesses, so these materials should be used in combination for reliable information.

Questionnaires

Questionnaires can be tedious to respondents, so only pertinent vital information should be requested. For example, physicians complete numerous questionnaires and are familiar with them. By explaining a questionnaire's value in maintaining or enhancing service for physicians, a manager can gain their cooperation; most will gladly share their comments in a short questionnaire.

Surveys

A popular survey method is a follow-up telephone call to recent customers. For example, this monitoring tool could be used to evaluate the service provided to those who request records or patient information from the department. Not only do the customers feel valued by the call but they willingly cooperate by responding to questions that can then become part of a monitoring process. Questions on the survey form used by the interviewer should include nonverbal communication also, such as "Was the customer's response spontaneous and positive in tone?"

Within health information services, surveys that include personal observations can generate a negative response to questions that are subjective, without careful planning. The surveyor can overcome this problem by assuming a questioning attitude, not a critical one. Several factors combine to create an activity, and any one of these factors, or a combination of some, could be a reason why variations from negative to positive may be significant. Employee interaction may be only one of the factors in the total process. By first encouraging a team spirit, a manager can defuse signs of negativism and uncover the reason for it.

One reason why it is important to use several methods and several types of data to monitor the effectiveness of a section is the importance the team will place on the criteria chosen for review. What is measured determines, to a great extent, where the team will choose to excel. Thus, a broad approach to auditing the processes builds concensus for excellence across activities within the team.

History of Total Quality Management for Monitoring Quality

The terminology used to describe the controlling function, especially as it relates to quality, is revised periodically. The term, **total quality management (TQM)**, was the standard for some time, notably in industry. Many articles, books, and manuals are available to assist in becoming familiar with TQM concepts and tools. This chapter gives an overview of TQM and includes a list of suggested readings for further study.

Several Americans introduced initial TQM theories; among these are W. Edwards Deming, Walter Shewhart, and Joseph Juran. AT&T initiated early efforts toward quality control. The Japanese learned from the theories of Deming and Juran by inviting them to present seminars in the 1950s and then developing the ideas further with their guru, Kaoru Ishikawa (Palmer, 1992).

As the Japanese began sharing their success stories, corporate America listened and responded. Deming was invited to consult with several major corporations, some of which significantly raised the quality of their products and lowered production costs. By the mid-1980s, articles appeared on the successes of these companies. Most of them were in the manufacturing sector of the economy (Robbins, 1994).

The health-care industry has watched this quality movement with interest, and seminars on Japanese-style quality circles, one component of the Japanese TQM system, slowly began to emerge by 1990. The quality assurance component of monitoring patient care retrospectively had been in place since the 1970s, with structure and form outlined by the Joint Commission on Accreditation of Healthcare Organizations (JCAHO). However, TQM necessitated a change in culture as well as in process management for continuous quality monitoring (vanMatre, 1992).

A significant study was published in 1990 by the National Demonstration Project (NDP) on Quality Improvement in Health Care that showed that the TQM model can be applied successfully in health-care institutions. In its 1992 *Accreditation Manual for Hospitals* (AMH), JCAHO stated it is "beginning a carefully planned transition to standards that emphasize continuous quality improvement." JCAHO had chosen to use the phrase *continuous quality improvement* in 1992 as it initiated a transition from the term *quality assurance*. These factors gave impetus for HIM professionals to gain a working knowledge of continuous quality improvement and share that knowledge as outlined in Chapter 16 (JCAHO, 1992). In its 1996 manual, the phrase used to describe all aspects of improvement is *performance improvement* (JCAHO, 1995).

As a review of the suggested readings reveals, the evolution of TQM for health-care facilities involves differences in details, but the basic success concepts remain the same. A working description of TQM today is put forth by George Box, a former director of quality: "TQM is the democratization of the scientific method" (Box, 1986). James Evans defines *scientific method* as "a systematic process in which a problem is identified, data are collected and analyzed, and valid conclusions are drawn from the analysis" (vanMatre, 1992).

To give focus in understanding TQM concepts, a useful model was developed and is shown in Figure 15-1. It is titled the D*A*T model with three critical elements: data, attitudes, and tools. The asterisk is the software symbol for multiplication, showing that TQM is the product of these three elements. Should one be absent, TQM is nonexistent (vanMatre, 1992). It was Peter Drucker who first emphasized the attitude component of TQM (vanMatre, 1992).

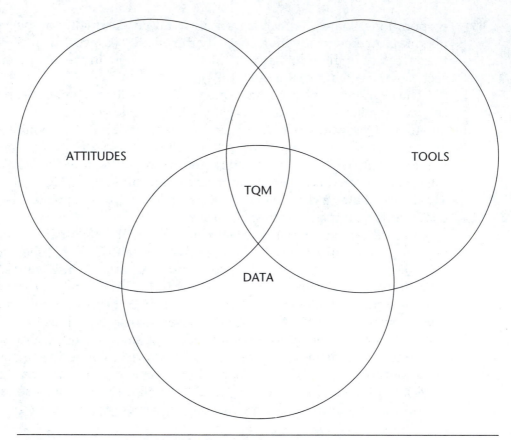

ATTITUDES

TOOLS

TQM

DATA

Figure 15-1. D*A*T Model for Total Quality Management

Recent Terminology Changes and Integrated Information Management

Continuous quality improvement has been used in the health-care industry to describe the continuous nature of QI where the process maintains a focus on customers and employees. However, the generic term, **performance improvement (PI),** best describes the philosophy of providing customers with better services, ideas, and products, and it is used interchangeably in this section.

The 1996 JCAHO *Comprehensive Accreditation Manual for Hospitals* (CAMH) standards emphasize an indicator measurement system that can offer meaningful measures of patient outcomes. The information management needed to implement this system, analyze it, and assess the resulting information for dissemination will challenge HIM professionals to utilize new terminology within the accrediting body of literature. Embedded in these data can be PI possibilities across the enterprise. Since JCAHO mandates the integration of information management, the PI possibilities are interdepartmental, and knowledgeable HIM professionals can offer expertise in assessing the needs and developing the systems.

Information Systems for Control

Theoretically, an MIS can be manual or computer based. Historically, managers relied on manual systems for the information to monitor the functions under their span of control until computer capabilities offered the opportunity to build systems based on computer-supported management applications. This is not to say that manual systems are no longer needed; they continue to be a component of the monitoring activity as discussed earlier.

A look at data as raw facts emphasizes the need for **integrated systems** to develop a true MIS. Data can be a collection of, for instance, listings showing the number of records coded for the week and the number of patients for whom billing data were sent to the billing department. Also available might be a record of the dates of discharges, the dates the bills were sent for payment, and the amounts of the bills. These bits of data can be listed in various activity reports. But, these discrete data are not useful to the manager for performance monitoring until they have been analyzed and processed. To reiterate, data are raw facts, numbers, dates, or quantities until they are analyzed, processed, and presented as information. Thus, an appropriate MIS system for HIM managers collects data, massages them, and turns them into meaningful information. Today it is possible to integrate information on interactive network systems that can become powerful tools for managerial decision making with outcomes that can then refashion the process.

The challenge of integrating data from the various systems throughout the facility creates an opportunity for HIM managers to be information innovators and strategic information resource professionals. As such, HIM professionals can maintain a vital role in the development of an MIS that will create efficient and effective systems monitoring productivity not only for health information services but for other departments as well.

To reach the goal of integrated data to serve the MIS customers, HIM managers and their staff should participate in the steps outlined in Figure 15-2, as the strategic plan relating to productivity is defined.

As the integrated systems are in the development phase, HIM managers and other customers should be able to say, "These are the key operating statistics my team leaders and I need to see every morning at 8 A.M. We want them presented in this format." They should feel assured that once the systems are in place, these performance tools will be online for monitoring operations.

Today's managers can then anticipate or identify problems almost as they occur using real-time decision support systems. No long delays will hamper their getting the needed information; alternatives can be identified quickly; what-if questions can be asked; and selection of the best alternative can be made efficiently.

As integration of data from the various facility systems progresses, it is likely there will be data islands where incompatible formats make integration impossible. HIM managers have the qualifications to participate on the team that resolves such difficulties and creates a control system that meets the needs of health-care facilities in the future.

---

1. Evaluate present flow of data and the points where decisions are made.
2. Determine source of the information needed at the points of decision making.
3. Analyze information requirements at these decision points.
4. Aggregate the decision needs and ensure needed data are collected only once.
5. Develop uniform data definitions.
6. Standardize documentation.
7. Ensure quality improvement data are available for analysis.
8. Assist in designing the integrated system; know what vendors have to offer and be a strategic resource in the decisions.

Figure 15-2.   Steps for Integrating Information Systems

Summary

Controlling is defined as ensuring that plans are accomplished through monitoring employee activities and then through remedial action to correct significant variations. Controlling can be considered normal, positive, future oriented, and dynamic.

To monitor performance continuously, managers use QI concepts that take advantage of MIS that have integrated system capabilities. As standards are set by managers and the teams, adjustments as MIS enhancements are brought online will become necessary. Increased information will mean that performance monitoring can become increasingly automated.

Four major steps set the stage for monitoring: (1) capturing data for measurement, (2) analyzing the data for comparison with the standard, (3) determining whether variations are significant, and (4) taking team/managerial action.

Subjective tools for monitoring include questionnaires, surveys of external customers, and surveys within a department.

Japanese firms have been successful in TQM activities, and health-care facilities in the United States are incorporating continuous quality monitoring in increasing numbers. The major elements in TQM are data, attitudes, and tools. JCAHO is using the term performance to describe the TQM process.

Integrated information systems are needed for developing the CPR as well as for monitoring quality activities. As HIM brokers disseminate meaningful information for these and other uses, they become the strategic information resource professionals of the future.

Review Questions

1. Outline the history of TQM, describing its adoption globally, and the modifications that increase its value in health-care settings today.
2. Describe how an integrated MIS assists in the controlling function and list eight steps in integrating data for performance measurement.
3. List three subjective monitoring methods and give one example of how each of these methods is best used.

References

Bissen, C. (1993). Ripples on the healthcare pond. *Journal of AHIMA, 64* (2), 4.

Box, G. (1992). Bayesian inferences in statistical analysis. New York, N.Y.: John Wiley & Sons, Inc.

Institute of Medicine (1991). Report of committee on computer-based patient records. Washington, D.C.: National Academy Press.

Joint Commission on Accreditation of Healthcare Organizations (1992). *Accreditation Manual for Hospitals.* JCAHO: Oakbrook Terrace, IL.

———— (1995). *Accreditation Manual for Hospitals.* JCAHO: Oakbrook Terrace, IL.

Palmer, L. (1992). Making data work. *For the Record, 4* (8), 1–11.

Robbins, S. (1994). *Management* (4th ed.). Englewood Cliffs, NJ: Prentice-Hall.

vanMatre, J. (1992). The D*A*T approach to total quality management. *Journal of AHIMA, 63* (11), 38–44.

Suggested Readings

Brunner, B. (1995). The use of work teams: A help or a hindrance to performance. *Topics in Health Information Management, 16* (1), 32–40.

Donnelly, J., Gibson, J., & Ivancevich, J. (1987). *Fundamentals of management* (6th ed.). Plano, TX: Business Publications.

Dowell, S., & Zieserl, R. (1992). Executive information systems technology and the health information management professional. *Journal of AHIMA, 63* (8), 62–64.

Hyde, L. (1992). Developing a quality management program for coded data. *Journal of AHIMA, 63* (1), 50–52.

Longest, B. (1990). *Management practices for the health professional* (4th ed.). Norwalk, CT: Appleton & Lange.

Markson, L., & Nash, D. (1994). Overview: Public accountability of hospitals regarding quality. *The Joint Commission Journal on Quality Improvement*, July, pp. 359–363.

Robbins, S., (1994). *Management* (4th ed.). Englewood Cliffs, NJ: Prentice Hall.

Rue, L., & Byars, L. (1986). *Management: Theory and application* (4th ed.). Homewood, IL: Richard D. Irwin.

Chapter 16

Controlling Through Total Quality Improvement

Learning Objectives

After completing this chapter, the learner should be able to:

1. List the results HIM managers can achieve when the model for integrated QI management is implemented in the department.
2. Identify changes in the culture of an HIM department when customers become the focus of activities.
3. Explain the value of a facilitator when educating HIM teams in QI concepts.
4. Give examples of the value of benchmarking as a tool for QI management.
5. Suggest appropriate rewards for employees and the reasons why managers may choose different rewards.

Key Terms

Benchmarking
Facilitator
Statistical modeling

Introduction

The emphasis on quality improvement concepts in corporate America in recent years is now visibly stretching into the health-care industry. Some seasoned professionals may say they have been practicing these concepts for years and rightly so. The difference is that quality improvement concepts are now being discussed in board meetings, in upper-level management committees, and down through the levels to the team planning a specific process change.

Adjectives used by board members, upper-level and middle management staff, and team members to describe their experience with quality improvement range from fantastic to frustrating. Why are some facilities so successful in adjusting their culture and why do others fail in their first attempt? These are questions this chapter explores as specific steps for success are outlined. But the major focus of the chapter is giving managers appropriate tools for success. Success is achievable for this paradigm shift as management and leadership styles are adjusted to meld quality improvement (QI) concepts with the best of the integrated management approaches of the past for managing into the twenty-first century.

References from several experts in quality improvement are listed at the end of this chapter; they offer information on specific QI skills. The references also include articles from current literature that will assist in understanding current thought as managers make this paradigm shift. This chapter discusses a manager's overall role in the process of quality improvement and gives broad managerial concepts for success, not details for implementing programs.

Integrated Management: A Contemporary Model

In the 1970s, health-care organizations took the first formal steps toward improving processes with the medical audit models that evaluated performance. During the 1980s, the Joint Commission on Accreditation of Healthcare Organizations (JCAHO) changed the audit models to include structure, process, and outcome quality measurement activities (Eubanks, 1992). HIM managers became familiar with these quality assurance activities. By 1990, a National Demonstration Project report confirmed that quality improvement techniques from industrial quality sciences, combined with quality measurement, could be beneficial to health-care facilities (Eubanks, 1992).

By focusing on the process or the system and using statistical quality control techniques, HIM managers can develop strategic plans that increase efficiency and effectiveness of the systems under their span of control. QI concepts emphasize that the employee, the physician, or the "other" department are not targeted for blame. And, people are considered only one element in the process—the procedures, the equipment, the materials, the resources—are all emphasized as being a part of the system's input. The outcome is influenced by appropriate changes and these are undertaken following statistical quality control steps. These changes create improvement because people have joined together to work on the process and make it happen.

Figure 16-1 gives a model for integrated QI management. As this figure shows, the emphasis is on **statistical modeling**. When a project is undertaken by a team, the results should include standardization of the procedures, elimination of non-value-added steps, and reduction of unnecessary variation—a tall order, but the following example illustrates the success stories.

---

1. Become familiar with QI management concepts through formal courses, seminars, review of literature.

    1.1. Network with peers.

    1.2. Share enthusiasm for integrated QI management models.

2. Use facility vision/mission plan and strategies to develop quality improvement strategies for department activities.

    2.1. Involve yourself in facility steering committees and information systems needs for the future.

    2.2. Standardize functions in the department to the extent possible for each section.

    2.3. Assist and empower management team and employees in each section to develop a quality improvement plan relating to their functions.

(continued)

Figure 16-1. Managing in the Integrated Quality Improvement Environment

3. Identify department customers—internal and external.

    3.1. Document internal and external customers, their needs, wants, and expectations, for the total department with assistance from the management team.

    3.2. Assist management team in documenting the customer needs, wants, and expectations for each section with assistance from each section team.

    3.3. Begin documenting perceived problem areas as teams discuss customers, information flow, timeliness, and present complaints.

4. Share QI management concepts with the management team and section teams during activities listed above and continuously as change is undertaken.

    4.1. Develop in-service programs for all levels of employees.

    4.2. Emphasize the long-range nature of the changes.

    4.3. Monitor reactions for resistance and defuse concerns.

    4.4. Empower employees to initiate ideas for quality improvement projects and steps for implementation.

    4.5. Separate formal training/quality improvement sessions from routine department activities.

5. Encourage team spirit among employees at all levels.

    5.1. Empower employees by giving increasing responsibility for their work environment.

    5.2. Change position titles and activity titles as ideas are generated by the teams.

    5.3. Coach the management team and section teams as needed.

    5.4. Prioritize quality improvement projects using input from the teams; choose initial ones carefully.

    5.5. Use an expert in quality improvement tools as the **facilitator** of project teams; use just-in-time training.

    5.6. Ensure that new employees have thorough initiation to process.

    5.7. Encourage interdepartmental and interdisciplinary interaction.

6. Ensure that information systems are in place for accurate data capture for use in statistical control techniques leading to validity in data dissemination.

    6.1. Review present systems used for clinical care, for interdepartmental and external customers, and for intradepartmental activities.

Figure 16-1.   *(continued)*

6.2. Encourage brainstorming and nominal technique sessions to anticipate information system needs for changing customer expectations.

6.3. Document future plans for information systems needed to meet data requirements for the future and present to administration.

7. Assure tools and release time for team members as they analyze data, retrieve data, and prepare presentations.

8. Network for effective benchmarking efforts.

9. Disseminate results of projects.

9.1. Encourage the management team and team members to share in presenting results of projects.

9.2. Share the learning experience and results throughout the facility as appropriate.

9.3. Share results of projects with internal or external customers as appropriate.

10. Reward achievement and extra effort.

11. Monitor activities and adjust process as necessary.

Figure 16-1. *(continued)*

▪ *Practice Example*

One HIM manager was receiving complaints from several physicians that half of their incomplete records were not available for completion in the physicians' work room. The manager and the three clerks involved in physicians' work room procedures met and discussed the problem. The clerks expressed their perception that the coding and utilization management section staff were at fault; records were taken without proper sign-out procedures being followed and the records were not returned promptly. A meeting of the two groups with the manager focused on the perceived people problems and ended with a concensus that each section would "try harder to follow procedures."

Two months later, the HIM manager again began receiving phone calls from the physicians. They expressed anger that the problem had not been resolved. During this time period, the manager had attended a seminar on integrated continuous quality management and was enthusiastic about this process approach to solving problems.

The manager invited the two groups to another meeting and this time explained the team approach, empowering the groups to use quality improvement techniques in finding the source of the problem and solving it. A facilitator, hired recently by the facility, assisted the team with just-in-time knowledge of the skills needed for this project. Physician staff members, chosen by the concerned physicians, were asked to be a part of the team. Flowcharting and monitoring of the demand for records revealed that the physicians received their incomplete records 63 percent of the time and that 58 percent of the unavailable records were for the copy service requests. In reality, 32 percent of the unavailable records were with the coding/utilization management section.

Representatives from the correspondence section were now asked to be a part of the team. The manager and the team worked diligently on this project and implemented their plan of action. At the end of 6 months, monitoring showed that incomplete records were available for physicians 89 percent of the time and the major use of those unavailable was for ongoing patient care. The team members were enthused with their success. By automating the system for pulling records for correspondence requests of incomplete records, the hours a record was unavailable for physicians shortened significantly.

At the next team meeting, the manager commended the team, encouraged them to continue striving for excellence, and asked for brainstorming ideas that might further reduce unavailable records. They suggested a daily list to physicians be instituted that showed the incomplete records taken to a patient-care unit for readmission. Fortunately, this could be implemented with the present system. Physicians appreciated this information and joined in the effort to reduce incomplete record days.

Periodic monitoring of the system showed a further reduction in the number of unavailable incomplete records. At the end of another 3 months, the available record rate was 95 percent. A graph was prepared to demonstrate this success. The HIM manager asked the team to share this quality improvement process with the rest of the department at an in-service meeting and further rewarded them with honorary badges for that day. The team also received a special commendation at the quarterly medical staff meeting. ■

Adjusting to Managing the QI Process

Education is one of the keys to success as managers begin using QI concepts. A seasoned manager has the advantage of a peer network within the facility and in the professional community, and can learn from the experiences of others. These experiences lend credence to the theory being learned in formal courses or seminars. Current professional journals are also excellent sources for both theory and experiences of others.

As students gain the formal knowledge of QI tools and anticipate using them in the work environment, they gain practical knowledge through practica and affiliations. Here they become acquainted with clinical practitioners and begin the networking that will hopefully continue throughout their professional careers.

In their first positions, new graduates will need time to become knowledgeable in the terminology and methodology used in their particular facility. By integrating the theory, the practical knowledge, and the facility-specific culture, terms, and techniques, new managers gradually unlock their full potential and they will gain confidence as experts.

Enthusiasm is known to be contagious. Some managers may hesitate to become enthusiastic for the integrated QI management model when they read that it takes more time. Look more closely at the success stories. Yes, the project takes longer from start to solution implementation, but there are trade-offs that can free a manager's time. As the move progresses toward sharing leadership tasks and empowering the team to find areas for improvement, managers are released from traditional managerial activities and are ready to be challenged in other areas.

Initially, managers may spend time developing strategies for the mission of the facility and in choosing global projects. These projects can then be narrowed to priorities at the departmental level. Other challenging tasks can include assisting the staff in making cultural adjustments, defining the department's customers, and prioritizing projects. But, once the teams are functioning smoothly with the team leader, managers can resist the temptation to micromanage and allow the process to work. By consciously concentrating managerial energies elsewhere, HIM professionals can enjoy job enrichment. Adapting the QI team approach to the unique features of the department and watching the teams meet their goals, managers can become advocates, sharing their enthusiasm for the process.

QI Planning Strategies

An enthusiastic HIM manager can impact implementation of quality improvement in the entire facility. By becoming knowledgeable through review of the literature, through seminars, and through formal courses, the manager can be an advocate and share the vision in meetings and in discussions with the management team. Offering to be a part of the steering committee is an excellent way to be involved personally and to have department involvement from the beginning. A background in systems, in data capture and analysis, and in statistical techniques gives HIM managers the expertise that will be of value for generating ideas and implementing change.

An example in *For the Record* explains how one HIM manager became so involved in the steering committee that when a facilitator was needed, she applied for and got the position! She is now a catalyst or coach to the numerous continuous quality improvement teams throughout the facility. Not only does she use her systems background but she finds her management knowledge and experience very useful (Palmer, 1993).

The first step in having measurable data for decision making is to update and standardize present procedures. Electronic exchange of information mandates the standardization of terms and techniques across all teams in the department. Standardized terms will be needed among all users in the facility. This will be an ongoing process as implementation takes place. At the same time, HIM managers can empower employees in each team to use unique and team-specific terms and techniques where feasible as they take increased responsibility for their work environment.

Using the facility-wide projects and the department projects, the teams can develop their strategic plan and prioritize projects. By assisting the teams in understanding how their projects enhance the department and facility-wide projects, managers can increase the sense of ownership employees feel toward their team. This enhances the success of the quality improvement effort.

Customer-Driven Attitudes

An exciting, appropriate, and pervading principle of quality improvement is the focus on the customers—their wants, needs, and expectations. As an HIM manager attends quality improvement seminars or a student learns techniques in a quality improvement course, customers of the department will become a major focus. Internal customers and their changing wants, needs, and expectations may be viewed differently. For instance, an employee may view demands from another department quite differently than a manager. Consider how coding technicians may view the multiple demands made by billing department employees when problems arise with codes and incomplete billing information. Their feelings about interruptions to correct problems may be viewed quite differently from managerial concerns between their manager and the manager of the billing department. In contrast, the billing department employees may perceive the interaction about the problem in another way.

Or, for example, consider students, spending practica or affiliation time with employees. They may or may not be impressed with the employees' understanding of the internal and external customers awaiting the product of their work. The view of students may be very different than the view of the employees.

Changing to a customer-driven cultural attitude is exciting, rewarding, and stimulating for employees. It can also be threatening. HIM managers will want to look for positive signs and respond with encouragement and rewards. Cultural change comes gradually and must flow from the top. As upper-level management focuses on customer-driven opportunities, managers at all levels can share enthusiastically with the employees in personal interaction, through in-service seminars, and through a story board. Most importantly, managers must "walk the talk" in their own management style.

By tackling the specific needs of a customer such as described in the previous example, employees will learn teamwork skills interacting with another department. Additional departments may also need to be involved as the source of the problem is uncovered, thus making the project truly interdisciplinary.

Quality improvement techniques call for the manager and the team to meet customer needs and then go beyond that, striving for excellence in performance by doing it better the next time, by anticipating future needs, and by staying one step ahead of customers in the strategic planning process. Inevitably there will be times when expectations of customers will need to be negotiated or reshaped.

Another aspect of the customer-driven and information-driven systems approach is the increased need for data. Think of the enhanced role of the HIM department in bringing standardized data capture systems to the integrated management effort as the facility moves toward an information-driven approach to excellence. By knowing the capabilities of the systems in-house and in the marketplace, the HIM broker will be able to explore options with customers. When another department requests information about capturing appropriate data for its needs, HIM brokers can offer suggestions.

As the strategic plan for the facility is developed and projects are prioritized, the opportunity to impact the decisions must be seized or it may be lost to others. It is the HIM broker who can take information needs outlined for the next 3 to 5 years and suggest how the present systems capabilities or future systems expansion can provide the needed data.

Exceeding the customers' expectations for information is the goal, and planning systems where staff members are involved in shared leadership can make that goal a reality.

Employee Education Needs

Employees will react differently to the same set of stimuli, making a broad approach necessary as QI concepts are presented to them. Some will be early adopters who will quickly learn the needed skills and embrace the change. Another group will tend to resist change and will require extra encouragement and support from managers as changes occur.

This resistance could be especially evident if the facility has a history of programs that started with fanfare but the commitment was not sustained and eventually the program was dropped. The HIM managers will need to emphasize that QI concepts will be integrated into the culture and activities of the department, and QI will impact their work environment over time and into the future.

A facilitator with the ability to present the tools and techniques in an informative yet interesting way should be on the staff of the facility and available to give in-service programs and special training sessions to teams. An effective learning tool is just-in-time education, where the section or team is instructed in the tools and techniques for a specific task as needed. Confidence in performing the task at hand is thus enhanced, which builds success in small steps.

Peter Drucker's advice to the Japanese in the 1950s continues to be valid today. He strongly recommends holding formal training sessions away from the routine activities. He states the pressure of work activities will detract from the learning experience and lead to failure as daily duties and set routines become the predominant focus. This situation makes clear the need for a budget that includes support staff to perform routine work while the staff members are in training.

Encouraging a Team Spirit

One of the benefits HIM managers can expect as integration takes place and cultural change occurs is an enhanced team spirit among employees. This should be increasingly evident throughout the facility as upper-level management supports the changes and demonstrates that leadership is with the people, not above them.

The AHA (American Hospital Association) journal, *Hospitals and Health-care Networks*, reports that one of the CEOs leading a TQM initiative applied the principles to his own telephone conversations by asking at the end, "Is there anything else I can do for you?" (Eubanks, 1992).

Coaching the sections as they are giving increased responsibility is also an important aspect of the HIM manager's role. This coaching should begin with upper-level management and flow to the HIM manager, who then educates the teams, thus empowering them to meet customer needs. Deming discusses a threat to empowering employees. That is, when crises occur, there may be times when managers, under pressure, return to making unilateral decisions. It is just a fact of life that this will happen. How managers respond when empowered staff members feel safe in taking the risk of confronting the boss is the issue (Hamilton, 1993).

Practice Example

A QI team began a scheduled meeting. As the team leader opened the meeting, she expressed anger with the department manager, who had reassigned several employees without discussing the reasons for doing so with the staff involved. The team leader was so upset that she stated she would resign as team leader. At this point, other team members supported her by stating they would resign from the team as well. They stated they felt betrayal when the manager had verbalized shared leadership with employee input in making decisions and then announced these changes on his own.

The department manager stood up, apologized to the team, and admitted that he had acted in the "old way of managing and controlling." This public admission in front of his boss, and then his request that the team point out future mistakes should he fail again, changed the tone of the meeting. The team leader expressed her support and respect for admitting a mistake and the members joined her in support. In fact, this interaction became a model for QI commitment throughout the facility and the empowered staff members felt comfortable taking risks in their quest for excellence (Eubanks, 1992). ■

As teams brainstorm and choose initial projects, the HIM manager should guide in the selection of the initial projects. As tools are used for the first time and techniques are being learned, success will be enhanced if the first projects are straightforward. While emphasis is placed on success stories, not all of the projects will culminate in success. What is important, when failure occurs, is a willingness to acknowledge failure honestly. Employees respect an honest admission of failure and a willingness to explore new options for solving a problem. Team members must be allowed to fail as part of the empowering process.

Since quality improvement projects are ongoing, it is inevitable that new employees will be hired for a team during any phase of the project. Human resources management should have monthly orientations for new employees to receive QI information; the HIM manager should assess the extent of involvement the new employee may have in QI activities before the formal orientation. A special session can then be held for the new employee, if warranted. New employees are customers, in a sense, needing information to perform their work effectively.

Despite obstacles to scheduling interdepartmental team meetings, developing such teams is an important facet in building team spirit across the facility. As interdepartmental teams work toward solutions that will benefit customers of the facility, this interaction promotes understanding of other disciplines among all staff members involved.

Managing Data Needs with QI

As brainstorming sessions create an increased need for data, few HIM managers will be confident that present systems are adequate for capturing and analyzing data to produce the needed information for proposed projects. Because of the importance of correct decisions when enhancing present systems or purchasing new ones, it is imperative that HIM managers update their knowledge in this area.

They must ensure that careful documentation is ongoing and then, through negotiations and with graphic descriptions, the manager can present the pros and cons of system needs to administration. Fortunately, resources are available from AHIMA and other professional organizations that can increase knowledge of software/hardware systems.

A team may find the solution to a problem blocked by a data barrier. In fact, as long as paper records are needed for ongoing patient-care requestors and for administrative requestors, these customers will experience frustrations. In the following example, one team was forced to look for interim solutions.

■ *Practice Example*

One facility averaging 700 record requests per day from staff throughout the hospital found customers and HIM department staff were frustrated with record movement problems. A quick review of policies and procedures showed (1) a time limit on returning these records was nonexistent, (2) there were records loaned to other departments by the hospital staff without notifying the HIM department, and (3) HIM staff had to go to the outguide in the permanent files to look for a record's location. As the HIM management team discussed where they should focus a pilot project for the first continuous quality improvement (CQI) effort in the department, it was unanimous that record requestors created the greatest challenges for the staff. For this problem, because the QI team would necessarily be interdepartmental, key managers from five other facility departments were surveyed to determine their interest in the project. The concensus was that HIM should undertake this pilot project. Each manager agreed to commit release time for a staff member to join the QI team.

The HIM operations manager had attended seminars and visited with other facilities with quality improvement models in place and became the facilitator for this project; there were seven people on the team. Use of CQI tools uncovered the extent of the problem and solutions were suggested. Purchase of an automated chart-tracking system was chosen as a main feature of the action plan. A second feature of the plan focused on policy revision for record movement.

An automated chart-tracking system was already approved for the next budget year; however, implementation would not be completed for at least 18 months. Despite this news, team members rallied and held another brain-storming session for an interim plan. They chose the following actions for this plan:

1. Ongoing patient-care request customers receive highest priority. A daily printout of scheduled admissions and ambulatory visits will be given to record movement clerks by 5 P.M. each day.

2. One record movement technician will change work hours to the second shift and pull and deliver these scheduled records.

3. Admissions will print out a record request for unscheduled patients in the HIM department as soon as registration is complete. These records will be delivered promptly.

4. Non-patient-care request customers will make requests at least 36 hours in advance of need. Computer terminals in the laboratory, utilization management, radiology, and billing departments will be upgraded to online requests.

5. Non-patient-care request customers will pick up their records at 8:30 A.M. for noon return and 1:00 P.M. for 4:30 P.M. return.

6. A manual card file of records signed out of the department will be maintained during the interim period.

Team members enthusiastically implemented the plan and revised policies and were supported by all departments. Team spirit and the improvement in record movement control were high; the team was looking forward to full implementation of the automated system the next year (Fletcher, 1992).   ◼

Managing the Tools for QI

The facilitator is an excellent resource in determining the tools needed for specific data analysis and retrieval. But the responsibility for assuring the availability of these tools rests with the HIM manager. Team members will become frustrated with deadlines should they lack the tools to complete their assignments. Another frustration comes when an assignment is added to a schedule already packed with routine activities. Time must be allocated for assignment completion as well as for meeting attendance.

Using Benchmarking as a QI Tool

Benchmarking is an important comparative data tool in performance improvement efforts. Benchmarking means research for new ideas by networking, reviewing the literature, or attending seminars on organizations and then adopting or modifying the best aspects of those organizations found to have outstanding performance. A definition is offered by author R. C. Camp in his book on benchmarking and this definition focuses on the networking aspects. He defines benchmarking as "the continuous process of measuring products, services, and practices against the toughest competitors or those companies recognized as industry leaders." Benchmarking ideas can improve department operations when incorporated into the quality improvement process (Camp, 1989).

Internal benchmarking refers to the process of looking for superior performance in other departments within the facility and adapting the best ideas into the HIM department processes. Competitive benchmarking is a form of external research that involves comparing the department's operation with those of competitors.

Networking develops into benchmarking when innovative ideas are exchanged and internalized. Sharing of information about the best practices is mutually beneficial; some health-care facilities are forming consortia for specific sharing of information. A new word being formed for this action is *coopetition*, where competitive health-care facilities share for the good of the community.

Managing the PDCA Tool

To generate ideas and data for monitoring one aspect of a process, managers can suggest that teams use the QI tool, asking participants to plan, do, check, and act (PDCA). By getting the team members involved and educated in using PDCA, HIM managers empower the team to create solutions to problems and then evaluate effectiveness.

Sharing the Benefits of Team Projects

The references are rich with ideas and examples for displaying the results of data analysis as presentations are prepared for others in the department, for facility committees, and for customers. The customers especially need to know the steps that were taken to reach a resolution, any revised procedures as a result of the project, and the action plan for monitoring of the system to assure needs continue to be met.

The presentations are an opportunity to emphasize that staff members involved all join in the common goal to achieve and maintain the highest level of facility-wide quality patient care.

Choosing Rewards for Employees

Knowing the team members, their preferences and interests, assists HIM managers in choosing appropriate rewards at the end of a team project. Rewards are best tailored to the values of the individual. Awards, verbal commendations, publicity in newsletter or bulletin boards, special parking spaces, or dinner tickets are some of the rewards that come to mind. It is usually better to vary the reward, to use creativity and innovation, rather than to plan a standard reward for each project. Many facilities have an "employee of the month" and there might be a "team of the year" special reward involving the whole facility. Rewarding the effort a team expends, even though present results may be less than optimum, is also important.

Quality Improvement and the Future

Periodic retrospective auditing has been a component of quality assurance activities, so managers are familiar with that process. Planning a monitoring program at the end of a project is important for continuous quality improvement. Hopefully, the monitoring will allow managers to anticipate problems before they erupt and customers become concerned.

An important aspect of the monitoring is the periodic review of systems that may have been installed since the formal project period ended. These new systems could change functions or enhance procedures across department sections.

As mentioned in Chapter 15, the term performance improvement is now being used by JCAHO to describe the process of improving quality.

Summary

Quality improvement concepts are introduced in this chapter as a part of the integrated management approach. For long-term success, upper-level management must lead in the quality improvement effort and cultural change, but there is much the HIM manager can do to promote the process, initiate personal and departmental change, and use appropriate tools as opportunities arise.

Tools and techniques for implementing specific QI concepts are found in the literature. A facilitator familiar with the use of these tools and techniques is an important member of the team; hopefully, a full-time expert will be hired by the facility for this purpose.

Quality improvement is a customer-driven, information-driven approach to solving problems using statistical control techniques for analyzing and presenting the information. This approach builds team spirit and increases a sense of ownership among staff members. Tools such as PDCA give structure to the approach.

Differing staff member personalities and values create a demand for innovative approaches to learning tools used and rewards given as change is undertaken. Experts in QI concepts can best lead in formal learning sessions that take place away from the work setting.

HIM managers have an opportunity for internalizing and using new leadership skills while integrating QI concepts into their present management styles. As staff members observe this change in their leaders, a sense of ownership for their own work ethic and environment can increase and enhance the team spirit. While coaching and facilitating this change, HIM managers may revert to old management approaches as facts of life impact the workplace. Apology then becomes a growth experience for all participants. Empowered employees need to be given permission to fail.

Increased data needs are to be expected, which increases the need for managers to maintain current knowledge of systems available and their capabilities. Benchmarking assists the managers in suggesting or implementing the best ideas in systems and procedures. Networking contributes to the sense of community.

Monitoring and making adjustments when variations are significant are the last steps in the process and can allow managers to anticipate future problems and avoid them.

Review Questions

1. Describe the role of a facilitator in QI implementation.
2. Explain how health information services develops a customer-driven attitude.
3. How do managers use the tool known as PDCA?

Field Practice Question

1. Develop a model for encouraging a team spirit among members of the record activity section of health information services in an acute care facility. The coding section is frustrated because the assembly/analysis team within the record activity section is increasingly unable to obtain and complete all discharged records within their procedural guidelines.

   In discussing the problem with the managers on the patient units, the record activity section manager and the assembly/analysis team leader discovered the patient care givers are holding records for completion because of the recent staffing change to 12-hour shifts from 7 A.M. to 7 P.M. They frequently need to complete documentation after 7 P.M. At present, the team members assemble and analyze the available records from 7 P.M. to 10 P.M., ready for coding the next morning.

   Plan a brainstorming session with the team to solve this problem; state who should participate in finding a solution; offer two creative ideas; and then give rationale for using these ideas as tools to build team spirit.

Case Study

A large clinic with 50 practicing physicians handles more than 400 patient appointments per day. Health information services is expected to have the record available for the physician at the time of each patient visit. And, loose reports are expected to be in the record and ready for review also. Those using the records are physicians, nursing staff, receptionists, and patient accounts staff.

Turnaround time for transcription is 24 hours. Laboratory and Radiation Therapy are located in the building and reports arrive from these offices several times a day. Registration and billing are a part of the MIS system, with the MPI and chart tracking with bar-code technology also a part of the system.

The manager of health information services chose to focus on availability of the complete patient record at appointment time as concerns regarding this issue were mounting. The quality improvement steps were undertaken, beginning with a monitoring instrument to determine present performance. This monitoring for 1 week revealed the following:

1. Loose report filing—record complete for patient visit 70 percent of the time.
2. Record availability for patient visit—80 percent of the time.
3. Record pulled and delivered to the reception areas by 6 P.M. on the day before appointment—90 percent of the time.
4. Reports arriving from Laboratory and Radiation Therapy within 24 hours (tests taking longer not included)—97 percent of the time.

Using the information from the 1-week monitoring data, develop the following:

1. Plan an interdisciplinary committee and suggest participants and items for discussion. Give rationale.
2. List alternative actions the committee can offer to raise the level of performance in all areas with the exception of #4.

References

Camp, R.C. (1989). *Benchmarking: The search for industry best practices that lead to superior performance.* Milwaukee, WI: Quality Press.

Eubanks, P. (1992). The CEO experience, TQM/CQI. *Hospitals*, June 5, pp. 36–38.

Fletcher, D. (1992). Continuous quality improvement for H.I.M. answers. Speaker, American Health Information Management Association. St. Louis, October 12.

Hamilton, J. (1993). Toppling the power of the pyramid: Team-based restructuring for TQM, patient-centered care. *Hospitals*, January 5, p. 3.

Palmer, L. (1993). RRA leads CQI. *For the Record, 5* (4), 7.

Suggested Readings

Berwick, D., Godfrey, A., & Roessner, J. (1990). *Curing health care: New strategies for quality improvement.* San Francisco: Jossey-Bass.

Bissen, C., & Fainter, J. (1993). Teaming up. *Journal of AHIMA, 64* (3), 4, 5.

Brassard, M. (1985). *The memory jogger.* Methuen, MA: GOAL/QPC.

Burns, D., Jr. (1992). Total quality means total change. *Advance for Health Information Professionals, 2* (15), 5.

Cassidy, B. (1991). Total quality management: An implementation strategy for excellence in the medical record department. *Topics in Health Record Management*, March.

Cassidy, B. (1992). Health information management professional's role in health care quality management. Speaker, American Health Information Management Association. St. Louis, October 14.

Cofer, J., & Greeley, H. (1993). *Quality improvement techniques for medical records.* Marblehead, MA: Opus Communications.

Deming, W.E. (1986). *Out of the crisis.* Cambridge, MA: Massachusetts Institute of Technology Center for Advanced Engineering Study.

Eubanks, P. (1992). The CEO experience, TQM/CQI. *Hospitals*, June 5.

Farrell, E. (1993). Quality assurance versus CQI: How one facility used the Deming process to increase quality. *Advance for Health Information Professionals, 3* (2), 10.

Fletcher, D. (1992). Continuous quality improvement for H.I.M. answers. Speaker, American Health Information Management Association. St. Louis, October 12.

Hamilton, J. (1993). Toppling the power of the pyramid: Team-based restructuring for TQM, patient-centered care. *Hospitals*, January 5, p. 3.

Hamilton, M. (1993). What does QI mean to MR. *Advance for Health Information Professionals, 3* (2), 9, 11.

Leebox, W., & Ersoz, C. (1991). *The health care manager's guide to continuous quality improvement.* Chicago: American Hospital Publishing.

Longest, B. (1990). *Management practices for the health professional.* Norwalk, CT: Appleton & Lange.

Management leadership critical to CQI success. The last word. *Hospitals,* July 20, p. 3.

Mastrangelo, R. (1992). It's important to work for quality improvement. *Advance for Health Information Professionals, 2* (1), 12. 13.

McBride, B. (1993). Quality improvement, making it happen. *Journal of AHIMA, 4* (3), 45, 46.

McKee, B. (1992). Turn your workers into a team. *Nation's Business,* July, p. 36.

McLaughlin, C.P., & Kaluzny, A. (1990). Total quality management in health: Making it work. *Health care Management Review,* Summer, pp. 7–14.

Melbin, J. (1992). The art of total quality management. *For the Record, 4* (13), 1, 4, 5.

O'Leary, D. (1990). CQI—A step beyond QA. *Joint Commission Perspectives,* March–April, pp. 2, 3.

O'Rourke, L. (1992). Healthcare organizations adapt benchmarking techniques from industry to make quality gains. *The Quality Letter for Healthcare Leaders,* September, pp. 2–10.

Palmer, L. (1993). RRA leads CQI. *For the Record, 5* (4), 7.

Patrick, M., & Alba, T. (1994). Health care benchmarking: A team approach. *Quality Management in Health Care,* Winter, pp. 38–47.

Plsek, P. (1994). Tutorial: Planning for data collection, part I: Asking the right question. *Quality Management in Health Care,* Winter, pp. 76–81.

Robbins, S. (1994). *Management* (4th ed.). Englewood Cliffs, NJ: Prentice-Hall.

Spath, P. (1993). Critical paths: A tool for clinical process management. *Journal of AHIMA, 4* (3), 48–58.

vanMatre, J. (1992). The D*A*T approach to total quality management. *Journal of AHIMA, 63* (11), 38–44.

Walton, M. (1990). *Deming management at work.* New York: G.P. Putnam's Sons.

Wear, P. (1993). Hope in Washington. Will it support quality healthcare? *Journal of AHIMA, 64* (3), 7, 8.

Zinn, D. (1993). Continuous quality improvement: Eliminating a transcriptionist shortage. *Journal of AHIMA, 64* (3), 70–75.

Chapter 17

Controlling: Productivity Measurement, Performance Standards, and Work Sampling

Learning Objectives

After completing this chapter, the learner should be able to:

1. Describe how organizing by product or service lines enhances managerial efforts toward productivity improvement.
2. List the steps in initiating productivity standards and the methods managers can use to involve team members at each step of the process.
3. Differentiate between data and the resulting information that can be used for performance measurement.
4. Explain why more information is not necessarily better information.
5. Describe the value of benchmarking in performance measurement activities.

Key Terms

Performance standards	Quantity
Product lines	Sampling
Productivity	Service lines
Quality	Service organizations

Introduction

The focus on customers and their needs continues to create paradigm shifts in health-care organizations in ways that impact all levels of managers and staff. This shift is mandating that HIM managers lessen dependence on carefully designed productivity measurements that tend to highlight the failure of specific employees. Rather, managers envision systems that will assist their self-managed teams in monitoring team effort and continually improving the work processes toward increasing customer satisfaction. As this paradigm shift occurs, team member cooperation toward mutual customer-oriented objectives and increased productivity will be a major focus for HIM managers.

Manufacturing organizations with well-defined inputs and outputs have been ahead of service organizations in this customer focus and in the creation of tools to meet increased productivity. Health-care facilities are typically labor-intensive organizations and offer products or services that can range from cardiac surgery to a clean room to a documented health record. With the increasing focus on efficiency and effectiveness, managers and department team members are hearing more and more frequently that they must "work smarter" to increase productivity and lower health-care expenditures. Working smarter includes using new technologies and work-flow patterns to increase productivity without working harder or longer hours (Kelly, 1993).

Too often **productivity** is defined simply as the ratio between input and output. This definition considers **quantity** and efficiency as the baseline factors in determining the level of productivity. But, effectiveness is equally important in service organizations, so **quality** has a shared importance. Quality is defined as the accuracy with which a task is completed while quantity is concerned with the number of task units produced per staff hour. Therefore, a better definition of productivity is the number of task units produced per employee hour that meet the established levels of quality (Brandt, 1994).

As teams are empowered to create redesigned environments using tools such as continuous quality improvement to increase customer satisfaction, they are given the responsibility of assisting in development of appropriate performance monitoring systems. These systems may include manual data-gathering methods, depending on the application and the setting. Increasingly, however, data are gathered electronically and the needed information is disseminated to the teams in the form they have requested. As HIM managers redesign departments with new equipment, work methods, and performance-measuring systems, increased productivity can become a reality. Empowered employees assist in the redesign and then, as self-managed teams, they create monitoring systems for their unique needs.

Measuring and improving team performance for increased productivity is a part of the controlling function of management. In practice, however, these processes lead back to the planning function, where objectives are developed to give reality to the organization's vision of the future. This chapter outlines steps for measuring performance and setting standards through team empowerment with a focus on process improvement. As paradigm shifts occur in health-care settings, these steps for measuring performance can keep pace with new expectations and systems.

The redesign or reengineering efforts discussed in previous chapters are the building blocks for this chapter. The focus now is on productivity improvement and the tools that can be used effectively to measure productivity once the planning vision efforts have defined the tasks and set the objectives for reaching customer-oriented goals through team effort.

Product Lines and Productivity Improvement Efforts

Before beginning the discussion of measurement efforts that will lead to productivity improvement, it is helpful to assess the direction managers should take in developing HIM product lines or services to meet customer needs. Managers in **service organizations** such as health-care facilities face new challenges as tools are adapted from manufacturing organizations to meet their needs. As redesign changes a department's structure from the traditional functional division to customer-focused services, productivity improvement tools will change also. HIM managers and their teams, who expend effort toward working more productively without working harder or longer, will now be creating services that customers want and will be discarding non-value-added tasks.

Writing in the *Harvard Business Review* in 1991, Peter Drucker outlines four tasks that managers in service organizations must undertake in their efforts at working smarter for productivity improvement. Figure 17-1 lists these tasks.

1. *Focus on defining departmental tasks.* Begin with the planning vision, then set objectives for reaching the goals within the guidelines set by upper-level management or regulations. Answer the following questions:

   a. What are the tasks for the department?

   b. What accomplishments can be documented to show completion of tasks?

   c. Why are present tasks being done and should they be done at all or in this way?

2. *Concentrate activities on the redefined tasks.* Observe work flow, make changes, redesign, and reengineer.

3. *Define performance.* Work with the team in setting standards and monitoring tools.

4. *Empower employees.*

   a. Build responsibility for productivity and performance improvement through continuous learning for each team member.

   b. Build responsibility within the team by asking team members to teach others through crosstraining and new employee orientation.

Figure 17-1.   Managerial Tasks for Productivity Improvement (Drucker, 1991)

The use of technology for monitoring activities is also emphasized by Drucker. Involving the teams in developing quality and quantity monitoring with the tools currently available is a starting point for improving productivity and performance (Drucker, 1991). HIM managers with access to new technologies, redesigned work processes, and self-managed diverse teams face opportunities for synthesizing these inputs into the outputs that will provide the best possible service to customers.

Service-Line/Product-Line Management

A matrix organizational structure serves well in **service-line** management as discussed in Chapter 9. As reengineering occurs in health-care facilities, HIM managers and their teams have the opportunity to become part of the matrix structures as multiskilled health professionals. Part of the thrust as this reengineering occurs should be to maximize department productivity and to utilize resources effectively (Campbell, 1990).

---

1. *Record completion services:* Assembly, analysis, incomplete and delinquent record processing, incomplete and delinquent record count, suspension list, monitoring of the unbilled diagnoses report

2. *Data and information services:* Coding (inpatient and outpatient), abstracting, DRG assignment, diagnosis and procedure codes for billing and research, cancer abstraction, MPI, census reconciliation, birth certificates, release of information, statistical reports, indices

3. *Record maintenance services:* Record filing, record retrieval, transcription report filing, ancillary departments report filing

4. *Transcription services:* History and physical examinations, discharge summaries, consultant reports, operative reports, radiology reports, pathology reports

---

Figure 17-2. Health Information Management Product Lines (Postal, 1990)

As HIM services are offered to internal and external customers, the needs and expectations of these customers can be ascertained and then incorporated into the service provided. In this way, rather than establishing production and quality standards by function, the focus is on the process and meeting the needs of the customer (Scott, 1990).

Susan Nelson Postal shares a suggested list of HIM **product lines** that will lay the groundwork for discussing customer-oriented productivity. This list is detailed in Figure 17-2.

With these service lines in place, HIM teams are ready to participate in designing a matrix structure that involves team members wherever the service is needed for the intended customers.

Initiating Performance Standards and Productivity Measurement

When **performance standards** are not in place as the change process begins, managers and team leaders are challenged with creating an environment where team members willingly embrace change and redesign the work processes. Steps for initiating performance standards, as outlined in Figure 17-3, will give direction to this effort. The first steps take managers back to the organizing function where the functional activity of the department was

1. Analyze present work processes and choose appropriate organizational changes as outlined in earlier chapters.
   a. Involve upper-level management.
   b. Include all employees in this process; have them assist in analyzing and documenting present systems.
2. Review present monitoring systems—electronic and manual.
   a. Develop a list of reports available and in use at present for each section/team.
   b. List capabilities of present automated systems for additional monitoring possibilities.
3. Coordinate the departmental changes with any changes occurring throughout the facility.
4. Develop priority list for creating appropriate customer-focused productivity measurements for sections/teams that include quality and quantity monitoring.
   a. Begin the changes with one or two motivated teams, with one where problems of quality and timeliness surface frequently, or with one where measurement can be quite straightforward.
   b. Plan methods for sharing the success stories of these pilot teams and set the pace for implementing performance improvement throughout the department.
5. Document standards for performance measurements that include quality, quantity, and other crucial factors.
   a. Review any productivity standard reports in use and establish present performance levels.
   b. Use benchmarking tools.
6. Adapt or upgrade monitoring reports and develop new ones as necessary during redesign/reengineering process.
   a. Request exception reporting where possible.
7. Use frequent team meetings to monitor progress and develop changes as needed.
8. Implement changes and continue the cycle.

Figure 17-3. Steps in Initiating Work/Productivity Standards

developed. Of course, when performance standards are already in place, managers can enter the steps in Figure 17-3 at the point where change is anticipated.

Figure 17-3 mentions quality as well as quantity in giving equal importance to doing the right things right the first time. Increased productivity can result when priority is given to both quality and quantity measurement as standards are developed.

Tools for Performance Measurement

One of the first measurement tools needing development as productivity monitoring is started is a listing of the terms that will be used in measuring performance with definitions that give every team member a clear picture of what the term means and how it will be used. These terms must be defined as standard units for comparison across teams and, when possible, throughout the facility and in benchmarking tools as well. As automation of data collection increases, this listing will need modification. Automated systems should be flexible enough to add additional collection units as needs arise.

Standardizing terms has benefits in areas such as transcription where performance standards are often utilized. According to Claudia Tessier, executive director of the American Association for Medical Transcription (AAMT), and Mary Brandt, director of policy and research for AHIMA, the need for standard terms became an acute issue recently. Tessier and Brandt took action, along with representatives from the Medical Transcription Industry Alliance, to develop a set of definitions for transcription quality and quantity terms. These published definitions can now be used by organizations developing standard units for performance measurement. The definitions are voluntary (Palmer, 1994).

Tools for Documenting Present Work Processes

By using present procedures and observation, teams can prepare documentation of their work process to use in performance improvement activities and productivity measurement. Figure 17-4 is a sample form that can be effective. Initially, emphasis can be given to the areas where monitoring will begin. Those tasks that are repetitive and would lead to the greatest

Section/Team: Date:

Work Process:

Critical Elements of the Work Process	Employee Hours Spent per Day	Estimated Monitoring Effort Needed*

*Choose One:

Simple—Automated or measurement tool available, little monitoring effort required.

Moderate—Manual, measurement tool available or little preparation time required, some monitoring effort needed.

Difficult—Manual, time-consuming to measure and monitor.

Figure 17-4.   Sample Form to Document Work Process (Courtesy of Hinsdale Hospital, Darice Grzybowski, RRA)

saving of time should be considered first. Another factor initially is data collection and the systems available to collect the needed data efficiently and with little or moderate monitoring effort.

Tools for Documenting Present Monitoring Systems

Knowing what is being monitored in a continuing fashion is the next step. Documenting these tools for each team and then examining the work processes as a total will assist the management team. Figure 17-5 is an example of this documentation from Hinsdale Hospital for the permanent filing team.

Tools for Documenting Standard Measurements

As standard measurements are developed unique to each work process and in agreement with the standard terms list, these measurements will serve as the baseline for performance measurement. A sample manual documentation sheet is detailed in Figure 17-6 for data collection in the permanent filing section at Hinsdale Hospital.

Benchmarking

National productivity standards are available to assist HIM managers in benchmarking tasks performed in health information services. Examples of two firms offering comparative database information are MECON and MONITREND. Firms such as these provide subscription services to healthcare facilities for benchmarking data, networking, and other services. Upper-level management may be receiving reports on nationwide or regional productivity standards from such firms. HIM managers who become informed about what is being used to benchmark productivity within the facility or in the region can utilize these tools also. Using comparative databases for assessing departmental monitoring systems gives managers the opportunity to determine whether their monitoring systems are adequate and comparable.

Figure 17-7 depicts a sample partial comparison report from MECON for medical records, using patient discharges. The first column gives the performance characteristics and the second column is data from the hospital. The next set of five columns enables a comparison of five hospitals with

HINDSALE HOSPITAL   QUALITY ASSESSMENT PLAN
HEALTH INFORMATION MANAGEMENT EFFECTIVE DATE:

AREA/FUNCTION: Permanent Filing

FREQUENCY/INTERVAL OF MONITORS/AUDITS: QUARTERLY

SAMPLE SIZE/SELECTION CRITERIA: 30 (15 inpt./15 outpt.)

CRITICAL ELEMENTS	MEASUREMENT TOOL	STD./THRESH	COMMENTS
1. Outside slips reconciled prior to record filed in folder	QA Work Sheet Record/Perm. File	100%	
2. Record filed in correct existing permanent folder	QA Work Sheet Perm. File Folder	100%	Permanent folder already exists.
3. Folder year label updated if necessary	QA Work Sheet Record/Perm. File Folder	100%–95%	
4. First outpatient record placed on fileback	QA Work Sheet Record	100%–95%	
5. Subsequent out-patient records filed in reverse chrono-logical order	QA Work Sheet Record/Perm. File Folder	100%–95%	
6. Outpatient facesheet tabbed if filing record when more than one outpt record	QA Work Sheet Record	100%–95%	
7. Permanent file folder created correctly	QA Work Sheet Record	100%–95%	
8. Records/folders filed neatly	QA Work Sheet Visual Check	100%–95%	

QUANTITY STANDARD (range)	HOW MEASURED	COMMENTS:
1. File 30–35 records/ folders per hour	Productivity Log	
2. 1–2 folders made/minute	Productivity Log	
3. Records filed daily	Productivity Log Visual Check	

(Maximum 10 records in sorter section remaining end of shift)
7/94

Figure 17-5. Documentation for the Permanent Filing Team (Courtesy of Hinsdale Hospital, Darice Grzybowski, RRA)

DATA COLLECTION/AUDIT FORM

H.I.M.

AREA/FUNCTION: Permanent Filing   COMPLETED BY: DATE:

UNITS #	NAME	PT TYPE	D/C DATE	O.G. RECON Y/N	FILED CORR Y/N	YR. LABEL UPDATED Y/N	FILEBACK OP REC. Y/N	OP FILED CORRECT Y/N	OP REC TABBED Y/N	FOLDER MADE CORRECTLY NAME: Y/N	UNIT #: Y/N	COLOR CODE Y/N	FILED NEATLY Y/N
				Y/N	Y/N	Y/N	Y/N	Y/N	Y/N	Y/N	Y/N	Y/N	Y/N
				Y/N	Y/N	Y/N	Y/N	Y/N	Y/N	Y/N	Y/N	Y/N	Y/N
				Y/N	Y/N	Y/N	Y/N	Y/N	Y/N	Y/N	Y/N	Y/N	Y/N
				Y/N	Y/N	Y/N	Y/N	Y/N	Y/N	Y/N	Y/N	Y/N	Y/N
				Y/N	Y/N	Y/N	Y/N	Y/N	Y/N	Y/N	Y/N	Y/N	Y/N
				Y/N	Y/N	Y/N	Y/N	Y/N	Y/N	Y/N	Y/N	Y/N	Y/N
				Y/N	Y/N	Y/N	Y/N	Y/N	Y/N	Y/N	Y/N	Y/N	Y/N
				Y/N	Y/N	Y/N	Y/N	Y/N	Y/N	Y/N	Y/N	Y/N	Y/N
				Y/N	Y/N	Y/N	Y/N	Y/N	Y/N	Y/N	Y/N	Y/N	Y/N
				Y/N	Y/N	Y/N	Y/N	Y/N	Y/N	Y/N	Y/N	Y/N	Y/N
				Y/N	Y/N	Y/N	Y/N	Y/N	Y/N	Y/N	Y/N	Y/N	Y/N
				Y/N	Y/N	Y/N	Y/N	Y/N	Y/N	Y/N	Y/N	Y/N	Y/N

7/94

Figure 17-6. Sample Manual Documentation Sheet for Data Collection in the Permanent Filing Section (Courtesy of Hinsdale Hospital, Darice Grzybowski, RRA)

⨀ MELCON-PEER$_x$
mecon

Facility :
Department : PATIENT–MEDICAL RECORDS**
Mecon ID : F5700–PATIENT INFORMATION MANGMNTRUNCT ROLLUP
As of : 04/30/94

Peer Facility Selection Criteria:
AVERAGE DAILY CENSUS : >=100 & <=280
FACILITY TYPE : General Acute
EXCLUDE : UHC

COMPARATIVE PERFORMANCE/CHARACTERISTICS	YOUR HOSP DATA	DEPARTMENTS SELECTED BY HIGHEST % OF MATCHING CHARACTERISTICS					SELECTED BETTER PERFORMERS Based on Outlined Ratios				GROUP PERFORMANCE PERCENTILES		
		F144* PATIENT 81%	F268* PATIENT 81%	F275 PATIENT 77%	F284* PATIENT 77%	F310* PATIENT 77%	F144* PATIENT 81%	F268* PATIENT 81%	F134* PATIENT 100%	F310* PATIENT 77%	25th	Median	75th
FACILITY INFORMATION													
Discharges	11407.0	18571.0	8640.0	13324.0	9217.0	11918.0	18571.0	8640.0	11407.0	11918.0	9217.0	11407.0	13269.0
Adjusted Discharges	17694.8	25164.4	13929.8	22437.7	11082.6	17545.3	25164.4	13929.8	17694.8	17545.3	13929.8	16604.7	18086.2
Regional Wage/Price Adj Factor	80.1	83.1	95.0	101.7	82.1	106.7	83.1	95.0	80.1	106.7	83.1	95.0	105.9
DEPT OPERATING STATISTICS													
100 Records Filed	2044.0	4060.7	°	1223.1	579.5	1029.3	4060.7	°	2044.0	1029.3	579.5	1223.1	2044.0
1000 Transcription Lines Provided	1881.1	3035.1	33.0	3345.2	1149.8	1610.9	3035.1	33.0	1881.1	1610.9	1149.8	1610.9	3345.2
Patient Records Completed	15330.0	86179.0	13493.0	76565.0	32176.0	61584.0	86179.0	13493.0	15330.0	61584.0	32176.0	61584.0	86179.0
Cases Tracked by Utilization Review	4660.0	13613.0	12793.0	20134.0	5308.0	9850.0	13613.0	12793.0	4660.0	9850.0	9850.0	12462.0	15910.5
Inpatient Days Initially Denied	196.0	226.0	0.0	72.0	57.0	261.0	226.0	0.0	196.0	261.0	62.0	165.0	226.0
Quality Assurance Chart Reviews	10690.0	13613.0	41116.0	35780.0	6378.0	11300.0	13613.0	4116.0	10690.0	11300.0	10471.0	13613.0	36554.0
Quality Assurance Studies	213.0	18.0	30.0	56.0	18.0	85.0	18.0	30.0	213.0	85.0	18.0	65.0	85.0
STAFF CONFIGURATION													
Paid FTEs	42.3	49.9	31.2	57.0	28.7	44.0	49.9	31.2	42.3	44.0	33.4	44.0	52.7
SKILL MIX													
Record Coder/Abstractor/Analyst %	11.8	18.2	°	39.4	36.4	9.9	18.2	°	11.8	9.9	11.8	18.2	36.4
Transcriptionist %	24.1	10.6	°	19.9	7.1	12.8	10.6	°	24.1	12.8	7.1	19.9	24.1
Utilization/Quality Mgmt Prof %	0.0	21.4	°	19.0	27.1	16.9	21.4	°	0.0	16.9	8.6	16.9	21.4
Management %	8.3	4.0	°	3.5	10.6	9.8	4.0	°	8.3	9.8	4.0	8.9	10.6
Other %	55.8	45.9	°	18.2	18.9	50.7	45.9	°	55.8	50.7	18.9	37.9	45.9
Hours Worked: Hours Paid %	89.4	86.3	88.3	87.5	88.4	88.6	86.3	88.3	89.4	88.6	88.0	88.4	89.0
Non-Payroll Hrs: Total Hrs Paid %	0.0	0.0	0.0	0.0	0.0	6.8	0.0	0.0	0.0	6.8	0.5	2.6	6.4
WORKLOAD/SERVICE INTENSITY													
Dept Specific OP Adj Discharges	20012.3	84413.6	13292.3	66620.0	25602.8	56752.4	84413.6	13292.3	66620.0	25602.8	56752.4	84413.6	31.2
RECORD COMPLETION MIX													
Inpatient %	57.1	21.5	65.4	20.5	36.0	21.4	21.5	65.4	20.5	36.0	21.4	21.5	36.0
Involved Outpatient %	42.9	°	34.6	48.9	8.0	78.0	°	34.6	48.9	8.0	78.0	°	78.0
Patient Records Completed/Adj Discharg	0.9	3.4	1.0	3.4	2.9	3.5	3.4	1.0	3.4	2.9	3.5	3.4	5.2
Patient Records Complete/Dept Adj Disc	0.8	1.0	1.0	1.1	1.3	1.1	1.0	1.0	1.1	1.3	1.1	1.0	1.2
Records Filed/Adj Discharge	11.6	16.1	°	5.5	5.2	5.9	16.1	°	5.5	5.2	5.9	16.1	11.9
Lines of Transcription/Record Complete	122.7	35.2	2.5	43.7	35.7	26.2	35.2	2.5	43.7	35.7	26.2	35.2	43.7

Figure 17-7. MECON Department Comparison Sheet (Courtesy of MECON)

matching characteristics. Next, the set of four columns depicts the better performers from among the comparing hospitals. The last set of columns gives percentiles.

Shown in Figure 17-8 is a partial sample of the baseline questionnaire that is completed when your hospital joins MECON. The answers to these questions place your department with other hospitals having the highest percentage of like characteristics for benchmarking purposes.

With productivity comparisons such as MECON, HIM managers have benchmarking tools to share with teams, to defend budget requests, and to use as a basis for networking with peers.

Tools Used in Creating New Monitoring Systems

Lastly, documentation of the new data collection systems that allow monitoring to occur must be created. Once in place, these tools will have wide usage; not only will the teams use them, but managers can document productivity data for the budget, annual reports, and rationalization of staffing needs. Then the reports showing team performance can be used in appraising the team as a whole or individuals on the team, should individual performance appraisals be a part of the controlling function.

As teams assess their capability to measure performance, emphasis should be focused on monitoring that will provide the greatest payoff. With the technology available to gather data indiscriminantly, care must be taken in choosing measurement tools appropriately. For example, the record maintenance team may perceive that there are inefficiencies in the exception reporting for monthly medical staff committee record review. More records are being pulled than needed. Since these are monthly medical staff retrievals, there will be minimal productivity savings by narrowing the exception reports so fewer records are targeted. Rather, effort spent correcting inefficiencies in the daily retrieval of patient records for scheduled admissions will have greater payoff. Setting priorities according to payoff allows corrections to be made in a consistent manner.

Work Sampling/Exception Reporting

In automated performance improvement monitoring systems, exception reports are requested as an efficient tool for taking subsequent action. In automated systems, while the data are collected continuously, deviations

MELCON-PEER$_X$™ Operations Benchmarking Database Service   05710

DEPARTMENT PROFILE QUESTIONNAIRE

MEDICAL RECORDS SERVICES WITH TRANSCRIPTION

This department maintains patient medical records including assembly, coding, abstracting, filing, and external correspondence. It also provides medical transcription service. It may perform birth registration, tumor registry, and financial chart audit functions.

Facility Code: PEER94   Reporting Period: 01/01/93 thru 12/31/93

Department #:   05710

Department Name: _____

Contact Person: _____ Title: _____ Phone: (__) ____-____

IMPORTANT: All data must relate to the time period and cost centers indicated above.

Part A - OPERATING and FINANCIAL STATISTICS

1. **PATIENT RECORDS COMPLETED** [_____]
Total discrete medical records completed. Exclude normal newborns. Refer to Data Coordinator Manual for description.

2. **INPATIENT RECORDS COMPLETED** [_____]
Total medical records of facility inpatients completed. This is a SUB-SET of A-1.

3. **INVOLVED OUTPATIENT RECORDS COMPLETED** [_____]
Total medical records completed of outpatients with invasive or other involved treatments requiring informed consent (E.D., cardiac cath, ambulatory surgery, etc.) This is a SUB-SET of A-1.

4. **RECORDS CODED FROM INCOMPLETE CHARTS** [_____]
Total medical records coded and released for billing from incomplete chart (i.e., without discharge summary & operative reports).

5. **RECORDS FILED** [_____]
Total medical records filed and re-filed. Refer to Data Coordinator Manual for description.

6. **LINES OF TRANSCRIPTION PROVIDED** [_____]
Total lines of transcription provided (either produced or purchased). Refer to Data Coordinator Manual for description.

7. **STAFF HOURS WORKED** [_____]
Total hours worked (productive). Include regular and premium time.

8. **STAFF HOURS PAID** [_____]
Total hours paid. Include regular, premium, and paid time off hours. Exclude on-call or standby time.

9. **RECORD CODER/ABSTRACTOR/ ANALYST HOURS PAID** [_____]
Total hours paid for medical record coding, abstracting, and analysis technical staff. This is a SUB-SET of A-8.

10. **TRANSCRIPTIONIST HOURS PAID** [_____]
Total hours paid for medical transcriptionist staff. This is a SUB-SET of A-8.

11. **OTHER HOURS PAID** [_____]
Total hours paid for all other staff not reported above. This is a SUB-SET of A-8.

12. **NON-PAYROLL HOURS PAID** [_____]
Total contract and registry staff hours paid by the department. Refer to Data Coordinator Manual if hours are unavailable.

13. **LABOR EXPENSE** [_____]
Total expense for labor resources that corresponds to STAFF HOURS PAID and NON-PAYROLL HOURS PAID. Exclude benefits such as FICA.

14. **OTHER DIRECT OPERATING EXPENSE** [_____]
Total other direct operating expense for professional fees, supplies, rental fees, dues, travel, etc. Exclude depreciation and interdepartmental transfers, e.g., maintenance and food transfers.

15. **SUPPLY EXPENSE** [_____]
Total expense for the department operating supplies. This is a SUB-SET of A-14.

16. **CONTRACT SERVICE EXPENSE** [_____]
Total expense for services (e.g., transcription, etc.) provided by outside contractors. This is a SUB-SET of A-14.

Figure 17-8.   MECON Department Questionnaire (Courtesy of MECON)

from the standard are separated out and exception reports are prepared to reveal problem areas. In manual systems, exception reporting is better accomplished through task **sampling** where periodic tracking shows problem areas. Increasingly, HIM managers will use automated exception reporting as an effective and efficient tool in measuring performance.

Summary

HIM managers are changing productivity measurement patterns in tandem with the changes that are occurring throughout the health-care industry. Redesign or reengineering department organizations based on a customer-oriented focus leads to the creation of teams responsible for product or service lines.

The emphasis on working smarter to increase productivity demands using new technology and tools for setting performance standards and monitoring results. Productivity is defined as the number of task units produced per employee hour that meet the established levels of quality.

Four major managerial tasks can improve productivity: (1) focusing on defining departmental tasks, (2) concentrating activities on these redefined tasks, (3) defining performance, and (4) empowering employees. HIM managers increasingly use automated tools in performing these tasks.

Initiating productivity standards involves several steps: (1) analyzing present work processes; (2) reviewing present monitoring systems; (3) developing a priority list for productivity measurements including appropriate facility-wide changes; (4) documenting standards for performance measurements that include quality and quantity; (5) upgrading monitoring reports, using exception reporting where possible; and (6) meeting with teams for progress reports, developing changes, and then monitoring the process periodically.

Standardization of terms used for measurement is an important tool as performance monitoring is initiated. This list of terms can be used regionally and nationally for comparison. Regional and national firms provide subscription services to facilities and their benchmarking reports are available for comparative data.

Manual methods of work sampling will continue to be used for specific application.

Review Questions

1. Define productivity and document specific quality and quantity items that the coding and reimbursement team might use in creating performance measurement tools.

2. Obtain a benchmarking tool from a department manager and review the comparison report with the report from MECON found in Figure 17-7. Be ready to discuss your findings in class.

References

Brandt, M. (1994). Measuring and improving performance: A practical approach to implementing a productivity program. *Journal of AHIMA*, 65 (7), 46–51.

Campbell, V. (1990). Product-line management defined. *Topics in Health Record Management*, June, pp. 1–8.

Drucker, P. (1991). The new productivity challenge. *Harvard Business Review*, November–December, pp. 69–79.

Kelly, C. (1993). New knowledge/service workers must raise their productivity: Working smarter is key. *Advance for Health Information Professionals*, 3 (19), 11.

Palmer, L. (1994). How do you measure quality? *For the Record*, 6 (13), 4, 5.

Postal, S. (1990). Product-line administration: A framework for redefining medical record department services. *Topics in Health Record Management*, June, pp. 24–33.

Scott, M. (1990). Who are the customers of medical record departments? *Topics in Health Record Management*, June, pp. 9–16.

Suggested Readings

Bishop, W. (1993). Operational analysis of department. *For the Record*, 5 (13), 8, 9.

Boston, C., & Vestal, K. (1994). Work transformation: Why the new health care imperative must focus on both people and processes. *Hospitals and Health Networks*, April 5, pp. 50–54.

Boyd, F. (1991). People and productivity in records management. *Records Management Quarterly*, April, pp. 28–33.

Brandt, M. (1994). Measuring and improving performance: A practical approach to implementing a productivity program. *Journal of AHIMA*, *65* (7), 46–51.

Donnelly, J., Gibson, J., & Ivancevich, J. (1987). *Fundamentals of management* (6th ed.). Plano, TX: Business Publications.

Drucker, P. (1991). The new productivity challenge. *Harvard Business Review*, November–December, pp. 69–79.

Fletcher, D. (1991). The system analysis as a tool for medical record department improvements. *Journal of AHIMA*, *62* (11), 38–54.

Hamilton-Corcoran, M. (1993). The incentive isn't in the lines: The quest for quality. *Advance for Health Information Professionals*, *3* (11), 10.

Kazandjian, V. (1991). Performance indicators: Pointer dogs in disguise—A commentary. *Journal of AHIMA*, *62* (9), 34–36.

Kelly, C. (1993). New knowledge/service workers must raise their productivity: Working smarter is key. *Advance for Health Information Professionals*, *3* (19), 11.

Longest, B. (1990). *Management practices for the health professional* (4th ed.). Norwalk, CT: Appleton & Lange.

Palmer, L. (1994). How do you measure quality? *For the Record*, *6* (13), 4, 5.

Robbins, S. (1994). *Management* (4th ed.). Englewood Cliffs, NJ: Prentice Hall.

Rue, L., & Byars, L. (1986). *Management: Theory and application* (4th ed.). Homewood, IL: Richard D. Irwin.

Strickland, B., & Coan, T. (1994). The relationship between innovation and continuous improvement. *The Journal of the HIMSS*, Spring, pp. 49–54.

Strickland, B., & Hardison, C.D. (1993). Continuous improvement in health care: Transforming the hospital department. *Quality Management in Health Care*, Fall, pp. 46–56.

Terry, J. (1992). Moving up to high performance. *Topics in Health Information Management*, November, p. 36.

Special Issues for Health Information Managers

Chapter 18

The Effective Committee

Learning Objectives

After completing this chapter, the learner should be able to:

1. List several reasons why managers choose to use committees and meetings for managerial tasks.
2. Weigh the advantages and disadvantages of using committees for decision making.
3. Identify the major techniques for group decision making and suggest appropriate uses for each.
4. Give the major responsibilities of a committee chairperson and committee participants.
5. Describe the components of a meeting agenda and state why each one is necessary.
6. Explain the value of each of the components that are a part of minutes.
7. Identify advantages and disadvantages for using computer technology to create electronic meetings.

Key Terms

Action plan

Coopetition

Delphi technique

Nominal group technique

Introduction

In health-care organizations, committees and meetings are frequently used to bring together employees of different disciplines to perform managerial tasks. Departments also use meetings to share the decision-making tasks with employees. These tasks vary widely, depending on the committee's purpose, but coordination is ideally achieved as the members work toward a common effort. HIM professionals may spend a significant portion of time sharing expertise as members of these various committees and as participants at meetings. In addition, informational meetings are a normal communication tool that managers use for in-service presentations and to keep staff informed. This chapter explores opportunities available to committee members and chairpersons to create efficient productive meeting environments that use this time wisely.

Negative comments are frequently made about committees and meetings, which may indicate they are sometimes used inappropriately. To minimize the negative aspects, the major advantages and disadvantages of choosing the committee method for accomplishing managerial tasks are detailed. A chairperson's role in using committees to fulfill department objectives is outlined. The responsibilities of committee participants are addressed. Members who choose to create a cooperative, effective group of decision makers have an environment where ideas are generated, alternatives are sought, and integrated decisions are made.

Interdisciplinary committees may be considered as a type of matrix structure that can be permanent or temporary. The temporary committee is also called an ad hoc committee. Monitoring the progress of ad hoc committees is the responsibility of the delegating manager who sets deadlines to ensure action, decisions, and/or recommendations. This temporary committee is then disbanded when its purpose ends. The permanent interdisciplinary committee offers opportunities for HIM professionals to be advocates of automated health information systems and other HIM issues.

Preparing and distributing agendas and minutes are covered next. These documents guide the meetings as the chairperson communicates the direction the meeting should take, publicizes decisions made, and then adds action plans to assure delegated responsibilities are clearly known.

Participating in electronic meetings is discussed in the last section of the chapter. Increasingly popular, electronic media can enhance member participation and shorten the time for making decisions.

Creating and Participating in Effective Meetings

Permanent, regularly scheduled committees are a part of the professional experience of HIM professionals. These meetings may be in health-care facilities, professional organizations, community organizations, or regional councils. By sharing in the responsibility for effective meetings, HIM professionals can assist in creating time-saving sessions and can impact the decisions made by the group. Guidelines for creating and participating in effective committees and meetings are shown in Figure 18-1. The structure of a temporary committee may be more informal, but the guidelines outlined in Figure 18-1 still apply.

1. *Delegated authority:* Formally designated groups receive authority from the person or group with delegating power. This delegation may be for an advisory, informational, decision-making, or coordinating committee or meeting. Authority is documented and specific. Ad hoc committees are given a time limit for action. The role and scope of committees is outlined and the membership may be specified.

2. *Membership:* Members should be kept as few in number as possible, but must include those with complementary skills and knowledge to effectively accomplish the objectives of the group. Assignment to a committee may be by position. When team members can select someone from among their ranks, that person should have communication skills for adequate group interaction and for sharing information back to the team.

3. *Chairperson:* Appointed by position usually, but may be chosen from among the members or designated because of expertise. Chairpersons should understand group processes, be able to hold respect, and have ability to set the tone for the meetings. Responsibility includes coordinating efforts toward meeting the objectives delegated to the group and delineated in the agenda. Items on the agenda can be delegated to others as desired.

4. *Agenda:* Planned by the chairperson, by the group, or structured according to the objective for that meeting. Prepared in advance, the agenda should have a time frame for each topic with the responsible presenter listed. With the agenda distributed in advance of the meeting, each member can be responsible for coming to the meeting ready to participate as items come before the group.

(continued)

Figure 18-1. Guidelines for Effective Committees and Meetings

5. *Recorder and minutes:* Assigned to someone with attention to detail and the time to prepare the minutes and action plans for timely distribution. Major points of each meeting, recommendations, decisions, and action plan items need recording. Minutes and action plans are then distributed as soon as possible following the meeting. In this way, activities that need accomplishing before the next meeting are not easily forgotten.

Figure 18-1. *(continued)*

The guidelines in Figure 18-1 suggest responsibilities for the members as well as the chairperson and the recorder. When committee members accept responsibility for effective committee participation, the recommendations and decisions made can often have greater accuracy and offer better solutions than a single individual would make. The disadvantages of committees and meetings are outweighed by the advantages (Longest, 1990). Also, the time and effort spent by HIM professionals and other participants can be satisfying.

Advantages of Committees and Meetings

Communication and coordination have already been mentioned as major reasons for gathering people into groups for presentations, brainstorming, and decisions. Figure 18-2 details specific advantages for using committees in making organizational decisions.

The advantages listed in Figure 18-2 offer valid reasons for HIM professionals to make committees and meetings an integral part of managing their departments, teams, and interdisciplinary activities. However, the disadvantages of meetings listed in Figure 18-3 are also valid and give reasons for judicious use of the group process.

While the group process disadvantages can be minimized through skillful chairing of meetings, the cost factor is difficult to contain. Keeping the members on a committee to a minimum and keeping within the time schedule for each meeting are two responsibilities the chairperson must accept.

1. Group judgment aids in improving the quality of a decision.
2. Group interaction stimulates creativity.
3. Interteam and interdepartmental committees coordinate activities toward meeting department objectives.
4. Committees enhance acceptance of decisions and group cohesion as the pooling of specialized knowledge aids in understanding.
5. Group decisions divide responsibility and thus can increase commitment and motivation toward goals as knowledge of the problem is enhanced through discussion.
6. Agendas, minutes, and action plans communicate information and lead to coordinated efforts by the group and then by the departments and/or teams represented by each member.

Figure 18-2.   Advantages of Using Committees in Decision Making

1. Cost of bringing groups of employees together to make decisions is high—employee salary time is significant.
2. Committees are time-consuming; decisions may need to be made and implemented in a shorter time frame.
3. Motivational deadlocks can occur when committee members have conflicts with the objectives; these deadlocks can create unrealistic compromises.
4. Divided responsibility can also be a disadvantage since members may not feel individual responsibility for decisions or recommendations.
5. Compromised decisions can be mediocre; therefore, when decisive action must be taken, one person may be better suited to making the decision. Committee recommendations can then be used for information only, not decision making.
6. Strong-minded, vocal members can control meetings; chairpersons may thus find it difficult to use group process methods effectively to assure everyone has the opportunity for input.

Figure 18-3.   Disadvantages of Using Committees in Decision Making

Techniques for Effective Group Decision Making

Managers have an array of techniques for use in group decision making, including consensus, voting, brainstorming, nominal group technique, and Delphi technique. Which technique is best suited to a particular need is the first decision. Then, when a decision is made to have group interaction, the type of group and the individual members must be decided. Decision by vote may be the best method, especially when every member has an equal stake in the action that results. Consensus building may be chosen as the most effective technique when the issue is not controversial and when there are benefits for the whole team, the entire department, or the facility.

Brainstorming, nominal group technique, and Delphi technique each have value in group decision making when a wide array of alternatives need to be evaluated before a final decision is made. These techniques are time-consuming, so the time factor must be considered.

Consensus Building

Managers may choose to use consensus for arriving at a group decision. When a consensus is achieved, each member of the group is accepting of the chosen solution to a problem—each member is able to support the decision and implement any plan of action necessary. The strength of consensus building lies in the participation of all members during the process, the use of sufficient time to resolve any items of disagreement, and the support of every member once the consensus is reached. Figure 18-4 details the basic guidelines for effective use of the consensus-building technique.

When consensus cannot be achieved, the chairperson can choose to ask for a motion, second the motion, and vote on alternatives. If time allows and the difficulty is with a lack of complete information on the item, it may be feasible to choose an ad hoc committee to gather the additional material and present it at a future meeting. For example, at an HIM department employees' meeting, one agenda item concerns the purchase of a divider to separate the customer reception area to give more privacy to the release-of-information staff. After a description of the proposed divider was presented, two group members had strong objection to it and asked that consideration be given to a divider they had seen in a hospital department in a nearby city. Because of a lack of consensus, the chairperson suggested an ad hoc committee be chosen to visit the other department and report back in 2 weeks. This action plan was approved and implemented. At the

1. Constraints from upper-level management will not prevent acceptance of group decision.
2. Manager can support and implement group decision.
3. Each group member has time to present views and alternatives for a solution.
4. Areas of disagreement are exposed, discussed, and resolved.
5. Areas of agreement are explored fully.
6. Use of bargaining or voting is avoided.
7. Support of decision is possible for all group members.

Figure 18-4.   Guidelines for Effective Consensus Building

next meeting, the chairperson called for a motion, a second, and a vote was taken on which divider to purchase.

Brainstorming

When an informal atmosphere where creativity can be encouraged is an appropriate setting for engendering ideas on a subject or a problem, brainstorming can be effective. Brainstorming generates creative ideas and develops concepts without typical group inhibitions or pressures toward conformity. Thus, it is an idea-generating process that encourages alternative suggestions. Managers have important tasks in preparing for brainstorming sessions, however. These are included in the suggestions outlined in Figure 18-5 for successful sessions. Some authors group brainstorming, nominal group technique, and Delphi technique together; here they are separated, with brainstorming being the most informal technique of the three (Umiker, 1988).

Nominal Group Technique

The generation of ideas for decision making is the first goal of **nominal group technique (NGT)**; however, the group session is highly structured and personal interaction is minimized. The chairperson's role with NGT is outlined in Figure 18-6 and emphasizes the independent thought of each member during the initial phase of the process. Research shows that NGT generates more unique ideas than brainstorming (Rue and Byars, 1986).

1. Develop a clear understanding of the subject or problem and a set of questions to begin the session.
2. Gather tools for the session such as flip charts/wall charts and writing supplies for recording ideas.
3. Ask someone who is not a group member to serve as recorder for the meeting.
4. Begin the session with an introduction to brainstorming technique and the goals of the meeting. The following points should be covered:
   a. Review the subject or problem to be discussed.
   b. Encourage each member to share ideas so there is a large quantity of input.
   c. Explain that no idea is considered too outlandish as ideas are generated, no criticism of ideas is allowed, and no value judgments are made.
   d. Explain that no praise of ideas is allowed.
   e. Remind everyone that during this idea-generating phase no discussion of an idea is allowed.
   f. Begin asking the prepared questions and have several ideas to offer that will generate thinking; at least one should be far-fetched.
5. Exhaust idea generation, making sure each group member contributes.
6. Cluster the ideas by grouping similar points together and assist the group in looking for patterns of similarity.
7. Encourage the group to suggest additional improvements from these clusters, refine wording, and develop alternatives for the subject or problem through consensus.
8. Inform the group of how the developed alternatives will be used.

Figure 18-5. Techniques for Successful Brainstorming

An advantage of using NGT is its unbiased approach to decision making. Group members work together without restricting independent thinking. Managers who choose NGT techniques to enhance decision making must be ready to accept the alternative ranked highest by the group if this was stated as part of the process. On the other hand, managers can use NGT process to bring forth several alternatives of high ranking that will then be developed further by the management team for a final decision.

1. Develop a clear understanding of the subject or problem and a set of questions to generate creative thinking.

2. Gather tools for the session such as pads of paper for members, flip charts/wall charts, and writing supplies for recording suggestions and priorities.

3. Ask someone who is not a group member to serve as recorder for the meeting.

4. Explain the NGT process to the group. The following points should be covered:

   a. Present the subject or problem.

   b. Distribute pads of paper and ask each member to silently think about the subject or problem and record ideas for later sharing.

   c. Emphasize that no talking is permitted during this phase unless a point of clarification is raised.

   d. Explain that during the recording phase each member will read one item at a time, around the group, in sequence, until all ideas are recorded.

   e. Encourage unusual ideas, quantity of ideas, and the value of piggybacking on someone else's idea once the list is exhausted.

   f. Emphasize that no criticism of ideas is made during this phase.

5. Begin the silent idea-generation phase; allow ample time.

6. Ask each member, in turn, to read one idea for recording on the flip chart; repeat in sequence until all ideas are recorded.

7. Cluster ideas and encourage evaluation and discussion of pros and cons.

8. Assign a letter of the alphabet to each idea or cluster of like ideas.

9. Ask members to record, on paper, their ranking of the ideas, using the letter assigned, prioritizing by order of importance. No discussion is allowed during this phase.

10. Pick up papers and record votes on the flip chart next to the corresponding letter. Total them for each idea.

11. Choose the ideas with the highest ranking (5 to 10 of them) for further discussion, refinement, and improvement.

12. Inform the group of how the ideas and rankings developed will be used.

Figure 18-6.   Steps for Successful Nominal Group Technique Meeting

Group members need to understand what use will be made of their product to enhance ownership of the eventual decision.

Delphi Technique

When time constraints are not present and group members are physically separated, a more complex technique can assist in futures planning. The **Delphi technique**, for instance, assists HIM managers employed by multihospital corporations in bringing a degree of standardization to health information activities among the facilities. The major features of the Delphi technique are listed in Figure 18-7.

Assessing the perspective of widely scattered members can also be achieved effectively with the Delphi technique. For example, selected members of a national organization such as AHIMA can be asked to offer ideas on a subject impacting the future of the association. Although the Delphi technique does not offer the advantages of face-to-face interaction as with brainstorming, fresh ideas can surface as expert minds consider alternatives and build consensus over time.

Sharing decision-making tasks, when delegated to those responsible for creating proposed changes, offers managers increased ideas and options. Committees can offer the appropriate setting for beginning the change process.

---

1. Identification of the subject or problem occurs and group members are chosen.
2. Questionnaires are carefully designed to elicit responses from group members toward solving the problem or developing ideas about the subject.
3. Group members complete this first set of questionnaires and return them for compilation.
4. Group members receive the compilation and a second questionnaire that will hopefully elicit new alternatives and narrow the options.
5. Compilation of the second set of questionnaires brings the group closer to consensus and another questionnaire is developed and distributed with the second compilation, if necessary.
6. Distribution of compiled information and new questionnaires continues until consensus is reached.

Figure 18-7.   Characteristics of the Delphi Technique

When HIM managers understand the alternative methods available to them for informing, sharing, obtaining ideas, and motivating, they can be effective chairpersons by choosing the most effective technique for the situation.

The Effective Meeting Participants

For truly effective meetings, all participants must understand why they are attending and then conscientiously fulfill their roles. While the chairperson sets the tone of the meeting, she cannot create success unless the participants are actively involved in fulfilling the goals for the meeting. This section looks first at the role of the chairperson and then at how the participants can contribute to group effectiveness.

The Chairperson

The manager of an HIM department in an acute-care facility participates in many committees and meetings. This section focuses on those meetings where she serves as chairperson. These meetings or committees are given various names such as management team meetings, administrative council, team quality improvement group, team planning group, department in-service meeting, or interdisciplinary team meeting. When a new group is formed, the members enjoy naming the committee and this ownership of the name can enhance their commitment to the objectives.

HIM professionals are involved in formal committees where legal protocol is mandated. The chairperson of such a meeting will want to use *Robert's Rules of Order* for motions and voting. A parliamentarian may be used to advise the chairperson of proper protocol. By preparing ahead of time and knowing just how the meeting will be conducted, chairpersons and members can participate confidently.

Regularly scheduled meetings can become boring committee sessions unless the chairperson uses creativity to stimulate ideas and present routine information in unusual ways. Figure 18-8 offers suggestions to keep regular meetings focused and positive.

The Members

When a committee meeting convenes, the participants bring to the meeting their unique ideas, expertise, personal biases, and concerns. Putting

Regular Meetings Within the Department

1. Decide whether routine items come before the group or are communicated by another route: newsletter, team leaders to team, E-mail, bulletin board.

2. Choose whether a scheduled meeting is needed—cancel unless needed. Schedule short meetings when the full time allotted is not needed.

3. Encourage each employee to place items on the appropriate agenda. Have the team manager review the item with the employee.

4. Include items pending from the last meeting: any previous items needing further action.

Special Meetings Within the Department

1. Announce well in advance.

2. Plan meetings for second- and third-shift teams as needed.

3. Define the objectives, role, and scope of the meeting, especially when authority is given for decision making.

4. Confirm the meeting with guest speakers and other invited guests the day before the meeting.

Interdisciplinary Meeting

1. Communicate with other department(s) regarding a meeting, structure of the meeting, and agenda items.

2. Offer to share responsibility for chairing the meeting, preparing the agenda, distributing background material and minutes.

3. Encourage teams to suggest agenda items.

Plans Common to All

1. Separate agenda into categories:
   a. Information-only items
   b. In-service presentations
   c. Decision-making brainstorming to gather list of alternatives
   d. Decision making solution to problem

Figure 18-8.   Planning Committees and Meetings

Chairing the Meeting

1. Begin the meeting with enthusiasm. State the objectives using action verbs. Repeat specific objectives as necessary for agenda items, changing the tone of the meeting appropriately.

2. Have material organized by agenda items; have notes of specifics to be mentioned.

3. Encourage participation by each member; ask for input by name, as needed.

4. Use active listening skills to gain a clear understanding of ideas.

5. Use a controlling mechanism to the extent necessary for reinforcing positive behavior or for keeping attention on the subject at hand.

6. Repeat decisions and motions for the recorder.

7. Use the consensus approach to decisions when feasible; when necessary, ask for a motion, a second, and call for a vote.

8. Allow the group to give opinions and suggestions without judgment, domination, sarcasm, or argument.

9. Be professional at all times, but with a sense of humor.

10. End the meeting on time by staying within the time frame for each agenda item.

Figure 18-8.   *(continued)*

aside personal interest and making decisions in the best interest of the department or the facility can be a challenge for the employees.

A major responsibility for members comes before the meeting itself. Reviewing the minutes of the past meeting and becoming knowledgeable about areas that are less familiar is a first step. Next, the action plan needs to be read as it may serve as a reminder of specific responsibilities with a deadline. By meeting action plan obligations within the time frame, members participate in creating a successful group and, in turn, success in the workplace. The third responsibility comes when the agenda for the upcoming meeting arrives. Reviewing the items, looking for any topics that have background material attached begins the preparation process for the meeting. This may include networking with experts or reading current journals or books to gain current knowledge on a topic.

An ongoing responsibility for committee members is to actively look throughout the workplace for problems, potential problems, and possible areas needing change to add to future agendas. Being a catalyst for quality improvement and for initiating paradigm shift proposals enhances the value of meetings and offers satisfaction to members.

During the meeting itself, effective members arrive on time, vary seating arrangements to avoid cliques, participate as active listeners, and offer ideas constructively. Each member can guard the time factor by refraining from bringing up issues that have little value for the item being discussed, or could more appropriately be resolved in another setting.

HIM professionals desiring to gain experience in meeting leadership can offer to present specific topics, or chair the meeting for a specific decision-making agenda item. Managers willing to offer growth experiences to their staff can be rewarded with increased enthusiasm and commitment.

Meeting participants who choose to combine competition and cooperation into the new term, coopetition, and actively cooperate to achieve the goals of the group, will find positive results. These results include motivation, enhanced communication, creative ideas toward problem solving, higher levels of productivity, and satisfaction (Donnelly, Gibson, and Ivancevich, 1987).

Documentation Tools for Committees and Meetings

Communication contributes to the success of the group process, and agendas, minutes, and action plans are important communicating components. This section details effective use of these documentation tools.

The Agenda

The value of creating structure for committee meetings through use of agendas was mentioned earlier. By attaching background material to the agenda and distributing it in advance of the meeting, chairpersons add to the ingredients for success. Agendas should be considered communication tools where committee members can both learn the direction the group is taking toward meeting the objectives and share in that move by suggesting agenda items.

Agendas consist of the committee name; date, time, and location of meeting; names of members when these vary; items to come before the group separated into those for information, those for formal presentations, those for brainstorming with alternatives, and those for decision-making solutions. After each item, the name of the person responsible, when other than the chairperson, is listed along with the time allotted for the item. A sample agenda for a team meeting is shown in Figure 18-9.

Having several extra agendas to give members who did not bring theirs is a realistic alternative to sharing or dashing off to make last-minute copies.

Community Hospital
Health Information Department
Agenda for Team Leader Meeting
Conference Room III, January 28, 19_ _, 2:00 P.M.

		Minutes
1. In-Service on New Exercise Room	Dr. J. Larson	15
2. Approval of Previous Minutes		
3. Old Business—Presentations		
3.1 Report on Task Force, DRG Update	Steve Conner	20
3.2 Policy for Record Tracking		5
4. Old Business—Brainstorming		
4.1 Weekend Coverage Request		15
5. New Business—Decisions		
5.1 Filing Change in Storage Area		10
5.2 Time Card Policy Change	Jean Weber	5
5.3 Lighting Problems, Transcription	Jim Walker	10
6. Information Only		
6.1 Farewell Reception for Mary Stevens Cafeteria, Room 2, February 6, 4:30 P.M.		
7. Adjournment		

Figure 18-9.   Agenda for a Team Leader Meeting

The Minutes

The minutes serve as a record of decisions made and are valuable legal documents showing when policies changed or when other changes occurred. This information is needed for accrediting and licensing bodies and shows the level of effective business practice. A facility may have specific guidelines for writing minutes, especially those involving medical staff attendance. The recorder then follows this format in writing the minutes.

The HIM department will need to maintain minutes of department meetings, showing the attendees and actions taken. Accrediting staff will ask for documentation that in-service programs involved all employees and covered a range of topics. And, of course, minutes complement the agenda as communication tools for the meeting members. When distributed promptly after a meeting, minutes reinforce the decisions made, act as reminders of activities still needed, and give the date of the next meeting.

The content of minutes may vary, the format differ, but the major components remain the same. Figure 18-10 shows minutes of a medical record committee meeting, chaired by a physician. Note that absent physicians are listed as excused for medical staff statistics.

The major components of minutes include:

1. Name of meeting, date, time, and location.

2. Those present at the meeting; should also include those absent to assure members unable to attend will receive a copy of the minutes.

3. Items brought before the group, with motions, votes, consensus decisions, actions, deferments; expressed in clear, concise language. Deadlines, persons responsible for future action are included.

4. Substantiating materials are attached to the official minutes such as outlines of in-service presentations, recommendations brought before the group from another committee, or supporting documents.

5. Name and title of the chairperson and of the recorder are indicated. This can be in the list of those present or as the final line of the minutes.

6. The action plans are also attached to the minutes and distributed.

Unless the meeting is quite informal, it is preferable to have a staff member who is not a member of the group as the recorder. Members should be given opportunity to concentrate on the issues, not on recording the actions.

Huffman Hospital

Health Information Services

Minutes of Regular Meeting Held February 12, 19__

Board Room II, 2:00 P.M.

MEMBERS PRESENT:	James Mitchell, Chairperson; Fred Brauer, Brian Dunbar, Thomas Evans, Marilyn George, Frances Johns, Alan King for John Mace, Frank Peterson, Maxine Peterson, GeorgeTaylor, Ruth Weisman, ex officio
MEMBERS ABSENT:	Barry Branson, excused; John Germann, excused; Roy Johnson; Geraldine Peterson
INVITED GUEST:	Marilyn introduced Janice Smith, management affiliation student from a nearby university.
DEVOTIONAL AND PRAYER:	Dr. Brian Dunbar presented a devotional thought from the Psalms and offered prayer.
MINUTES OF PREVIOUS MEETING:	The minutes of the meeting held January 11, 19_ _, were reviewed as distributed and approved.
ON UNIT ANALYSIS:	Marilyn George presented the results from the 2-month trial study on on-unit analysis. The sample study was done on Unit Three with two medical record professionals spending time on the unit each day for coding and analyzing the records. The handout showed the statistics from the study. It is attached to the official minutes.
	A motion was made by George Taylor that Unit Four be added to Unit Three for another 2-month study and that Marilyn report back to the committee at the end of another 2 months. There was a second and the motion was VOTED unanimously.
DEATH RECORD REVIEW:	The practice of reviewing the death records at the end of each meeting was discussed. Since these death records are only those that a reviewing physician feels should be discussed in committee, there was general consensus that these records could now be reviewed by the newly formed departments for each service.

(continued)

Figure 18-10.   Medical Record Committee Minutes

Dr. Mitchell asked Marilyn to prepare a memo to that effect for each of the medical staff department chairpersons.

Frank Peterson showed the committee members an architect's drawing of the proposed remodeling of the medical record services office suite. Dr. Mitchell asked whether the placement of the door opening from the physician's lounge had been cleared with the Chief of Staff.

Further discussion and approval of the drawing will be tabled until Frank talks with the Chief of Staff and has further information for the committee.

INPATIENT FACE SHEET: Discussion continued on the changes proposed for the inpatient face sheet as part of the new admitting computer system. Dr. King presented the views of the OB/GYN Department and discussion followed.

It was moved by Dr. King and seconded that a final decision on the proposed face sheet changes be tabled until the Executive Committee of the Medical Staff can discuss the statement above the signature line.

RATIONALE: Because of the negative feelings of many physicians to the statement, Dr. King and Dr. Mitchell felt that the Executive Committee should look at this statement and recommend alternatives to the committee before proceeding.

The VOTE to table a decision and send this statement portion to the Executive Committee was passed by a six-to-four margin.

NEXT MEETING: A special meeting is called for 2 weeks from today (February 26) to discuss the inpatient face sheet statement recommendation from the Executive Committee.

ADJOURNMENT: 3:40 P.M.

_____
James Mitchell, M.D., Chairperson

_____
Sally Green, Recording Secretary

Figure 18-10.   *(continued)*

The Action Plans

A very successful meeting can be held with all the members enthusiastic about the direction of the plans as they leave the meeting. But, success can be halted in its tracks if an **action plan** to remind members responsible for follow-up activity is lacking.

The action plan includes the committee name, date of the meeting, action to be taken, member(s) responsible for the activity, and deadline for completion. Figure 18-11 is an example of the action plan following the meeting described in the minutes shown in Figure 18-10. When the member assigned to an action plan was not present at the meeting, the chair-

---

Huffman Hospital

Health Information Services

Action Plan for February 12, 19_ _, Meeting

1. Death Record Review

ACTION: Memo to Medical Staff Department Chairpersons

BY: Marilyn George

DEADLINE: Within week

2. Face Sheet Changes

ACTION: Refer to Executive Committee

BY: Alan King

DEADLINE: February 15

REPORT BACK: February 26, Special Meeting

3. On-Unit Analysis

ACTION: Perform another 2-month study

BY: Marilyn George

DEADLINE: Report at April 8 meeting

4. Placement of Door into Physician's Lounge

ACTION: Discuss with Chief of Staff

BY: Frank Peterson

DEADLINE: Report at March 10 meeting

Figure 18-11. Action Plan

person, recorder, or another member can amplify the task description, verbally communicate the objective, and answer any questions the member may have.

Effective Use of Electronic Meetings

Combining sophisticated computer technology with the nominal group technique to enhance decision making offers advantages over the traditional meeting. With a computer embedded in front of each group member, ideas can flow to a projection screen on the wall and be read instantly. As issues are presented to the group and ideas are flowing via computer, anonymity offers honesty and speed. In addition, chitchat is eliminated, everyone can key in ideas at the same time, and members can piggyback their ideas with speed.

As use of electronic meetings becomes popular, some managers concede that those who are slow typists may have great ideas but do not get them all on the screen within the time frame. And, those who contribute the best alternatives do not get credit for them (Robbins, 1994). To lessen these disadvantages, an alternative is to use face-to-face discussion after idea generation and initial priorities are set, to gain the informational richness of verbal interaction at that point. Busy HIM professionals will appreciate the ability to use electronic meetings for intradepartmental and interdisciplinary meetings as large facilities install the technology to increase staff efficiency.

Summary

Meetings and committees are an integral part of the group process within health care, and managers spend a significant portion of their time as members, committee chairs, or participants in informational meetings.

Making meetings effective demands effort on the part of the chairperson and each participant. This effort is worthwhile because the advantages of using committees in decision making outweigh the disadvantages. The advantages include improving the quality of a decision, stimulating creativity, increasing coordination, solidifying group cohesion, and enhancing commitment.

Major disadvantages of using committees for decision making are the cost of bringing groups of employees together, the time factor, motivational deadlocks, lack of individual responsibility for decisions, consensus that may lead to mediocre decisions, and strong-minded members who may control the meeting.

Managers have responsibility for choosing the best technique for group decision making; these techniques include consensus, voting, brainstorming, nominal group technique, and Delphi technique. Chairpersons may change from consensus to a vote when an issue becomes controversial. Informing participants of how the product of their efforts will be used is an important component when the chairperson wishes an array of alternatives for a later decision.

Agendas, minutes, and action plans communicate with group members and serve as legal documents. Agendas include a time limit for each item and are distributed with background material before the meeting. The recorder uses clear, concise language in the minutes to describe the meeting and the actions taken. Items that need further action are documented in an action plan that serves to remind members of later assignments.

Using computer technology for electronic meetings can shorten the time in making a decision, and can offer anonymity and honesty. To take advantage of face-to-face discussion, the chairperson may choose to end the meeting with verbal interchange as refinement of alternatives is undertaken.

Review Questions

1. What qualities would you like to see in the chairperson of a committee where you are a member?

2. List five techniques managers can use for group decision making. Which technique would the manager of a coding and reimbursement team most likely use for gathering proposed workstation designs for the team's area of the new department? The alternatives are to be submitted to the department manager in 10 days. The final decision will be made by the construction planning team.

3. What is the follow-up document that accompanies the minutes? Who uses this document and why?

4. Obtain copies of the agenda and minutes from a recent meeting and analyze them for effectiveness in serving as communication documents.

5. Attend a committee meeting, take minutes, and prepare the minutes for distribution.

References

Donnelly, J., Gibson, J., & Ivancevich, J. (1987). *Fundamentals of management* (6th ed.). Plano, TX: Business Publications.

Longest, B. (1990). *Management practices for the health professional* (4th ed.). Norwalk, CT: Appleton & Lange.

Robbins, S. (1994). *Management* (4th ed.). Englewood Cliffs, NJ: Prentice Hall.

Rue, L., & Byars, L. (1986). *Management: Theory and application* (4th ed.). Homewood, IL: Richard D. Irwin.

Umiker, W. (1988). *Management skills for the new health care supervisor.* Rockville, MD: Aspen Publications.

Suggested Readings

Donnelly, J., Gibson, J., & Ivancevich, J. (1987). *Fundamentals of management* (6th ed.). Plano, TX: Business Publications.

Huffman, E. (1994). *Medical record management* (10th ed.), J. Cofer (ed.). Berwyn, IL: Physicians' Record Company.

Longest, B. (1990). *Management practices for the health professional* (4th ed.). Norwalk, CT: Appleton & Lange.

Robbins, S. (1994). *Management* (4th ed.). Englewood Cliffs, NJ: Prentice Hall.

Rue, L., & Byars, L. (1986). *Management: Theory and application* (4th ed.). Homewood, IL: Richard D. Irwin.

Terry, G., & Franklin, S. (1982). *Principles of management* (8th ed.). Homewood, IL: Richard D. Irwin.

Umiker, W. (1988). *Management skills for the new health care supervisor.* Rockville, MD: Aspen Publications.

Chapter 19

Managing the Time Factors of Managers and Employees

Learning Objectives

After completing this chapter, the learner should be able to:

1. Define discretionary time and explain why managers wish to increase this resource.
2. List five tools and techniques that offer better time management.
3. Describe use of a master list for organizing activities to be completed; include time management features of this tool.
4. Describe the techniques that can reduce stress relating to time management.
5. Contrast urgent management problems or items with important managerial problems or items, and state the role of priority setting in managing crises effectively.
6. Explain why delegating to employees can lead to increased career satisfaction for managers.

Key Terms

Discretionary time
Response time

Introduction

Time is a resource each of us has in equal allotments; how the precious minutes are used is up to us. Although the phrase "saving time" is frequently heard, managers can only spend time—saving it is not an option. When engaged in each of the four management functions—planning, organizing, leading, and controlling—HIM professionals utilize time as a resource. This chapter offers suggestions for using the scarce resource of time efficiently and effectively.

The HIM profession is comprised of a wide range of functions, each demanding attention and activity from busy managers. This heightens the awareness that time is a valuable resource. When a variety of activities simultaneously confront busy managers, they tend to focus on the most urgent ones—not necessarily the most important. This can create tension for managers. By taking a few moments to focus on end results and then setting priorities and delegating appropriately, managers can schedule their time and their staff's time most effectively.

Because time expended in an HIM department is so closely tied to the budget, managers can experience stress when budget allocations and time used to accomplish objectives are not in alignment. For example, HIM managers and employees can be pressured to meet deadlines—such as 3-day billing information submission without adequate coding and reimbursement staff—but they lack the staff resources for success in this instance. Stress related to time management can be caused by other factors also and suggestions for reducing such stress are outlined in this chapter.

Implementing the tools and techniques for time management gradually leads to confidence. HIM professionals soon find that setting priorities and delegating tasks to empowered employees are integral to the functions of planning, organizing, leading, and controlling. The last section of the chapter emphasizes setting task priorities and delegating when possible to release personal time for other opportunities.

Time as a Resource

Planning personal activities for the day, for the week, or for the year mandates that managers choose how time will be expended. When the return on invested time is considered just as important as the return on invested money, managers begin to give increased value to this scarce resource. Unfortunately, while employees experience automation and other job enhancements with resulting higher productivity, managers are frequently asked to increase their responsibilities and effort without comparable job enhancements that would increase managerial productivity. Thus, the managerial tasks are increased, creating a demand for efficient use of time. This situation is especially true in health care, where the trend is to reengineer with flattened organizational structures, adding to the responsibilities of middle management. This increased responsibility offers an additional reason for health information professionals to utilize time management principles wisely.

A look at possible time wasters in the typical HIM department gives focus to the principles for effective time management. Figure 19-1 provides a list of common time wasters that can keep HIM professionals from prioritized activities already planned for the week. These time wasters are, in part, uncontrollable since they are responses to legitimate requests, problems, or demands initiated by someone else. The time needed to complete these uncontrolled requests is called **response time**. When response time can be shortened, **discretionary** or controllable time is increased.

Increasing discretionary time is the goal as the time wasters outlined in Figure 19-1 are scrutinized for action. A closer look at the challenges out-

---

1. Crisis situations demanding immediate attention. No plan in place to solve the problem.
2. Unexpected walk-in interruptions or telephone interruptions from employees, customers, peers, upper-level management.
3. Lack of clear instructions to proceed on a project.
4. Need for additional information or material to complete report or project.
5. Meetings, scheduled or unscheduled, that are poorly run.
6. Disorganized desk with stacks of unfinished projects.
7. Procrastination and difficulty saying "no" to requests.
8. Lack of effective automated executive support system.

Figure 19-1. Possible Time Wasters for HIM Professionals (Ensman, 1994; Umiker, 1988)

lined in Figure 19-1 offers insights that can be helpful in reducing these time wasters.

Crisis Situations

Certainly not every crisis situation can be avoided. The goal is to decrease their frequency and disruption. During the planning functions, programmed decisions can be documented for the teams as suggested in Chapter 4. Recurring problems can then be handled by the teams in line with the policies. Managerial planning reduces the frequency of crisis situations and increases discretionary time for both managers and employees.

Unexpected Interruptions

Personality differences offer a plethora of ways managers choose to handle interruptions. Some managers gradually make everyone aware that they have an open-door policy except for time periods needed for concentrated work. Choosing a special time of day when the door is closed for an hour or two is then accepted well. Managers who choose to close their doors for longer periods can be accepted well also when they increase their visibility by employing management by walking around (MBWA) techniques. Appropriate assertive comments to upper-level management can also lessen interruptions. Comments such as, "Thank you for deferring our conversation this morning while I was busy completing the medical staff report," lets upper-level management know that you will inform them when important items take precedence over interruptions.

Information/Material/Instructions Needs

Many reports and projects are monthly or yearly requests and it is possible to plan and organize for them. Documenting what is needed, and having this information routinely gathered will reduce the time wasted in preparing for the next report. Taking a critical look at each project when it first arrives can provide impetus for asking questions and setting in motion the gathering of material and information. Then, when there is time to work on the project, the information and material will be ready.

Meetings

Chapter 18 offers suggestions for effective meetings. Poorly run meetings that are chaired by someone else challenge the members to create a climate that encourages change toward effectiveness.

Disorganization/Procrastination

The tools and techniques described in the next section offer ideas for putting disorganization and procrastination on notice that they will not be tolerated. Personality types tending toward disorganization can take small steps toward using these tools and techniques; time management enhancement makes the effort worthwhile.

Employee Time Management

By utilizing effective time management techniques themselves, HIM managers are role models for the team members. When emphasis is given to reducing time-wasting habits through in-services, bulletin boards, newsletter spots, and E-mail, additional impetus can quicken the pace of change. The raised awareness level regarding time management encourages employees to look for time wasters and eliminate them.

One way to raise awareness is by creating incentives for teams who ferret out time wasters; this creates enthusiasm. Allowing the members to initiate action when specific team members have time-wasting habits offers advantages. For example, when one employee is habitually taking longer to perform a task, such as opening correspondence and keying in information, the members may request a time and motion study for opening and sorting the correspondence.

Team leaders can reduce time wasters by assuring:

1. Orientation and training are thorough.
2. Instructions are clear and documented so team members do right things right the first time.
3. Policies and procedures are current and understood by team members.
4. Duplication of activities is minimized.
5. Socializing and personal activities are reserved for break and lunchtime.

Tools and Techniques for Time Management

To some extent, time management remains an individualized process. Just as each of the time wasters in Figure 19-1 can create greater difficulty for some HIM professionals than others, so the tools and techniques outlined in this section have greater usefulness for some managers than they will have for others. This situation relates to personality types, for HIM professionals carry their personality types into the workplace and their methods for handling time management are as varied as their personality types. By utilizing the tools and techniques outlined in Figure 19-2 that best match their personality organizational types, busy managers can develop time management plans that will increase discretionary time.

---

1. *Activity log:* Keep an activity log in 15-minute intervals for at least 2 weeks to determine how time is spent. It can be on an appointment calendar or automated log. Record as activities are done, not at the end of the day. At the end of each week, categorize the activities and total the minutes. Analyze how time is spent and look for time wasters. This log analysis brings into focus how time is actually spent and offers opportunity for change.

2. *Objectives:* Plan or update personal and departmental objectives. List activities that need to be initiated to accomplish objectives needing action; include deadlines when appropriate.

3. *Desk file/computer file:* Use file drawer in desk as a working file, not just for storage. Prepare file folders for items that are frequently used for quick reference—a file for each employee or team—to drop in an informal note of commendation, concern, or family item, for example. Prepare file folder for each unfinished project or request that now resides on top of the desk and place in drawer. Keep top of desk work space clear except for item being done at the moment.

   Complement use of desk file with a computer file. Since requests come in hard copy in many situations, a desk file cannot be totally replaced in most facilities.

4. *Master list:* Create a master list or "to do" list either on computer or in an 8½-by-11-inch ruled binder. Attack clutter and stacks on the desk first, then activities from the list of objectives, and subsequently periodic reports. Indicate date that item made the master list and a deadline for completion.

Figure 19-2.   Tools and Techniques for Time Management

a. Go directly to master list when accepting a request and write it down; do not record on small pieces of paper.

b. Cross through items as they are completed; tear out page when majority of items on it have been completed; rewrite unfinished items and dates, when using binder; on computer, move completed items to an inactive list, or delete completely.

c. Keep master list available at all times as a working document; review it before leaving for the day to set priority projects for the next morning.

d. Prepare file for daily mail items that cannot be cared for at once. Place item on master list with date and completion date, when necessary.

5. *Daily organizing techniques:* By taking the actions outlined above, the desk is now uncluttered, the working files are out of sight in the drawer or on computer, and the master list is less than two pages. Discretionary time is increasing, and some daily organizing techniques can increase that time even further.

a. *Beginning-of-day planning:* The real slaves of time are those who dash in the last minute every morning, stressed and out of breath. What a difference arriving at least 10 minutes early—at least most mornings—can make. Those 10 minutes will offer the opportunity to look at the appointment log (computer or desk calendar) for the day. Make sure items needed for appointment are ready and note on master list any that still need completion. Review master list for priority items for the day. Circle or star those that have highest priority. Check any messages that may have come in; record or discard appropriately. Now, meet the challenges of the new day.

b. *Mail techniques:* Mail for the department can be sorted by a receptionist, secretary, or team manager. Choose the best time of day for the mail and concentrate on it then. Label and place in the "out" basket any items that need rerouting. Place items in working file folders as needed; have folders for committee meetings or team meetings and place items in these folders for future announcements or discussions. Use computer to respond to requests that can be answered immediately or to request information needed before responding. Use telephone, voice mail, or E-mail for requests or responses. Use file folders and master list for other items. Choose to delegate requests when possible. Scan magazines, journals, or reports for key information; clip articles for later reading and place in "to read" basket. Do find time to read and share them.

Figure 19-2. *(continued)*

Tools and Techniques for Reducing Stress in Time Management

Reducing stress related to time pressures can increase productivity for HIM professionals and increase their feelings of well-being at the same time. The June 27, 1994, issue of *For the Record* (Palmer, 1993) has an editorial on stress and the immune system. The stress-reduction techniques listed in the article include two techniques that relate to time management: (1) slow down and (2) tackle problems one by one, not all at once. To slow down need not mean to get less done. Slowing down better relates to increased efficiency through the tools and techniques outlined in Figure 19-2. There will be increased discretionary time to slow down and enjoy other aspects of the health information profession and career goals.

Tackling problems one by one is valued advice for beginning the morning thinking time, when the challenges for the day can seem overwhelming. By creating a mindset that prioritizes the tasks and then concentrates on one task at a time, busy managers reduce stress for themselves and set the tone for the staff as well. Each manager must choose the most effective work schedule for himself by understanding his productivity cycle. Doing the most difficult priority item at the time of day when energy levels are highest is important. Also, big projects like the budget have many individual items that can be tackled one by one, delegated, or divided into tasks that better fit the schedule. By always thinking of big projects in terms of divided units, HIM managers can reduce stress and not waste time slots that may be just long enough for one divided unit, but not for a whole project.

Priority Setting and Delegation

The difference between handling urgent problems or items and important items has been mentioned briefly. An example of an urgent problem is when the HIM manager finds the team responsible for release of information upset because the team leader is at a meeting, the copy machine is down, and an attorney is expected in an hour to pick up the copy of a record for court. Rather than assuming crisis responsibility by taking the record, going to another department, copying the record, and having it ready for the attorney, the manager—with priorities in mind—could spend a few minutes interacting with the team. By asking questions about where another copy machine might be available, how to get permission to use it, and then allowing the team members to work out solutions to their urgent problem, the manager has empowered them. At the same time he has helped them—with ideas—and used minimal time in doing so.

In the "Managers Who Make a Difference" below (Nelson, 1993), the manager of a department at a 186-bed hospital found that empowering employees to assist in solving time-constraint problems brings rewards. Both she and her staff were commended for developing cohesive interteam groups and working smarter to accomplish a project.

Managers Who Make a Difference

Debi Nelson, manager of health information services at Trinity Hospital in Minot, North Dakota, enlisted the creative effort of her employees in solving a problem. Through teamwork and extra effort, they met time constraints and stayed within the budget.

The problem facing Debi and the department teams was not an overnight crisis, but the impetus for taking action—an upcoming accreditation visit—offered no time extension for completing the task. And the task was one of those low-priority, time-consuming projects managers have difficulty working into the busy routine of everyday activities—purging the files. The shelving was packed with patient records and in some sections records had to be pulled before there was room to file the completed folders. A crisis indeed, but no extra budget for temporary personnel and no time from other duties to release a team member full-time to complete the project. Time management solutions had to include a working smarter philosophy since other team priorities demanded the time available.

With the cost and time constraints in mind, Debi and her staff began brainstorming for ideas. The consensus grew that each employee would have a stake in completing the purging project and enthusiasm grew because everyone wanted to solve the problem. Working on Saturdays, every other week, was chosen as an alternative. Since the file area was totally available for purging on Saturdays, concentrated energy could be devoted to the project. The staff signed up to work on alternate Saturdays, giving a team of half the employees each week. In order to avoid overtime costs, each employee took leave on another day during that week.

(continued)

The project started with great enthusiasm and teamwork. Purging was accomplished without the many interruptions that would occur on a weekday and the change of pace was enjoyable. But it was a big project and Debi sensed a decline in morale before long. She discovered that giving up part of the weekend was beginning to take its toll. A second brainstorming meeting was called to find another alternative.

The following adjustment in the schedule was chosen: Half of the staff dedicated every other Wednesday to purging. The routine work was covered by the remaining staff and interruptions for questions, telephone calls, and other demands were kept to a minimum. Purging was organized with each team dedicating half of its members every Wednesday—coding, transcription, record analysis, release of information, and record activity. The high morale that characterized the beginning of the project returned and teamwork efforts increased.

Well before one accreditation surveyor had opportunity to step into the department and view the file area, it was orderly with records easily found on request. And, upper-level administration commended Debi and her department staff for finding a solution to a thorny problem, solving it together by utilizing time wisely, and staying within the department budget. As other backlogs occur, Debi and her staff now have confidence they can use time effectively to solve them also.

In Chapter 16, tools for delegating and empowering teams encouraged HIM managers to choose new tasks and responsibilities as increased discretionary time allowed. At the same time, increased responsibility is likely to be thrust upon HIM managers as reengineering takes place in health-care settings. But, as busy managers delegate tasks to empowered teams, they can accept increased responsibilities with confidence that by letting go of some tasks the new ones will be manageable. Knowing how much time a new task will take can be difficult to judge initially, so the need for extra effort may be present at first. However, the professional who accepts changing paradigms and actively creates new methods and tools to accomplish tasks can grow professionally and find greater career satisfaction. When accepting new responsibilities, astute HIM professionals will take time to ensure they have a clear understanding of the tasks involved before beginning. This will save revision time later and increase confidence. Successfully executing new responsibility offers managers the opportunity to be seen as professionals with advancement potential.

Summary

As a scarce resource for HIM managers, time cannot be saved; it can only be used. This use may be in uncontrolled or response time to perform managerial functions and the activities of the department in response to requests, demands, or problems. In contrast, discretionary time is that part of a manager's time that is controllable. By increasing discretionary time and then organizing it effectively, managers can experience professional growth and career satisfaction.

Five tools and techniques that can be utilized by HIM professionals to minimize time wasters are (1) an activity log, (2) a list of objectives for direction and motivation, (3) desk files and computer files, (4) a master list, and (5) daily organization with first-hour planning and mail techniques.

The master list is a working tool that keeps all tasks recorded, ready for setting priorities and delegating appropriately. This master list can be in a binder on the desk or it can be in a computer file. It could very well be a combination of these if the computer file is not instantly available.

By increasing discretionary time available, HIM professionals can reduce stress that relates to time management. Tackling problems one by one is helpful, and, since discretionary time is frequently in short blocks of time, breaking projects down into divided units increases the likelihood that these short blocks of time will not be wasted.

With practice, priority setting can become a part of daily techniques, especially when crises occur. When HIM managers view these urgent problems and prioritize them into other activities scheduled for the day, delegating and empowering are useful tools.

As teams are empowered to be self-managed, delegating becomes a skill. This can increase the time available for accepting new responsibilities and career growth and satisfaction.

Review Questions

1. Choose one of your typical weeks and keep an activity log with 15-minute intervals. Star those activities that represent uncontrolled response time. Total the remainder of activity times to determine the discretionary time available to you each week.

2. List five tools and techniques that can minimize time wasters and critique the use of each. Be prepared to discuss your ideas in class.

3. Interview an HIM manager to determine how he handles urgent management problems versus important managerial problems. Ask for some specific experience to bring to class for discussion.

References

Ensman, R. (1994). How well do you manage time? *Advance for Health Information Professionals, 4* (9), 21.

Nelson, D. (1993). Saving time on purges. *For the Record, 5* (1), 11.

Palmer, L. (ed.) (1993). Stressed out. *For the Record, 6* (13), 4.

Umiker, W. (1988). *Management skills for the new health care supervisor.* Rockville, MD: Aspen Publishers.

Suggested Readings

Appelbaum, S., & Rohrs, W. (1981). *Time management for healthcare professionals.* Rockville, MD: Aspen Systems.

Bishop, W. (1993). Managing conflicting priorities. *For the Record, 5* (6), 9.

Ensman, R. (1994). How well do you manage time? *Advance for Health Information Professionals, 4* (9), 21.

Huffman, E. *Health information management* (10th ed.), J. Cofer (ed.). Berwyn, IL: Physicians' Record Company.

Meyer, J. (1990). *If you haven't got the time to do it right, when will you find the time to do it over?* New York: Simon and Schuster.

Nelson, D. (1993). Saving time on purges. *For the Record, 5* (1), 11.

Robbins, S. (1994). *Management* (4th ed.). Englewood Cliffs, NJ: Prentice Hall.

Umiker, W. (1988). *Management skills for the new health care supervisor*. Rockville, MD: Aspen Publishers.

vonOech, R. (1990). *A whack on the side of the head: How you can be more creative*. New York: Warner Books.

Chapter 20

Managing Change as a Health-Care Professional

Learning Objectives

After completing this chapter, the learner should be able to:

1. List the major forces that are creating a mandate for change in the health-care industry.
2. Give three categories where change typically occurs in health-care organizations.
3. Identify major challenges that face HIM professionals initiating change in both acute-care facilities and ambulatory settings.
4. Define revitalization and explain why change experiences are needed for professional career growth.
5. List four underlying reasons why employees may resist change and explain the rationale for each.
6. Discuss six steps managers can take to reduce resistance to change.
7. Explain the factors that offer value to the role as broker of health information.

Key Terms

New vision
Organizational development (OD)
Revitalization

Introduction

Multiple megatrends are shaping the health-care industry and most of these trends impact the HIM profession to some extent. From the paradigm shift toward integrated delivery systems to increased ambulatory care, the pressures to obtain accurate, timely health information appear to consistently increase. These shifts to an information-driven health-care setting, where communicating health information via technological tools reigns, add to the impetus for HIM professionals to increase analytical, assessment, and evaluation skills. The need to embrace expanded communication roles will also increase. As professional organizations develop contemporary definitions of the profession that emphasize a combination of knowledge in medical science, health data needs, confidentiality/legal issues, systems thinking, and information technology, changing roles will emerge.

Accepting shared responsibility for the development of an integrated longitudinal computer-based patient record (CPR) that will meet customer needs through integrated networks, HIM professionals can find new opportunity for **revitalization** of their professional vision. HIM professionals can choose to accept responsibility for being change agents in shaping future health-care trends, articulating a **new vision**, and molding a contemporary definition of the profession that is understood by their customers. In fact, learning the necessary skills for implementing change successfully may be the most important factor for career growth (Longest, 1990).

This chapter explores the inevitable changes that are impacting the health-care industry and suggests three major categories of change: technical, structural, and employee/interpersonal relationships. Next, the challenges and rewards of embracing change and proactively planning, organizing, and implementing change activities are discussed. Change offers opportunities for career advancement and the next section revisits briefly the opportunities outlined in Chapter 1. This section also shows why HIM professionals need periodic revitalization to stimulate a new vision that can lead to expanded roles, excellence, and excitement in the workplace.

Creating an environment for reducing resistance to change is a crucial skill for change agents. The next section looks at some factors that cause resistance, and methods that managers can use to create a sense of ownership and belonging among employees to lessen the resistance.

The last section of the chapter takes a broad look at managing and brokering health-care information into the twenty-first century.

Change Is Inevitable

The strategic planning that consumes a significant portion of managerial time and effort is, more often than not, in response to perceived forces that result in a revised vision, new objectives, and improved customer relations. These forces may be external to the enterprise, or they may come from internal pressures.

External Forces

Government laws and regulations regarding health care are an example of external forces that may be anticipated by managers. Or, the laws and regulations can change quickly, leaving health-care managers to react by initiating change. Community growth or the actions of other health-care institutions may be anticipated—these external forces result in changes that impact how a facility meets the needs of its customers. Notice that the word *anticipation* is used to describe these examples of external forces. If the SWOT analysis is not performed and strategic planning is neglected, the facility will not have an anticipatory, proactive approach to change. Instead, top executives and middle management will be reacting to the imposed changes when the pressures mandate action. The example of government laws and regulations, enacted quickly, shows that despite the SWOT analysis, reactive change is sometimes necessary. However, innovative organizational changes do not take place in a reactive environment.

Internal Forces

Internal forces also create an environment for organizational change. At the extreme, the objectives of the facility can be revised when a new upper-level management team is employed—with resulting vision and cultural changes. Other internal forces that stimulate change for HIM professionals frequently involve technology with new equipment that demands retraining for new skills among the employees. Anticipating and planning for such change offers opportunity for revitalization for the HIM managers and the teams involved.

An unfortunate internal force for change involves dissatisfied employees and results in increased stress and behavior problems. Resistance to change causes dissatisfaction and stress; these issues are discussed later in this chapter.

Major Categories of Change

Strategic planning is crucial to managing organizational change from the internal and external forces mentioned above. When organizational change is undertaken, it typically involves one or more of the three major categories of change. These categories are (1) changing the technology, (2) changing the structure, and (3) changing employees/interpersonal relationships. Figure 20-1 briefly describes activities that HIM professionals will perform as these major categories of change are undertaken.

As the details in Figure 20-1 suggest, a balanced approach to creating change includes a combination of appropriate elements from these three categories as managers look for the tools and techniques that will bring successful results. Since internal and external pressures that bring change

---

Changing the Technology

External forces may be the likely reason for new equipment such as computers, or for new software. As integrated delivery systems increase and networking becomes commonplace, standardization will mandate additional hardware and adaptable software. This will necessitate revised policies, revised procedures, and retraining of employees. On the surface, these changes may not appear to involve any major change in the objectives planned for the department. However, it is likely that technology changes will provide a catalyst for change in the other two categories as well as with organizational redesign and team-building relationship enhancement.

Changing the Structure

As discussed in Chapter 8, organizing the department is not a static process. Innovative organizational changes to flatten the managerial structure, to create self-managed teams, or to decentralize some sections are redesign or reengineering options. Utilizing facets of organizational design best suited to their unique settings, HIM managers can use structural change to create efficiencies and effectiveness that will offer excellence to their customers. Such changes will involve the redesign of positions, of position descriptions, and of the work flow to better meet customer needs. With implementation of these structural changes, attention must be given to the last category—interpersonal relationships.

(continued)

Figure 20-1. Major Categories of Change

Changing Employees/Interpersonal Relationships

Changing interpersonal relationships in response to planned technology and structural changes is crucial to success. The redesign of a department where employees are empowered through creation of self-directed teams results in increased responsibility and authority for these teams. With such major changes, the department may need consultants with expertise in **organizational development (OD)**. OD is defined as a focus on techniques to change people and their interpersonal work relationships (Robbins, 1994). Consultants in OD can assist in preparing employees for change by offering sensitivity training, team building, and interteam development techniques. Effective communication of the vision, objectives, and benefits of the changes are also needed.

Figure 20-1. *(continued)*

are inevitable, HIM professionals must continually seek a proactive stance in meeting the challenges. While not possible with every pressure, anticipating and planning in a proactive manner offers rewards as outlined next.

Change: The Challenge and the Rewards

In the preceding sections several reasons for implementing change activities in an HIM department are offered. The advantages of planning and implementing innovative organizational change where there is anticipation of external or internal factors are then emphasized. When the management team anticipates and then plans strategically, the opportunities for success are enhanced. With success comes rewards that can include satisfied customers, motivated employees, recognition for change-agent excellence, or personal career advancement.

Within the Department

The principles outlined in Chapter 19 for effective time management are crucial to meeting the challenges facing HIM professionals in anticipating and preparing for change. When the pressures of uncontrolled response time do not allow reflective, creative, periodic thinking and planning time, the challenge of anticipating change and instituting strategic departmental planning can go unrealized. The resulting stress only increases as dependency on crisis management becomes more and more commonplace. Revitalization of the vision cannot take place.

By taking the steps outlined in Chapter 19 and managing time effectively, not only can stress be lowered, but HIM managers can begin to envision rewards as they anticipate, plan, and implement change in their roles as innovators, systems thinkers, and technology-wise brokers of health information. The increasing demand for data capture, analysis, integration, and dissemination will result in a wider distribution of knowledge among employees as they serve the customers of health information. Managers who recognize the advantages of educating and empowering teams with increased knowledge, skills, and responsibilities will be rewarded with visionary teams that give excellence to customers and are motivated to accept the next responsibility.

Within Ambulatory Settings

Mergers, managed care, integrated delivery systems, HMOs (health maintenance organizations), and like terminology are used to describe the trend toward the growing networks of health-care providers and insurers. Increasingly, the trend is to provide the full spectrum of care for contracted patients. In response to this trend, developers of EPR and related information systems are accelerating the pace of open, interoperable, integrated health-care information systems that can lead to a functioning CPR network. As patient care moves increasingly into the ambulatory arena, HIM professionals have the opportunity to build careers within the ambulatory setting. Being part of the teams that shape delivery of health-care patterns for the future can be rewarding.

Within Other Settings

Challenge and reward face HIM professionals who choose careers in diverse settings such as those outlined in Chapter 1.

Professional Revitalization and New Vision

To revitalize is to offer enriched opportunities for personal growth that energize people and stimulate them to perform at their optimum. Busy HIM professionals may have difficulty finding the time and expending the effort to scan the environment, think critically, and adjust their vision for the future on a periodic basis. But for personal growth and for collective professional growth, it is essential. Professionals who take the time, at least every 5 years, for this revitalization process, can be the leaders, thinkers, and planners who take the HIM profession into future successes.

To create a new professional vision means to view the future with imagination and clear thinking that can be shared with others. Through leadership this shared vision brings a community of individuals together, working toward the same objectives. The process of change can then occur.

Specific steps toward revitalization and creation of a new vision are outlined in Figure 20-2. These steps offer professionals an opportunity to develop visionary skills and leadership. Each step is discussed below.

Step 1: Create Time for Planning

Comparing the present vision with accomplishments gives HIM professionals insight into the direction they have taken during the period. While a major revitalization and a new vision is of value every 5 years or so, a yearly

---

Step 1. Create time for planning: Set aside time to revisit the past and plan for the future.

Step 2. Initiate activities for growth: Initiate professional growth planning such as taking formal courses in leadership, critical thinking, systems thinking; read current literature; attend seminars and workshops.

Step 3. Practice new thought patterns: Practice using new thought patterns that lead to proactive mode; be information focused.

Step 4. Embrace creative tension: Embrace creative tension that leads to cognitive dissonance; resolve through focus on ultimate vision.

Step 5. Share the new vision: Share the new vision with the management team; articulate and integrate plans into action.

Figure 20-2.   Steps toward Revitalization and New Vision

assessment is equally valuable. In fact, Peter Drucker, in *Managing the Non-Profit Organizations*, suggests a yearly self-assessment that focuses on a review of the past year, a comparison with the goals for that past year, and a vision for the future (Drucker, 1990). This evaluation will require setting aside personal time, away from external pressures, and then answering several questions in a search for revitalization. These questions should include:

1. What have been my major successes in the past year and have they given my customers, my employees, and myself satisfaction?
2. Have I enriched my position over the past year so that I have added responsibilities and enrichment?
3. What do I want to be remembered for and am I progressing toward that goal? What adjustments do I need to make to remain stimulated to achieve this goal?
4. Have I served as mentor to others as I introduced change over the past year?

By answering these questions, HIM managers can review the direction of their careers, their work environment, and then make the necessary adjustments that keep them focused on the ultimate vision.

Step 2: Initiate Activities for Growth

Lifelong learning activities assist in maintaining the focus of revitalization and offer opportunities to change thinking patterns. Because traditional health information activities have focused on objects such as the physical medical record and its contents, courses in systems thinking have special value.

Step 3: Practice New Thought Patterns

Breaking away from routine thought patterns and reactive modes of behavior can take great effort. HIM managers who make that effort find creating a satisfying and rewarding new vision stimulating. The resulting revitalization has benefits for the HIM professionals, for their work environment, and for the collective profession.

Step 4: Embrace Creative Tension

In Chapter 12, cognitive dissonance was discussed as a sense of uneasiness created by a difference between reality and hopes. HIM professionals can create an environment where creativity takes root and empowered teams envision and build systems that will close the gap between reality and the vision.

Step 5: Share the Vision

Leadership involves visionaries who can motivate others to move toward the vision. By articulating the objectives and vision to the working teams and persuading each employee toward the best effort, the shared vision can become reality.

Shaping the Curve

Each professional has a lifetime career curve and the shape of that curve is the responsibility of the individual. Figure 20-3 depicts a curve that illustrates the career of an individual who chooses to enter the health-care industry as an HIM professional and is initially enthused about her job and the profession. As the years go by, however, she appears to be waiting for someone else to parade the next new vision into her professional life. When that does not happen, when she does not reach out for revitaliza-

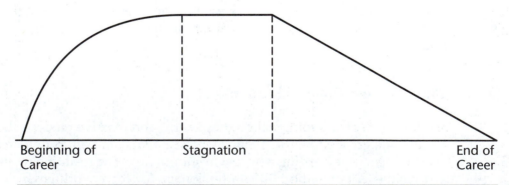

Figure 20-3.   Lack of New Vision Experience

tion, for growth, nothing happens. Instead she stagnates and the result is the flat curve seen in Figure 20-3. The curve begins normally and then flattens out as there is no stimulation to create a new vision experience.

Reed Powell, guest professor at Claremont Colleges, Claremont, California, suggests in the Management for Change course, that professionals need revitalizing every 5 to 9 years. Mr. Powell states that revitalizing is not the same as promotion; in fact, with revitalization, the job title may not change. Revitalizing means continuing education, job enrichment, and increased breadth of experience. For example, a manager who has spent the last 5 years with a fairly stable department chooses to stretch herself and her staff by becoming informed about creating a departmental business venture. Planning with the transcription and reimbursement teams, she then chooses to develop transcription and coding services for a newly opened urgent-care center across town. By initiating a plan to become a revenue-producing department in this entrepreneurial manner, the HIM manager can revitalize her own professional spirit and create new vision experiences for the transcription and reimbursement teams as well. The curve in Figure 20-4 has a new vision experience just beginning, and this demonstrates the growth of revitalization.

To avoid stagnating, of course, HIM professionals may choose promotion by educating themselves to become CIOs, vice presidents, or managers of ambulatory settings. Advanced education, growth experiences, and men-

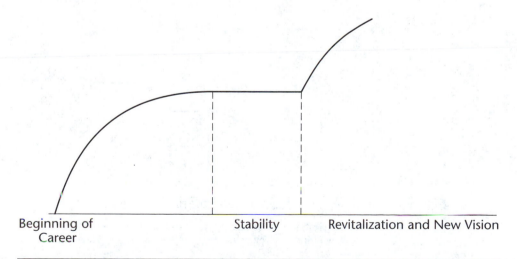

Figure 20-4. New Vision Experience

toring are three steps that professionals may utilize in the new vision process. Figure 20-5 offers a lifetime glimpse of new visions that can keep HIM professionals excited about their daily activities and revitalized over the life of their professional careers.

Scarring and Self-Protection

Revitalization is not without risks. Mr. Powell cautions that when problems arise, scarring and self-protection may result. These factors can be counterproductive to new visions and will be setbacks on the path to continual growth curves for HIM professionals. Negative attitudes can result when professionals reach out for revitalization and are hindered in their plans. For example, after 5 years as regional manager of a copy service firm, an HIM professional chose to grow by returning to school and obtaining a master's in business administration. When a position opened within the firm for a vice president on a national level, the regional manager applied for the position, and, after several weeks of infighting and political maneuvering, did not receive the promotion. This experience scarred her to the extent that she left the health-care industry and protected herself from further pain by taking a staff position in a stable food product business.

Figure 20-6 offers a pictorial review of this experience. The curve that showed promise has flattened and the scar may prevent further new births. Mentoring can guard against the self-protection that arises following a pain-

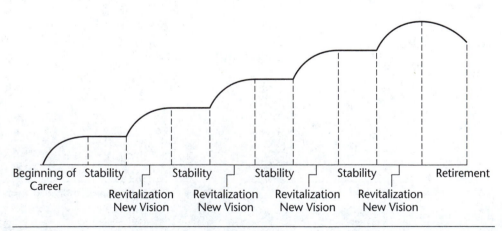

Figure 20-5.   Lifetime New Vision Experiences

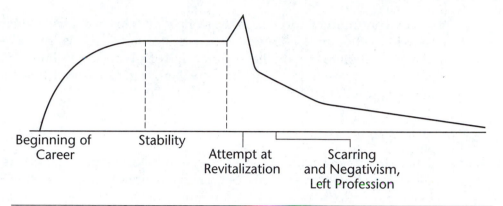

Figure 20-6.   Scarred Attempt at a New Vision Experience

ful scarring. When a seasoned HIM professional assists in restoring self-confidence to a scarred colleague, new vision experiences can revitalize and renew the spirit. The disjointed curve in Figure 20-7 offers a realistic view of the value that mentoring can have in the life of a scarred professional.

Entrepreneurial HIM professionals can extrapolate these personal growth ideas for their businesses also. Starting a new business that offers services or products in health care can be exhilarating, and when riding the crest of success, entrepreneurs may feel they are on top of the world. This euphoria can lead the professionals to feel their business will stay

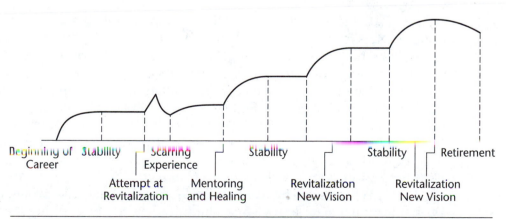

Figure 20-7.   Scarring and Healing with Mentoring Experience

there by continuing to do things the same way. This is a fallacy; their business will decline unless they have a series of new visions, revitalization, and a dedication to stay on the leading edge of advancing technology. Businesses will have the declining curve of Figure 20-3 without this constant effort for growth.

Emerging Roles for Advancement

As megatrends in health care continue, new roles emerge that offer opportunities for HIM professionals. Several have already been mentioned, but other possibilities expand the vision. For example, in Chapter 11 mention was made of community health information networks (CHINs) and their role in the developing network for a CPR. As responsibility for creating databases, maintaining confidentiality, and disseminating meaningful reports becomes focused, HIM professionals can fill the opportunity niches that will emerge for accomplishing these activities. By joining committees, councils, and associations, HIM professionals will stretch their imagination and sharpen their skills for fulfilling future needs.

Standardization efforts as health-care networks grow can offer an attractive niche also. From insurance forms to smart card technology, standardization will enhance the speed of change toward the CPR, and HIM professionals can find opportunities for career paths within the vendor community. Developing new tools and techniques to assist in data capture, analysis, integration, and dissemination of health information are also roles that can bring satisfaction to HIM professionals as vendor employees.

As relationships between physicians and hospitals change, there are opportunities to create niches where HIM professionals can carve out their roles. Some hospitals are creating physician support services departments with broader objectives than the typical medical staff office. Especially when these departments are involved in the automatic transfer of patient information, HIM professionals may find fulfilling careers implementing new technologies and managing such departments. As the range of ventures and contracts between physicians, hospitals, and insurance firms continues to expand, additional opportunities for challenging careers are created for HIM professionals with a vision of the future.

The legal profession has captured the hearts of some HIM professionals. With additional legal knowledge, these leaders are now filling key roles within professional associations, the government, and health-care facilities. As legal decisions are made regarding national health information networks, confidentiality, or standardization, the direction provided by these experts adds to the esteem of the profession. Participating in legal health-care activities offers rewards to many HIM professionals.

Consulting firms attract HIM professionals looking for career changes. The wide range of roles within consulting offers the opportunity to be on the leading edge of health-care changes in specialty areas of interest. Some entrepreneurs choose to transition into self-employment by creating new companies while phasing out present positions. For example, recruiting firms have been started by HIM professionals. Perry Ellie, an RRA, began HIM Recruiters in Largo, Florida, while teaching at a local junior college (Detwiler, 1993). Ellie emphasizes the value that his health information background and experience have had in his business.

Being personally accountable for career advancement and choosing their personal best time for new growth experiences brings rewards to HIM professionals. Those who innovate change for the future and not just react to pressures mandating change are the true visionaries.

Reducing Resistance to Change: Creating an Environment for Change

Employees bring their total past experiences into the work environment and these experiences likely include attitudes about change. To better understand the human element of resistance to change, then, requires that managers know their team members and be environment creators for reducing resistance to change. Implementing more than one change reduction method to meet the needs of individual team members may be necessary.

The most likely reasons for resisting change fall into four major categories. These are outlined in Figure 20-8. As underlying causes of resistance, they must be addressed; if only the symptoms of these causes are addressed, resistance will likely erupt again.

Awareness of the reasons for resistance to change offers advantages to HIM managers. Now they can be masters of the change process, not prisoners of the symptoms prevalent when change is planned. These advantages allow managers to review resistance factors and then take specific

Change creates uncertainty: Uncertainty upsets equilibrium and resistance may continue until there is a return to status quo. For example, when there is concern that team members may lose their jobs, the status quo can return when team members learn jobs will be lost only through attrition.

There is a fear of loss: Employees feel secure in their familiar settings. Change creates a fear they may lose what is already possessed or they may not be able to learn new equipment and new methods.

There is team pressure to resist: When the change is perceived to alter status symbols within the team or break up informal relationships, there can be pressure from some team members to resist. This can create tension for other members who must choose between following friendship pressures or employer initiatives. The price of cooperation may then be perceived as too high.

There is a belief that proposed change is not in the best interest of the department: There could be instances when resistance is valid. When valued employees have rational reasons for resistance, managers who listen to these reasons and review the options may avoid mistakes.

Figure 20-8.   Reasons for Resistance to Change

steps. These are outlined in Figure 20-9 and can reduce resistance as managers become environmental creators by utilizing steps that are appropriate to the situation.

Becoming a Broker of Health Information Resources

Responding to the change initiatives outlined in this chapter can leave HIM professionals breathless. Because the health-care industry is playing catch-up as it moves from the information age into the communication age, change and turmoil will continue. In this turbulence, finding the time to take a deep breath and make time for a personal assessment will demand discipline. Unique confidentiality and legal issues have hampered past change initiatives in health care and will continue to bring stress to HIM managers in their role as change agents.

At the root of change, however, are the familiar terms *efficiency* and *effectiveness*. Vision and objectives may be adjusted as the industry moves into new frontiers, but efficiency and effectiveness remain the energizing

Communicate: Reduce uncertainty by communicating the need for change. Schedule meetings to be sure all shifts are covered. Assure that interdepartmental teams impacted by the changes also have the information. Share success experiences of others. Stay positive and enthusiastic. Be as specific as possible. Use all the communication tools available—people learn through different avenues. Use the grapevine judiciously. Be an active listener.

Educate: Insist on adequate training for all involved team members. Have teams share in changing policies and procedures—educate them in the process. Build credibility and trust of all levels of management, if necessary. Share the background reasons for change through in-service. Use vendor knowledge when possible.

Participate: Enlist help from team leaders and informal leaders. Involve those who have negative feelings; make them a part of the change process to facilitate a sense of ownership.

Facilitate team building and interpersonal relationship enhancement: Update the teams involved by offering team building and interpersonal relationship enhancement programs. Incorporate specifics about the changes into these programs.

Negotiate and reward: Offer alternative change options, when feasible, to allow negotiation in decision making. Offer rewards throughout the change period, especially verbal rewards. Offer fun time to release tension and build commitment.

Evaluate and make corrections: Evaluation of the changes must be ongoing; resistance can return quickly when problems erupt. Make necessary corrections, communicate, and stay positive.

Figure 20-9.   Steps for Reducing Resistance to Change

goals of managers. With these goals, offering excellence to customers as information is communicated using the latest technology will continue to guide managerial action. Disseminating accurate, timely data and database information by presenting them in a format that meets the expectations of diverse customers remains a goal that will keep HIM professionals focused. This goal translates into having the skill and knowledge to develop health-care databases that are flexible, dynamic, and interactive. Moving the health-care industry through these change initiatives takes cooperative effort among many professionals, with each one contributing specific skills.

To stay on the leading edge of change, HIM managers must develop anticipatory skills, must be knowledgeable by reading or scanning a wide range of articles and books, and must be familiar with vendor applications. Becoming acquainted with tools, techniques, and systems for the profession requires consistent effort. Developing the EPR, the CPR, and the information superhighway for communicating health-care information will challenge the skills and knowledge of health information brokers. Technical tools such as CD-ROM health-care applications, smart card applications, network technology such as Ethernet, optical imaging, and others will become familiar terms. But, anticipating and having the technical knowledge are only the beginning.

To be brokers of health information, HIM professionals must also have managerial skills for becoming proactive change agents. As such, they must be willing to take risks, to initiate change, and to develop a sense of destination for themselves and the profession. Using powerful communication tools, knowledge, and skills will allow health information brokers to take part in the exciting future of health care that can lead to lasting wellness for the customers in the community or traveling the globe.

Summary

External forces continue to exert pressure on the health-care industry to change. Because of confidentiality and other issues unique to health care, transition from the information age into the communication age has been hampered in the past. HIM professionals must become proactive change agents in solving these issues and be a part of moving the industry forward. Internal pressures also demand change, frequently in step with those demanded by external forces.

The major categories of change are (1) changing technology to meet the needs of integrated delivery systems, (2) changing the structure, with present trends toward flattening the organizational design, and (3) changing employee/interpersonal relationships, which includes responding to such initiatives as team organizational structure and CQI. Organizational development consultants are useful in communicating the vision, objectives, and benefits of change.

The challenges to HIM brokers during these turbulent times are many and varied, but the rewards within acute-care departments, within ambulatory settings, and for professional advancement create incentives that make the challenges worthwhile.

New vision experiences keep managers from stagnating. By revitalizing their professional life every 5 to 9 years, HIM professionals renew their spirit and energize themselves and their employees. The broad range of career opportunities in health care offer endless options for professionals seeking career advancement and unique satisfying roles.

Resistance to change can be anticipated. Underlying reasons that lead to resistance include uncertainty, fear, team pressures, or vested interests. Steps that can reduce this resistance include communication, education, participation, team building, rewarding, and ongoing evaluation. Knowledgeable managers can journey successfully through the maze of change with their teams and reengineer their departments into models with systems in place, ready for the communication age and poised for the future.

Review Questions

1. Give the five steps that HIM professionals can take toward revitalization.

2. Choose one of the four factors for resistance to change and discuss reasons for the resistance.

3. Choose one of the steps for reducing resistance to change and discuss the rationale for its effectiveness.

Field Practice Questions

1. Interview an HIM manager who is planning a departmental change. Prepare a table that shows the following:
   a. Planned change—separate the change into subsets showing how a change in one factor of the department will create the need for changes in other factors.
   b. State which of the three major categories of change is involved for each subset of change planned.
   c. List some challenges the manager will face for each of the subsets of change.

> **d.** Offer some possible reasons why the employees may resist the proposed changes.
> **e.** Discuss steps the manager can take to reduce the resistance reasons offered above.

2. Interview an HIM professional who has changed career paths at least twice. Prepare a curve line that shows revitalization and any self-protection efforts taken because of scarring experiences.

References

Detwiler, M. (1993). Designing a life. *For the Record, 5* (23), 7.

Drucker, P. (1990). *Managing the non-profit organizations.* New York: Truman Talley Books.

Longest, B. (1990). *Management practices for the health professional* (4th ed.). Norwalk, CT: Appleton & Lange.

Robbins, S. (1994). *Management* (4th ed.). Englewood Cliffs, NJ: Prentice Hall.

Suggested Readings

Balloun, J., Stebbins, L., & VonBergen, C. (1995). The emerging need for transformational leadership in health information management. *Topics in Health Information Management, 15* (3), 39–45.

Bissen, C. (1995). From business process engineering to business process innovation. *Journal of AHIMA, 66* (2), 49–51.

Brandt, M. (1995). Developing an information management plan. *Journal of AHIMA, 66* (5), 24–33.

Brunner, B. (1992). Health information in the computer era. *Topics in Health Information Management*, November.

Cohen, W., & Murri, M. (1995). Managing the change process. *Journal of AHIMA, 66* (6), 40–47.

Detwiler, M. (1993). Designing a life. *For the Record, 5* (23), 7, 24.

Donnelly, J., Gibson, J., & Ivancevich, J. (1987). *Fundamentals of management* (6th ed.). Plano, TX: Business Publications.

Drucker, P. *Managing the non-profit organization.* New York: Truman Talley Books.

Gennusa, C. (1994). Ambulatory care settings require strong HIM skills. *Advance for Health Information Professionals, 4* (13), 8.

Gibbons, M. (1994). Major changes loom in health care. *Advance for Health Information Professionals, 4* (4), 22–24.

Harris, S. (1994). Riding the information wave with CD-ROM information sources. *Advance for Health Information Professionals, 4* (20), 20, 21.

Hospital of the future (1992). *Modern Healthcare,* July, pp. 47–65.

Johns, M. (1995). Issuing the challenge: Creating leadership for health information management. *Topics in Health Information Management, 15* (3), 1–9.

Kuntz, L. (1993). Breaking out of the mold. *For the Record, 5* (9), 16–18, 27.

Layman, E. (1995). A model to implement and sustain change. *Journal of AHIMA, 66* (7), 52–55.

Longest, B. (1990). *Management practices for the health professional* (4th ed.). Norwalk, CT: Appleton & Lange.

Palmer, L. (1992). Facing the future. *For the Record, 4* (19), 20–23.

Powell, R. (1986). Management of change course notes. Claremont, CA: Claremont Colleges.

Robbins, S. (1994). *Management* (4th ed.). Englewood Cliffs, NJ: Prentice Hall.

Rue, L., & Byars, L. (1986). *Management: Theory and application* (4th ed.). Homewood, IL: Richard D. Irwin.

Chapter 21

Personal and Professional Career Management

Learning Objectives

After completing this chapter, the learner should be able to:

1. Describe the content of professional resumes and state four principles that guide in their preparation.
2. Explain four reasons for writing a cover letter that introduces the resume.
3. Give three major reasons for careful planning prior to a position interview.
4. List 10 major personality organizational types and explain how each type tends to organize personal work.
5. Describe five major tools and techniques for effective personal and office time management.
6. Offer five opportunities HIM professionals have to enhance personal and professional growth.

Key Terms

Chronological resume
Cover letter
Functional resume

Introduction

Managing professional career goals and personal life with the same enthusiasm that brings success to the workplace is an important HIM activity. This chapter includes five areas of emphasis for personal and professional career management:

1. Preparing resumes and cover letters
2. Preparing for interviews
3. Managing personal time
4. Planning for positive performance evaluations
5. Investing personal effort toward professional growth

Specific rules to guide in these activities are offered with suggestions from practitioners who already have successful careers.

Personal Planning for a Professional Career

This section is devoted to personal planning for a professional position. As you have internalized the management planning principles of this text, you may have discovered some that apply directly to your personal life. Have these concepts been helpful this week in day-to-day experiences? At first it may take conscious thought to develop patterns of planning practice; then it will become a way of life. It is rewarding to develop the skills in using management concepts for planning your professional future. Your first position following graduation will be very important to you. No less important is the position you will hold 5 years later. The strategic planning undertaken now may determine whether you will stretch yourself to reach each plateau at the time interval planned today. Flexibility and contingencies are discussed as important components in organizational strategic planning; they are equally important in your professional planning. Setting attainable goals with alternatives, should change occur, gives reality to long-range personal planning.

Two excellent beginnings for creating a vision for the future are (1) to read a variety of publications on the profession and (2) to listen to successful practitioners. A vision will take shape as you read and listen to the variety of opportunities available. Lock into the one that excites you and become a part of the dynamic future of health-care. In this industry devoted to the healing arts, there are options in the future that may be unheard of today. This demonstrates another reason for flexibility in long-range planning.

To create the image you wish to project and to be noticed in the marketplace, take time to prepare a winning resume. This resume and its cover letter introduces you and sets the tone for an interview.

Planning a Resume

A resume is a summary of your work experience and education. It is an advertisement to create an interest in you. Resumes take careful thought and preparation; they are an introduction to a prospective employer, and yet, by definition, a resume is quite impersonal. A cover letter sent with the resume serves as a bridge between you and the potential employer. Sincerity and honesty, however, can be expressed in both the resume and the cover letter. The following principles will guide in preparing a resume:

1. Make it interesting enough to secure an interview.
2. Make it visually attractive.
3. Make it brief but informative.
4. Personalize it.

To assist in the creation of a winning resume, the following guidelines offer ideas for taking these principles into action.

Choosing the Best Format

Resumes may be in chronological format, functional format, or in a combination approach. The following descriptions of these three formats will facilitate in choosing the best one for you.

Chronological

The **chronological resume** is the best known and widely used. It is arranged with the most recent information/experience first and then descends in reverse chronological order and ends with the oldest experience or information. This format makes it easy to review career progress from one step to the next. Obvious gaps in work history can be readily seen.

Functional

To emphasize overall skills and abilities, the **functional resume** downplays dates. In fact, specific dates are omitted. The work history is defined by specific examples of experience and responsibilities. Previous positions may or may not be included. The focus is on responsibilities and accomplishments.

Combination Approach

Combining chronological and functional formats, the combination approach is becoming increasingly popular. Transferable skills or capabilities used in a variety of positions are emphasized. This format pinpoints job titles, dates, and past employers. Its strength is that both career direction and depth of experience can be shown. Figure 21-1 details the resume for an RRA after 5 years of employment. The chronological format is followed in this resume example.

In contrast, Figure 21-2 shows the resume of a graduating student who returned to school after her children had all entered first grade. This resume is prepared using a functional format.

Writing Your Resume

The following rules for writing resumes give guidance in documenting your background. Most are listed as positive action, but a few of the guidelines include specific things to avoid:

Rule 1. Heading: Start with your name, address, and telephone number. Place your name on every page. Do not use the words, "Resume of ..." Include your business telephone number if appropriate. Check your answering machine message—be sure it is professional in tone.

Rule 2. Career objective: Use a career objective if desired and if your objective will relate to the position for which you are applying. Make it specific and allow it to give focus to the remainder of the resume. The

Don Smith
100 Park Avenue
Anytown, U.S.A. 10000
(714) 555-0000

Employment History

November 1992
to Present

Anytown City Hospital
Anytown, U.S.A.
Manager, Health Information Department

- Managed department, planned expanded department
- Implemented enhanced information system
- Assisted in planning Home Health Care Division

June 1990 to
November 1992

Community Hospital
Anytown, U.S.A.
Team Leader, Record Activity

- Reorganized physician work room
- Implemented automated incomplete record system

September 1988 to
June, 1990

Anytown City Hospital
Anytown, U.S.A.
Part-time responsibilities while attending college included record activity, coding, and abstracting

Education

B.S. in Health Information Management, June 1990,
City College, Anytown, U.S.A.

Professional Credentials

Registered Record Administrator (RRA), October 1990
Certification #111222

Affiliation/Membership

American Health Information Management Association

Figure 21-1.   Resume for Don Smith, RRA

Resume

Mary Jones   200 State Street
(222) 333-4444   Anytown, Florida 55555

Career Objective

To enter the Health Information Management profession as a systems specialist and manager, strengthening my management and systems abilities and gaining the experience necessary to become a leader in clinical data management.

Past Responsibilities and Accomplishments

- Installed a membership tracking software package and maintained records for the church.
- Organized and directed yearly charity fund-raising events for the civic club in my community.
- Received the Faculty Recognition Award this year at Anytown University.

Education

- Graduated from Anytown University this year with a Bachelor's Degree in Health Information Management.
- Graduated from Anytown High School with emphasis in the computer career track.

Professional

- Member of the American Health Information Management Association. Will take the credentialing examination this fall.

References available upon request.

Figure 21-2.   Functional Resume for Mary Jones

cover letter is an alternate place for the career objective and allows the resume to be used when applying for various positions. The career objective can then be tailored in the letter toward the specific position.

Rule 3. Work experience or education first? Either can come first. When work history is scanty, education is best placed first. List most recent education or work experience first and proceed in reverse chronology.

Rule 4. Main headings: Plan headings that will guide or lead into the information. Headings should catch the eye and be visually compelling. Be conservative rather than gimmicky. Some basic headings are:

Career Objective	Education
Employment Experience	Professional Education
Work History	Certificates and Licenses
Business Experience	Special Skills
Professional Highlights	Technical Skills
Selected Achievements	Relevant Experience
Memberships	Publications

Rule 5. Phrases versus sentences? Be concise; use phrases rather than complete sentences. Avoid use of pronouns such as "I" or use of third person to refer to yourself. Use parallel sentence structure. Make every word count.

Rule 6. Vocabulary: Avoid abbreviations except for degrees such as B.S. Use vocabulary related to the profession.

Rule 7. Action verbs: Use action verbs to describe your responsibilities. Examples are:

administered	delegated	interviewed	reduced
analyzed	designed	lectured	revised
assisted	developed	managed	selected
communicated	directed	monitored	supervised
conducted	evaluated	organized	taught
controlled	formulated	performed	trained
coordinated	implemented	planned	translated
created	initiated	proposed	wrote

Rule 8. Gaps in work history: Avoid obvious gaps by using a functional format. Homemakers can avoid obvious references to time spent at home. Rather, highlight volunteer or unpaid experience in the community or social organizations that can parallel responsibilities in a work environment. For example, "Developed training manual for Girl/Boy Scouts."

Rule 9. Previous employer information: Omit reason for leaving a previous employer. Never include salary requirements or previous salary. Never list name of a supervisor. The formal application will request this type of information.

Rule 10. Accomplishments: Include special awards, superior grade-point average, extracurricular activities, and other accomplishments that are relevant.

Rule 11. Publications: List names of publications with information on when and where they were published.

Rule 12. Personal information: Omit information such as birthdate, marital status, hobbies, health status, and a photograph. Employers are looking for valuable employees, not friends, and in most instances this information is not appropriate.

Rule 13. References: Rarely include references in a resume. If you wish to use the term as a line item, state "Available on request." Should the prospective employer have requested references, list them on a separate sheet.

Rule 14. Appearance: Use cream, white, buff, or light gray high-quality paper. Use standard-size paper with no borders. Print on one side only. Use boldface, italics, and underscoring with discretion. Proofread carefully; have someone else proofread also.

Rule 15. Attachments: Never attach transcripts or letters of recommendation. When these are specifically requested by a prospective employer, include them as separate sheets in the packet of material. Do not place in a report cover. Mail with cover letter.

Rule 16. Individualize for employer: Be prepared to make changes in your resume to create it specifically for a prospective employer.

Preparing the Cover Letter

A well-written **cover letter** introduces you to the prospective employer and neutralizes the tone of the more impersonal resume. The cover letter should be written as carefully as the resume as it may be used as a screening tool. It should be addressed to a specific person when possible.

As you explain what you can do for the prospective employer, emphasize what you can contribute to the organization. By using simple direct language and correct grammar, you can avoid being stiff and impersonal. The first sentence should catch the attention of the reader and the last sentence can suggest an interview.

The cover letter should include the reason for the contact. Are you responding to an advertisement? Are you writing at the suggestion of a mutual friend? If a specific skill was mentioned in the advertisement, refer the reader to the resume where your skill is described.

Lastly, review your resume and cover letter. They should project a positive, professional image that represents your unique personality. Resumes are a mainstay of modern business and are worth the effort spent in creating one that will advertise your skills.

Planning for a Position Interview

Within a university or college setting there are many sources of information regarding possible positions following graduation. Once your resume is ready, begin exploring options and making appointments for interviews. Exposing yourself to several interviews gives you experience in the interview process and builds your confidence.

An excellent person with whom to begin your professional interview is the HIM manager at your affiliation or internship facility. Even though there may not be an opening at the facility, the manager may be willing to mentor you through this first interview. Also, asking a clinical supervisor or one of the instructors to critique your interview skills can create a great learning experience.

Guest lecturers in your courses also give good opportunities for interviews. A professional who gives time to students by lecturing is often willing to give you an interview and then critique your skills. Ideas for possible positions and future interviews may also come from guest lecturers.

Making the appointment for an interview should be at a time favorable for both of you. Choose a time when you can relax and not be rushed, and certainly a time when the manager can give you his undivided intention. Set aside time to prepare for the interview. Learn details about the facility by reading reports, brochures, or newspaper articles. Become familiar with the vision of the facility, its success in maintaining that vision, and how the community needs are being met.

Preparing yourself to answer questions about technical details of the position for which you are applying is also crucial to success. This is enhanced by reviewing past experiences and using the 1-2-3 story technique to demonstrate your competence. This technique involves stating a problem that occurred, describing how you solved it, and then emphasizing the positive results of your action. You may even wish to write out some responses you would give to typical questions to reinforce your memory.

Planning your attire for the interview avoids last-minute problems. Professional conservative attire is a must, but just as important is choosing well-fitting comfortable clothing that will allow you to focus on being yourself.

A winning resume, interesting cover letter, and professional attire will contribute to projecting the desired image employers are seeking. But it is the interview, where the chemistry between interviewee and the manager connects, that really counts. Expressions of confidence, interest, commitment, and competence will win the position.

Planning for Positive Performance Evaluations

As new visions are anticipated, HIM professionals can prepare for making that growth step by maintaining a professional attitude, by wearing attire that projects a professional image, and by assuring that regular performance evaluations are a part of the personnel file. Busy managers and busy vice presidents to whom they report may not be documenting faithfully the spontaneous informal commendations that are verbalized or put in memos following rewarding efforts.

Judy Cordeniz, a busy HIM manager in California, considers carefully written evaluations an important part of professional growth and future opportunities. She offers insights in the following practice example.

Practice Example

Several years ago, Judy managed health information services and utilization management in a 200-bed facility with multiple service. During the 2 years she was a part of the management team in this facility, she was under three different vice presidents. Two of these vice presidents were not familiar with health information processing activities. When Judy reached out for new opportunities and began the interview process, she became concerned that the information in her personnel file may not reflect her managerial skills adequately.

In pursuing this concern, Judy found that indeed the performance appraisals and information in her file were very sketchy, and several of the accomplishments for which she had been highly commended at the time were not mentioned. In tracking the appraisal and minimal raises she had received, the pattern she saw emerging was extremely disappointing, and Judy determined to assist the documentation process in the future. She took the following steps:

1. Maintained a running "to-do" list of projects, not just the big important ones, but projects of all sizes and importance.

2. Prepared a summary of accomplishments for the appraisal period and submitted this to the vice president shortly before her scheduled evaluation.

3. Prepared a list of current projects including their status and submitted this with the summary of accomplishments.

4. Outlined professional goals and objectives as chosen at the beginning of the period and assessed strengths and weaknesses in meeting these goals and objectives. This was also submitted with the summary of accomplishments.

5. Submitted a copy of the summary of accomplishments, the list of current projects, and the goals and objectives to the human resources department for her file.

At the performance appraisal, the vice president used Judy's documentation as a tool for jogging the memory and the resulting documentation for the personnel file was accurate. Judy also found that she received the raise she felt was deserved.

Judy has continued this successful pattern of activity since that time, and reports continuing accuracy and completeness of the documentation in her file.   ■

Judy's experience with changes in upper-level managers is not unique. In today's health-care environment, new visions and opportunities appeal to managers, and change in reporting responsibilities will continue. Through personal documentation of accomplishments, middle managers can be assured that the human resources department has complete and accurate information (Cordeniz, 1995).

Personal Time Management

This section brings into focus the importance of personal planning for effective time management. In Chapter 19 the more formal aspects of managing time are outlined. Additional informal aspects of time management are covered here. Utilizing these aspects can lead HIM professionals to a better understanding of how they function at their best.

Sunny Schlenger and Roberta Roesch (1989) have identified major personality organizational types in their book, *How to Be Organized in Spite of Yourself*. These types relate to organizing work, which is important in time management, because organizing is so clearly tied to the time needed to complete tasks. Exploring the strengths and weaknesses inherent in these organizational types is useful for our discussion of the tools and techniques that create efficiencies in task performance.

The names Schlenger and Roesch have given to these major organizational types are quite descriptive and their meanings follow:

1. *Hopper*—likes to have several projects going simultaneously; jumps from one to the other without completing any of them.
2. *Perfectionist plus*—believes he can complete all the projects on time, but gets so involved in details of doing them right that he is not satisfied when one is finally completed.
3. *Allergic to detail*—enjoys being a part of planning committees, but loses interest when completing projects.
4. *Fence sitter*—puts projects off because she has trouble making decisions since she fears not making the right one.
5. *Cliff hanger*—enjoys the excitement of planning, but leaves detail work to the last minute with deadlines pressuring him.
6. *Everything out*—works best when everything she needs or might need is on the desk around her.
7. *Nothing out*—hiding things from sight helps him feel in control; hates to see clutter.

8. *Right angler*—believes she is organized when piles are arranged with perfectly straight edges.

9. *Pack rat*—compulsion to save everything as it might be needed some day.

10. *Total slob*—believes he has more important and creative things to do than stay neat.

Several of these personality organization styles demonstrate a pattern that leads to time wasted looking for items that are either buried in clutter, buried in neatness, or hidden from sight without proper labels. Schlenger and Roesch suggest making minor organizing changes such as using identified file folders but keeping them out on the desk, or using stacked desk trays and organizers to hold project materials. With conscious effort at putting things into the labeled trays and organizers, the time spent looking for things will be minimized.

The technique of breaking down projects into several small or divided units will assist several of the organizational-type managers. Once the tasks are smaller, smaller blocks of time can be used effectively to complete the projects in manageable steps. Keeping these divided units together in a folder or tray until ready to put the project all together will keep time wasted to a minimum.

While most HIM managers will not fit neatly into just one of the personality organizational types depicted by Schlenger and Roesch, a personal appraisal of tendencies toward one or more of the types can lead to a conscious effort at reducing time wasters.

Professional Growth

HIM managers are constantly stressed by the need to monitor the latest computerized innovations or last week's technological systems change. This demand for ongoing new knowledge increases the need to review and glean information from health-care and computer journals and magazines. They are valuable resources, and reading and scanning several at least monthly is a habit to begin now and to continue for the rest of your professional life. Becoming acquainted with successful HIM managers enhances the knowledge of new graduates; having them serve as mentors is a valuable growth experience. Seeing systems installed and functioning in facilities is another valuable resource. Visiting with vendors at professional meetings is an excellent avenue for obtaining current technological information.

Journals and newsletters from the American Health Information Management Association (AHIMA) and other associations are most beneficial. Examples of alliance associations are the Health Information Management Systems Society (HIMSS), the American Management Information Association (AMIA), the Healthcare Financial Management Association (HFMA), and the Healthcare Innovations in Technology Systems (HITS). Through networking experiences with other professionals, HIM managers can enhance their understanding of capabilities and trends in managing health-care information into the future.

Summary

Preparing well-written resumes using the 16 rules outlined in this chapter offers HIM professionals the opportunity to walk into a position interview with confidence. Other confidence-building items include a personalized cover letter and attire that creates the desired impression.

Resumes can be prepared using a chronological format where significant dates are included in reverse order. The functional format may prove advantageous when it is preferable to emphasize skills and abilities. A combination of the two formats may also be used where skills and abilities are emphasized selectively.

Major personality organizational types have been identified and play a role in how professionals organize work and utilize time. Understanding your organizational type can be helpful in using inherent strengths and downplaying weaknesses.

HIM professionals who make a personal effort to network with peers, read a broad range of literature, and attend professional meetings grow personally and professionally.

Review Questions

1. Describe several tasks you will undertake in your personal planning for your first HIM position following graduation.

2. List the major features of a resume. Which format will be most appropriate for you?
3. Interview a classmate to determine tendencies toward one or more of the personality organizational types as suggested by Schlenger and Roesch (1989). Ask questions that relate to the descriptions under each type; then document the significant findings for class discussion.

References

Cordeniz, J. (1995). Personal sharing and discussion with the author.

Schlenger, S., & Roesch, R. (1989). *How to be organized in spite of yourself.* New York: New American Library.

Suggested Readings

Bellows, L. (1995). Sharpening your negotiation skills. *Journal of AHIMA, 66* (8), 34–39.

Brandt, M. (1995). Thinking outside the box: New opportunities for HIM professionals. *Journal of AHIMA, 66* (1), 52, 53.

Dowell, S., & Fainter, J. (1992). President's message: Personal QI plan. *Journal of AHIMA, 63* (5), 4.

Fry, J. (1992). Designing your medical record career path: Successfully integrating work and family responsibilities. *Journal of AHIMA, 63* (4), 55–61.

Hamilton, M. (1993). Good job market plus job hunting. *Advance for Health Information Professionals, 3* (9).

Lancaster, H. (1994). You, and only you must stay in charge of your employability. *Wall Street Journal* (XCIV/4).

Scheele, A. (1992). Interviewing for the top. *Working Woman*, June, pp. 30, 31.

Schlenger, S., & Roesch, R. (1989). *How to be organized in spite of yourself.* New York: New American Library.

Weber, S. (1995). Strategies for negotiating preemployment agreements. *Journal of AHIMA, 66* (8), 64–67.

Glossary

Action plan   The document that assists committee members with delegated responsibilities by reminding them of tasks and deadlines; prepared and distributed immediately following committee meetings.

Actuating   A term sometimes used for the third function of management; emphasizes the responsibility of managers to motivate all members of the team to strive toward objectives.

Adhocracy   See organic structural design.

Attitudes   Evaluative statements that reflect how an individual feels about objectives, events, or people.

Authoritarianism   The measure of a person's belief in status and power differences among people in organizations.

Authority   The rights inherent in a managerial position to give orders and expect them to be obeyed.

Benchmarking   The search for the best practices among like entities or past practices that lead to superior performance.

Bottom-up budgeting process   A philosophy that encourages participation of all employees in planning priorities and objectives for the budget year.

Broker of data   A negotiator, an intermediary, or a person entrusted with the transmission of health-care data.

Business plan   A plan that documents details of a proposed project or new business that includes a mission statement, a description, the proposed market, the budget, and a plan for evaluation.

Centralization of authority   The concentration of decision-making authority that lies with upper-level management.

Certainty   A decision situation in which the manager can make a correct decision because the outcome of each alternative is known.

Channel   The medium by which a message travels from sender to receiver.

Chronological resume   A summary of one's work and education experience in reverse date order.

Clinical decision support systems Automated systems that guide health-care professionals in making decisions regarding patient care.

Clinical management Automated systems capable of managing all aspects of direct patient care.

Closed systems Systems that are not influenced by their environment and do not interact with their environment.

Cognitive dissonance An incompatibility between two or more attitudes or between behavior and attitudes.

Committee structure A structure that brings together a range of individuals from across functional lines to solve problems or develop proactive alternatives before problems exist.

Communication The transferring and understanding of meaning.

Community health information network (CHIN) An integrated health information system capable of transferring health-care information to caregivers in the community, regardless of the setting.

Compressed workweek A schedule where employees work four 10-hour days.

Computer-based patient record (CPR) Patient health information captured and stored electronically as a patient record; in a system designed to support users by providing accurate data for patient care, analysis, and dissemination as needed.

Conflict The perceived incompatible differences that result in interference or opposition.

Conflict resolution An action by managers to resolve conflicts through accommodation, force, compromise, or collaboration.

Consistency perception The process of organizing and interpreting sensory impressions in order to give consistency and meaning to the environment.

Consultant One who gives professional advice and services in the field of his or her specialty.

Contingency approach An approach that recognizes and responds to situational variables as they arise.

Continuous quality improvement A health-care term that is patient or employee focused, used to describe a constant cycle of improvement.

Controlling The management function that ensures activities are being accomplished as planned and corrects any significant deviations.

Coopetition A term that describes the environment where groups in competition with one another can cooperate to achieve the goals of the larger group to which they belong.

Cover letter An introductory document that accompanies a resume sent to a prospective employer.

Creativity   A thinking process that combines ideas in a unique way to produce new and original concepts.

Critical pathways   Automated systems created to lead the physician toward patient care in an interactive manner.

Customers   Those persons who use the services provided or have a stake in the success of an organization.

Decision-making process   A series of steps that include identifying a problem, developing and analyzing possible alternatives, selecting the best alternative, and monitoring its effectiveness.

Decision support systems   Automated systems capable of guiding the user in making decisions.

Decoding   The retranslating of a sender's message.

Delphi technique   A group decision-making technique where members do not meet face to face.

Departmentalization   The process of formalizing the structure by grouping employees together according to their specialized activities.

Directing   A component of the leading function of management that emphasizes giving assignments and instructions, guiding employees, and overseeing activities.

Discretionary time   Time that is under the control of managers to use wisely.

Division of labor   See specialization of labor.

Electronic data interchange (EDI)   The exchange of information that will become possible through community and regional health-care networks as the information highway becomes reality.

Electronic patient record (EPR)   An electronic path toward the CPR that includes databases, integrated work flow, optical disk storage, and paper documents.

Electronic meeting   A committee or group meeting where decisions are made with linked computer technology.

Empowerment   The process of increasing the decision-making discretion of employees.

Encoding   The converting of a message into symbols.

Entrepreneur   A person who conceives a product or service idea, pursues opportunities for innovation, and starts an organization.

Ergonomics   The design of products, processes, and systems to meet the requirements and capacities of those people who use them.

Executive information systems (EIS)   An automated database system with timely information for top executives.

External environment   Outside forces that potentially affect a department or total organization's performance.

Facilitator A professional with expertise in leading group discussions, especially in quality improvement efforts.

Feedback A process for determining whether the receiver of a message understood it.

Fixed budget A budget that assumes a fixed level of services, sales, or productivity.

Flextime Flexible work hours where employees work a specified number of hours per week, but are free, within limits, to schedule their own hours.

Followership The theory that managers spend more time following leaders up the organization than in leading those down the organization.

Formal leader The manager appointed to lead an entity and have responsibility for the activities within that entity.

Formalization The degree to which an organization relies on rules and procedures to direct the actions of employees.

Functional departmentalization The grouping of activities by functions performed.

Functional resume A summary of a person's work and education experience that emphasizes skills and downplays dates.

Gantt chart A bar chart that graphically shows the work planned and completed on one axis and the time span on the other.

Grapevine The informal communication network.

Human relations approach An approach that emphasizes the important role humans play in the success of an organization, and states a satisfied employee will be a productive one.

Human resources approach A managerial approach that focuses on human behavior.

Incentive pay Wages paid to employees on the basis of productivity, for example, transcriptionists paid per line or keystroke.

Incremental budget A budget that allocates funds to departments for the new budget period based on allocations of the previous budget period.

Informal leader The leader chosen by members of the group to lead the group in certain attitudes and behaviors.

Informal planning The planning done by managers that is not formally documented for present or future use.

Information superhighway An electronic networking ability that allows access to accurate up-to-date health-care information on a patient at point of service, regardless of geographic area.

Integrated model of management A model that uses of the best features of information theories to develop a health-care management model that integrates new technologies into the management model of the future.

Integrated systems A system where data and information on separate automated applications are integrated to allow invisible transfer of information among them.

Interim organizational models A model that creates a design documenting a temporary structure while reengineering continues to occur.

Internal environment Forces within the organization but outside the department that potentially affect the department's performance; factors within the department that affect its ability to perform effectively and efficiently.

Intrapreneur A person who creates an entrepreneurial spirit within an organization.

Job characteristics model A framework for analyzing and designing jobs that identifies five primary job characteristics, their interrelationships, and impact on outcome variables.

Job description The written statement summarizing what an employee does, how it is done, and why it is done.

Job design The way in which tasks are combined to form a complete position.

Job scope The variety of activities within a position description and the frequency with which each activity is repeated.

Job splitting The practice of splitting one full-time position into two positions with one part-time employee performing lower-level skills and another part-time employee performing the remaining tasks.

Knowledge couplers The term given to an automated decision system created by Dr. Lawrence Weed that assists physicians in making patient-care decisions.

Leadership The ability to inspire and influence attitudes and behaviors of group members in accomplishing objectives.

Leading The management function involved in motivating employees, directing others, resolving conflicts, and selecting effective communication channels.

Locus of control A personality trait with two components; internal, where people believe they control their own fate and external, where people believe they are pawns of fate.

Longitudinal patient record The creation of a record that encompasses patient health-care information from all sources, over time, for use and update by caregivers.

Machiavellianism A measure of the degree to which people are pragmatic, maintain emotional distance, and believe that ends justify means.

Management A process of activities for creating objectives and for teaming with people to meet these objectives through efficient and effective use of resources.

Management by objectives (MBO) A system where performance objectives are jointly planned by manager and employee with periodic review of progress and rewards based on this progress.

Manual A book containing policies, rules, and procedures for a department, a section, a team, or an employee. Also called a handbook, guidebook, or data quality manual.

Matrix organizational structure A design that assigns specialists from departments to work on one or more projects led by a project manager.

Mechanistic structural design A structure that is high in complexity, formalization, and centralization.

Message A purpose to be conveyed.

Mission statement The documentation of the purpose of an organization.

Moderator A person skilled in group techniques who leads a committee or group through a decision-making process.

Modified organic design An organizational design for departments within a mechanistic structure that has aspects of adhocracy structure with few levels of control.

Monitoring A process of taking the action necessary to be aware of the quality and quantity of employee activities that may be performed by manual or electronical means.

Motivation A willingness to exert high levels of effort to reach departmental goals, conditioned by the ability to satisfy some employee need.

Multiskilled health professional A person crosstrained to provide more than one function, often in more than one discipline.

Narrative style A writing style used in preparing manuals that begins each statement with action verbs and uses incomplete sentences in outline format.

Network structure An organization that chooses to rely on other organizations to perform some basic business functions on a contract basis.

New vision The creation of new professional career goals as the result of assessment and revitalization efforts.

Noise Disturbances that interfere with the transmission of messages.

Nominal group technique A decision-making technique in which group members are physically together, but operate independently.

Nonprogrammed decisions Decisions that are unique and thus require custom-made solutions.

Objectives Statements that outline desired outcomes to give direction to an organization and its employees. Can be synonymous with goals.

Open systems Dynamic systems that interact with and respond to forces in the environment.

Open-mode environment A specific work space that encourages creativity and original thinking.

Operational plans Plans that detail the action of each department or team that will lead to achievement of the overall objectives.

Organic structural design   A structure that is low in complexity, formalization, and centralization.

Organizational development (OD)   A system of techniques to motivate people and improve the quality of interpersonal work relationships.

Organizing   The management function that determines what tasks are to be done, who shall do them, the reporting structure, and at what level decisions will be made.

Paradigm shift   The changes that take place as present models of activity no longer meet the needs, and pressure mounts for a shift to new models.

Participative approach to management   A management style where managers consult with employees and use their suggestions in making decisions.

Patient-focused centers   Direct-care units where multiskilled health professionals provide all of the patient activities and care, such as admitting the patient, performing diagnostic examinations, caring for the patient, and coding patient diagnoses.

Perception   The process of organizing and interpreting sensory impressions in order to give meaning to the environment.

Performance evaluation and review technique (PERT network)   A diagram that graphically shows the relationships among the various activities of a project and estimates time needed for each activity.

Performance standards   The expectation that performance will meet a set level of quantity and quality.

Personal, fatigue, and delay factor (PFD)   Employee nonproductive time that is deleted from productivity statistics.

Planning   The management function concerned with defining goals, establishing strategy, and creating plans to guide the coordinated effort of employees to meet the goals.

Policy   A decision-making guide that establishes parameters for taking action and meeting objectives.

Position depth   A practice where employees are given an increased degree of control over their tasks.

Position description   See job description.

Position design   See job design.

Position enlargement   A practice that offers employees horizontal expansion of activities and an increase in scope.

Position enrichment   The practice of enriching positions by expanding the tasks vertically, usually with planning and evaluating responsibilities.

Position rotation   The practice of lateral transfers of employees among jobs involving different tasks.

Position specification   A statement of the minimal acceptable qualifications that an employee must possess to perform a position successfully.

Power   The capacity to influence the decision-making process.

Problem avoiders   Managers who tend to ignore signs of problem eruption.

Problem seekers   Managers who actively look for opportunities to alleviate potential problems before they occur.

Problem-solving process   See decision-making process.

Procedure   The series of interrelated steps that are documented and used to give standardization to routine tasks or structured problems.

Process approach to management   A process where management performs the functions of planning, organizing, leading, and controlling in a circular and continuous manner.

Process innovation   See reengineering.

Product lines   The organization of activities by products or services offered to the customers.

Productivity   The overall output of products and services produced per employee hour that meet the established levels of quality.

Programmed decisions   A repetitive decision that is documented to handle routine problems.

Quality   The degree to which an activity produces a product or service that meets the standards set for that activity.

Quality improvement   The philosophy that processes, management, and employees all benefit from efforts to provide better service, products, and ideas focusing on the customer.

Quantitative approach to management   The use of quantitative techniques, usually computerized, to improve the decision-making process.

Quantity   The ratio between input and output.

Rational model in decision making   A model where the manager behaves rationally in making decisions by following the steps and maximizing every alternative before the final decision is made.

Reengineering   The process of changing business practices to maintain quality, reduce costs, improve performance that involves fundamental rethinking and redesigning processes.

Resources   An organization's resources are the skills and abilities of employees, the monies available for producing its products or services, and the physical plant and equipment.

Response time   Uncontrollable time spent responding to requests, demands, and problems initiated by others.

Results management   See management by objectives (MBO).

Resume   A summary or brief account of one's background—work experience and education.

Revitalization   A growth concept where professionals consciously stretch their horizons and gain new visions for the future.

Risk   The decision maker has some information but must calculate the likelihood of specific outcomes.

Rule   An explicit statement that requires definite action be taken or not taken in a given situation.

Sampling   The process of measuring productivity by making a series of observations at random.

Satisficing decisions   Decisions that meet the decision maker's minimum standard of acceptance for the situation.

Scientific approach to management   Scientific procedures for finding the best way to accomplish a task, introduced by Frederick W. Taylor.

Section/team managers   Managers whose span of control covers one section of a department or one team within a section or a department; also called team leader, team coordinator, section leader, or section coordinator.

Self-esteem   An individual's degree of like or dislike for him or herself.

Self-monitoring   A personality trait that measures an individual's ability to adjust his or her behavior to external situational factors.

Service lines   A management concept where activities are organized around the service offered to a like group of customers.

Service organizations   Organizations that offer services to their customers in contrast with manufacturing organizations that offer products.

Single-use plan   A plan that is created to cover a unique problem and is rarely used; also called a nonprogrammed plan or decision.

Space modeling   The layout model created to depict the plans and decisions made for a physical environment that includes ergonomic principles.

Span of control   The number of employees a manager can direct with efficiency and effectiveness.

Span of management   The number of employees a manager can direct efficiently and effectively. See also Span of control.

Specialization of labor   An organizing concept where employees specialize in skilled tasks that may then be grouped for efficiency.

Staff authority   Authority that supports, assists, and advises managers of line authority.

Stakeholder   Any constituency in the environment that is affected by an organization's decisions and policies.

Standing-use plan   A plan that is created when repetitive or routine decisions are made; also called programmed plan or decision.

Statistical modeling   A model that uses information systems data as a base for quality improvement management.

Strategic planning A planning process that documents long-range objectives, develops activities to achieve the objectives, and allocates resources to those activities.

Stress A dynamic condition in which an individual is confronted with an opportunity, constraint, or demand related to what he or she desires for which the outcome is perceived to be both uncertain and important.

SWOT analysis An analysis involving an organization's strengths and weaknesses and the opportunities and threats in its environment.

Systems approach to management A theory that views an organization as a set of interrelated and interdependent entities.

Task force A temporary structure created to perform specific, well-defined, usually complex tasks using members from various organizational departments.

Template A plastic pattern for drawing scaled layout furniture.

Top-down budgeting process A philosophy where upper-level management plans the priorities and objectives for the budget year and disseminates these to others in the organization.

Total quality management (TQM) A management philosophy that recognizes employee involvement in meeting customer needs and expectations.

Transitional planning A process that offers a new paradigm for planning that begins by designing a bridge to the future.

Two-dimensional templates A set of scaled card stock cutouts, representing office furniture, for use in moving around layouts until desired configuration is taped in place.

Uncertainty A situation where the decision maker has no certainty about the probabilities associated with the situation.

Unity of command The principle that an employee should have one and only one manager to whom he or she is directly responsible.

Variable budget A budget that recognizes and gives consideration to adjusting costs as volume fluctuates.

Vision An idealized goal that proposes a new future for an organization.

Work sharing A practice where work is shared across all shifts, or where one full-time position is shared by two part-time employees.

Work transformation See reengineering.

Zero-based budgeting (ZBB) A budgeting system where each budget request requires justification in detail regardless of past allocation.

Index